SUSTAINABLE INDIA

TOWARDS 2075: ROADMAP FOR HARMONIOUS LIVING IN 150 BLUE GREEN CITIES

Palash Tayal

Chennai • Bangalore

CLEVER FOX PUBLISHING
Chennai, India

Published by CLEVER FOX PUBLISHING 2024
Copyright © Palash Tayal 2024

All Rights Reserved.
ISBN: 978-93-56489-31-8

This book has been published with all reasonable efforts taken to make the material error-free after the consent of the author. No part of this book shall be used, reproduced in any manner whatsoever without written permission from the author, except in the case of brief quotations embodied in critical articles and reviews.

The Author of this book is solely responsible and liable for its content including but not limited to the views, representations, descriptions, statements, information, opinions and references ["Content"]. The Content of this book shall not constitute or be construed or deemed to reflect the opinion or expression of the Publisher or Editor. Neither the Publisher nor Editor endorse or approve the Content of this book or guarantee the reliability, accuracy or completeness of the Content published herein and do not make any representations or warranties of any kind, express or implied, including but not limited to the implied warranties of merchantability, fitness for a particular purpose. The Publisher and Editor shall not be liable whatsoever for any errors, omissions, whether such errors or omissions result from negligence, accident, or any other cause or claims for loss or damages of any kind, including without limitation, indirect or consequential loss or damage arising out of use, inability to use, or about the reliability, accuracy or sufficiency of the information contained in this book.

Table of Contents

1. The burning passenger train — 13
2. The Holy Grail — 22
3. Rebuilding natural wealth — 42
4. Health is wealth — 64
5. Live in the city — 102
6. Urban infrastructure — 132
7. Large scale natural farming — 142
8. Sustainable consumption — 175
9. Five star destinations — 205
10. Green transportation — 214
11. Make it large — 237
12. Sustainable energy balance — 413
13. Indian citizen — 447
14. People love people — 458
15. Independent economy — 526

Chapter wise summary

Chapter 1 - The burning passenger train

The Indian subcontinent has been devastated by the continuous state of conflict since the 10th century A.D. The fertile and diverse natural ecosystem that nurtured an evolved human society is fast headed down the path of irreversible environmental degradation.

Chapter 2 - The Holy Grail

Sustainability is the supreme purpose of humanity. A pure focus on sustainability will not only rescue the subcontinent but will also lead to the most optimal form of development. India is uniquely placed to build the world's first sustainable economy by 2075.

Chapter 3 - Rebuilding natural wealth

India will need to forego human settlement in the mountains, create a dense forest cover on >55% of land area with wide riparian cover along the rivers, minimize the use of groundwater, build lakes for complete water security, regulate livestock rearing, and divert water to the Thar.

Chapter 4 - Health is wealth

Sustainability and health are mutually dependent and can together guide decision making for systems and individuals. Health is the most rewarding individual purpose - a perfectly fit individual is in harmony with the surroundings and leads the most fulfilling life.

Chapter 5 - Live in the city

Bringing everyone to live together in ~130 equal high-rise cities is the core structural shift for India to become sustainable. The move will maximize resource efficiency and quality of life and minimize inequality.

Chapter 6 - Urban infrastructure

Each city should be spread over an area of ~2,000 sq km with an urban green cover of ~800 sq km, urban blue over ~500 sq km, high-rise buildings and mobility infrastructure over ~500 sq km and sports infrastructure over ~200 sq km.

Chapter 7 - Large scale natural farming

Aligning with a balanced nutritious diet and producing indigenous varieties at scale in their natural habitats, will minimize agricultural land requirement (~100 Mha), maximize agricultural productivity and quality, keep the soil nourished and nurture thriving local ecosystems.

Chapter 8 - Sustainable consumption

The natural orientation of Indian consumers, systems and industries can help India leapfrog rampant consumerism and achieve the optima of sustainable consumption. By going back to natural products, materials and supply chains, and the culture of minimalism, the Indian population can reinstate harmonious existence with its environment.

Chapter 9 - Five star destinations

By adhering to the highest standards of responsible development, India can create the most attractive tourist destinations without disrupting the local biomes. A five-star treatment of the countryside will also make every Indian a five-star traveler.

Chapter 10 - Green transportation

Speed capping, use of green hydrogen, development of sustainable energy storage (vehicles and utilities), and scale are the key drivers for ensuring safety, sustainability, and efficiency in transportation. Walking, cycling, electric trains (metro and intercity), green hydrogen / battery powered shared cars, mini-buses, & commercial vehicles, and long haul flights, emerge as the logical options for travel and logistics in an 'urban only' India.

Chapter 11 - Make it large

From $400 billion (FY21), Indian manufacturing needs to be scaled up to ~$5 trillion - infrastructure related (~$1.5 trillion), sustainable consumption (~$3.0 trillion), and green transportation (~$500 billion). Focus on sustainability will minimize production requirements and increase the competitive advantage of domestic enterprises. Consolidating each industry into a few large players is pivotal for efficient and indigenous expansion. Initial rapid transformation towards a focused, efficient and sustainable manufacturing set up will be critical.

Chapter 12 - Sustainable Energy Balance

India can strike a sustainable energy balance around 22,000 TWh (~2.5 times the current primary energy consumption), by increasing industrial energy efficiency by ~60%, building over 10,000 GW of solar capacity, and embracing sustainable consumption, along with ubiquitous electrification.

Chapter 13 - Indian citizen

Responsible family planning, progressive asset ownership, minimum wages, healthy work policies, social security and pension, will enable a high standard of living for every Indian.

Chapter 14 - People love people

Formalization and institutionalization of services will enable India to fully exploit the power of its people towards ensuring sustainable production and consumption. The resulting size of the services industry would be around $23 trillion with a workforce of nearly 60 crore people.

Chapter 15 - Independent economy

The pursuit of sustainability as the supreme national objective is the best strategy for India to strengthen its economy in the near term and eventually gain economic independence. With focused investments towards the core structural changes and by garnering global support, India can achieve a real GDP of ~$28 trillion and a nominal GDP of ~$150 trillion in about 50 years.

Preface

Sustainable India is the culmination of a millennium of struggle, the emergence of a global leader, the impending resource cliff, and the collective learning and consciousness of humanity. It is the solemn proclamation of one of the world's most productive ecosystems that has been ravaged by conflict and continues to sacrifice its resources to defend against unsustainable geopolitical forces.

The population explosion post independence, accelerated industrial development over the last 3 decades, and dissemination of western consumption patterns, has led to a rapid deterioration of natural resources. The degradation has reached alarming levels and the on-going distributed development will drain India's natural wealth beyond recovery. The deterioration is all pervasive, deep rooted, and the various issues are heavily intertwined, rendering compartmentalized interventions (e.g. farm laws) unsuccessful and incremental gains inadequate.

Simultaneously, India has built leading capabilities across industries and is now possibly the most advanced intellectual superpower. Along with the capability and perspective India has acquired, it has also given itself the opportunity to step back and build a viable plan for building a sustainable future. 'Sustainable India' is the output of 2.5 years of dedicated research that started with a hypothesis that sustainability can solve every problem for India. The value creation discovery of the optimal model is based on the positive correlation between sustainability, health, safety, equality, efficiency, quality, productivity and economy.

The vision, strategy and transformation plan has been developed using globally accepted standard methodologies and by leveraging publications of leading professionals, researchers, engineers and experts in both Government and private sector institutions (global and India). The best practices have been applied to the subcontinent and the evolved Indian culture has formed the bedrock of guiding principles for determining the ideal structure, consumption and production patterns on the subcontinent.

The document recognizes the challenges of enacting the proposed transformation, and outlines the mechanism of financial engineering and ground level execution details for overcoming key roadblocks, while leveraging the existing institutional, industrial and cultural foundations.

The book provides an actionable plan for the Government to realistically drive the transformation over the next 50 years clearly specifying the structural changes, the reorientation of each industry, occupational changes, consumption patterns and code of conduct. The recommendations in each area are meant to ensure sustainability and certainty of execution. Besides acting as a strategic guide for the government and industry, the book is meant to build broader consensus, which is critical for enacting change in the world's largest democracy.

The book is also meant to advance the global frontier of sustainability and act as a resource for people and Governments across the globe.

Introduction

Sustainability refers to maintaining an ecological surplus (biocapacity minus ecological footprint) and bringing down the consumption of non-regenerative resources to negligible levels.

Most countries in this world don't even have the chance to become sustainable as they are not self-sufficient. This fundamental deficiency creates the necessity to trade and is the key determinant of their bargaining position in imports as well as exports. Self-sufficient countries and closely integrated regions have the bargaining power on everything. The favorable bargain translates into higher prices, larger economy, and a stronger currency. The stronger currency further increases their share of value in any trade. Self-sufficiency is critical for countries to adopt all best practices for maintaining and enriching the environment & the people, and factor those costs into the price of products and services. Dependent countries are simply unable to avoid resource extraction by the more powerful.

India is the only country in the world that is self-sufficient in natural resources and is now very close to having a full spectrum of industrial capabilities.

Amongst the six biogeographic regions of the world, the tropical and subtropical regions (Sub Saharan Africa, Latin America and Indo-Malay) display the highest levels of biodiversity and are also much older environments. Coupled with higher renewable energy availability, these regions are self-sufficient to sustain large human populations. The high bio and resource diversity enables dense settlements and minimizes trade requirements. This significantly reduces requirements for infrastructure, transportation, manufacturing, processing, packaging, logistics etc. Besides, all forms of production are less resource intensive in these regions. India, along with Brazil and Argentina, are the only large biodiverse countries in these regions, and India is by far the leader in industrial capabilities amongst these.

Therefore, India has the unique opportunity to become the world's first sustainable nation and guide geopolitics, macroeconomics, trade, finance, development, industry, consumption and code of conduct that enables the creation of sustainable regions and nations across the globe.

"Sustainable India" is a comprehensive game plan to revitalize nature and transform India into a sustainable superpower. The transformation blueprint is based on a novel strategy of making sustainability the supreme national objective. The overarching pursuit of sustainability gives rise to an optimal development model, and maximizes natural wealth, quality of life and strength of the Indian economy. The transformation blueprint smoothly facilitates core structural changes while leveraging frontier capabilities and the evolved Indian culture. The pure focus addresses all sovereign objectives most effectively, makes every Indian a willing participant, as well as garners global support for the transformation.

A sustainable India will also lay the foundation of a global transition towards delinked self-sufficient regions with minimal inter-regional trade. Global trade accounts for ~$32 trillion of the ~$90 trillion global economy and is the primary cause of ecological deficit and resource burden across regions. The gradual reduction of inter-regional trade will enable each region to evolve their own model of sustainability. Humans in each region will re-adapt to the region's environment and resources and correspondingly transform their patterns of settlement, development, industry and consumption. Dependent countries will no longer need to abuse their own resources to pay for imports.

Besides the direct impact due to inter-regional trade elimination, there will be indirect ripple effects (larger than the direct impact) associated with regional readaption. First, several product categories will disappear in the absence of material availability. E.g. Plastics and batteries may disappear with the unavailability of oil & gas or Li. Second, more durable products would be built and mainly for important needs. Functionality and mechanical engineering will reign supreme. Third, regions will find ways to minimize the energy and resource requirements - use of natural light, green modes of transportation, use of natural fibers for apparel, sharing economy etc. Most importantly, every region will accelerate a complete move towards efficient settlements (high-rise urban) that structurally minimize resource and energy requirements.

The re-adaption will enable people in each region to reconnect with nature and people at a much deeper level and focus on increasing the natural endowment. The resulting harmony will lead to a state of everlasting fulfillment. Natural supply chains will bring real joy. The experience of consuming fresh regional produce will be religious and would curb the desire for the global basket.

Delinking will automatically enable each region to become self-sufficient and to engage its workforce meaningfully towards sustainability. The occupational hierarchy will disappear as regions become responsible for doing everything themselves. The pure distinct identity of each region and its people will flourish, and the world will be a friendly place.

Synopsis

The fertile and diverse ecosystem of the Indian subcontinent has been devastated by the continuous state of conflict since the 10th century A.D. Environmental deterioration has reached alarming levels and unrestrained distributed development will drain the natural resources beyond the point of recovery. A pure focus on restoring the health of the environment and its people will not only rescue India but will also guide the most optimal form of development.

India is uniquely placed to build the world's first sustainable ecosystem and economy. The subcontinent is naturally endowed with abundant resources and still has the opportunity to follow the path of moderation. The decisive government over the last decade has accelerated capability development and enabled swift execution at all levels. India has arrived and can now reorient itself towards readiness in 10-15 years for indigenously building a sustainable India by 2075.

To create eternal harmony with nature, India will need to advance towards living in the city, create dense forests on more than 55% of land area with wide riparian cover, and build an extensive network of rivers, lakes and canals. Large-scale natural farming can meet the nutrition requirements with high quality produce from just ~100 Mha while maintaining soil health.

Bringing everyone to live together in ~130 equal high-rise cities is the core structural shift for India to maximize its natural wealth and resource efficiency, as well as to create the most fulfilling life experiences. The seemingly impossible transition can be smoothly facilitated over 50 years by adopting modularization for efficient, equitable and high-quality development. By offering attractive financial compensation and formal employment for relocation, the

Government will also enable urban development and higher economic productivity.

Each city should be spread over an area of ~2,000 km2 with an urban green cover of ~800 km2, urban blue (city's lake) over ~400 km2, high-rise buildings and mobility infrastructure over ~500 km2 and sports infrastructure over ~200 km2.

Mixed-use high-rise development will facilitate a reversal to natural products, materials and supply chains and a culture of minimalism. It would also enable the creation of a green transportation system. As people migrate to the cities, high quality development of the countryside will also become viable. Urban Indians will become responsible with systematic dissemination of family planning, progressive asset ownership, minimum wages, healthy work policies, social security and assured pension.

Consolidating each manufacturing industry is pivotal for efficiently meeting the industrial needs of the transformation and beyond. Nation's pivot towards sustainability will minimize production requirements, increase the competitive advantage of domestic enterprises and best leverage people's working capacity. Initial rapid transformation towards a focused, efficient and sustainable manufacturing set up will be critical before India initiates capacity expansion.

India can strike a sustainable energy balance by achieving benchmark industrial energy efficiency, building over 10,000 GW of solar capacity and embracing sustainable consumption, along with ubiquitous electrification. Formalization and institutionalization of services will enable India to fully exploit the power of its people.

The transformation can be viably and efficiently executed in four phases: i) concentration, consolidation and capability building (15 years), ii) capacity expansion (10 years), iii) steady growth (20 years), and iv) stabilize (5 years). Building indigenous full spectrum capabilities and regulating consumption would be critical to limit dependency during subsequent scale up.

The pursuit of sustainability as the supreme national objective is also the best strategy for India to strengthen its economy in the near term and eventually gain economic independence. Government led investments will drive growth in Phase I and II, with industrial expansion and formalization of services taking over eventually. India will gain more macro-economic control as it ramps down trade (Phase II onwards) and builds sufficient solar (end of Phase III). Real GDP gains will gradually start translating to concomitant appreciation of the INR. India would be generating a surplus on all fronts and the balance sheet will be backed by its own assets.

With focused investments towards the core structural changes and by garnering global support, India can achieve a real GDP of ~$28 trillion (2020 prices) and a nominal GDP ~$150 trillion in the next ~50 years, making the Indian economy larger than the US (~$140 trillion).

1. The burning passenger train

The Indian sub-continent that stretches from Hindukush in the west, Himalayas in the north, Pat-kai hills in the northeast, and Sri Lanka in the south, has a unique history of being formed by the breaking away of a landmass from Africa. The collision of this plate with the Eurasian plate resulted in the formation of the Himalayas, the tallest mountain range of the world.

The land of four distinct seasons, India is the most productive ecosystem in the world. Latitudinal location results in optimal levels of sun throughout the peninsula. The abundant water bodies around the sub-continent create moisture laden winds during the summers. Substantial precipitation is caused by the presence of abundant highlands (Himalayas, Western and Eastern Ghats, etc.) right across the path of the southwest monsoon winds. Direct rainfall and the mineral rich rivers flowing from the Himalayas, the Sahyadris and the Eastern Ghats have created the most fertile land mass in the world.

No wonder then that flora and fauna thrived here in all its brilliance. The flora of India is one of the richest in the world with an estimated 18,000 species of flowering plants in India, which constitute some 6-7 percent of the total plant species in the world. India is home to more than 50,000 species of plants, including a variety of endemics[1]. As the world's fifth largest megadiverse country[2], India has some of the world's most bio-diverse regions with four distinct biodiversity hotspots and is home to 7.6% of all mammalian, 12.6% of all avian, 6.2% of all reptilian, 4.4% of all amphibian, and 11.7% of all fish species.

---

[1] Species Diversity in India; ENVIS Centre: Wildlife & Protected Areas (Secondary Database); Wildlife Institute of India (WII)

[2] Biodiversity Theme Report, Williams, J. 2001

A natural consequence of India's rich biodiversity was the possible evolution of the human species[3]. It has been established that human life originated simultaneously in Africa, Europe and India. The species Homo heidelbergensis (a proto-human who was an ancestor of modern Homo sapiens) inhabited the subcontinent of India centuries before humans migrated into the region known as Europe.

Human evolution on the subcontinent was followed by the development of the world's largest ancient civilization - the Indus Valley civilization. Even though agriculture was the mainstay of these ancient Indian civilizations (Harappa, Mohenjodaro, Dravidian), these were basically urban civilizations where people lived in well-planned and well-built towns, which were also the centers of trade. The ruins of Mohenjo Daro and Harappa show that these were magnificent merchant cities - well planned, scientifically laid, and well looked after. They had wide roads and a well-developed drainage system. The houses were made of baked bricks and had two or more storeys.

Eventually, several kingdoms developed and flourished across different parts of the Indian subcontinent - Magadha, Haryanka, Shishunaga, Nanda, Maurya, Shunga, Gupta, Kushan, Harsha in the north-west, Kalinga and Kamarupa in the east, Chera, Chola, Pandyan, Satavahana, Vakataka, Kadamba and Pallava in the south.

With a population of 60 million in the 1st century AD, the subcontinent was flourishing. The population growth was minimal in the Classical and early Medieval eras resulting in a total population of ~67 million (6.7 crore) by 10th century AD. India was called the Golden Bird (earned the title 'Land of the Golden Sparrow', from the Romans) and contributed nearly 25% of world's GDP at this point.

Subsequent invasions into the subcontinent resulted in the decimation of around 50 million people and also accelerated

---

[3] India at the cross-roads of human evolution, R Patnaik, P. Chauhan, Nov 2009

the population growth. While the population growth was 5-10% per century till the 15th century, it increased to over 40-60% per century during the next 4 centuries. From ~100 million in 1500, the population of the subcontinent reached ~200 million by 1820. And by 1941, the last census before partition and independence, the subcontinent had a population of ~390 million.

After the partition, the population growth accelerated even further, and by 2011, the population of the subcontinent was in excess of 1,550 million or 155 crores, much ahead of China which stood at 1,344 million. India has achieved the highest population density amongst the top 50 countries by land area; the subcontinent has the 7th largest land mass with an area of 4.2 million sq kms.

The population explosion completely sidelined the associated development that was needed to maintain the quality of life. The subcontinent's share of world GDP declined to 3% (nominal) and ~8% (PPP). India was ranked ~150 out of 196 on GDP per capita i.e. income levels (2011), #124 in terms of literacy levels, a key determinant in the productivity of people, and #135 on life expectancy, a key indicator of the level of human development.

To make this worse, the uncontrolled human activity relentlessly destroyed the natural ecosystem and reduced the biocapacity of the region.

In the Vishnu Purana, one of the earliest published texts of the subcontinent, there is a reference to vanas (forest) existing across the length and breadth of the country[4]. Before the rise of the agrarian civilization, the subcontinent was inhabited by tribal societies. Being very few in number, these tribes received plenty for their sustenance from the natural growth in the forests. Even during the rise of the various indigenous civilizations, trees were worshiped and forests

---

[4] Nature worship in India and forests in ancient India, Forests in ancient and modern period", Nabendu Mondal, The University of Burdwan

were carefully preserved by the various rulers. The largest deforestation occurred during the Mughal era. As they came from arid lands, there was no concept of forestry or forest preservation. With their indifference, significant forest cover was lost to provide for timber, cultivation and energy. Even during the British presence on the subcontinent, forests were destroyed to increase grain production, provide wood for various industries, build railways and at times simply to prevent the locals from hiding in the forests. By the time of India's independence, India's recorded forest cover had reduced to 68 million hectares, around 20% of the total land area. Even though forest preservation became more important post independence, the primary (very dense) forest cover has now reduced to around 10 million hectares, just over 3% of the total land area[5]. "What we are doing to the forests of the world is but a mirror reflection of what we are doing to ourselves and to one another." - Mahatma Gandhi

The massive wipeout of forests, which are carbon sinks, along with rising levels of air pollution, have naturally resulted in temperature increases in the subcontinent. During the 20th century itself, the average temperature in the subcontinent has increased more than 3 degrees celsius. During the Covid months, the temperature decreased 3-5% on average as compared to last year, clearly indicating the impact of human activity on temperature. Himalayan glaciers lost billions of tons of ice — equivalent to more than a vertical foot and half of ice each year—from 2000 to 2016. That's double the amount of melting that took place from 1975 to 2000, revealing that the ice loss is accelerating with rising temperatures[6]. Forest fires have become commonplace due to the interdependence of irresponsible human settlements,

---

[5] India state of forest report 2021, Forest Survey of India, Ministry of Environment Forest and Climate Change

[6] Acceleration of ice loss across the Himalayas over the past 40 years, Department of Earth and Environmental Sciences, New York and Department of Geography, University of Utah

lower rainfall, higher temperatures, drying rivers and degraded soils.

Rivers, which are the lifeline and connect the entire subcontinent, are supposedly the most polluted in the world and water levels in most of them have reduced drastically. Unplanned growth has led to the use of water bodies as dumping grounds for sewage and industrial effluent. According to India's Central Pollution Control Board, 63 percent of the urban sewage flowing into rivers (some 62 billion liters a day) is untreated. It is estimated that around 70% of surface water in India is unfit for consumption. Be it Ganga, Yamuna, Brahmaputra, Kaveri, Narmada, Sabarmati, Damodar, Cooum, Mithi or Ulhas, large stretches of these rivers are considered dead zones, with oxygen levels too low to support most fish life.

Release of pollution upstream lowers economic growth in downstream areas. The World Bank suggests a reduction of over 33% in GDP growth in these regions. In middle-income countries like India where water pollution is a bigger problem, the impact increases to a loss of almost half of GDP growth. Another study estimates that downstream areas (from the centers of pollution) experience a 9% reduction in agricultural revenues and a 16% drop in agricultural yields[7].

In addition, riverbanks, riparian woodlands, wetlands, and floodplains have been claimed over time by agriculture, infrastructure, slums, offices, and housing developments - all of which have narrowed natural river channels, distorted flow and inhibited the natural absorption of the river water into the surrounding lands. This has resulted in enhanced flooding around all major Indian rivers and loss of biodiversity in the region.

The Chennai floods took nearly 300 lives, damaged thousands of homes and businesses, and paralyzed the

---

[7] The Costs of Industrial Water Pollution to Agriculture in India, "Essays on the Economics of Water", Nicholas W. Hagerty, Department of Economics, Massachusetts Institute of Technology, June 2018

airport, which is partly built over the Adyar River, all leading to an estimated $3 billion in losses to the city's economy. The flood brought attention to the assault on the region's natural systems, with marshland shrinking by 45 square miles from 1980 to 2010.

A similar disaster unfolded in Mumbai on July 26, 2005 when an unprecedented monsoon deluge drowned the financial capital, killing more than 900 people, damaging a quarter-million homes, and causing an estimated $2 billion in economic losses. This inundation made Mumbai residents suddenly aware of the presence of the Mithi River in their midst. A modest channel that begins in suburban hills, the Mithi winds 11 miles down to the Arabian Sea. For much of its run, the river is a glorified sewer serving small workshops, slums, housing, the airport, and a business center. All were inundated on that fateful day when the conjunction of high tide and extreme rain caused the river to overflow its banks and flood the city. The airport's runway had been built over the river, narrowing the channel and forcing it into a 90-degree bend, and a new office district had been built on wetlands. One satellite study found that from 1966 to 2005 the width of the Mithi was reduced by almost 50 percent, while mudflats had shrunk by 70 percent[8].

All the farming states of India (Assam, West Bengal, Bihar, Uttar Pradesh, Kerala, Gujarat, Karnataka, Madhya Pradesh, Tamil Nadu, Goa, Orissa, Andhra Pradesh) were severely affected by floods in 2019.

The subcontinent has also witnessed the depletion of all its water reservoirs i.e. lakes, ponds etc. A large number of shallow lakes have been completely lost to farming and other human activities. Most of the remaining ones have either been reduced to swamps, or drastically reduced in size and volume. They are now also heavily polluted with sewage and industrial disposal. As per the Central Water Commission

---

[8] Dying Waters: India Struggles to Clean Up Its Polluted Urban Rivers, Yale School of Environment, Vaishnavi Chandrashekhar, Feb 2018

(CWC), most reservoirs in 2019 have 30-80% less water as compared to the 10 year average. Western and Southern states have been impacted the most - 83% reduction in Andhra Pradesh, 71% in Maharashtra, 43% in Tamil Nadu, 38% in Kerala, 36% in Karnataka and so on. The 10 year averages are themselves much below the water levels seen in these reservoirs before the population exploded. In 2015, water level had declined in over 60% of the wells across India over the last 10 ten years.

The cost of environmental degradation in India is estimated to be INR 3.75 trillion ($80 billion) a year. The health costs relating to water pollution are alone estimated at about INR 470-610 billion ($6.7-8.7 billion per year)[9].

India is literally burning itself up to keep going. And unlike the developed economies, that are at least generating financial returns from the exploitation, India is not even able to do that.

India is largely a consumption driven economy with very low investment in building capabilities for the future. Nearly 60% of the Indian economy is based on private consumption with only ~11% investment in fixed capital. China, on the other hand, has 40% private consumption and 40% investment in fixed capital. India was left behind during the Industrial Revolution and is now decades behind on capabilities across several industries. India is ranked around 60 globally on innovation, the most important factor that determines industrial competitiveness.

India does not have even a single enterprise that generates non-linear financial returns for the economy. We are absent from the list of top 50 companies globally by revenue or profit. Imagine the contribution companies like Apple, Samsung, Foxconn, Walmart, Amazon, Sinopec, Shell, Volkswagen, Toyota, General Motors, Berkshire Hathaway,

---

[9] World Economic Forum

United Health, Mckesson, AT&T, Huawei, Google, Microsoft, Facebook etc. make to their respective economies.

Truth be told, India has never had the time or the resources to step back and build indigenous capabilities to nurture a self-sufficient and independent ecosystem, the way it naturally was. Indians simply became followers, allowing foreign players to control the direction of their industries. Local Indian counterparts have never been able to compete on either quality or efficiency. India never consolidated its efforts and ended up having a distributed production environment with a plethora of small and medium enterprises across the length and breadth of the country. These enterprises could obviously never achieve the scale efficiencies of the foreign players and build defensible capabilities across the value chain. We have ended up becoming dealers, assemblers, distributors or retailers, completely dependent on the core creators.

India simply ends up sacrificing the environment and its people to somehow compete with the large efficient companies. To save costs, the industrial units avoid using clean sources of energy, managing their waste, or cleaning the pollution they generate. They keep the wages so low that the employees can never follow an environmentally friendly and healthy way of living.

Government policies are reactive and incremental as they are severely constrained by external dependencies, insufficient internal availability of investment capital, business lobbying, and fear of public backlash. Environmental regulation is evolving in functional silos and enforcement is compromised at various levels. Policy making is primarily driven by national security and the development agenda, and the environment is almost always sidelined or deferred, especially in front of the latter.

India is so far down this path of natural disaster, that instead of trying to reverse the process of destruction, people are just adopting artificial solutions to avoid the consequences on their personal life. To avoid the heat people are using air conditioners, for clean water they are using water purifiers, for clean air they are using air purifiers, and so on. People are simply increasing the rate of burn and environmental degradation.

India is now in a situation where its very existence threatens life on the subcontinent. India is the most fiercely competitive market and society of the world. Indians have already exploited every inch of the available land. The competition is so intense, that Indians have no hesitation in taking shortcuts, breaking rules or the code of conduct. India is soon likely to reach a stage where resources will become extremely scarce and the fight for survival will become uncontrollable. "Cultivating and conserving diversity is no luxury in our times. It's a survival imperative." Vandana Shiva.

2. The Holy Grail

Before the Covid pandemic, India had been steadily marching ahead on the path to becoming a developed nation. In 2018, the GDP per capita on a PPP (Purchasing Power Parity) basis was $7.8k with a total GDP (PPP) of $10.5 trillion. As cost of living is fundamentally lower on the subcontinent (lower energy requirements, higher land fertility etc.), PPP numbers reveal the real story. The developed nations have a per capita GDP (PPP) above $40k, around 5 times of what we have. On a PPP basis that is very significant. But if India were to achieve the same in say the next 30 years by 2050, when it is likely to have a population of 1.65 billion, the size of the economy would reach around $65 trillion (PPP) or around $15-20 trillion (real terms). That represents an year on year annual growth of 6.25%. With the world GDP expected to be around $270 trillion, India would be back to having a significant share of the world GDP like in the Golden Age.

This linear surge is very tempting to say the least, but as with most things in this world, there is always a catch. Well, there are several challenges if India goes down the path of achieving glory in the world's GDP rat race.

First, this reflects a significant shift in world order and there would definitely be resistance, given that the Indian economy is well integrated now with global supply chains. China sustained its rapid surge in times when the world was not as integrated and connected as it is today. There was little competition for China during those growth years (1980-2010) and language was a strong barrier preventing any leakages. Today apart from China, there are other manufacturing powerhouses like Mexico, Vietnam, Indonesia and Malaysia. Given that these powerhouses are highly advanced in their capabilities and also have good investment availability, moves by India to increase share of the global trade would be readily countered. India will also start facing increasing scrutiny of operations and higher tariffs from the countries whose domestic industries come under threat.

With the developed economies witnessing a slowdown in growth and a rise in unemployment, there has been an increasing shift from open markets towards protectionism over the last decade or so[10]. While direct tariffs have been avoided, subsidies for domestic players and increased trading requirements have been more popular measures. Iron & steel and automotive have been the most negatively impacted industries of late. Hidden protectionism is only likely to increase further[11].

India's experience with Free Trade Agreements (FTAs) also lays bare the uphill battle it faces in its attempt to grow trade. Three out of four of our major FTAs have resulted in a trade deficit. These were with South Korea, Japan and ASEAN. We only generated a trade surplus through our South Asian Free Trade agreement[12].

Second, large foreign players are gradually eating into the domestic consumption pie and will increasingly limit India's ability to generate investment capital for nation building. Over the last three decades, India has already seen domination by foreign entities in some of its core consumption sectors viz. consumer electronics, FMCG, and automotive. More recently India is witnessing the rich and higher middle income segments develop and exercise preference for premium global brands especially in clothing, home appliances, kitchenware, packaged food, furniture, toys etc.

---

[10] Rising Protectionism Signals Valuable Lessons Have Been Forgotten, International Institute for Sustainable Development (IISD), Per Altenberg, Jul 2021

[11] Trend toward trade protectionism expected to continue in 2020, weigh on growth, Craig Wong, Canadian Press, Dec 19, 2019

[12] Free Trade after RCEP: What Next for India?, Observer Research Foundation, Nandini Sarma, Apr 2020

Third, the export orientation of several core industries will increasingly drain critical resources. Agricultural produce, petroleum crude and products, and base metals, are among the top exports sectors for India. These are essential resources for infrastructure development and self-sufficient consumption.

Fourth, India's high manpower intensiveness in industrial production will create a drag on its ability to increase competitiveness. Automation and technology products have the highest impact on low skilled and high volume jobs. Given the manpower intensity in India, technology adoption will be slower, resulting in lower efficiency and investment attractiveness.

Fourth, the Indian economy will need to bear the burden of a very large unemployed population. As the latest technologies do get adopted, India is likely to witness high levels of unemployment. There is still 50-60% of the population residing and growing up in villages and towns. All of them are at risk of not finding any worthwhile employment in the new economy. That will create a huge strain on government expenditure and drastically reduce its ability to sustain economic growth.

Fifth, both the public and private sector lack the ability to make the required investment in fixed capital to mobilize large scale manufacturing. Large scale manufacturing has been built across the world with the availability of risk-free capital. Government funds, large corporations generating sustained profits, big insurance companies and pension plans, and big banks with low NPAs, typically provide capital for such investments. While India has seen the emergence of these entities, capital availability is still nowhere close to the levels of investment required for building gigafactories.

Sixth, India's ability to innovate and produce for the world is not likely to change, and so nonlinear contribution to the economy seems unlikely. Innovation is a process and necessitates having leading edge capabilities to start with.

Given the position of our existing industries, we are likely to just keep playing the catch-up game. Also, innovation is becoming increasingly difficult and sizable capital is needed to develop something novel and valuable for the world.

Seventh, the current economic growth and competitiveness will be negatively impacted once Indians start paying taxes. Amongst the large emerging nations, India has the lowest tax to GDP ratio of ~11%. Most developed nations have the ratio above 35%; even other emerging economies have the ratio between 20% and 30%. Even though the Government has simplified taxation with the introduction of GST, compliance remains abysmally low. There are several reasons for the same but primarily it is low incomes, high competition and absence of effective enforcement mechanisms (digital adoption, severe penalties, linkage to citizenship benefits, etc.). As and when the compliance challenges are solved, the increased taxes will negatively impact both the supply and demand curves, and in turn will dampen economic growth in the short to medium term.

Increasing liberalization across sectors of the economy has driven higher growth post 1990 and since 2000. The Indian market has seen a flood of investment from multinational corporations (MNCs) looking to grab a share of the expected consumption growth. Foreign companies have already entered all sectors and will eventually overcome roadblocks for complete market dominance. The only significant internal driver was the development of the IT industry but even that is largely dependent on the business environment of the US and Europe.

Liberalization was really the only option for the Indian government in the 1990s to build the economy and generate resources to fend off threats from hostile neighbors. It was also the best way for Indian companies to get connected with the larger global industries and learn from them. India has indeed reaped these benefits - the defense capability is way past deterrence and moving towards increasing collaboration. India has indeed built a large base of experts in every field who are helping create domestic counterparts to the multinationals.

But staying on this path for too long would lead to economic colonization. Most of India's manufacturing and services sectors (automotive, FMCG, food & beverage, home appliances, electronics, electrical, glass, textiles, furniture, toys, sports, heavy engineering, insurance, hospitality, communication etc.) would be foreign controlled in the next 30-40 years. With very few large domestic corporations, India will lose economic control to foreign entities and with that lose the capability to act on its other critical sovereign objectives. The liberalization led development path would largely be governed by what the world wants as against what truly makes sense for the subcontinent.

What India needs today is a clear vision of what it really wants and needs to channelize all its efforts in that direction. India currently has several long-term objectives - increasing GDP, becoming self-sufficient, unifying the subcontinent, reducing population and income inequality, building infrastructure, improving health, becoming a smart society, rebuilding its natural wealth, providing equal opportunities, keeping its people happy etc.

Nordics, which comprises the world's most developed countries, has already achieved most of the above objectives. Even though they have an ecological surplus, they are now focusing all their efforts towards sustainability. Experts predict that their largest glaciers will completely melt away in the next 50-75 years[13].

Even Western Europe, which is home to the next set of developed economies, is now prioritizing sustainability. France, where temperature has been rising steeply, is now

---

[13] Norwegian mountain glaciers in the past, present and future, University of Bergen, Jan 2008

taking a lead in driving the sustainability agenda globally. They apparently have a significant ecological deficit.

Essentially these countries have largely developed as much as they could and are now moving towards sustainability.

They are doing so not just because they care for the environment, sustainability also presents a huge business growth opportunity. Whoever builds capabilities for sustainability will eventually also lead in the global business environment.

Sustainability by definition is the ultimate human purpose. Earth has gone through many cycles of creation and destruction of life. These have occurred as earth moved between the greenhouse and ice age periods.

Greenhouse periods are much hotter with very high carbon dioxide levels and are characterized by an explosion of life forms. The high temperature eventually leads to volcanic activity and formation of large mountains. Mountain formation saps carbon dioxide and results in chilling of the earth, and a transition to the Ice Age.

In the Ice Age or the Ice House periods, ice caps form at the poles and there are sheets of ice over water. Within the Ice House there are shorter cycles of glacials and interglacials.

We're living in a mild interglacial of a long-term Icehouse. Temperate climate for many millennia has allowed the human population to expand to what it is today.

But now due to the ongoing anthropogenic greenhouse gas emissions, the Earth is heading towards a greenhouse Earth period. The accelerated melting of the polar ice caps and the mountain glaciers, and changes in the amount of water stored in lakes and rivers on land, is likely to result in a damaging rise in sea levels. In the worst case scenarios, polar ice caps might completely collapse resulting in a severe rise in temperature.

Even though there is no broad consensus yet on the timelines, all the research reveals an accelerated degradation of the environment over the last 20 to 40 years. The population explosion and industrial revolution have literally put the earth on fire and polluted the air, land and sea like never before.

So, halting this march towards devastation is clearly an imperative for humanity. Not only do we have to stop the degradation but we have to actually reverse the direction of climate change.

While humans have caused the greatest devastation, we are also the most evolved life form and the only ones with the ability to create things and enact change. "In Marsh's view man was an agent of destruction as well as regeneration, with the potential, as he so beautifully put it, to be a 'restorer of disturbed harmonies." - Ramchandra Guha, Environmentalism: A Global History.

We have developed a deep understanding of every component of the earth's ecosystem. We know what the planet is made of and how the different elements interact with each other. We know the consequences of all types of human activity and have now also learnt the principles of sustainable living.

We have the capability to revitalize ecosystems and make flora and fauna flourish in a natural manner. We can even build systems and structures to control phenomena and prevent disasters.

We have the unique capability to reverse climate change and then stabilize the environment. We can achieve the optima where there is perfect balance between human activity, the earth's natural resources and the environment.

Stabilizing temperature, volume of ice, sea levels, amount of rainfall, ground water levels, volcanic activity and other movements in the earth's crust, is that ultimate human purpose.

Once we achieve balance with nature, there is literally nothing much left to do. We can then just find more ways to play, have fun and keep increasing life spans, without disturbing the harmony with nature.

Sustainability would necessitate fundamental changes in the way we live. Every aspect of human activity needs to be relooked at from a sustainability lens. That would lead to changes in what and how we consume and produce, and hence would require new products, new services, maybe the reintroduction of old products and services that are more sustainable or can be made so by rethinking the supply chains and the modes of delivery. Sustainability will therefore create most of the new opportunities and drive growth across industries.

India today has the unique opportunity to become the global leader in driving sustainability. Even though India is large, it is more flexible than the leading economies given that most of the development is yet to happen. The subcontinent has been bestowed with nature in all its glory and therefore the natives have always been very deeply integrated with it. Indians worship rivers, mountains, the clouds, trees, animals, birds, fruits, grains and literally everything that nature has provided. The subcontinent's ecosystem is our natural habitat and all aspects of our life have evolved in a deep alliance with the local environment. Our festivals and foods celebrate the seasons, and our eating habits show respect for all forms of life. We dance when it rains, rise with the birds and sleep when trees do. The best perfume for us is when dry sand meets rain.

The dream of Indian society has always been to achieve perfect harmony with nature. They have always aspired to fly with the birds, and move with the sun, wind and water. Indian batsmen rely on timing, not hitting the ball hard.

Indians have always had the supreme consciousness - they realize that only when Mother Earth is healthy would they be healthy. We have always believed that if we just take care of the mother, she will take care of her children. The linkage between the environment and humans is the foundation of the Indian cultural heritage, and Indians have always known that preserving and enhancing natural wealth will have the most direct, positive and meaningful impact on their lives. "Respect for nature is an integral part of our culture and has been passed across generations. Protection of the environment comes naturally to us." - Narendra Modi, Prime Minister of India.

Now, there are three distinct alternatives for India to go about achieving sustainability.

The first alternative entails focus on becoming a developed nation and then moving towards sustainability. The second alternative is to follow a sustainable development model as also propagated by the United Nations. And the third alternative is to just focus on sustainability and do everything that's needed for it.

Alternative 1 - Development first

As for the first alternative, India will take at least 50 more years to get anywhere close to becoming a developed nation. The development will further accelerate the pace of environmental degradation and cause irreversible damage beyond the point of recovery. Melting of glaciers, depletion of coal, oil, precious metals, minerals, polluted soil, are just some of those consequences. New Delhi, which used to attract some of the best global talent, is now fast declining on the choice list due to the environmental degradation. Already 27 out of the top 30 polluted cities in the world are on the subcontinent.

The development will most likely be haphazard driven primarily by cost and return consideration of the investors. Even though the planning authorities have developed some thinking around having industrial zones and economic zones in various cities, they have limited understanding of what needs to be done where. With the current development mindset, India will essentially end up doing everything everywhere resulting in lower efficiencies, minimal synergies, and inability to create globally competitive Indian enterprises.

The country will end up developing consumption behaviors that disregard necessity, nature, purity, balance and health. In the haste to develop fast, the natural habitat will be compromised. We are likely to see palm trees everywhere just because they grow faster. GMOs would have captured most of India's agricultural produce. And India may end up creating the world's largest waste processing and management companies.

Given the capitalist nature of the development focus, India would still end up having a large percentage of poor, lower middle class, minimally educated and low skilled population. High inequality and resource constraints will result in a hyper competitive society of spineless people with low levels of trust, empathy, satisfaction, authenticity, creativity and self belief.

'Development first' will essentially be the fastest pathway towards irreversible resource drain, environmental degradation and economic colonization. The development first approach will likely find favor with the global business environment but will be more expensive and lead to higher levels of foreign control. The large global companies will execute resource intensive development that caters to lavish lifestyles. India will also face higher sanctions in this path resulting in higher costs for the economy. On this path, India will soon exhaust its natural resources and become a fully dependent economy.

Alternative 2 - Sustainable development / climate change / decarbonization / ESG

As the name suggests, sustainable development is about simultaneously working on the twin objectives of sustainability and development of both people and the environment. Eradicating poverty, creating peace, removing gender inequality, reducing income inequality, providing equal opportunity, giving land and property to everyone, ensuring healthy lives, achieving food security, ensuring water availability, achieving sustained economic growth, creating decent employment for all, building infrastructure, making consumption sustainable, combating climate change, preserving natural wealth and ecosystems, and so on are some of the key objectives in this approach.

While these objectives are indeed very charitable and humanitarian, the current global business environment is really not geared to support these. Defense companies do not want peace in the world, health companies would lose profitability if they provided free or cheap medications, real estate and infrastructure developers do not want to encourage individual ownership, investors will not discourage innovation that increases efficiency and reduces manpower dependence, companies will not have the same pay for all, and so on. And so one might get some CSR allocation towards these sustainable development goals, but that would really not move the needle on the deep rooted systemic issues.

Sustainable development possibly makes sense for developed regions like North America, Europe, Russia and Australasia, where the population density is low and resource burden is not significant. The resource burden has also been greatly optimized by these regions by establishing global supply chains to import raw materials, agricultural produce and resource intensive industrial output. In these regions, even inefficient distributed development, will not lead to resource constraints for at least the next 500 years.

They are only faced with the problem of climate change, a subset of sustainability. Given that the world together is responsible for climate change at a local level, the developed world is focused on the agenda of climate change across the globe. For decadal and longer timescales, global mean changes explain at least 60% of local change for most of the planet[14].

Emissions are the primary contributor of climate change and therefore the developed world is concentrating all its energies towards decarbonization. Besides, even though the developed world has been outsourcing industrial production to Asia and South America, they are still major contributors to the total global emissions as they have a sizable share of carbon intensive energy generation and industrial production in their own countries.

And instead of pursuing development and consumption patterns to reduce the use of organic matter, they are attempting to avoid the release of emissions into the environment. In essence, they are burning more to sustain their lifestyles with the use of energy and resource intensive technologies. This is further accelerating the depletion of fossils and non-renewable resources.

By building the global narrative around climate change and decarbonization, the developed world is simply solving the only problem that they face, with little regard to the problems of others or the disastrous consequences in simply addressing climate change.

For the developing world, a blind focus on climate change and decarbonization will increase economic dependency (cost of technology upgrades) in the short term, further force export of raw materials, produce and output, and lead to a faster drain of resources and economic colonization. India has already committed to climate action goals and is witnessing a flurry of investment activity across industries for decarbonization as well as steady growth of exports.

Now even if you assume noble intentions, expecting the world to pump in billions of dollars of free money in the name of sustainable development to help clean up the great Indian

---

[14] Global vs local, Nature Climate Change, Oct 2015

mess, would essentially be day dreaming. Not to say that the world has not tried, it has, but has never seen any real change happening on the ground as a result. India has to start acting seriously on the clean up before it's too late, and then maybe with some genuine progress, the world will join the bandwagon and with real positive intent.

And the Indian government clearly does not have the resources to simultaneously work on the twin objectives of sustainable development on its own.

The broad-based approach fails to prioritize the structural shifts needed to move towards equitable development and sustainability. It is essentially an attempt to treat various symptoms of the problem without really diagnosing or dealing with the core issue. Sustainable development is essentially being penny-wise and pound foolish. It is letting people continue on the path of distributed development with poor levels of resource efficiency. Instead of making production and consumption truly sustainable, sustainable development is about finding smart work-arounds for shifting the environmental liability to others.

While carbon accounting might encourage some companies to become greener, it also makes fundamentally unsustainable companies seem technically acceptable and allows them to keep fueling unnecessary consumption.

Enterprise, social and governance (ESG) standards are the latest entrant to corporate sustainability. They are being welcomed across the world, as the system minimizes direct Government intervention and brings in well incentivized private players to manage themselves. The standards that have been developed by the World Economic Forum, the International Business Council and the Big Four accounting firms are designed to improve the financial performance of a company in a changing world, not vice versa. They also bear no connection to natural boundaries.[15] Both the core 22 and

---

[15] ESG investing isn't designed to save the planet, Harvard Business Review, Aug 2022

expanded 34 metrics are structured to align with the UN's 2030 Agenda for sustainable development. Each of the Big Four has been made the leader for a key area: principles of governance (led by Deloitte), planet (led by PwC), people (led by KPMG) and prosperity (led by Ernst & Young).

ESG ratings don't measure a company's impact on the Earth and society. In fact, they gauge the opposite: the potential impact of the world on the company and its shareholders. Marketing materials of ESG funds often make lofty statements about social or environmental aspirations, but the fine print reveals that the real goal is to assure shareholder profits. According to Henry Fernandez, CEO of the leading ESG ratings provider MSCI, ESG doublespeak has confused most individuals, many institutional investors, and even some portfolio managers. ESG funds are based on unregulated ESG ratings. ESG ratings, in turn, are built on comparative rankings of industry peers not on universal standards. This is why fossil fuel companies can have better ESG ratings than makers of electric vehicles. In addition, the data underlying ESG ratings are incomplete, mostly unaudited, and often dated. There are multiple ongoing efforts to standardize ESG reporting, but, for the foreseeable future, ESG investors will not have access to comparable, accurate measures, making it nearly impossible to attribute results or make impact claims.

Most importantly, the boom in ESG investing helps to create the impression that the trillions of dollars needed to finance the transformation to a low carbon economy are on the way. This misconception likely relieves pressure on necessary regulatory reforms and the massive public private partnerships that are required to avert the increasing threats to environmental and social welfare. If so, this deferral would represent the latest installment of a 50-year trope positing that market based voluntary action can supplant the need for public regulation of private externalities.

As but one illustration of the limits of voluntary action, consider Coke's voluntary efforts to reduce one of its most material ESG risk factors: water usage. After years of effort and NGO partnerships in close to 100 countries to save and replenish local watersheds, Coke declared itself "water neutral" in 2015 — five years ahead of its self-selected target. In part as a result, Coke's ESG rating via MSCI is "AA," or market leader. However, Coke's chosen boundary for water neutrality is the water used in manufacturing, distribution, and cooling, not the more than 90 percent of water it estimates that it uses in its agricultural supply chain, primarily in the fields to irrigate farmed sugar.

Sustainable development, along with its associated approaches (climate change, decarbonization, ESG etc.), are simply avoidance mechanisms that are unlikely to deliver any real impact. They are venetian blinds that are pushing out the urgent need for action by Governments and are enabling the corporate to suppress the activism. They are preventing the introduction of structural reforms needed to shut down unsustainable enterprises and to facilitate sustainable lifestyles.

The approach fails to recognize that it is essentially our natural environment that determines the way we act and the kind of society we build. Humankind thrives where nature flourishes, and when humans over exploit natural resources, the society deteriorates.

Alternative 3 - Lead with sustainability: just focus on rebuilding our natural wealth and creating harmony with nature.

Sustainability means the ability to maintain resources at a certain rate or level or avoidance or the depletion of natural resources in order to maintain an ecological balance. At its most literal level, 'sustainability' refers to the quality of a state or process that allows it to be maintained indefinitely. While the term can be applied to any spatial scale, the most obvious and relevant application for humanity is to the planet earth or more broadly the ecosphere, which includes both biological and physical components of the planet[16].

Sustainability has also been defined as the indefinite survival of the human species across all regions of the world[17]. While the focus on humans could be considered narrow, human survival also depends on the survival of other life forms and the continuity of all ecosystems. And given that human population is now the biggest threat to sustainability and the fact that humans are the most superior beings on the planet with the collective consciousness and capabilities to enact change, human perspective becomes central for achieving sustainability. The United Nations defined (1987) sustainability as "meeting our own needs without compromising the ability of future generations to meet their own needs".

The variability of human needs is higher as compared to that of resource availability. Besides, it is more feasible to adjust needs based on resource availability rather than attempting the opposite. Therefore, the resource perspective becomes even more fundamental and also helps establish clear principles that can guide human progress towards sustainability.

For humans to flourish indefinitely, a sufficient stock of all resources should always be available. During the 1970s and '80s when industrial advances were significant (also the time when the sustainability narrative was initially framed), resource requirements seemed an uncertain variable. Since then, humanity has indeed found solutions for sustainable living in almost all areas. And with diminishing returns on core technology and focus shifting towards experience in this century, the current estimates of resource requirements should now be fairly accurate.

---

[16] Chemistry of the climate system, Möller, Detlev

[17] Global sustainability: Toward Definition, Diana Liverman, Robert Merideth

An ecological surplus (biocapacity[18] minus ecological footprint[19]) ensures availability of regenerative or renewable resources and the continuity of all natural ecosystems. While most of the earth's resources regenerate, some are not replaced quick enough to keep pace with consumption and are termed as non-renewable resources[20] (minerals and metal ores, fossil fuels, and groundwater in certain aquifers).

While humanity has developed solutions to minimize the consumption of non-renewable resources, their use is still needed for capital formation (infrastructure, machinery, etc.) and as well as for certain on-going requirements (appliances, equipment, electronics, batteries and other non-durable products). Sustainability would therefore first and foremost restrict usage of non-regenerative resources to at least keep the majority of these reserves intact. Second, consumption for capital maintenance, upgrades, and redevelopment, and for the on-going requirements, should be brought down to negligible levels.

By doing so, we will also have the best chance of stabilizing temperature, volume of ice, sea levels, amount of rainfall, ground water levels, volcanic activity and other movements in the earth's crust, and ensure indefinite survival of human population in the true sense, although the quantum is likely to be lower given the current ecological deficit and stage of development across the globe.

So, at a high level, India would become sustainable if it maintains ecological balances and brings down the depletion of non-renewable resources to negligible levels. "We, the present generation, have the responsibility to act as a trustee of the rich natural wealth for the future generations."- Narendra Modi, Prime Minister of India.

---

[18] Global Footprint Network

[19] Mathis Wackernagel and William Rees, University of British Columbia (early 1990s)

[20] Earth systems and environmental sciences, Elsevier 2013

At first glance, it seems like an impossible and boring thing to do. Also, there is no precedence to visualize what this kind of focus would entail. This is a novel approach and involves a new set of challenges and opportunities. Given the way Indians have spread themselves far and wide into every corner of the subcontinent, such revitalization really seems daunting. The current stock and rate of consumption of various resources presents a very grim scenario.

Well, the good news is that science, engineering, technology, systems, processes and behaviors have rapidly evolved globally that present solutions to every sustainability challenge we face today. Over the last two decades, technology has dramatically changed the spectrum of possibilities for mankind. It has brought in efficiency in the way we live and operate in workplaces or at home. Most importantly it has allowed the dissemination of the world's collective wisdom. Whether it is large scale forestation, restoration of natural habitats of different flora and fauna, building dams, lakes, or canals, sustainable real estate, large scale monitoring and surveillance systems, creating sustainable products, or ensuring safety for everyone, today we have the ability to achieve whatever we set our minds to. "The climate crisis has already been solved. We already have all the facts and solutions. All we have to do is to wake up and change." - Greta Thumberg, climate activist.

A certain segment of population, even in India, has already developed the understanding and is leading the sustainability charge by their choices and actions. But unless there is national consensus, the high cost of sustainability will eventually even dissuade those who are making the attempt.

The entire Indian society will have to genuinely unite towards the cause to really make it happen. India's accumulated knowledge and collective wisdom would be needed to plan this transformation and to make it happen without adversely affecting anyone.

While for some the prospect of a thriving and beautiful natural environment itself is motivating to dedicate themselves fully to the cause, others will only make an informed judgment. To do so, we need to dig deep into what a pure sustainability focus would entail.

Can a selfless devotion to achieving balance with nature lead to the welfare of the masses? Will it solve the problem of poverty and income inequality? Will it help India achieve economic prosperity and guide the nation towards building the right infrastructure? Will it help everyone get high quality education and healthcare? Will it help achieve peace and safety for all? Will it help everyone find meaningful employment and opportunities to realize their potential? Will it help create an eclectic social infrastructure?

Is it viable for India to make this shift? Does it present an opportunity for India to lead the world into the 22nd century?

Maybe, India is the rightful torch bearer and should lead the charge towards humankind's greatest mission. The Indian subcontinent is the world's most productive, valuable and diverse ecosystem, has undergone the highest extent of damage, is still far from being developed, and is home to a population with an inherent love for nature and people, high levels of intelligence and logical thinking capabilities.

For pretty much no fault of ours, we had to sacrifice millions to defend our motherland. Indians have thwarted all foreign attempts to capture their homeland over the centuries. Our farmers have broken their back over the last century to give India the chance to survive and build a nation. Indians have come to be known as the most hard-working over the last few decades as they have learnt from the world and built their domestic industries.

It is now possibly India's chance to bring it all together and reclaim the position of being the most evolved civilization - a place where all human beings can enjoy prosperous and fulfilling lives and where economic, social and technological progress occurs in harmony with nature.

Sustainability presents the biggest and lasting business opportunity for the world. Green technology and sustainability is expected to have a GDP share of 20% in the next 10 to 20 years. The market will keep growing over the next 100 years as the world transitions towards complete sustainability.

Sustainability presents a unique opportunity for domestic businesses to dominate the Indian market. Local enterprises will gain significant supply chain and cost advantages making it nearly impossible for foreign businesses to stay viable.

Indians and the broader global society just need to give the Indian polity the confidence to swiftly enact regulations that enable the transformation towards sustainable living in India. Indians are a family, and they need to behave like one to make their home the most beautiful for the children.

3. Rebuilding natural wealth

"The wealth of the nation is its air, water, soil, mountains, forests, minerals, rivers, lakes, oceans, scenic beauty, wildlife habitats and biodiversity... that's all there is. That's the whole economy. That's where all the economic activity and jobs come from. These biological systems are the sustaining wealth of the world." - Gaylord Nelson

The natural wealth of the Indian subcontinent includes the four watersheds (Himalayan and Karakoram range, the Sahyadris, the Aravallis, and the Vindhyas and Satpura ranges), the rivers that flow from them, the various natural lakes, the different types of forests, our fertile lands, and the coastal areas.

The mountains are a critical source of water, electricity, fruits, medicinal herbs, and minerals. They serve another very important purpose. They provide a physical screen within which the monsoon system operates and are the source of the great river systems that water the plains below. As a result of erosion, the rivers coming from the mountains carry vast quantities of alluvium that enrich the plains.

Over time mountains have witnessed a steady increase in human settlements. J&K, Ladakh, Himachal Pradesh, Uttarakhand, Nepal, Sikkim, Bhutan and Arunachal Pradesh are Himalayan states with a total population of nearly 6 crores. And another 3-5 crore people live in the other mountain ranges of India. So, a total of around 10 crore people live in the mountains on the subcontinent.

Besides earning their own livelihood, these settlements have also served the needs of the nation. They have been the eyes and ears in protecting India's borders and have also helped extract various resources for consumption in the plains.

But conservationists, scientists, and administrators have expressed growing alarm about the rapid deterioration of the Himalayan environment over the past thirty years or so[21].

Human settlement has triggered a vicious downward spiral of environmental degradation across the Himalayan range (2400 kms). The level of degradation is largely proportional to the population density of the different regions. A significant majority of the population is rural and subsistence. Their dependence on agriculture, horticulture and on wood for energy and construction has led to massive deforestation. Over 50 percent of the forest cover has been wiped out across the range.

Extensive animal husbandry and use of biomass as fuel has further created immense pressure on the flora and reduced fertility. Soil erosion and landslides have increased dramatically leading to destruction of the natural flora.

Deforestation has impacted the hydrological cycle, decreasing the level of rainfall. Reduced rainfall and human exploitation have resulted in lower water levels of the rivers and streams and in drying up of springs and wells.

The increased runoff from the mountains has intensified siltation of reservoirs, caused abrupt changes in the course of rivers, and aggravated flooding in both upstream areas and downstream plains. Siltation in the plains has severely impacted the land productivity. Hydroelectricity projects have also become increasingly unviable due to the increased silting.

Development in the mountains, especially road construction, has only accelerated the degradation with increased footfall and commercialization of the exploitative activities. The large influx of tourists is accommodated in lodges that utilize

---

[21] The theory of Himalayan environmental degradation: what is the nature of the perceived crisis?, United Nations University

significant timber and that are unable to process the massive amounts of waste generated.

The waste generated in the mountains not only pollutes the mountains but also the rivers. Most tributaries of rivers like the Ganges, Indus and the Brahmaputra are already fairly polluted before they reach the foothills. Siltation and pollution of the rivers has also increased diseases in the downstream areas.

Several attempts have been made by local, national and world organizations to solve the problems of the locals and ensure sustainable development. The attempts have possibly been well meaning at times but all of them ignore the singular reality of the mountain habitat - mountains are not meant for human settlement.

Most of the Himalayan range (Hindu Kush, J&K, Nepal, Bhutan) was settled by war refugees. The earliest settlements in Himachal and Uttarakhand were restricted to the foothills. The natural settlements on the subcontinent were in the plains.

Now even if you attempt to enable development that mitigates the degradation to some extent, that development becomes outrageously expensive and unviable.

To reverse the process of degradation and rebuild India's greatest natural wealth, there is really no other solution than a complete evacuation of the Himalayan settlements. Living in these ranges needs to be eventually forbidden.

Any other compromise that we come up with might reduce the speed of degradation but will never help us realize the true value of these mountains.

Maybe ten years ago, it would have seemed impossible to manage and extract value from the Himalayas without allowing human settlement. But today technology solutions are available for almost everything. Advanced systems can be deployed to monitor human activity. Large horticulture firms can remotely monitor crops and use aircraft to send workforce for picking and transporting to the hub city. The five-star properties for tourism do not require local residents outside their own premises. They have extremely evolved processes and equipment, and well-trained employees.

Although nature is very reactive and would tend to heal itself once substantial evacuation is done, significant investment would still be needed to clean up the clutter and revitalize the natural habitats.

Once the natural habitats are restored, the subcontinent will accrue several direct and indirect benefits.

1. Abundance of fresh glacial water for the entire subcontinent

2. Significant increase in the contribution of hydroelectricity to India's energy mix

3. Increased land productivity in the plains

4. Reduction in average temperature and increased rainfall in the plains

5. Increase in volume and quality of fruits

6. Decrease in illegal cross border trade

7. Decrease in infiltration.

As one would expect, most of the mountain states have a fiscal deficit[22]. Evacuation of human settlement and technology enabled efficient value extraction will also help generate a significant fiscal surplus from the region.

In the case of the Aravallis, the environmental disaster includes certain other dimensions, but the extent of damage is similar if not more.

The Aravalli range is 690 km long and spans across the Indian states of Gujarat, Rajasthan, Haryana and Delhi. Over 60-70%

---

[22] State budget documents (Uttarakhand, Jammu & Kashmir, Himachal Pradesh), Government of India

of the forest cover in the Aravalli region has been lost in the last 50 years. But the most significant damage has been due to the rampant mining that has taken place. Over 30% of the hillocks have completely vanished[23].

This has led to significant reduction in rainfall, drying up of many rivers, large decreases in ground water levels and conversion of vast tracts of land into barren lands or desert. "In India, more than 70 per cent of the underground aquifers were dead, the rivers polluted, and a large portion of earlier water zones had turned gray or black." - Dr. Rajendra Singh, Waterman of India, who brought back to life seven dead rivers in Rajasthan in 1985.

The duration of the rainfall season has decreased from 101 days in 1973 to just 25 days in 2009. The groundwater levels in the adjoining areas have gone down to 10m from 150m originally. Banas, Luni, Sahibi, Indori and Sakhi are some of the rivers that have largely dried up and all the other rivers have seen a significant reduction in water levels. The widening gap in the Aravallis is resulting in the spread of the Thar desert into eastern Rajasthan, the Indo-Gangetic Plains, Haryana and western Uttar Pradesh. Sand pollution has increased substantially on the eastern side of the range. Many indigenous plant species have been lost completely.

While several regulations have attempted to curb mining, deforestation and other damaging activities, none has truly attempted to genuinely preserve the range. As long as there are settlements near the range, the degradation would continue in some form or the other.

Again, the only way to save these mountains is to steadily remove all settlements from the area. The mountains and adjacent land for at least 10 kms on either side needs to be completely evacuated eventually and brought under the forest department.

---

[23] Aravallis broken beyond repair, Jitendra Choubey and Shagun K, DownToEarth, April, 2019

The story of the Eastern and Western Ghats is again very similar[24]. The Western Ghats run to around 1.6 lakh sq km, spread across Kerala, Tamil Nadu, Karnataka, Goa, Maharashtra and Gujarat. Eastern Ghats run from northern Odisha to Tamil Nadu through Andhra Pradesh and Karnataka.

These mountains are the source of several rivers and support an extremely valuable and pristine ecosystem. Over 15 rivers originate in the eastern ghats and 5 cross through them. They are in the top 10 biodiversity hotspots of the world. The Western Ghats are much higher than the Eastern Ghats and have a larger number of waterfalls, reservoirs and lakes.

Deforestation has been rampant in these jungles. Large scale plantations and monocropping have depleted native vegetation. Valuable trees like sandal and medicinal plants now face extinction. Extraction of bauxite and magnesite has also led to large scale forest clearance. Illicit collection of firewood and grazing has also been rampant.

Several industries have been established in the forests and adjoining areas resulting in air, water and soil pollution. Unregulated tourism runs amok in these mountains and creates tonnes of untreated waste.

Deforestation and quarrying have led to a drastic increase in flooding in Kerala, Tamil Nadu, Karnataka and Maharashtra. And simultaneously several rivers, waterfalls and reservoirs are on the verge of drying up. Water levels in the largest rivers of the south have been decreasing rapidly. Groundwater levels have also declined sharply in the entire region.

Again, it is the scores of villages and towns in the Ghats and adjoining areas through which all the damage is enacted. These need to be resettled in the cities and the entire range

---

[24] PIL wants permanent body to preserve eastern and western ghats, Mohamed Imranullah S., The Hindu, March, 2020

and an area of at least 10 km on either side needs to be completely isolated.

Forest cover in the hill districts of the country is 2,84,006 sq km, which is 40.30% of the total geographical area of these districts. Complete evacuation of hill districts will enable forest cover on at least 80% of the area. That would mean an addition of 2.86 lac sq km of forest, which is 8.75% of our total land area.

Ever since the dawn of civilization on the subcontinent, we have revered our mountains like gods. And over time mountains have clearly established the damaging consequences of coming too close to them. For the scientifically inclined, it is easy to understand that mountain habitats will flourish only if left untouched. They are a valuable shared resource of the world, not just the subcontinent. Any attempt to gain personal benefits from them is an act against society. Naturally thriving mountain ranges will generate unimaginable wealth for the subcontinent. We just need to harvest that wealth with our collective wisdom.

The subcontinent has over 400 rivers that originate in the four mountain ranges (watersheds). Several tributaries in the mountains eventually join in the plains to form the main river systems of India. Ganga, Yamuna, Brahmaputra, Indus, Narmada, Godavari, Krishna, and Kaveri are some of the largest rivers in the plains.

These rivers are the natural source of fresh water needed for irrigation, drinking and industry. They carry a volume of around 2000 cubic kilometers annually. India's water requirement was 761 cubic kilometers in 2010, only 40% of the water available in the rivers. We used 688 cubic kilometers for irrigation, 56 cubic kilometers for municipal and drinking water applications and 17 cubic kilometers for industry.

But India uses river water for only around 30% of its total requirement. The remaining 70% requirement is met by pumping out groundwater. Around 80% of the drinking water and around 60% of our irrigation needs are fulfilled with groundwater.

Groundwater use is not sustainable and has severe ripple effects on nearby ecosystems. India is the world's highest user of groundwater, accounting for 25% of the total groundwater used globally. The excessive use of groundwater has resulted in lowering of the water table, increasing energy costs for extraction, increased contamination of the groundwater, and depletion of natural flora. Groundwater has a major contribution in river volumes. The increased drying up of rivers is also a result of depleting groundwater levels. Additionally, the loss of micro-fauna in groundwater is leading to lower quality of surface water.

The British had built an extensive canal irrigation system in India, but India was unable to develop and maintain the network of canals to fulfill the farming requirements[25]. Instead, farmers switched to pumping out groundwater on their own. Municipalities and industry also did the same given our inability to appropriately use river waters.

In northern and central parts of India, the water table has reached an alarmingly low level. Unlike rivers, ground water takes several years and at times decades to recharge. We therefore have to completely phase out the use of groundwater. Groundwater depletion will eventually dry out the rivers as well and leave us with nothing. In any case, rivers are the natural source of fresh water for consumption by life on the earth's surface. The water in Indian rivers is also full of minerals that enhance land productivity.

But to drive that shift from groundwater to surface water, we need to 1) protect the rivers, and 2) build ample and

---

[25] Past, Present and Future of Canal Irrigation in India, Tushar Shah, International Water Institute, Colombo

widespread storage capacity, and 3) and a robust distribution network.

The rivers on the subcontinent are one of the most polluted in the world. Sewage discharged from cities, towns and villages is the predominant cause of water pollution in India. The levels of BOD (a measure of pollution with organic matter) are severe near the cities and major towns. The fecal coliform levels are 3-12 times higher than permissible levels. Industrialization along the river belt is polluting the water with chemicals and other industrial effluents. Human settlements along the course also dump their garbage directly into the rivers.

The best and natural protection for rivers is forest. Trees serve as natural sponges, collecting and filtering rainfall and releasing it slowly into streams and rivers, and are the most effective form of protection for maintaining the quality of river water. Forest cover has been directly linked to drinking water treatment costs. The more the forest in a source water watershed, the lower the cost to treat that water. Forests provide these benefits by filtering sediments and other pollutants from the water in the soil before it reaches a water source, such as a stream, lake or river. Having a buffer of forestland by streams and riverbanks also helps prevent erosion of sediment into the water and helps to recharge the water table by allowing water to enter the ground. Even the shade of trees plays an important role in the lives of certain fish. Fish species, such as trout and salmon, are sensitive to changes in water temperature and will only lay their eggs in cool water, which is where the role of shady trees comes in.

Riparian or riverside forests prevent collapse of riverbanks and are the most effective and cost-efficient natural solution for preventing floods. Constructing artificial banks is not only extremely costly but also damages the local ecosystem.

Brazil also has hundreds of rivers like India and is the only country in the world with stringent regulation to maintain riparian buffer zones[26]. The regulation aims to protect both water resources and biodiversity. The no-harvest zone varies 30 to 500 meters on each side depending on the width of the river. No private property is allowed in these zones.

Given the extent of damage already done on riverbanks of India, we need a much more stringent regulation. India needs to have a riparian buffer zone between 100 m and 2 kms on each side to fully protect our rivers. We need a blanket regulation for the entire country applicable to all types of natural rivers and streams.

This would require evacuation of all settlements that fall in the ambit of the proposed regulation whether it is in the form of a city, town, village or slum. We are talking about relocating more than 20 crore people.

With clean rivers, we will have around 2000 cubic kilometers of freshwater flow available. But due to various constraints of topography and uneven distribution over space and time, only 600-700 cubic kilometers of the river flow can be utilized for the various requirements. That still leaves a deficit of around 100 cubic kilometers against the 2010 total requirement of ~800 cubic kilometers. By 2025 India is estimated to need 900 cubic kilometers and by 2050, the requirement would be around 1200 cubic kilometers. India is therefore staring at a severe shortage even after it fully protects the rivers.

Effective storage in dams, lakes and other forms of reservoirs is therefore essential. India currently stores only 6% of its annual rainfall or 253 cubic kilometers, while developed nations strategically store 250% of the annual rainfall in arid river basins[27]. With total rainfall of ~4,000 bcm, India should ideally store more than 10,000 cubic kilometers (or bcm) in

---

[26] Forest and land use policies in private lands: an international comparison - Argentina, Brazil, Canada, China, France, Germany, and the United States, Joana Chiavari, Christina Leme Lopes, Climate Policy Initiative, October 2017

[27] Integrated hydrological data book 2016, Central Water Commission, Government of India

reservoirs. The total storage capacity of dams in India is around 180 cubic kilometers.

India can create sufficient storage by building dam reservoirs and lakes. While rivers are the primary source for dam reservoirs, lakes can be fed by rivers, rainfall or both. Now, nearly 1200 cubic kilometers of river water flows into the Indian Ocean every year and there is 2000 cubic kms of untapped rainfall every year. India can have some level of water security if we can create a storage capacity of at least 1000 cubic kms spread across the country.

The large dam reservoirs of India like Indira Sagar, Nagarjuna Sagar, Srisailam, Bhakra, and Rihand have a storage capacity of around 10 cubic kilometers. The large lakes of India viz. Chilika, Rajsamand, Sambhar Salt, Upvan, Shivajisagar, Punnamada, Wular, Pangong Tso, and Maharana Pratap Sagar, have a storage capacity of over 5 cubic kms.

A hundred similar lakes will create a capacity of 500 cubic kms. Currently, there are around 500 lakes of different sizes that are currently in a deplorable state, with both surface area and depth reduced significantly. They are also severely polluted with urban and industrial waste.

India also possesses several valleys that can be transformed into huge lakes. There are over 50 valley areas in India that present the opportunity for lake restoration. Ladakh, J&K, Himachal and Uttarakhand, have enormous valleys that were originally filled with water. We also have natural valleys in the states of Maharashtra, Andhra Pradesh, West Bengal, Tamil Nadu, Orissa, Madhya Pradesh and the northeast.

The combined development of lakes in these large natural valleys (average volume of 50 bcm) and of urban lakes (each with a volume greater than 10 bcm), can enable India to reach the strategic storage levels.

Development of each lake would be a massive project. The development and restoration would involve land reclamation for the lake and catchment area, digging, dredging and desilting the lake to achieve maximum depth, building silt traps, restoration of inflow and outflow channels, balancing infrastructure, cleaning up the accumulated waste and pollution, diverting sewage discharge, development of the lakefront and reintroduction of flora and fauna.

Lake restoration or development will need significant investment and the nation's intent to overcome all hurdles. Given that India has the manpower and all the required capabilities, what we really need is the country's focus and contribution from everyone in the development effort.

Besides acting as a source of freshwater for irrigation, drinking and industrial purposes, lakes truly boost the environment and the economy of the region. Proper lake function can ease the impact of floods and droughts by storing large amounts of water and releasing it during shortages. Lakes also work to replenish groundwater, positively influence water quality of downstream watercourses, and preserve the biodiversity and habitat of the area. Lakes have a cooling effect on the nearby environment and also help increase air quality. Lakes create prime opportunities for recreation, tourism, and residential high-rises. Digging, dredging and desilting also provide the much-needed construction materials for other infrastructure development.

Dam reservoirs are usually built in mountains or the foothills to enable hydroelectricity generation. India currently has 180 cubic kms of storage capacity and another 150 cubic kms of capacity is in the works. The installed hydroelectric capacity is 44,594 MW, or 13.5% of its total utility power generation capacity. India's hydroelectric power potential is estimated at 148,700 MW, around three times its current capacity. Full potential realization will cover around 40% of India's current power demand. That will also help India achieve nearly 500 cubic kilometers of water storage capacity in the dam reservoirs.

Extensive distribution infrastructure would be essential to fulfill irrigation, drinking and industrial requirements. Nearly 90% of the total water consumed is for agriculture. Hence, building a robust irrigation network is most critical.

Irrigation in India mainly relies on groundwater well based systems and network of major and minor canals from Indian rivers. In 2013-14, 51% of the agricultural area was covered by irrigation and only 36.7% was reliably irrigated. The remaining 2/3rd cultivated land in India uses groundwater or is dependent on monsoons[28].

Canals irrigate 14-15 million hectares, which is less than 10% of the total arable land of 160 million hectares[29]. India's existing canal network is designed to move 300 cubic kilometers of water and has the capacity to irrigate 37 million hectares. Hence, there is a need to triple the canal and pipe irrigation network to reliably irrigate more than 100 million hectares without the use of groundwater.

Connecting urban municipalities and industrial zones to the rivers, lakes and reservoirs is also critical as the groundwater depletion is severe in the cities.

Availability of assured water supply increases agricultural productivity by almost 100%[30]. Canal and pipe irrigation will also help improve groundwater levels which further enhances productivity and quality of produce.

India is bestowed with the world's most diverse and fertile lands. We have several different types of soil spread across the country. Around 45% of the land is made of alluvial soil that has been enriched by the Himalayan Rivers. It is the most productive and delivers the highest quality food crops and vegetables. Canal irrigation is most critical in this region to ensure continuous enrichment with Himalayan minerals.

---

[28] Food and Agriculture Organization, The World Bank

[29] Annual report 2017-18, Ministry of Agriculture & Farmers Welfare

[30] Food and Agriculture Organization, The World Bank

Black and red soils cover the rest of India, except mountains and the desert. While not as productive as alluvial, all these soils are natural habitats for different types of food, cash, plantation and horticulture crops.

Population growth has led to damaging levels of agricultural expansion. India has the highest land area under agriculture in the world. While the official figures are 160 million hectares of farmland, some estimates suggest 190 million hectares being under some form of agriculture. The most troubling fact is that it represents 60% of the country's total land area. In comparison, the United States and China have only about 10% of their land under cultivation. Most countries have a similar percentage (10-20%) and only a very few have 20-30% agricultural land. To be sustainable, India will need to limit cultivation to around 30% of its land area which is nearly 100 million hectares.

The excessive farming has damaged natural habitats and resulted in severe levels of soil degradation[31].

Agriculture has expanded through deforestation and removal of natural vegetation, converting forests to farms, cultivating steep slopes and marginal lands. People living in villages consider all trees and plants nearby to be a free commodity that they can use - for fuel, feed, construction, furniture, handicrafts, and a whole host of other uses.

The Indian farmer, rich or poor, does not have the option to care about soil and environmental damage, and does whatever it takes to make money and sustain their family. They cultivate what they need and whatever fetches the best price, not what's natural. They excessively use pesticides and fertilizers and have been economically forced to grow GM varieties. They have no choice but to dump sewage into the land or nearby rivers, streams or canals. Fire is their best friend that they use for cooking, burning crop residue and all

---

[31] Soil Degradation in India: Causes, Major Threats, and Management Options, Milkha S. Aulakh and Gurjant S. Sidhu, Banda University of Agriculture & Technology, National Bureau of Soil Survey and Land Use Planning

kinds of waste, leading to significant air pollution. They domesticate animals for milk, meat, eggs, fur, leather and wool, resulting in excessive grazing, animal discharge and destruction of the region's natural ecosystem.

India has one of the largest livestock in the world, with around 46 crore chicken, 30 crore bovines (cattle and buffalo), 14 crore goats, 7 crore sheep, and 1 crore pigs[32].

Livestock farming is one of the leading causes of deforestation, water pollution, soil degradation and biodiversity loss[33].

Livestock farms create waste in a concentrated land space, which is often poorly managed. The high volumes of animal waste coupled with the lack of recycling of nutrients to replenish the soil, causes deterioration of soil and water quality of the adjacent areas of the farm.

The livestock water requirement is nearly the same as that of the total human population in India. Buffalo's feed itself has an irrigation requirement of nearly 500 cubic km. Most of it is obviously supplied by groundwater and rainfall.

In addition to requiring large volumes of water, livestock also depend on land resources for grazing. Indian pastures sustain a total of over 50 crore livestock grazing on about 12 million hectares of land. This implies an average of 42 animals grazing per hectare of land, higher than the recommended threshold of five animals per hectare. The area of degraded pasture lands is steadily increasing especially across the meat producing states. As much as 70% of the agricultural land gets degraded in places with high intensity livestock farming. It is also the major cause of soil erosion. The Indian herdsman considers all open lands and especially forests to be their own. They merrily go to any place that has some greenery for their

---

[32] Annual reports, Ministry of Animal Husbandry, Dairying and Fisheries

[33] How is India's meat industry impacting the environment, Yashika Kapoor, India Bioscience, Oct, 2019

herd to feed on - no wonder then that a herd of cattle, goats or sheep is a very common sight in India.

Besides, meat generated from livestock is an inefficient source of calories. It accounts for 17% of global calorie intake, but uses twice that amount of land, water and feed. Scientists estimate that animals must be fed up to 10 kilograms of grain to produce just 1 kilogram of meat. The world's cattle alone consume a quantity of food equal to the caloric needs of 8.7 billion people – more than the entire human population on Earth.

A pure vegetarian diet requires only 1,137 liters of water per day, while a meat-based diet requires more than 15,160 liters of water per day. Milk is far more efficient than meat: it takes five times as much feed to produce protein in the form of meat than in milk. Natural dairy farming is literally the only form of animal husbandry that makes logical sense.

Animal husbandry can never be environment or animal friendly and is clearly not essential for human needs. Animals thrive in their natural habitat where they are a part of a highly evolved and complicated food chain. And the natural ecosystem itself flourishes when left untouched by humans. One really does not need meat in the Indian climatic conditions. Besides the supremely diverse and nutrient rich Indian vegetation does not leave any void that needs to be plugged with meat.

A significant reduction in animal rearing for meat production will lead to a sizable increase in forest cover and a large reduction in agricultural land and water requirements.

One of the core problems in India is the private land ownership and the resulting distributed nature of agriculture. Once you buy land, you feel you have the right to do anything - grow what you want, build a home the way you like, produce as many children as possible, get a lot of servants and animals to live and work for you, set up a small business, organize events and so on. You just burn the trash or dig a hole for it. With the world's highest population density, private owners have exploited every inch of land available on the subcontinent.

At a very fundamental level, the thought that we own a piece of land is completely flawed. How can we own something that has existed for time immemorial and will exist even after we die. Neither did we have a role in its creation nor can we preserve it on our own. We are by the land, land not by us.

Land is a finite and connected resource. Human activity on any land parcel has consequences for adjoining lands and people living there. It is a shared resource, and the entire society is responsible for its correct usage and preservation. Government is the entity that transcends generations and that represents the interest of all. The government can ensure land usage that benefits the current and future generations.

China has three times the land India has and almost the same number of people. To prevent the exploitation by its rapidly surging population, China gradually phased out private land ownership (rural and urban) after the Chinese Communist Revolution in 1949. Now, there is only state ownership or collective ownership. Rural collectives own all the agricultural land.

If India has to evolve into a truly progressive family that intends to preserve and enrich its natural wealth, Indians will need to give up private land ownership. Only the government or government bodies that are geared to make the right decisions should own land in India. These bodies should be structured to prioritize the enhancement of India's natural wealth while meeting the collective needs of the society.

Cultivation needs to be governed by a deep understanding of every region's soil, climate, native flora & fauna and their interlinkages. The agriculture industry needs to be fully formalized and farming practices strongly regulated before the damage becomes irreversible.

Public companies need to be formulated that fully own and operate all primary agricultural activities. Agriculture is one the most evolved professions in the world and there is really not much scope for innovation. Clearly defined processes are needed to manage all parts of the farming value chain. Public companies need to employ people for managing, executing and controlling these activities. It is time for India to overhaul the slavery culture in the agriculture industry and give people a respectable profession and life. When the Indian government starts taking responsibility for every citizen and starts caring for every person, every individual will start thinking of the collective benefit. And that is when nature will blossom.

Forests have suffered the most at the hands of agriculture and now represent just around 24% of our land area[34]. This even includes all trees outside the recorded forest areas. Actual forest cover is just under 22%. Europe is the only other region on the globe that is bestowed with a natural environment as rich and diverse as the Indian subcontinent. Almost all countries in Western Europe have a forest cover above thirty percent with some even having as high as 60%.

India emits half the amount of greenhouse gasses and has nearly 75% of land as compared to the EU. Our population is three times that of the EU. Now if you include the forest cover of Russia, which is considered to be the lungs of Europe, the average forest cover for the region is around 45%.

But European countries are also experiencing a perceptible rise in temperature. Paris keeps recording the highest temperature every subsequent year. So, even Europe's forest cover is proving to be insufficient to fully act as a carbon sink.

The most environmentally conscious nations like Sweden, Japan, Korea, and Brazil have around 60% forest cover.

---

[34] Annual report 2017-18, Ministry of Environment Forest and Climate, Government of India

But an even bigger issue with India is the density of our forests. The average growing stock measures the volume density of wood in forests. In India the average growing stock per hectare in forest has been estimated as 56 cum[35]. The average for Europe is 163 cubic meters. For Switzerland it is 350 and Germany 320[36].

So the 24% green cover that we have in India translates to 8% by European standards and 4% by German standards. That clearly brings out the extent of damage we have caused and why India feels so hot and polluted.

Very dense forests cover just 3% of India's land area today but are spread across all states. Even Rajasthan has 78 sq km of very dense forest. So, very dense forest is possible almost everywhere in the subcontinent.

Much like the mountains, India's coastal zone is another extremely ecologically sensitive area that presents a huge opportunity for preservation and enhancement. India has a ~6000 km long coastline on the mainland that has been severely damaged by human settlement.

The coastal zone is a transition area between marine and territorial zones. It includes several distinct but interdependent ecosystems such as shore, wetland, mangrove, mudflat, seagrass, salt marsh and seaweed.

When left to thrive, these ecosystems build up to create a natural defense against the turbulent ocean.

Shore, wetland and mudflats act as a barrier to waves from eroding land in the interior. The roots of mangrove trees trap mud, sand, dirt and floating debris. As soil builds up, different mangroves take over, and eventually the area converts to land and the shoreline moves further into the ocean.

Many sea-grass species produce an extensive underground network of roots and rhizomes which stabilizes sediment and

---

[35] Ministry of Environment, Forest and Climate Change, Government of India

[36] Forest growing stock, increment and fellings, European Environmental Agency

reduces coastal erosion. The long blades of sea-grass slow the movement of water which reduces wave energy and offers further protection against coastal erosion and storm surge. Furthermore, because sea-grasses are underwater plants, they produce significant amounts of oxygen which oxygenate the water column. These meadows account for more than 10% of the ocean's total carbon storage.

India has a sizable coastal settlement that has damaged these ecosystems. Around 15 crore people live in coastal areas of India. Most of them are poor and extensively consume wood and marine organisms for subsistence.

Tourism has further exacerbated the problem. Developmental activities are often carried out without properly understanding the coastal dynamics, leading to long-term damage.

Excessive fishing along the coast has led to extinction of several species and is rapidly degrading the marine ecology. Fishing operations and industrial processing also discharge massive amounts of waste that deplete marine life.

Hard structures like sea walls, dikes, breakwaters, groins and jetties, have all been proven to negatively impact the natural coastal defense mechanism. They are expensive and are only meant to protect businesses looking to monetize the specific area.

The coasts and coastal water form a critical segment of our shared wealth. As a responsible society, we need to adopt the most advanced approach towards rebuilding the coastal ecosystems and extracting value in a sustainable way. Water-tight processes and controls need to be institutionalized to prevent personal interests from damaging the coastal environment.

The latest thinking advocates inland movement of all human settlement and restoration of the natural ecosystems, as the only viable solution towards protecting our coasts. Protected coastal zones need to be carved out all along the shoreline covering at least all areas within 10 km of the shores. Human settlement and industrial operations need to be moved out of the protected zone. Fishing industry needs to be owned and operated by the government with no individual or private participation allowed. India needs systems and models that prioritize coastal enrichment over monetization.

The last big chunk of our natural wealth is the Thar desert. It has a total area of 2 lac sq km with nearly 1.7 lac sq km in India. It represents around 5% of India's total land area.

People living in the desert mainly depend on animal husbandry. Surprisingly, around 45% of the country's wool is produced in the Thar with Bikaner being the largest Mandi. Overgrazing by animals has further degraded the already arid soil. Groundwater has completely disappeared in most places.

The desert obviously receives minimum rainfall due to the lack of any green patches to ensure precipitation. Churu, which has the lowest green cover in the desert, also records the highest temperature.

The Thar Desert is a result of mankind's neglect. The subcontinent has sufficient surface water that could have been diverted to these areas. The Indira Gandhi canal was a good step in the direction but was too small to really transform the desert into a green zone.

Based on the desert greening done in the Middle East, desert greening needs around 0.25 cubic km of water per 1000 sq km of desert area[37]. Therefore, to green the 2 lac sq km of the Thar Desert, 50 cubic km of water would be needed.

The Indus River system has sufficient surplus that can be used for greening the desert. All the five key rivers of the Indus system originate right above the Thar Desert but flow westward largely due to the Indus Water Treaty. It has an

---

[37] Data on water requirement for desert greening, "Environmental Politics in the Middle East", Harry Verhoeven, Georgetown University Qatar, Center for International & Regional Studies, Oxford University Press

inflow of ~200 cubic km but the current usage out of that is only around 105 cubic km[38]. 30 cubic km of unused water directly goes to sea and another 60 cubic km is lost naturally or is unaccounted for. These are glacial waters and will eventually convert the arid lands into alluvial plains.

---

[38] Pakistan - Getting more from water, William J. Young, Arif Anwar, Tousif Bhatti, Edoardo Borgomeo, Stephen Davies, William R. Garthwaite III, E. Michael Gilmont, Christina Leb, Lucy Lytton, Ian Makin, and Basharat Saeed, World Bank Group, 2019

4. Health is wealth

Health is the most rewarding individual pursuit for humans. It is the core around which everything else revolves. Health essentially determines the processing power of our body. A healthy body and mind efficiently absorb from the environment and enables swift development.

Healthy people glow like diamonds and attract like magnets. Their movements are effortless as if they are moon-walking. Their minds are at peace and they are always in a kind of blissful paradise. They are in such harmony with their environment that they seldom crave external glory or gratification. They are never running towards lofty goals or ambitions. They live in the moment and make the most of it. They enjoy every breath they take, every move they make. They run for the sheer joy of running.

They are confident, clear-headed people, but are also humble, flexible and transparent. That also makes them curious, great listeners and fast learners. They are sharp and rational. They possess incredible stamina and retention, and therefore build a lot of substance over time. Filled with positive energy and optimism, they are able to make the best of every situation.

They easily step up and can quickly change gears when need be or when the going gets tough. They are mentally strong and extremely resilient in the wake of failures.

They are great social animals - charming, friendly, and never abrasive. They never get defensive and are genuinely selfless in their behavior. They are not looking to build their own personal empires but rather want to make the world a better place for everyone. They are extremely conscious and display supernatural awareness of whatever transpires around them.

Healthy people are great at whatever they do. With an abundance of positive energy, composure and focus, they are extremely productive individuals. They have pride but not any ego and work wonderfully with team members without ever being confrontational. They are not driven by expectations, but usually exceed them all. They do not subscribe to the 'whatever it takes' mentality - they just do the right thing!

Unlike any other quest, health is a lifelong journey. It is the only endeavor that impacts you directly and in real time. Neither money nor anything else in the material world can give you the fulfillment that your healthy body and mind will.

Health is a state of complete physical and mental well-being. A person with good physical and mental health is likely to have bodily functions and processes working at their peak. The state of our mind is also deeply linked to the state of our other organs.

Our genes and the environment determine the state of our health. Genes are the basic physical and functional unit of heredity. They control the process by which physical or mental qualities pass from parent to child. Children inherit approximately 23,000 genes from their parents. Our environment or the experiences leave a chemical "signature" on genes[39]. That determines whether and how the genes are expressed. Experiences essentially change the chemistry that encodes the genes. These changes typically occur in cells that comprise organ systems, thereby influencing how these structures develop and function.

Genes have also evolved over thousands of years based on the local environment. The natural evolution over time also makes human bodies most suited for the local ecosystem. Africans will thrive in Africa, Indians in the Indian subcontinent, Europeans in Europe, East Asians in East Asia, and so on.

India is unique in its geographical diversity and has been a melting pot of several cultures. The cross mingling across the

---

[39] Early Experiences Can Alter Gene Expression and Affect Long-Term Development, National Scientific Council on the Developing Child, Center on the Developing Child, Harvard University

subcontinent has led to development of genes that are suited for a broad spectrum of environmental regimes.

While the environment is the primary determinant of human health across generations, in our lifetime, genes do play a significant role.

Genes provide the foundation for the entire body. They define the markers of all our physical features, sexual orientation, behavioral traits, nature of our body systems, quality of our organs, and our susceptibility to diseases.

Our environment that includes nutrition, climate, parents, friends, family, education, community etc. provides the building blocks for creating the structure over the genetic foundation. Genes also govern the body's receptivity towards the environmental influences. The ease with which you develop muscle mass, for example, is a highly inherited trait. But in essence, except for a few things, the environment has sufficient influence in determining every aspect of human health. Health problems are mainly environmental and the right environment can even help overcome genetic deficiencies.

From the earliest moments of life, the interaction of heredity and the environment works to shape who children are and who they will become. While the genetic instructions a child inherits from their parents may set out a road map for development, the environment can impact how these directions are expressed, shaped or even silenced.

Our blood group and the color of our eyes rarely change at all during our lifetime. Hair color is also driven by genetics. Even our skin color depends primarily on genes. Excessive exposure to sunlight or a lack thereof, especially during the development years, will definitely alter the skin tone. Nevertheless, a healthy body will have glowing skin whatever be the skin color.

Our facial features like our jaw structure, lips, nose, cheeks, ears, are predominantly (~80%) influenced by genetics[40]. Health of the pregnant mother and non modifiable environmental factors viz. trauma, infections, burns, tumors etc. can influence changes in facial features. Leaving aside facial deformations, all faces are attractive when devoid of excess fat. The fat on our face is completely environmental and linked to the overall fat excess in the body. Inadequate hydration and smoking also damage the face.

Voice is one of the key components of the human personality. Our genes naturally shape the larynx. Males have larger vocal folds and therefore tend to have their father's voice. Females with lesser folds tend towards the mother's voice. The language we speak also seems to have a big impact on our voices[41]. In India, one is likely to have a deeper voice if their native tongue is Haryanavi, Punjabi, Bagri, Magahi, Bhojpuri or some of the Hindi dialects of Uttar Pradesh. Children's vocal cords tend to adapt strongly to their parent's voices.

Genetics defines the range of our physique i.e., the size and shape of our body, but what we actually achieve is largely a function of the environment we grow up in.

About 60 to 80 percent of the difference in height between individuals is determined by genetic factors, whereas 20 to 40 percent can be attributed to environmental effects, mainly nutrition[42]. The most important nutrient for final height is protein in childhood. Minerals, in particular calcium, and vitamins A and D also influence height. Because of this, malnutrition in childhood is detrimental to height. In general, boys will reach maximum height in their late teens, whereas girls reach their maximum heights around their mid-teens. Thus, adequate nutrition before puberty is crucial

---

[40] Facial Genetics: A Brief Overview, National Center for Biotechnology Information, National Institute of Health, Oct 2018

[41] Are Voices Genetic?, Annie Lennon, Apr 2019

[42] How much of human height is genetic and how much is due to nutrition?, Dr. Chao-Qiang Lai, Scientific American, Dec, 2006

for reaching the top end of your genetically determined height range.

People of any height can be healthy as long as they have the right body proportions. The Vitruvian Man is a highly regarded representation of the ideal human body proportions. It puts man at the center of both a square and a circle, with the implication that man is in harmony with the world around him. There is a beautiful harmony in nature and what reflects that harmony will itself be beautiful.

"For the human body is so designed by nature that the face, from the chin to the top of the forehead and the lowest roots of the hair, is a tenth part of the whole height; the open hand from the wrist to the tip of the middle finger is just the same; the head from the chin to the crown is an eighth, and with the neck and shoulder from the top of the breast to the lowest roots of the hair is a sixth; from the middle of the breast to the summit of the crown is a fourth. If we take the height of the face itself, the distance from the bottom of the chin to the underside of the nostrils is one third of it; the nose from the underside of the nostrils to a line between the eyebrows is the same; from there to the lowest roots of the hair is also a third, comprising the forehead. The length of the foot is one sixth of the height of the body; of the forearm, one fourth; and the breadth of the breast is also one fourth."

It further states that "...in the human body the central point is naturally the navel. For if a man be placed flat on his back, with his hands and feet extended, and a pair of compasses centered at his navel, the fingers and toes of his two hands and feet will touch the circumference of a circle described therefrom. And just as the human body yields a circular outline, so too a square figure may be found from it. For if we measure the distance from the soles of the feet to the top of the head, and then apply that measure to the outstretched arms, the breadth will be found to be the same as the height, as in the case of plane surfaces which are perfectly square."

The skeletal structure is the basic foundation for the body proportions. Head size, neck length, and length of arms, legs and trunk, define the basic proportions of the human body.

Research indicates that the environment is a powerful force influencing body proportions[43]. Only 40% to 75% of inter-individual variation in the body proportions are attributable to "genetic effects". During the years of growth and development, more or less of total food, essential nutrients, and physical activity (and the type of activity) influence the body proportions. Bone mass and strength have a strong dependence on nutrition and have minimal correlation with the level of exercise. Bone structure and proportions are largely established by the time you reach adulthood[44]. We achieve peak bone mass in our early 20s, and after that it declines. Regular consumption of the mineral-supplemented diet could be beneficial in preventing the loss of bone mass and strength with age, even if you don't exercise.

While body proportions might seem like a thing of beauty, they are also associated with health risks viz. overweight (fatness), coronary heart disease, diabetes, liver dysfunction and certain cancers. Poor bone health naturally leads to problems related to osteoporosis - weak and brittle bones.

The adult skeleton makes up 7-15 percent of the body weight. Water is generally the largest portion of the body, accounting for about 60 percent of total weight[45]. The rest is pure muscle and fat tissues, which vary considerably between individuals. About 75 percent of the body's water content is found in muscles. Fat accounts for only about 10 percent water content as it retains much less water than muscles. Skeletal muscles are the largest body organ comprising ~40% of the body

---

[43] Leg Length, Body Proportion, and Health: A Review with a Note on Beauty, Health & Lifespan Research Centre, School of Sport, Exercise & Health Sciences, Loughborough University

[44] Skeletal growth and the changing genetic landscape during childhood and adulthood, Human Biology Symposium, American Journal of Biological Anthropology, December, 2012

[45] Your Body Composition Shapes Your Health, Ask the Scientists

mass. Even under severe obese conditions, skeletal muscles comprise 25% of the body mass.

We have nearly 600 muscles in our body that help us move, lift things, pump blood and even breathe. We can mainly control the amount of skeletal muscles. Healthy muscles let you move freely and keep your body strong. They not only help you enjoy sports, dancing, and other fun activities, but also help become efficient and enthusiastic in performing various daily chores. Strong muscles keep your joints in good shape and also decrease your body's susceptibility towards gaining fat. Skeletal muscle exercise increases energy expenditure (skeletal muscles uptake ~75% of ingested carbohydrates from meals), stimulates secretion of beneficial myokines (increases fat burn and enhances activity of several body functions) and increases insulin sensitivity (control blood sugar levels). An increase in skeletal muscle mass may directly lead to reduced body fat composition. An increase in muscle mass will increase the amount of food you can fully digest. Good muscle mass can significantly reduce the tendency of weight gain in Indians. Late teens and twenties are the best years to build muscle as your body is fully grown and you have high testosterone levels.

Low muscle mass results in reduced strength, increased risk of sudden body function decline, poor balance, increased blood sugar levels, metabolic disorders, poor bone health, and hormonal imbalances.

While we need a little essential fat for storing energy and keeping the body warm, excess fat creates the biggest and largest number of health risks for the body. Fat stored in the belly is the most risky as it affects the functioning of critical organs such as the liver, kidneys, pancreas, intestines, and heart. It can increase your risk for diabetes, heart disease, stroke, artery disease, musculoskeletal disorders and some cancers. Fat is also stored under the skin all over the body in the limbs, hips and buttocks. This affects the circulatory system and creates hormonal imbalances that further increase appetite and blood sugar levels.

Some other complications associated with excess body fat are shorter lifespan, increased blood pressure, gallbladder disorders, sleep apnea, menstrual abnormalities, respiratory disorders, compromised immune function and increased stress levels.

Insufficient body fat, however, decreases body insulation, energy reserves, cushioning for organs, cardiovascular function, immune health, ability to recover from exercise and illness, testosterone levels and menstrual health.

Obesity is a vicious downward spiral that completely ruins your life. You become an eyesore for yourself and everyone, your movements are labored, you avoid doing things that you ideally should, get irritated and angry when interacting with others, and try to aggressively control conversations in a bid to avoid personal attacks. Fat is essentially negative energy and unless you burn it, it comes out as such in your actions and behaviors. Excess weight also makes you highly prone to injuries and accidents. It also drastically impedes your ability to recover and at times results in further injuries when you exert yourself for speedy recovery. Fat people are unable to find any satisfaction from the world and end up gratifying themselves with various forms of excessive and unnecessary consumption. Negative energy and poor metabolism impact your ability to think straight and clouds your judgment. Life becomes a real burden, and you just can't see the positive in anything that happens around you. Instead of living in harmony with your society, you end up trying to create a secluded world for yourself where you can do as you please. You become a bad influence on your family and friends and turn into a social liability.

You are overweight if your BMI is above 25[46]. That is the Lakshman Rekha one should never cross. A BMI in the range

---

[46] Assessing Your Weight, Centers for Disease Control and Prevention

of 21-24 is ideal. Around 21, you will most likely have no unnecessary fat in the body. Around 23, you will either have ideal muscle mass and strength or you might have some little amount of fat still left and lower than ideal muscle mass. The best sportsmen in soccer (especially forwards and playmakers), badminton, swimming, tennis, gymnastics, track & field and cycling have a BMI in the ideal range. People within the ideal range should increase muscle strength without going past a BMI of 24.

Being overweight or obese is almost completely controllable. Even though genes determine our propensity for weight gain, a combination of a healthy diet and regular exercise results in a fit body for everyone. Being fit is the most fulfilling lifelong pursuit and given that weight has the biggest bearing on fitness, we should measure our weight regularly.

To prevent weight gain, we need to control both the volume and type of food we eat. The volume control is most critical and if exercised well, will let you eat all types of food.

Chewing your food thoroughly is the only way to achieve real and lasting volume control.

Chewing helps to break down the food and enables the digestive system to fully do its job. Digestion involves the breakdown of food into smaller and smaller components, until they can be absorbed and assimilated into the body. Chewing, in which the food is mixed with saliva, begins the mechanical process of digestion. The more you chew the more saliva you create and as saliva contains digestive enzymes, the better the digestion.

Chewing might seem like a tedious thing to do but people who chew thoroughly will confirm that it actually results in a far superior eating experience. Slow eating allows us to relish the taste at a very granular level. We are able to appreciate each and every ingredient. You truly start enjoying the eating experience. We also develop a much better understanding of all that goes into preparing a dish as well as the difference in quality of various ingredients. Rigorous chewing takes time and every meal will last much longer. Given that everyone loves eating, chewing gives you the opportunity to extend one of life's simplest and most central activities.

Chewing ensures that you eat only as much as the body needs. When eating slowly, you start burping as your stomach reaches capacity and you know very clearly when to stop. People who eat fast end up burping long after their stomach is full. For fast eaters, slowing down will cut down their intake by more than half. And you end up enjoying more for a longer duration.

One truly grows up as a person when one learns to chew. Slow eating helps the body to efficiently absorb and assimilate what's eaten. Over time, that also translates into greater awareness of your surroundings, people and their actions. Your detail orientation increases, and your head becomes clearer. You start enjoying one thing at a time and making good choices. Instead of ordering thalis or gorging on buffets, you would always prefer one well-made dish. You become a more focused and responsible person. Slow eating is a sign of confidence, security and being in harmony with the world. You become relaxed and much better at handling pressure situations.

For thorough chewing, one needs to take small bites (eat like a bird / don't bite more than you can chew). People who do so also become smooth in getting things done. They don't look for instant gratification and enjoy the long game. They become adept at slowly reaching greatness.

Slow eaters develop a very strong antenna for value and quality. They easily determine what truly adds value in terms of taste and nutrition. They start enjoying pure, natural and unprocessed things. They enjoy fresh cottage cheese, boiled eggs, salad, fresh fruits, and minimally cooked vegetables. They become much less dependent on add ons like curries, rotis, paranthas, breads etc. Eating matar paneer with a couple of rotis becomes an indulgence. Quality matters so much to slow eaters that they would rather go empty stomach than eat substandard things.

Besides volume, what you eat influences weight gain as well. To prevent weight gain, we need to control the intake of foods with high carbohydrates, especially rice, roti and bread. Once you start chewing thoroughly, high carb foods feel like a waste. Yes, you might still indulge in a little perfectly made pulao, lemon rice, bajre ki roti, or fresh warm bread, but you will do that only on occasions and in a very careful manner.

Increasing the proportion of fruits in our diet is a sure shot way to prevent weight gain. After air and water, fruits are the next closest natural connection we have with Mother Earth. They are high in nutrients and relatively low in calories. They are also high in water and fiber, which help you feel full. Because of this, you can typically eat fruit until you're satisfied, without consuming a lot of calories.

Apples and citrus fruits, like oranges and grapefruit, are among the most filling. Whole, solid fruit is much more filling than puréed fruit or juice, which you can typically consume a lot of without feeling full. For the average person, fruit is safe in almost any amount. Unless you are intolerant or are following a very low-carb or ketogenic diet, there really is no reason to limit your intake. Most studies show health benefits with 200-400 grams of fruit per day[47]. Fruits should not be treated like an add-on that you eat before a meal. Fruits should ideally be one of the three meals in a day or be at least one third of whatever you consume in a day.

The Indian subcontinent is home to a rich variety of fruits around the year. The Indian variety of almost all fruits is one of the most superior in the world. So whoever can, should consume as much fruit as possible.

In India, we are surrounded by unhealthy foods. Restaurants, sweet shops, street vendors, neighbors, family and friends,

---

[47] How Much Fruit Should You Eat per Day?, Kayla McDonell, Healthline, March 2017

religious establishments, and even the content you watch entices you with the sight, smell and talk of unhealthy foods. You do need strong willpower to resist the temptation and exercise control while consuming the widest array of the tastiest and richest food in the world. But once you start controlling, you will realize that Indian society has always had health at its core and our customs and recipes have actually been built for healthy consumption. The large unhealthy diets were really meant for people engaged in hard manual labor. And yes, nobody will really stop you if you want to overeat. Others usually benefit either monetarily or otherwise at the expense of your eating. But once you start displaying that control yourself, people actually appreciate it and you will also start getting the best quality and service.

Regular exercise is also essential for preventing weight gain. Strength training helps build muscles that improve metabolism. The body can digest more if you have good muscle mass. And Cardio directly burns calories - more the cardio more the burn. Research suggests doing 150 minutes of moderate cardio every week to prevent weight gain[48]. If you can do more, you can eat a little more.

Research continues to suggest that healthy diet and regular exercise are paramount for the smooth functioning of all body systems - circulatory, digestive, endocrine, exocrine, immune, nervous, urinary, reproductive, respiratory, and musculoskeletal.

A healthy diet provides the nutrients needed to nourish the various systems. All eleven organ systems in the human body require nutrient input to perform their specific biological functions. No energy means no work output. Overall health and the ability to carry out all of life's basic processes is fueled by nutrients.

All body systems perform best when we have no extra fat in the body, eat a nutritious and balanced diet, have good

---

[48] Physical Activity for a Healthy Weight, Centers for Disease Control and Prevention

muscle mass, and exercise regularly. And since all organs are very intricately connected and dependent on each other, we perform best when every part of the body is completely healthy. Our capacity to eat (without gaining weight) is also the highest when all organs are perfectly healthy and we have good muscle mass.

The Circulatory System (Cardiovascular System) transports nutrients to all other parts of the body and is therefore the most critical body system. The system consists of the heart, blood, and blood vessels.

Our heart works beat by beat, second by second for 24 hours a day, never resting. Over the average lifetime, our heart beats about 2.5 billion times. Heart ailments are the number one cause of death among women and men globally and in India[49]. Genetics contribute significantly to heart diseases or coronary artery diseases (CAD). But healthy lifestyle choices can significantly reduce the risk even for people with a family history of heart problems. Maintaining a healthy lifestyle (regular exercise, no smoking and healthy diet) throughout life will always result in the highest possible heart capacity and longevity for anyone.

Heart disease conditions emerge when plaque, which is made of fat and cholesterol, builds up inside the coronary arteries which supply oxygen-rich blood to the heart muscles. When plaque builds up, it restricts blood flow to the heart's chambers, which can lead to heart attack, sudden cardiac death and stroke[50].

So, eating food loaded with fat and cholesterol, poses the biggest risk to our hearts. Fried foods, curries, meat, sugar and sweets, rice and roti are the biggest culprits in the Indian diet. India is the diabetes capital of the world and also has one of the highest incidence rates for cardiovascular diseases.

---

[49] National Burden Estimates of healthy life lost in India, 2017: an analysis using direct mortality data and indirect disability data, Ministry of Health and Family Welfare, Government of India, 2019
[50] European Society of Cardiology

Indians need to radically shift their diet towards heart healthy fruits, vegetables and whole grains to protect their heart. Some of the heart healthy foods available in most Indian cities are leafy green vegetables, whole grains (whole wheat, brown rice, oats, rye, barley, buckwheat and quinoa), berries, walnuts, beans, tomatoes, almonds, seeds, garlic, olive oil, carrots, sweet potato, orange, melon, and papaya.

Additional fat in the body also has serious implications for the heart. The heart needs to pump a lot more when there is extra fat. Fat creates resistance at various points in the body, making the heart work harder to pump through the blood. Excess fat in the liver leads to lower sugar metabolism, which increases the level of blood lipids and triglycerides, and results in higher risk of heart diseases.

The heart is also a lump of muscle and we can make it stronger through rigorous cardio. People who do three or more hours of exercise every week can have larger and stronger hearts. Well-trained athletes can have much larger hearts due to the effects of exercise on the heart muscle, similar to the response of skeletal muscle. Having optimal muscle mass also reduces anger levels.

The resting heart rate (RHR) is the key metric of our hearts and is very simple to measure. Place your index and middle finger on your wrist just below the thumb, or along either side of your neck, so you can feel your pulse. Use a watch to count the number of beats for 30 seconds and double it to get your beats per minute. While a heart rate is considered normal if the rate is between 60 and 100 beats per minute, most healthy relaxed adults have a resting heart rate below 90 beats per minute. People with RHR near the low end of the range have a high degree of physical fitness. High RHR is linked with lower physical fitness and higher blood pressure, body weight, and levels of circulating blood fats.

People with a healthy heart are also better able to handle stress and moments of anger. The emotion of anger begins in the brain and results in the release of hormones. These stress hormones act on different parts of the body but mainly the heart. They cause a rise in our blood pressure and an increase in our heart rate. Our hearts beat faster to pump blood more quickly to certain parts of the body, like the muscles, so that we are ready to act, if we need to. And when the rate exceeds a certain limit, we get uncomfortable. And that leads to outbursts and violence in a bid to quickly relieve the stress or the stress hormones being generated. If the RHR is low, we have a wider cushion before reaching the outburst limit.

The brain is part of the central nervous system. The main function of the central nervous system is to sense changes in the external environment and create a reaction to them. All nerve impulses travel by the movement of charged sodium, potassium, calcium, and chloride atoms. These are some of the essential minerals in our diets—essential because they are absolutely required for central nervous system function. Nerves communicate with each other via chemicals built from amino acids called neurotransmitters. Eating adequate protein from a variety of sources will ensure the body gets all of the different amino acids that are so important for central nervous system function. We can protect our senses from the effects of aging by maintaining a healthy weight, blood pressure and sugar levels, exercising regularly, getting enough sleep, and not smoking or drinking alcohol.

Heredity and environment contribute differently to the development of different parts of the brain[51]. Heredity has a greater impact on IQ and language than on motor and sensory skills.

In terms of environmental influences, the quality of a child's experiences in the first five years have the most lasting impact on brain development and child's ability to learn and

---

[51] The changing impact of genes and environment on brain development during childhood and adolescence: Initial findings from a neuroimaging study of pediatric twins, Rhoshel K. Lenroot and Jay N. Giedd, June, 2010

succeed in school and life[52]. A newborn baby has all of the brain cells (neurons) they'll have for the rest of their life, but it's the connections between these cells that really make the brain work. Brain connections enable us to move, think, communicate and do just about everything. The early childhood years are crucial for making these connections. The connections needed for many important, higher-level abilities such as motivation, self-regulation, problem solving and communication are also formed during this period. It's much harder for these essential brain connections to be formed later in life.

A young child's daily experiences determine which brain connections develop and which will last for a lifetime. The amount and quality of care, stimulation and interaction they receive in their early years makes all the difference. Loving relationships with responsive, dependable adults are essential to a child's healthy development. Parents and caregivers who give attention, respond and interact with their child are literally building the child's brain. That's why it's so important to talk, sing, read and play with young children from the day they're born, to give them opportunities to explore their physical world, and to provide safe, stable and nurturing environments.

Technology has democratized intelligence. In today's world, if you just have a clear head, focus and good memory, you can acquire all the knowledge you need to be as intelligent as the best. Interestingly, these traits all have more to do with metabolic health than we might think. We have good metabolism when the glucose levels are fairly stable and in a healthy range. That is when the body efficiently uses glucose and fat for stable energy and mental clarity, a process called metabolic flexibility. If glucose levels are frequently high because of our dietary and lifestyle decisions, our body doesn't get the opportunity to "learn" how to harness fat for energy efficiently. This puts us in the position where if we

---

[52] Research on child development, First Things First, Arizona, United States

don't have constant access to glucose, we may feel lethargic and mentally foggy. We may be most familiar with these sensations in the "post-meal energy slump," a plummeting of focus and energy levels that comes after eating a massive carby meal.

For acute mental alertness and clear thinking, glucose must be systematically delivered to your brain. But excessive glucose levels in the blood can cause a loss of cognitive function and chronically high blood-glucose levels can damage brain cells. Spending an hour each on a light breakfast and a light lunch is the best way to keep the mind alert and fresh throughout the day. Optimal glucose metabolism depends on the intake as well as on the performance of several body organs such as the GI tract, heart, lungs, liver etc.

Brain-boosting foods that contain antioxidants, such as flavonoids or vitamin E, B vitamins, healthy fats, and omega fatty acids, are essential for healthy brain development and for reducing cognitive decline during adulthood. Berries, nuts, citrus fruits, eggs, seeds, certain spices, leafy greens, veggies like cauliflower etc. are some of the good foods for the brain.

Our lungs provide the oxygen for all body organs and form the core of our respiratory system. The lungs have a two-fold job of delivering oxygen to the bloodstream while removing carbon dioxide from the body. Every cell in the body draws oxygen from the blood and deposits carbon dioxide as waste into the bloodstream.

Lung function and lung capacity determine how efficiently the lungs deliver oxygen and get rid of carbon dioxide[53]. Lung capacity indicates how much air your lungs can hold. It also affects how quickly air moves in and out of your lungs. Your level of lung function also determines how well the lungs deliver oxygen and remove carbon dioxide from the

---

[53] Research on Lung Function, Lung.org

bloodstream. Lung function has to do with how efficiently the body uses the oxygen it receives. Whereas lung capacity can be improved, lung function cannot. This means improving your lung health is about improving your lung capacity.

Total lung capacity (TLC) increases from birth to adolescence and plateaus at the age of around 25 years. The maximum capacity in a typical adult is around 6 liters. After the age of 35, the lung function starts declining gradually, and one would normally lose around a liter of the capacity by age 65. A number of factors can accelerate your lungs' aging, including smoking, exposure to air pollution, and repeated respiratory infections. Obesity is also a cause of reduced TLC.

In India, around 55% of the chronic obstructive pulmonary diseases (COPD) are due to air pollution and nearly 25% are due to smoking. The Indian subcontinent has the poorest lung capacity in the world. In a global study, the Indian subcontinent fared the worst amongst all distinct global regions and had ~31% less lung capacity than Europeans[54].

Air pollution is at a hazardous level because of the greasy and fatty foods we cook and the extensive use of fire. Industrial and vehicular pollution is rampant and unchecked as we have to build an economy to fend off the lurking dangers. Smoking is indicative of the stress and hyper competitive nature of our society. It is a social evil we have succumbed to over the last few centuries.

To improve the health and capacity of our lungs, we need to protect them from all kinds of pollutants and do aerobic exercises. While reducing air pollution requires strong government intervention, there is a lot that one can do to protect one's respiratory system. If you smoke, quitting is without a doubt the best way to help your lungs' health. Aerobic exercise can't increase lung function, but improve lung capacity. Including some resistance workouts in your

---

[54] Global differences in lung function by region (PURE): an international, community-based prospective study, PURE-BREATH Study Investigators, Sep 2013

regular routines increases the intensity and variability of your workouts. That raises your heart rate and makes you breathe harder, which ultimately improves lung capacity. Even core and upper body exercises (chest and shoulder presses and dead-lifts) that strengthen the chest, shoulders and back muscles, improve the body posture and enable us to take fuller breaths.

Stronger lungs and heart will reduce the shortness of breath and rapid breathing that people experience under stress and conditions of anger and anxiety. When under mental pressure, the heart rate and breathing rate increases. Simultaneously, both the blood vessels and air pipes constrict resulting in decreased flow of blood and air. As a result, the delivery of glucose and oxygen to the brain, which is essential for mental processing, is inefficient and our ability to focus and make decisions is hindered. If your heart and lungs are strong, with low RHR and high lung function, the constriction of blood and air pipes under pressure situations does not affect brain performance. The blood and air flow remain at levels that allow delivery of sufficient glucose and oxygen to the brain for functioning normally.

When you are physically active, your lungs and heart work harder to supply the additional oxygen your muscles demand. As your physical fitness improves, your body becomes more efficient at getting oxygen into the bloodstream and transporting it to the working muscles. That's one of the reasons that you are less likely to become short of breath during exercise over time. Some types of exercise can also strengthen the muscles of the neck and chest, including the diaphragm and muscles between the ribs that work together to power inhaling and exhaling. Both aerobic activities and muscle-strengthening activities can benefit your lungs. Aerobic activities, including swimming, give your lungs as well as the heart the kind of workout they need to function efficiently. Muscle building activities build core strength, improving your posture, and toning your breathing muscles. Breathing exercises in particular can strengthen your diaphragm and train your body to breathe more deeply and more effectively.

Eating fruits rich in antioxidants and flavonoids viz. berries, bananas, apples and tomatoes slows down the decline in lung function.

The digestive system is the window to overall good health and has the biggest impact on the functioning of most organs. The digestive system is the cornerstone between eating and having adequate fuel and nutrition for the body to thrive.

A healthy digestive system will minimize the tendency for weight gain, ensure smooth functioning of various body systems, lead to stronger immunity towards illness or infection, and result in high energy levels and glowing skin. If your digestive system isn't strong you may not be effectively absorbing all the nutrients and energy from the food you are eating.

Single ingredient foods in their most natural form are familiar to the body and will be broken down more efficiently. Examples include whole grains and legumes, fruits and vegetables, lentils, nuts and unsaturated oils. Foods high in saturated fat, fatty meat and convenience foods, high sugar and refined foods with added preservatives and emulsifiers can inhibit digestion and lead to stomach discomfort, bloating, inflammation and lethargy. Foods high in fiber content give a good workout to the digestive system and enhance metabolism.

Digestion starts in the mouth when you salivate and then chew your food to break it up. If you are a fast eater or don't chew food properly, it's only partially broken down before swallowing. After eating, standing or stretching out the midsection to facilitate movement through the stomach and intestinal tract, avoids cramps or indigestion.

The small intestine is where most of the fuel from food is absorbed into the bloodstream. Early on in the small intestine is where all the essential nutrients like glucose, iron, zinc, magnesium and other water-soluble vitamins are absorbed. Further down amino acids and fats and fat soluble vitamins are absorbed.

The large intestine is where the insoluble parts of food, from foods high in fiber, that cannot be broken down are fermented and prepared for removal. This part of the digestive system is where water is reabsorbed, and hydration plays a role. Good bacteria in this part of the intestine contribute to the fermentation of fibers and protect the intestinal lining.

The gut (gastrointestinal tract) health strongly influences the immune system, mood, mental health, endocrine system, skin conditions and cancer. A person has about 300 to 500 different species of bacteria in their digestive tract. Diet and gut health are very closely linked. Avoiding processed foods, high-fat foods, and foods high in refined sugars is extremely important, as these foods destroy good bacteria and promote growth of damaging bacteria. There are also a number of foods you can eat that actively promote the growth of beneficial bacteria, contributing to your overall health. Foods that enhance gut health are high fiber foods such as legumes, beans, peas, oats, bananas, berries, asparagus, and leeks, garlic and onion, fermented foods such as curd, yogurt, kimchi, sauerkraut, tempeh, miso, kefir etc. and collagen rich foods viz. mushrooms and dairy products.

Liver is the most important accessory organ of the digestive system and is the largest internal organ of the body. Weighing in at a little over one kilogram, your liver is a complex chemical factory that works 24 hours a day. It processes virtually everything you eat, drink, breathe in or rub on your skin; in fact, the liver performs over 500 functions that are vital to life[55].

---

[55] Research on Liver Function and Nutrition, Canadian Liver Foundation

The liver's main job is to filter the blood coming from the digestive tract, before passing it to the rest of the body. The liver detoxifies chemicals and metabolizes drugs, makes proteins that are important for blood clotting and other functions, and is responsible for manufacturing cholesterol and triglycerides. Carbohydrates are produced in the liver and the organ is responsible for turning glucose into glycogen that can be stored both in the liver and in the muscle cells. The liver also makes bile that helps with food digestion.

The liver is a resilient organ and thus also gets ignored. Because of its wide-ranging responsibilities, your healthy liver can come under attack by viruses, toxic substances, contaminants and diseases. However, even when under siege, the liver is very slow to complain. People who have problems with their liver are frequently unaware because they may have few, if any, symptoms. Your liver is such a determined organ that it will continue working even when two-thirds of it has been damaged.

Alcohol is by far the biggest problem for the liver and alcohol related liver problems are one of the top 15 contributors to loss of healthy lives in India. The liver is responsible for processing this alcohol and detoxifying your blood. Breaking down alcohol is only one of the various vital functions performed by your liver. This means it can only handle so much alcohol at once. Alcohol can be toxic to the liver (hepatotoxic), especially in high doses, and long-term alcohol abuse is a common cause of liver diseases.

The liver is the world's most efficient factory. It helps power your body by storing and releasing energy when you need it. Your liver plays a key role in converting food into the chemicals essential for life and it is therefore important to make food choices that optimize liver health.

To keep the liver functioning at its best, we should eat small regular meals, drink 6 to 8 glasses of fluids a day, eat a variety of whole foods including fruits and vegetables, protein sources (legumes, lean meats), whole grains (quinoa, wild rice), dairy (low-fat yogurt, milk and cheese) and sources of healthy fat (nuts, avocado, fatty fish), increase your intake of fresh fruits and vegetables, and maximize consumption of raw vegetables with high sulfur content (i.e. broccoli, brussel sprouts, cabbage, cauliflower, garlic and onions).

To prevent developing a fatty liver, moderate your consumption of saturated fat and simple sugar. When it is full of fat, the liver cannot perform all of its 500 functions, and it can become progressively more damaged to the point of developing cirrhosis and even cancer.

While the solid waste is removed through the large intestine and rectum, liquid waste removal is done through the urinary system. Kidneys and bladder are the main organs of the urinary tract.

Kidneys filter waste products, excess water, and other impurities from the blood. These waste products are stored in the bladder and later expelled through urine.

In addition, the kidneys regulate pH, salt, and potassium levels in the body. They also produce hormones that regulate blood pressure and control the production of red blood cells. They are responsible for activating a form of vitamin D that helps the body absorb calcium for building bones and regulating muscle function.

Maintaining kidney health is important to overall health and general well-being. By keeping kidneys healthy, the body will filter and expel waste properly and produce hormones to help the body function properly.

Diabetes, high blood pressure, obesity, smoking and cardiovascular diseases negatively impact the functioning of kidneys and the bladder. Maintaining a healthy weight and not smoking are the best ways to prevent damage to the urinary tract. Smoking irritates the gallbladder and significantly increases the risk of bladder cancer and other urinary tract issues. Caffeine is also an irritant for the bladder and should be consumed in moderation. Indians should avoid excessive consumption of chai every day.

Benign prostate is a common problem for males, especially over the age of 50. An enlarged prostate creates an obstacle in the urinary tract and can lead to several urinary problems such as high frequency, strong urge, involuntary leaking, difficulty starting urination, straining to urinate, incomplete bladder emptying, weak or intermittent urine stream, dribbling after urinating etc. Smoking and high caffeine are known to both cause and enhance these problems.

The most common causes of kidney disease in India in both men and women are Diabetes and Hypertension. India also has a high incidence of kidney stones, especially in North India which is a stone belt. A hot and long summer season where you pass thick urine due to sweating, insufficient and unclean water intake, and a diet that is rich in stone forming elements, are the key reasons for kidney stones being a common problem in India.

The reproductive system comprises internal and external organs in males and females that work together for the purpose of procreation.

The male reproductive system consists of the testes and the penis. The testes are carried in an external pouch called scrotum where they remain cooler than the body temperature to facilitate sperm production.

The external structures of the female reproductive system include the clitoris, labia minora, labia majora and Bartholin's glands. The major internal organs of the female reproductive system include the vagina and uterus — which act as the receptacle for semen — and the ovaries, which produce the female's ova. The vagina is attached to the uterus through the cervix, while the fallopian tubes connect the uterus to the ovaries. In response to hormonal changes, ovum, or egg is released and sent down the fallopian tube during ovulation. If not fertilized, this egg is eliminated during menstruation.

Fertilization occurs if a sperm enters the fallopian tube and burrows into the egg. While the fertilization usually occurs in the oviducts, it can also happen in the uterus itself. The egg then becomes implanted in the lining of the uterus, where it begins the processes of embryogenesis (in which the embryo forms) and morphogenesis (in which the fetus begins to take shape). When the fetus is mature enough to survive outside of the womb, the cervix dilates, and contractions of the uterus propel it through the birth canal.

The health of the reproductive system, more broadly referred to as sexual health, drives both our physical and mental health[56]. Sexual activity includes masturbation, intercourse, non-penetrative sex etc. Besides serving the purpose of reproduction and being pleasurable while you are at it, sexual activity is an important cog in the overall health wheel.

Sex and sexuality are a part of life. Aside from reproduction, sex can be about intimacy and pleasure. Sexual activity, penile-vaginal intercourse (PVI), or masturbation, has an important role to play in our physical, intellectual, emotional, psychological and social well-being[57].

Some of the benefits you can get from sex include lowering blood pressure, burning calories, increasing heart health, strengthening muscles, reducing your risk of heart disease, stroke, and hypertension, and increasing libido.

Physical fitness and sexual activity reinforce each other. People with active sex lives tend to exercise more frequently and have better dietary habits than those who are less sexually active. Good physical fitness results in higher performance and better experience in sexual activity. Improvement in the body's flexibility, strength and endurance increases the number of positions you can try in

---

[56] Reproductive System: Facts, Functions & Diseases, Kim Ann Zimmermann

[57] The Health Benefits of Sex, Pamela Rogers, medically reviewed by Debra Rose Wilson, October, 2018

sexual intercourse. Fat people are severely restricted in their ability to have any form of sex.

In a study of immunity in people in romantic relationships, people who had frequent sex (one to two times a week) had more immunoglobulin A (IgA) in their saliva. IgA is the antibody that plays a role in preventing illnesses and is the first line of defense against human papillomavirus, or HPV.

Your body releases oxytocin, also called the "love" or "intimacy" hormone, and endorphins during an orgasm. The combination of these hormones causes sedation, and results in better sleep.

Sexual activity can provide full or partial relief from migraines and cluster headaches. Over 60 percent of people suffering from migraine or headaches reported improvement when they were sexually active during the attacks.

A recent review found that men who had more frequent penile-vaginal intercourse (PVI) had less risk of developing prostate cancer. One study found that men who averaged having 4.6 to 7 ejaculations a week were 36 percent less likely to receive a prostate cancer diagnosis before the age of 70.

For men, sex may even affect your mortality. One study reported that men who had frequent orgasms (defined as two or more a week) had a 50 percent lower mortality risk than those who had sex less often.

For both men and women, having an orgasm increases blood flow and releases natural pain-relieving chemicals.

Sexual activity in women can improve bladder control, reduce incontinence, relieve menstrual and premenstrual cramps, improve fertility, build stronger pelvic muscles, help produce more vaginal lubrication, and potentially protect you against endometriosis, or the growing of tissue outside your uterus.

The act of sex can help strengthen your pelvic floor. A strengthened pelvic floor can also offer benefits like less pain during sex and reduced chance of a vaginal prolapse. One study shows that PVI can result in reflexive vaginal contractions caused by penile thrusting.

Women who continue to be sexually active after menopause are less likely to have significant vaginal atrophy, or the thinning of vaginal walls. Vaginal atrophy can cause pain during sex and urinary symptoms.

Sex can serve as a natural way to relieve stress. A 2019 study looked at the effect that intimacy with a partner had on cortisol levels. Cortisol is a steroid hormone that circulates through the body in response to stress. The researchers found that expressions of intimacy, whether sexual or not, helped to bring cortisol levels in both males and females back within normal range. Sex triggers the release of oxytocin, endorphins, and other "feel-good" hormones, which may be responsible for this stress reducing effect.

Frequent sexual activity, whether with a partner or alone, can make you look younger. This is partially due to the release of estrogen during sex.

Sex can help you connect to your partner, thanks to oxytocin. Oxytocin can play a role in developing relationships. You may find that consistent, mutual sexual pleasure helps with bonding within a relationship.

Coupled partners often have increased relationship satisfaction when they fulfill one another's sexual desires. You may find positive growth in your relationship when you're able to express yourself and your sexual desires.

Masturbation can offer many of the same benefits as sex, but also has its own advantages, including enhanced sex between partners, understanding your own body, increased ability for orgasms, boosted self-esteem and body image, increased sexual satisfaction, treatment for sexual dysfunction etc.

Masturbation is considered entirely safe and has fewer health risks attached. When practiced alone, there is no risk of pregnancy or sexually transmitted infections (STIs). According to Planned Parenthood, it increases mental well-being not mental illness or instability like some myths suggest.

Sexual activity in general is associated with various risks. The risks of sexual intercourse include unwanted pregnancy and contracting a sexually transmitted infection such as HIV/AIDS, which can be reduced with availability and use of a condom or adopting other safe sex practices. Contraceptives specifically reduce the chance of pregnancy.

Sexual activity involves sociological, cognitive, emotional, behavioral and biological aspects. One needs a lot of maturity, knowledge and sound decision making to rightfully engage in sexual activity.

Adolescents face the highest risk of negative consequences from sexual activity because their brains are not neurally mature. Several brain regions in the frontal lobe of the cerebral cortex and in the hypothalamus that are deemed important for self-control, delayed gratification, risk analysis, and appreciation are not fully mature. The prefrontal cortex area of the human brain is not fully developed until the early 20s or about age 25. Partially, because of this, young adolescents are generally less equipped than adults to make sound decisions and anticipate consequences of sexual behavior.

There is evidence of the presence of an evolved culture in India before the 10th century that promoted sexual health. But in those times, India was rich and people were not fighting everyday battles for survival and earning a livelihood. The high levels of illiteracy, an education system that fails to ingrain health perspective in the right manner, and poor living standards of the masses, mean that sexual health is largely ignored and unable to improve the overall health of Indians.

The immune system comprises several types of white blood cells that circulate in the blood and lymph. Their jobs are to seek, recruit, attack, and destroy foreign invaders, such as bacteria and viruses. Other less realized components of the immune system are the skin (which acts as a barricade), mucus (which traps and entangles microorganisms), and even the bacteria in the large intestine (which prevent the colonization of bad bacteria in the gut).

Immune system functions are completely dependent on dietary nutrients. In fact, malnutrition is the leading cause of immune-system deficiency worldwide. When immune system functions are inadequate there is a marked increase in the chance of getting an infection. Children in many poor, developing countries have protein- and/or energy-deficient diets that are causative of two different syndromes, kwashiorkor and marasmus. These children often die from infections that their bodies could normally have fought off, but because their protein and/or energy intake is so low, the immune system cannot perform its functions.

Other nutrients, such as zinc, selenium, copper, folate, and vitamins A, B6, C, D, and E, all provide benefits to immune system function. Deficiencies in these nutrients can cause an increased risk for infection and death.

Equally important to remember is that multiple studies show that it is best to obtain your minerals and vitamins from eating a variety of healthy foods.

Both under-nutrition and overnutrition compromise the health of the immune system. People who are obese are at increased risk for developing immune system disorders such as asthma, rheumatoid arthritis, and some cancers.

The endocrine system is made of a complex system of glands that include hypothalamus, pituitary, pineal, thyroid, parathyroid, thymus, adrenal, pancreas, ovaries and testes. The glands secrete hormones, which travel through the bloodstream to various organs and tissues in the body.

The hormones tell these organs and tissues what to do and how to function. Body functions that are controlled by these hormones include metabolism, blood sugar levels, growth and development, sexual function and reproduction, heart rate, blood pressure, stress response, appetite, sleep, and body temperature.

Adequate nutrition is critical for the functioning of all the glands in the endocrine system. A protein deficiency impairs gonadal-hormone release, preventing reproduction. Children who are malnourished usually do not produce enough growth hormones and fail to reach normal height for their age group.

The hormone system is responsible for the linkage between obesity and the development of Type 2 diabetes. Over consumption of high-fat and high-sugar foods makes muscle, fat, and liver cells resistant to the pancreatic hormone insulin. When cells are resistant to insulin they do not take up enough glucose and fatty acids and so glucose and fatty acids remain at high concentrations in the blood.

Hormone levels that are too high or too low indicate a problem with the endocrine system. Hormone diseases also occur if your body does not respond to hormones in the appropriate ways. Stress, infection and changes in the blood's fluid and electrolyte balance can also influence hormone levels.

Hormones released from the pituitary (also considered the master gland) and adrenal glands have the most impact on mood states. Cortisol is released from the adrenal glands to manage stress. Adrenaline, another hormone released from the adrenal glands, regulates heart rate, blood vessel and air passage diameters, and metabolic shifts. High adrenaline levels correspond to high levels of happiness. Oxytocin, hormone released from the pituitary gland, causes a wide spectrum of behavioral and physiological effects mediated through receptors within the brain, such as maternal, sexual and social behaviors. Oxytocin contributes to happiness as it facilitates relationships with others and is associated with positive social behaviors.

The master regulator of the endocrine system is the hypothalamus. It releases the hormones that signal the pituitary gland, which then send signals further downstream to your other glands. Essentially, it acts as the initial signaler for the adrenal glands, thyroid gland, and the ovaries and testes.

The hypothalamus also plays a key role in energy balance and metabolism. Not only does the hypothalamus control the thyroid hormone, which plays a significant function in regulating metabolism, but it also directly influences appetite through sending and receiving signals involved with insulin, leptin, and ghrelin. Thus, the hypothalamus is part of two of the major signaling pathways involved in energy homeostasis, and thereby dysfunction could lead to obesity and associated disorders.

Good physical health results in good health of the hypothalamus and the endocrine glands. There is a significant correlation between positive mood and physical health. Researchers find a strong relation between local areas of the brain that manage weight and metabolism and areas that control cognition and emotions. Fatness is a risk factor for depression and significantly decreases the quality of life.

Hypo and hyperthyroidism are the next biggest disorders of the endocrine system. The thyroid gland is found in the front of the neck below the larynx, or voice box, and has two lobes, one on each side of the windpipe. 42 million people in India have thyroid disorders and hypothyroidism is the most common of thyroid disorders in India, affecting one in ten adults.

In hypothyroidism, your thyroid gland doesn't produce enough of certain hormones, most importantly ones that regulate metabolism. Women, especially those older than age 60, are more likely to have hypothyroidism.

Some of the most common symptoms are weight gain or inability to lose weight in spite of exercise, feeling cold, fatigue, dry skin, puffy face, among others. The more severe your hypothyroidism, the more weight you are likely to gain. Hypothyroidism develops slowly. Symptoms may go unnoticed for a long time, and they may be vague and general. The only way to obtain a concrete diagnosis is through a blood test.

The prevalence of hypothyroidism in India is 11%, compared with only 2% in the UK and 4·6% in the USA. This is possibly linked to long-standing iodine deficiency in the country, which has only been partly corrected over the past 20 years.

Apart from iodine deficiency, exposure to cyanogenic compounds, unregulated use of pesticides, exposure to endocrine disruptors and contaminated drinking water can be likely causes.

Hormonal imbalances also lead to stress and anxiety. Women are especially vulnerable to mood swings around their menstrual cycle.

The endocrine system and fitness go hand in hand. During exercise, several hormones (adrenaline, noradrenaline, growth hormone and cortisol) function together to mobilize fuel for the production of ATP (energy) for the exercise.

These hormones affect the cells on three primary target tissues (fat, liver and skeletal muscle) during exercise. When they bind to receptors on fat cells, fat storage is inhibited and fat mobilization is enhanced for energy. When they bind to receptors on the liver, glycogen is broken down into glucose for readily available energy. When they bind to receptors on skeletal muscle, stored glycogen is broken down into glucose and the uptake and utilization of fatty acids for energy is increased.

With exercise there is a greater demand from muscle tissue for blood glucose for fuel, causing blood glucose levels to drop. Glucagon levels consequently increase with exercise and insulin levels are simultaneously suppressed.

Exercise increases the number of receptors at the target tissues, strengthens the chemical bond between hormone and its receptor, and improves blood hormone levels.

Right nutrition is also essential for maintaining good endocrine health. Eat foods low in glycemic index (or GI, meaning they raise blood sugar slowly), and rich in protein. Consume nuts such as almonds, walnuts, pistachios, and pumpkin seeds, and use unsaturated oils like olive oil, flax oil, sesame oil and ground nut oil. Eat whole grains like buckwheat, brown rice, ragi and quinoa and other millets. Avoid or minimize caffeine, alcohol, fried foods, processed meat, peanuts, saturated fat, full-fat dairy, artificial sweeteners, and simple carbohydrates or simple sugars like white bread, sweets, pastries, etc.

The functioning of various body systems and organs is interdependent. A change in the levels of functioning of one organ has an impact on the functioning of several other organs and systems.

Our consumption and levels of exercise determine the health of the various body systems. To keep health in the best possible condition, we need to eat healthy and exercise regularly. We should eat only as much as the body needs in terms of energy and nutrients. A healthy diet is about volume, balance and quality. Weight has the biggest negative impact on all body systems and so controlling the amount of food is most critical. We should eat different types of foods to ensure supply of all required nutrients. And the higher the quality of food we eat, lesser is the amount of undesired food that the body needs to process. We need to exercise regularly to build the optimal muscle mass and ensure smooth functioning of all body systems. Optimal muscle mass maximizes the volume of food we can eat in a sustainable manner.

We are in perfect shape when all body systems are healthy. It is a state where there is complete harmony within the body organs and systems, as well as between the body and the environment.

There is nothing better in the world than being in a state of perfect health. A healthy person is in a constant state of exhilaration, elevated consciousness and positive energy. All other pleasures and joys in the world are momentary and dependent on external factors.

A perfectly healthy person does not crave for gratification from anything or anyone. He or she is in a pure state of joyous equanimity and does not need things like smoking, alcohol, meat, oily and / or high carb food, or adventurous activities that involve unnecessary risks. Every living breathing moment is so fulfilling that they don't need to pamper themselves by going out of the way and getting fancy. They don't need to drive fast or do long unhealthy vacations in the mountains. They have a lean mindset and are not hoarders as they are confident in their abilities to always be productive. They are not looking to get ahead of people, they just feel the energy and enjoy the presence of other people. The positive energy flowing through the body is the best gratification anyone can experience.

Healthy people are sporty. Not only can they actually play various sports, their flexible and energetic body and mind makes them open and good at learning and doing almost anything. Whether it is cooking and cleaning at home or working professionally, they will always perform well. Their mental faculties enable them to think rationally and engage in tough conversations without getting agitated.

A strong health perspective is essential for maintaining the state of perfect health. The state of perfect health does not last in today's unhealthy environment. Almost everyone reaches the state of perfect health when they are kids or during their youth. But only a few are able to sustain it. That is largely because we do not have the perspective to understand the importance of staying healthy. By the time most of us understand, we are so far down the path of being unhealthy that it becomes nearly impossible to come back. The world around us presents unhealthy options in front of us and unless we have a health perspective, we end up making unhealthy choices.

An evolved health perspective is our best friend to stay in a healthy zone. An assessment of the health impact always helps in making the right judgment in pretty much everything. Whether the choice is related to an activity, a consumable, a non-consumable item or a person, thinking about health implications is most critical.

The world around us, more so in the Indian subcontinent, is full of health risks. You are surrounded by unhealthy foods, air, water, and unhygienic and dirty societies, shopping centers, offices and public places. At every corner, you will find dozens of merchants vying to get a piece of your health, whether it is the panwala, or a thela selling oily and fatty food, a liquor shop or a mithai shop. Some of the biggest business houses are essentially selling unhealthy items - cigarettes, sweets, candies, snacks etc. And the business environment is evolving towards delivering death to your doorstep. You are being bombarded with offers specifically targeted at your weaknesses. We live in a world where a fairly large percentage of the population has been forced into earning its livelihood by indirectly killing others. In India, engagement with our social circle, even our friends and family, creates health risks, as we typically do unhealthy things when we get together. Health consciousness is our weapon to anticipate and avoid various health risks.

The journey of health is challenging and needs a lot of focus, patience and perseverance. You may need to sacrifice certain material and seemingly important pursuits to regain health and get to perfect shape. But don't even think twice when making that healthy choice. And while it does take time, and will be challenging, you will realize that it was worth its weight in gold! Every healthy moment is far more valuable than an unhealthy one. Even in today's material world, health is the biggest and most important asset.

The most difficult part is getting on to the health bandwagon. Once you get on, health momentum will self-sustain the move forward. There will be temptations along the way. But if you internalize that health is a lifelong pursuit, it will really not matter even if you fall for some. You will eventually get there!

When you are in the health zone, your head starts getting clearer and you are able to make better decisions. Better decisions usually lead to better outcomes, and you get into a cycle of continuous improvement.

You gradually realize that it is all or nothing. All unhealthy habits are linked to each other. Alcohol leads you to smoking as well as excess food intake. Smoking leads you to drugs as well. Obesity leads to laziness, anger, violence and drives you towards taking shortcuts in life. When you are in the health zone, you don't feel the need for anything unhealthy. Eventually your mind and body do not experience and acknowledge pleasure or fulfillment from anything unhealthy. You stop looking for cheat days, festivals, occasions or opportunities to indulge.

While a healthy person is a positive influence on society, an unhealthy person is a social liability. They are low on productivity, indulge in unhealthy and excess consumption, and are health risks for others. Health is therefore a public and social concern. Governments, communities and individuals need to do whatever they can, without taking unnecessary health risks, to prevent unhealthy behaviors and activities, and encourage healthy living.

Healthy people have sustainable demands. Earth can support the requirements of healthy individuals and communities. They are in harmony with their surroundings and their needs are basic and optimal. They just need the essentials (water, nutritious food) in a timely manner. Their food requirements can be met with minimal and enriching agricultural output. They have minimal consumption of meat, sugar, carbohydrates (rice, wheat) and consume varieties (e.g. nutri cereals, natural varieties of rice etc.) that are beneficial for both health and the environment. In scorching summers, they stay cool with just a fan or a splash of water. Their clothes last forever as their bodies stay in shape. They just need the floor, mattresses and cushions, no chairs, tables or sofas. And so on...

Healthy people are not dependent on material pleasures for gratification, which further reduces the material burden on earth's resources. They don't need fancy clothes, cars, lights, crockery or ornaments. They derive most pleasure from simplicity and fulfillment from functionally efficient items that best serve basic needs. They are confident and clear headed and make good decisions. They are conscious of the environment and the impact of every individual action.

Healthy people like to operate mechanically efficient products that also help exercise different parts of their bodies. They don't need smart products that are much less durable, constantly require upgrades and use limited materials in the earth's crust. Their behavior is nonabrasive and they embrace everyone in the society. They don't look to circumvent problems of safety by creating new products for the elite, but rather work towards solving inequality, the primary cause of various societal issues.

Healthy communities thrive with sustainable and equitable infrastructure and systems. Functionally efficient housing with evolved social and community systems are preferred by healthy families. They are not running away to create their own isolated row house, mansion, or bungalow, but rather want to live in vibrant densely packed neighborhoods. They have good sex with their partners and feel the energy of beautiful people around them. They prefer walking, running and cycling instead of using private guzzlers, and like traveling in shared transportation modes. They encourage the development of community centers, sports and entertainment infrastructure.

A healthy environment breeds healthy people and creates a beautiful self-sustaining cycle of human evolution and nature's enrichment. Systemic and individual decisions anchored around sustainability and health are likely to be the most optimal.

5. Live in the city

The way we live is the primary driver of our health and that of our planet. Human settlements have the maximum impact on the environment. And the state of our health is heavily dependent on the physical environment we live in. Better health leads to better quality of life. Hence, the quality of life, health and environment are positively correlated with each other. So, environment friendly human settlement is also best for health and quality of life.

Cities are the densest form of human settlement. The most crowded cities have a population density of more than 10,000 people per sq km. Dhaka, Kolkata, Mumbai, Karachi, Chennai, Delhi, Surat, Hyderabad, Ahmedabad, Bengaluru, Lahore, Kanpur, Patna and Varanasi are some of the densest cities on the Indian subcontinent and in the world.

Most livable cities[58] are Vienna, Melbourne, Sydney, Osaka, Calgary, Vancouver, Tokyo, Toronto, Copenhagen and Adelaide. Among these, Tokyo has the highest density of ~6000 people per sq km but most of them have a density in the 1000-1500 people per sq km range.

New York City has more than 30,000 people per sq km and even Paris has more than 25,000.

A population of 1.5 billion will need 1.5 million square kilometers if we created cities with a density of 1000 people per sq km. That is around 45% of India's total land area. But if we lived in cities with more than 10,000 people per sq km, we would only need around 5% of the total land area.

To be sustainable we have no option but to live in cities with an overall density of more than 10,000 per sq km. We need at least 40% of land area to be covered by forest and eventually

---

[58] Global Liveability Index 2022, Economist Intelligence Unit; scores cities on stability, healthcare, culture & environment, education and infrastructure

around 55% to truly drive sustainability. We have ~46% land under agriculture and even with efficiency gains, we will need anywhere between 30-35% land for agriculture. 6% of the land is completely barren (desert or snow) and another 5-10% is currently uncultivable.

According to the 2011 census of India, 68.84% of Indians (around 833.1 million people) live in 640,867 different villages. There are 4,000 cities and towns in India. About 300 cities have a population over 1,00,000, around 30 have population over 10 lacs and seven cities have population more than 30 lacs. Delhi, Mumbai, Kolkata, Hyderabad, Chennai and Bengaluru metropolitan areas have a population of more than a crore.

We essentially have human settlement everywhere. We did that to monetize every inch of the land and natural resources and also to prevent occupation by outsiders.

Small settlements like most Indian villages and a large percentage of towns derive their life support or basic economic needs usually from land or nature based activities such as farming, logging, mining etc.

Then we have a large number of small and mid-sized towns and cities that were built to perform a certain activity that still remains their dominant function. Examples of these specializations are Industrial (Salem, Coimbatore, Modinagar, Jamshedpur, Hugli, Bhilai), transport (Dhulia, Itarsi), commercial (Saharanpur, Satna), mining (Raniganj, Jharia, Digboi, Ankaleshwar), cantonment (Ambala, Jalandhar, Mhow, Babina), education (Roorkee, Varanasi, Pilani, Prayagraj), religion (Mathura, Puri, Tirupati, Haridwar), tourist (Nainital, Mussoorie, Shimla, Jodhpur).

Across the world, small settlements, whether it is a village, town or a small city, do not have the scale and the capability to stand on their own. Insufficient local resources and demand mean that such settlements are almost entirely dependent on the outside world to provide infrastructure, products and services. They lack the resources to build anything meaningful organically. Demand is insufficient for retail, manufacturing or services ventures to be built by local people.

They are unable to generate enough value to invest in creating essential public infrastructure and safety mechanisms. Utilization of any form of infrastructure is low whether it is for healthcare, education, residential, commercial, energy, water, waste management, telecom, transportation, sports, entertainment etc. And given the high capital and / or resource requirements for creating high quality infrastructure, small settlements are unable to justify and make these investments. Law enforcement is more difficult in scattered settlements leading to higher crime rates. Insufficient administrative resources and the influence of local industry makes rule of law extremely ineffective. Human rights that include civil, cultural, economic, political, and social are sacrificed. Quality of healthcare and education suffers. There is rampant discrimination, inequality, injustice, abuse, corruption and bureaucracy. People from small towns and mid-sized are some of the most fired up and motivated employees in large cities as they never want to go back.

Even the mid-sized cities lack the diversity that is critical for independent existence. The few organizations that control the local economy have too much leverage and end up paying poorly. The small businesses in other areas do not generate enough to offer good employment. The best talent migrates to the mega cities and these smaller settlements are further weakened. Over time their core industry also loses out to the big brothers in the metros.

These communities just recklessly damage the natural environment for their survival. Smaller settlements have a mismatch between what people need and what they offer. And so they end up monetizing the natural resources in all possible ways causing irreversible damage. Sustainability is compromised to meet basic requirements and also to plug the aspirational gap. People recklessly use wood, exploit water resources, and use ad hoc methods (burning, dumping etc.) to manage waste. Weak rule of law results in local businesses flouting all environmental norms to stay afloat. Across the world, these smaller settlements are flat, and are therefore inefficient and not sustainable.

The small settlements including mid-sized cities are likely to remain incapable, inefficient and unsustainable. The extent may vary depending on whether they are in a developed, developing or an underdeveloped country. Lack of scale and diversity prevents them from building world class capability. They will never be able to compete with the big cities in an open market environment and will end up settling for a second-rate economy, lower standards of living and a compromised environment.

On the other hand, large mega cities across the world are all capable and independent. There are around 50 cities in the world with a population of over 50 lacs, and all of these have a thriving economy, with several well-developed industries.

These large cities are becoming extremely efficient. Most of them are in the process of going completely vertical, with tall skyscrapers taking over both residential and commercial real estate. Besides land use, urban developers are able to drive efficiencies in cost of real estate development, energy use, water management, sanitation etc. Transportation is getting efficient due to high density, quality infrastructure and technology adoption in these cities. They have the resources to build world class public infrastructure whether it is parks, stadiums, lakes, cultural centers or any other health, leisure or administrative infrastructure. High volumes improve supply chain efficiency of consumer goods. Sharing has become feasible in these cities and reuse has now become common for electronics, furniture, and several other products.

In the developed world, cities win the head-to-head energy efficiency matchup in transportation thanks to their mass transit systems and denser layouts, which promote walking and bicycling. Small-town and suburban residents usually have to drive themselves to get around, which isn't cheap. Urban U.S. households own an average of 1.8 vehicles each, compared with 2.2 for each rural household[59]. Urban families also drive about 11,000 fewer kms annually than their rural counterparts.

Even per capita residential energy consumption is lowest in dense urban households as compared to rural (~12% higher), towns (~20% higher) and suburbs (~30% higher)[60]. Free standing homes by nature need more energy for heating and cooling. Additionally, urban developers are able to use advanced design and engineering to maximize efficiency of energy use.

The largest cities might not be the most livable but are still the most attractive for people. Most of them are cosmopolitan and diverse. They give access to every possible product or service one can think of, that too with an ample number of options to choose from. The abundance of markets, events and activities keeps people on their toes. The society is hyperactive and does not give you a chance to breathe a lonely moment. Employment is usually available for everyone.

Most large cities, especially in the developed world, are also taking big strides towards sustainability. The residential and commercial high-rise developments in these cities are central towards creating a sustainable model of living. They are encouraging development of green buildings, usage of clean sources of energy, and electric vehicles. They are adopting technologies and processes to reduce industrial pollution and to effectively manage all kinds of waste.

---

[59] Split of US energy consumption across key segments, US Energy Information Administration

[60] Trends in urban land expansion, density, and land transitions from 1970 to 2010: a global synthesis, Environmental Research Letter, March, 2020

The megacities of the developed world represent the frontier of human evolution. Each and every human need has been thought of and addressed in these cities. They are the ones leading research and development across various industries. Every large company has a sizable presence in these cities. People in these cities use the latest and the best products and services.

They are leading the world towards the model of responsible human settlement. The diversity of people and activities makes city dwellers appreciate the impact of every human behavior and action on the larger society and the world. The lines are clearly drawn for everything and there are boundaries you cannot cross. People make responsible choices as there are real consequences of good and bad decisions. Raising a family in a large dense city requires couples to plan well and actually commit themselves towards raising their children. A minimum standard of life is being ensured for every individual with several benefits mandated by some of the most progressive and powerful city governments. People pay their taxes.

There is also a growing class of neo urbanites who live at the intersection of health, technology and sustainability. They are constantly toning their bodies - they regularly go to the gym, walk or run in the park, attend dance, fitness or sports classes. Their diets include super-foods and they are constantly expanding their repertoire of healthy recipes. They buy natural and organic and carry their own bags.

But these large cities are overburdened. The population has become larger than what they could practically sustain. Instead of developing green cover and other essential public infrastructure around the dense core of high-rise development, the metropolitan areas have expanded manifolds with suburban development. Traffic congestion is frustratingly high in all these mega cities such as New York, Chicago, San Francisco, São Paulo, Mexico City, Tokyo, Rome, Paris, London and so on.

"The disadvantages of a decentralized, spread-out urban area are tremendous, and the environmental damage of urban sprawl cannot be ignored. As a large city, Tokyo must be used more efficiently, and the population density increased." - Minoru Mori, one of Japan's most powerful and influential building tycoons.

Indian metros (New Delhi, Mumbai, Kolkata, Bengaluru, Chennai, Hyderabad, Pune) have exploded over the last couple of decades and their destructive sprawl is widening at a fast clip. They are witnessing increasing levels of inefficiency, excessive consumption, congestion, inequality, pollution and environmental degradation. The real estate development is haphazard and lacks responsible urban planning. High quality development is being done in isolation by circumventing the masses and leading to higher resource intensiveness and poor efficiencies. Apartment complexes are being built with their own power back-ups and adhoc water supply systems. Forests are being encroached to build the most prime residences. To let the affluent keep moving, the Government is building over-bridges, a relatively resource intensive form of development. It is now rare to find roads flanked and covered with trees.

There is excessive competition to live in these cities. To get in and survive in these cities, people have to work their guts out, belong to a rich family, be highly talented, be incredibly intelligent or be ready to literally do anything. The work culture is cutthroat whether you are working for a bank or a restaurant.

Income and quality of life varies significantly in most of these large mega cities, whether in the developing or the developed world. Large metros have higher rates of income inequality mostly because they tend to attract more residents at the extreme opposite ends of the economic spectrum. Big cities often draw wealthy residents to high-paying industries; at the same time, these metro areas offer the poor their only shot at some form of employment. High levels of wealth and modern infrastructure coexist with areas characterized by deprivation and a dearth of services. Underinvestment in infrastructure and public transportation prevents some urban residents from accessing good jobs, education and services.

These large cities are trapped in a vicious cycle of encouraging poverty. The hyper competitive environment is making governments, enterprises and individuals ignore the basic minimum standards of living that are essential for any form of employment. There is literally no reason why a person doing essential jobs such as cleaning, gardening, construction etc. should be poor. Enterprises and individuals also avoid paying taxes that further prevents investment needed to uplift the poor.

The vicious cycle continues unabated mainly because there is an abundant supply of people from smaller cities, towns and villages. Villages, towns and smaller cities have small economies, low incomes and low-cost of living. They are home to a disproportionate share of the poor population. A sizable proportion of people working in the large cities take up low end jobs because that is still enough for them to provide for their families back home while living in poverty themselves in the city. The wages and working conditions are so poor in the smaller settlements (towns and villages) that people just want to run away. People who have the money abuse the availability of cheap labor by engaging people for jobs that are really not needed and are essentially a form of waste creation and over consumption.

Agriculture was a basic need for which most of the smaller settlements were created. Farming is an essential job and people working across the agricultural value chain should be part of mainstream society. And like any other industry, it will be most productive, efficient and high quality when capable and professional organizations carry it out. The yields would be much higher if the farms had no settlement and the operations are planned and executed centrally by people living in the cities. In today's world, every land and natural resource-based activity can be managed from the cities. Transportation has evolved so much that cities can easily manage all activities within a radius of 150-200 kms.

The low-cost agricultural settlements reduce the real value of the agricultural industry. Agriculture managed in a rural environment does not recognize several costs such as fully loaded labor costs, environmental costs, etc. And that is true of all industries that operate in smaller settlements.

Even in a developed world scenario where you end up developing smaller settlements, inequality remains. The sleepy towns and cities are just trade hubs for farm produce and have retail stores to cater to local demand. With no meaningful industry, such settlements eventually transform themselves to cater to tourists, in a bid to generate enough income. "Dull, inert cities, it is true, do contain the seeds of their own destruction and little else. But lively, diverse, intense cities contain the seeds of their own regeneration, with energy enough to carry over for problems and needs outside themselves." - Jane Jacobs, American Canadian journalist, author, theorist and activist.

Essentially, the size of a settlement determines the size of its economy, capability and resource availability. But the levels of income and quality of life are influenced by the nature of surrounding settlements. In a large city that is surrounded by several small settlements, there will be sizable inequality. Similarly in villages, towns and small cities, there will be suppressed incomes and significant poverty due to the presence of large powerful cities nearby.

We also realize that the development of a large number of smaller cities and towns is inefficient and unsustainable. The low population density and the higher number of settlements significantly increase the amount of development that needs to be done. The cost of provisioning energy and water, developing roads, managing waste, sewage and other public infrastructure increases significantly. Cost of delivering basic services is 30 to 50 percent cheaper in concentrated population centers than in sparsely populated areas[61].

Housing expansion in smaller settlements is extremely erratic and inefficient. People build single and double storey houses of different shapes and sizes. In towns and cities, individual homes are usually built on plots sold by local development authorities, and in rural areas and smaller towns, the development is completely random.

Smaller settlements including small cities are unable to justify high-rise development and also lack the capability to do so. Because of their scale, tall buildings demand alignment and coordination between several stakeholders including owners, developers, planners, architects, and engineers. Construction of these buildings requires an extra cost premium because of their need for sophisticated foundations, structural systems to carry high wind loads, and high-tech mechanical, electrical, elevator, and fire-resistant systems. Rural settlements and small towns just don't have the money to get such high-rises built. In smaller cities, tall buildings become unprofitable due to low occupancy rates. The economic climate just does not allow recuperation of the high capital investment and operational costs.

A core problem of low value small settlements is the high fertility rate. The linkage of childbirth with land & property ownership and political control has been at the root of high fertility rates in such settlements. Also, farmers and other people living in rural and small city environments typically do not have any form of insurance or retirement benefits. Smaller settlements are just not geared to provide a caring and engaging environment for the elderly. Hence, a lot of people just produce kids to provide and care for them when they get old. Families pressurize young couples to produce so they can find the heir to their small empires, whether it is a farm, a trading business, a retail shop, a service business, or a

---

[61] Trends in urban land expansion, density, and land transitions from 1970 to 2010: a global synthesis, Environmental Research Letter, March, 2020

manufacturing set up. The low-cost of living also drives people to produce without being bothered about financial consequences. A large proportion just produce kids because of social norms and peer pressure without really knowing why they are actually doing it. And of course, a large percentage of these children then migrate to large cities in search of a better life.

Women's rights are heavily compromised in smaller settlements. They have a deeply ingrained culture where women are just birthing, cooking and cleaning machines. Their education is considered worthless, and they are not allowed to develop skills for becoming an independent individual. Crimes against women such as violence, eve teasing, and abuse are common and very difficult to police. They do not have sufficient surplus to build social systems and do not have the scale to make these systems efficient and viable. The informal nature of the economy prevents the contribution of women's work (women typically work 12 to 13 hours more per week than men in rural areas[62]) to be recognized which translates into complete dependency on the male counterparts and a cause for abuse.

Living only in large cities is the only logical way forward for the world. We need to come together as responsible and conscious humans. We need to live together, think together and operate as a society rather than acting in individual interests. We can't let people rot because we think they are responsible for their own misery. We need to acknowledge the efforts of prior generations that have enabled us to figure out the way to live in harmony with the world around us. It is now our responsibility to get everyone onboard the principles of efficiency and sustainability. Everyone needs to appreciate that efficiency, sustainability, health, quality of life and equality are all dependent on each other. Living together in large cities is the core structural change needed to strike the

---

[62] https://www.ifad.org/en/web/latest/-/photo/ten-things-to-know-about-gender-equality-and-rural-poverty

chord of positive reinforcement between these interdependent variables.

Tall buildings are the most important aspect of large cities that deliver efficiency, sustainability and quality. Vertical development allows the large cities to minimize residential and commercial land use. By increasing the number of dwelling units per acre, cities not only go a long way towards meeting their sustainability objectives, but also become competitive, resilient, and great places to live[63]. Dense arrangements help preserve open spaces, a core goal of sustainability. The essential open spaces include natural areas in and around cities and localities that provide habitat for plants and animals, recreational spaces, farm and ranch lands, places of natural beauty, critical environmental areas (e.g., wetlands), and recreational community spaces. Protection of open space ensures appropriate use of prime farm and ranch lands, and prevention from flood damage. The availability of open space provides significant environmental quality and health benefits that include improving air pollution, attenuating noise, controlling wind, providing erosion control, and moderating temperatures. Open space also protects surface and ground water resources by filtering trash, debris, and chemical pollutants before they enter a water system.

Tall buildings can support dense arrangements and help in preserving open and natural spaces by accommodating many more people on a smaller amount of land area than can low-rise buildings. When developments expand vertically, public space, agricultural lands, and wilderness remain untouched. Tall buildings maximize building area with a minimum physical footprint. Accommodating the same number of people in a tall building of 50 stories versus 5 stories, for example, requires about one-tenth of the land.

---

[63] Tall Buildings and Urban Habitat of the 21st Century: A Global Perspective, School of Architecture, University of Illinois at Urbana-Champaign, Urban Planning and Policy Department, College of Urban Planning and Public Affairs, University of Illinois at Chicago, July, 2012

Commercial and residential towers free the ground plane for ample green space, which supports human connectivity and social vibrancy. Through his "Towers-in-the-Park" model, Le Corbusier advocated the high-density city mainly for the purpose of increasing access to nature. Freeing up spaces for parkland brings about "essential joys" of light, air, and greenery. This supports creating healthy and walkable communities as well.

Vertically developed cities would be the most energy efficient form of human settlement. They have many energy-effective attributes such as agglomeration, savings in auto fuel and travel time, and reduction in losses in power lines, etc.

A new generation of tall buildings, "green skyscrapers," further improves energy efficiency, and helps to combat global warming. Tall building design that incorporates energy-saving technologies also can substantially reduce CO_2 emissions. Green skyscrapers dubbed "zero energy" buildings have the potential to produce as much energy as they consume or can act as "batteries" by producing even more energy than they consume, and are described as "positive energy" buildings, and can deliver energy to the city's power grid[64].

Vertically configured buildings also facilitate more efficient infrastructure. Simply put, a 500-unit single-family subdivision requires many more roads, sidewalks, sewers, hydro lines, power and gas lines, light standards, fire hydrants, etc., than that of a tall building, which allows integrating these systems efficiently in a dense manner. Therefore, tall buildings will be crucial in creating sustainable cities.

Concentration of multi-story development will reduce costs and energy involved in transportation and urban services. Compact development reduces driving from 20% to 40%.

---

[64] Sustainability and the 21st Century Vertical City: A Review of Design Approaches of Tall Buildings, Kheir Al-Kodmany, Aug 2018

Compact development also maximizes the opportunity for combining journeys. Lunch hours and journeys to and from work can be utilized for errands such as shopping, banking, and going to the library or dry cleaners. In doing so, people will maximize the efficiency of their journeys.

Clustering of tall buildings also fosters urban synergy among the diverse activities and specialized services. The high concentration of activities creates "knowledge spillovers" between firms in the same sector and across sectors that lead to increased innovation. In a denser and varied environment, knowledge can spill into unintended fields, and a significant share of knowledge transfer occurs informally. Since knowledge is generated and transmitted more efficiently via local proximity, economic activity based on new knowledge has a high propensity to cluster within a geographic region. The presence of an abundance of firms offering similar products spurs competition, innovation, and efficiency. Agglomeration improves economies of scale and can increase productivity through access to denser markets. Access to competing suppliers helps firms procure more efficient, cheaper, and more appropriate inputs.

Vertically built cities will significantly enhance the quality of life for everyone. People will not need to maintain properties themselves, drive long distances, and will escape the feelings of loneliness and isolation experienced in suburbs and smaller settlements. High-rise urban development provides plenty of socio-cultural activities and services that cover daily needs such as shopping, groceries, and healthcare within walking distance. Tall buildings encourage central living and working. They beautify and revitalize neighborhoods, improving the quality of life by minimizing or eliminating social ills such as crime.

India stands to gain the most from the model of sustainable living and is in a unique position to lead the world towards living only in large urban centers.

The developed world will find it extremely difficult to move to a model of living only in large urban cities. Significant development and investment have already happened in their villages, towns and suburban areas. The migration to large cities will therefore be much more costly given that people have a good quality of life and there will be higher resistance to migration as well.

India has one of the worst Gini coefficients (measure of inequality) in the world. It is largely due to the vicious cycle that is rampant between our large cities, smaller cities, towns and villages. We have been following a flat model of urbanization by letting people build their own independent houses on plots of land carved out by development authorities. This model of development has resulted in India having one of the poorest and decreasing levels of urban land use efficiency.

But India is still largely undeveloped across its length and breadth and high-quality development has only started very recently. India might still not have indigenous capabilities across various industries to build a fully urban and sustainable India, but we have sufficient capability in all areas to make it happen. We now have the unique advantage of having enough people to get anything done.

Besides, once we focus our development efforts on building just the large cities, our capabilities will significantly enhance. The size of these cities will make all the development financially viable and also allow India to leverage global finance and development capabilities.

A few simple guiding principles will help identify the cities India should build and live in. One, all of them should be equal in size. Two, none should be located in an eco-sensitive region. Three, they should be able to efficiently monetize the natural resources. Four, they should maximize efficiency and competitiveness of various industries.

We also understand that an independent mega city takes shape above a population of 1 crore and cities with populations over 2 crores start becoming too big. Therefore, to sustain a population nearing 150 crores, India should build around 100 equal cities. Each city should have a minimum population of 1 crore and a cap of 2 crore.

These large cities will cover a large area and cannot be developed too close to one another. At a minimum density of 10,000 people per square km, a city with 1 crore people will be spread over 1000 sq km (~35 km diameter). With 2 crore people, the city will need an area of 2000 sq km (~50 km diameter). The cities should therefore have a minimum distance of 100 km between them.

Delhi (3 crore), Mumbai (2.5 crore), Kolkata (1.5 crore) and Bengaluru (1.3 crore) are the biggest cities. All four need to continue the vertical transformation and enforce the 2-crore population cap. Talent from these cities will be needed in any case for building the other cities.

Next are Hyderabad (1 crore) and Chennai (1 crore) that have become overcrowded due to their largely flat layouts. Ahmedabad (80 lac), Surat (72 lac), and Pune (66 lac) are the only other cities with a population above 50 lacs. They are also extremely crowded due to horizontal and poor-quality development.

All these 9 cities have multiple well-developed industries and have a robust economy. These 9 cities are at different stages of going vertical with high-rise development happening at a fair clip in each.

But the quality of life is still poor in these cities as development is way behind the needs of their existing population. It is likely to remain so and predicted to actually get worse given current trends of infrastructure investment. Inequality is high in these cities as the wealthy are able to find unlimited cheap labor to literally do anything for them.

Enforcement of minimum living standards and benefits can drive these nine cities towards an ideal state.

The next set of well-established cities are Jaipur (40 lac), Lucknow (37 lac), Kozhikode (36 lac), Kanpur (32 lac), Indore (30 lac), Kochi (30 lac), Nagpur (29 lac), Coimbatore (29 lac), Thiruvananthapuram (26 lac), Patna (25 lac), Bhopal (24 lac), Agra (22 lac), Visakhapatnam (22 lac), Vadodara (22 lac), Nashik (21 lac), Vijayawada (20 lac), Ludhiana (19 lac), and Rajkot (19 lac).

While none of these are economic powerhouses, each of these has a few known large enterprises across multiple sectors. Cost of living is lower and has allowed India to build cost-advantage based manufacturing capability across various industries. Foreign companies in both IT and manufacturing are also using these cities for their cost advantage.

High-rise development has started in these eighteen cities although it is very minimal and lower quality as income levels are lower as compared to the 9 top cities.

32 cities with population above 10 lacs (1 million)

Kollam (19 lac), Madurai (18 lac), Meerut (17 lac), Raipur (17 lac), Jamshedpur (16 lac), Aurangabad (16 lac), Jabalpur (15 lac), Jodhpur (15 lac), Tiruppur (15 lac), Ranchi (15 lac), Asansol (15 lac), Varanasi (14 lac), Dhanbad (14 lac), Amritsar (14 lac), Prayagraj (14 lac), Gwalior (14 lac), Kota (14 lac), Chandigarh (12 lac), Guwahati (12 lac), Mysore (12 lac), Trichy (12 lac), Bareilly (13 lac), Aligarh (12 lac), Moradabad (12 lac), Bhubaneswar (12 lac), Bhilai (12 lac), Jalandhar (11 lac), Solapur (11 lac), Salem (11 lac), Saharanpur (11 lac), Warangal (10 lac), Siliguri (10 lac)

55 cities with population above 5 lacs (500,000)

Guntur (9 lac), Cuttack (8 lac), Gorakhpur (8 lac), Bikaner (8 lac), Amaravati (8 lac), Nellore (8 lac), Belgaun (8 lac), Muzaffarnagar (7 lac), Mangalore (7 lac), Bhavnagar (7 lac), Rourkela (7 lac), Nanded (7 lac), Gulbarga (7 lac), Jamnagar (7 lac), Jhansi (7 lac), Jammu (7 lac), Erode (7 lac), Kurnool (7 lac), Malegaon (7 lac), Tirupati (7 lac), Bokaro (7 lac), Durgapur (7 lac), Patiala (6 lac), Mathura (6 lac), Kolhapur (6 lac), Jalgaon (6 lac), Ajmer (6 lac), Ujjain (6 lac), Agartala (6 lac), Rajahmundry (6 lac), Tirunelveli (6 lac), Gaya (6 lac), Udaipur (6 lac), Bilaspur (6 lac), Panipat (6 lac), Akola (5 lac), Sangli Miraj Kupwad (5 lac), Kakinada (5 lac), Devanagere (5 lac), Bellary (5 lac), Bhagalpur (5 lac), Latur (5 lac), Rohtak (5 lac), Sagar (5 lac), Bhilwara (5 lac), Brahmapur (5 lac), Muzaffarpur (5 lac), Ahmadnagar (5 lac), Kadapa (5 lac), Anantapur (5 lac), Sambalpur (5 lac), Vijaypura (5 lac), Chandrapur (5 lac), Nizamabad (5 lac), and Bathinda (5 lac).

So we have 114 cities with a population of around 5 lacs or more that are around 100 km or more away from each other. We have not included any mountain city. We have also chosen only one city in cases where there are multiple cities forming a large metro area.

A state-wise assessment of these cities will help us refine the list. We need to ensure sustainability, coverage and efficiency while selecting the list of equal cities across India.

We only have Jammu in the entire region of J&K and Ladakh so far. The entire Ladakh and Kashmir valley are extremely eco sensitive regions and should not be inhabited. Kashmir valley is a natural location for India's largest lake. The total population of the state is around 1.5 crore, and the mainstay is agriculture and allied activities. The terrain in the region makes most industries unviable in the region. The region has enormous water and mineral resources and also has large hydroelectric potential. Jammu is well located and sufficient to efficiently manage horticulture and other activities suitable in the region.

We have not included any city from the state of Himachal Pradesh as it is completely mountainous. We will need to find a city or two in the foothills to efficiently manage horticulture, consumer goods, pharmaceuticals, textiles, hydroelectric power generation and tourism industries.

Pathankot in current Punjab, and Una in Himachal could be ideal locations. Pathankot can be a hub for both J&K and Himachal. The total population of Himachal is only about 75 lacs.

Now in the land of the five rivers, Punjab, we have identified Ludhiana, Amritsar, Chandigarh, Jalandhar, Patiala and Bathinda. The state has 3 crore people with agriculture being the mainstay of the majority. Punjab also has several other industries such as consumer goods, electrical goods, machine tools, textiles, sports, fertilizers, steel etc. The six cities are well spread out to efficiently cover the entire land area and manage the manufacturing units across the state. Over time, manufacturing can be further consolidated closer to the chosen cities. Industrial consolidation will bring scale efficiencies and enhance competitiveness. Significant gains can be made in terms of forest area and water table enhancement by limiting settlement to these cities.

In Haryana, we have identified Panipat and Rohtak so far. We have excluded Gurugram and Faridabad as they are part of Delhi NCR. Haryana has a total population of around 3 crore people and contributes nearly 15% of India's agricultural produce with only 1.5% of the area. One can deduce that there is almost no forest cover left. It also has well developed auto, steel, textiles, oil refining, dairy and food processing industries spread across Gurugram, Panipat, Faridabad, Hisar and Sonipat. From a geographical coverage and industrial presence standpoint, Hisar would fit well into the list of equal cities. To manage the large remaining area on the western side, Hanumangarh would possibly need to be developed as well.

Coming down to Rajasthan, we have identified Jaipur, Jodhpur, Kota, Ajmer, Udaipur, Bhilwara and Bikaner. Rajasthan's population is 8.25 crore and it has more than 10% of the country's land area. Even though there is a large desert, there is still a case for at least another city. The development of Jaisalmer and / or Barmer is important from a coverage standpoint and can help in greening the large desert area on the western side.

Now in the mountain state of Uttarakhand, we only have Roorkee in our list as it is in the foothills. Uttarakhand has a total population of around 1.2 crore. The relevant industries are horticulture, food processing, pharmaceuticals, hydro power and tourism. Haldwani is well located to cover the eastern half of the state.

In Uttar Pradesh, the most populous (23 crore) and third most dense state of the country, we have identified Lucknow, Kanpur, Agra, Meerut, Varanasi, Prayagraj, Bareilly, Aligarh, Moradabad, Saharanpur, Gorakhpur, Muzaffarnagar, Jhansi and Mathura. Muzaffarnagar is well covered by Saharanpur, Roorkee and Meerut. There is also a case for some consolidation in the Agra, Mathura and Aligarh region. Kannauj plugs the coverage gap in the center and also has a distinct perfume industry. Ayodhya will be developed in any case. UP has 7.3% of the country's land area. It forms the biggest part of the rich alluvial plains that sit in the lap of the Himalayas. Another city around Govind Ballabh Pant Sagar will plug the coverage gap in the southeast region of the state.

In Bihar, we have Patna, Gaya, Bhagalpur and Muzaffarpur. The state has a population of 13 crores and 2.86% of India's land area, making it the densest state in the country. It lies at the foothills of the Himalayas with several rivers flowing through it. 80% of the people depend on agriculture and forest cover is less than 8%. The land produces some of the highest quality fruits (mangoes, litchi and bananas) and vegetables (potatoes). There are also some mineral deposits (bauxite, dolomite, glass, cement, mica and salt). There is a large untapped hydroelectric power potential in the state. Some consumer goods and agro based companies do have units in small industrial towns such as Hajipur, Dalmianagar, and Barauni. Darbhanga, Munger and Bihar Sharif are other notable cities. Steel, other metals, paper, cement, chemicals are other industries present in the state but there are no large-scale operations. One or two more city locations can be identified from amongst these industrial towns that efficiently cover the state's geography and industry.

Both Northern UP and Bihar have some of the best climate regimes. They are ideal for developing another 2-3 cities that efficiently and sustainably monetize the foothill areas and the Himalayan range above them. Lakhimpur, Bahraich, Motihari, Sitamarhi, Janakpur, Madhubani, and Purnia are possible locations for these additional cities.

In the northeastern region, we have identified Guwahati and Agartala. The total population of the seven northeastern states is a little over 5 crores. Dimapur, Jorhat and Dibrugarh are three other sustainable city locations that will ensure complete coverage of the region. We have not included Imphal as it is a natural lake formation that could be restored over time.

In West Bengal, we have identified Kolkata, Asansol, Durgapur and Siliguri. The state has a population of 10 crore and is the second most dense. West Bengal also depends mainly on agriculture and has one of the highest proportions of agricultural land. Rice, sugarcane, oil seeds, jute, wheat, potatoes, mango, jackfruit, and bananas are produced extensively across the central and southern delta region. The northern areas produce high-quality tea, oranges, apples, pineapples, ginger, and cardamom.

The state's two industrial belts lie along the Hugli and Damodar rivers. Steel, oil, petrochemical, shipping, auto, chemicals, fertilizers, wagons, electronics, paper, jute and textile companies are present across the various industrial cities and towns. It might make sense to also develop Kharagpur and Haldia for coverage as well as trade competitiveness. There is still a large uncovered area north along the border with Bangladesh. Berhampore and Malda are ideally located to efficiently cover the same.

In Jharkhand and Chhattisgarh, we have identified Ranchi, Raipur, Dhanbad, Jamshedpur, Bokaro, Bhilai and Bilaspur. The total population of the two states is nearly 7 crores. Dhanbad and Bokaro are ~70 km apart and can be merged. One city in the northeast of Jharkhand is needed to ensure coverage. Deoghar or Dumka could be possible locations. Another gap is in the northwest region of Chhattisgarh which could be plugged with a city around Ambikapur.

In Madhya Pradesh, we have identified Indore, Bhopal, Gwalior, Jabalpur, Ujjain and Sagar. The state has a population of 8.5 crore and 9.4% of the country's area. There are coverage gaps in the northeast, east and southern regions of MP. Satna, which lies in the limestone belt and contributes ~10% of India's cement production, perfectly plugs the gap in the northeast. Chhindwara is one of the largest cities in the Satpura range and is ideally located to manage the southern region. It also has multiple industries viz. pottery, leather moots and ornaments of zinc, brass and bell metal. In the eastern region, another city can be developed in the Shahdol division, which is rich in mineral resources viz. coal, fireclay, ochers and marble.

In Orissa, we have identified Bhubaneswar, Cuttack, Raurkela, Sambalpur, and Brahmapur. The total population is 4.7 crore, and it covers 4.7% of India's geographical area. Bhubaneswar and Cuttack can be merged as one city given the proximity. Balasore and Jeypore can be included to cover the eastern and western extremes of the region.

In Andhra Pradesh, we have identified Visakhapatnam, Vijayawada, Guntur, Rajahmundry, Kadapa, Tirupati, Anantapur, Nellore, Kurnool, and Kakinada. The total population of the state is 9.2 crore, and it covers 4.9% of India's land area. Vijayawada and Guntur can be merged as one city. Rajahmundry and Kakinada may also be merged.

In Telangana, we have Hyderabad, Warangal and Nizamabad. The state's total population is 4 crore and it covers 3.5% of the country's area. The three cities along with those in Andhra adequately cover the region.

In Maharashtra, we have identified Mumbai, Pune, Nagpur, Nashik, Aurangabad, Solapur, Amaravati, Nanded, Malegaon, Kolhapur, Jalgaon, Sangli Miraj Kupwad, Latur, Akola, Ahmadnagar, and Chandrapur. The state has a population of 12.5 crore and occupies 9.4% of the country's land area. Kolhapur and Sangli can be merged. Ahmednagar district is well covered by Aurangabad, Pune and Nashik.

In Gujarat, we have Ahmedabad, Surat, Vadodara, Rajkot, Bhavnagar and Jamnagar. The state has a population of 6.5 crore and has 6% of India's land area. The selected cities would be able to efficiently manage the state's natural resources and related industries.

Along the long western coastline, we need to include Panaji in the state of Goa.

In Karnataka, we have identified Bengaluru, Mysore, Belgaum, Mangalore, Gulbarga, Devanagere, Bellary, and Vijayapura. It has a population of 7 crore and 5.8% of India's land area. These 8 cities are well spread out across the state.

In Tamil Nadu, we have Chennai, Coimbatore, Tiruppur, Madurai, Trichy, Salem, Erode, and Tirunelveli. The state has a population of 8.5 crore and has 4% of India's land area. Coimbatore, Tiruppur, Erode and Salem are within 60 km of each other and present a case for consolidation with the textile industry being common across them.

In Kerala, we have Kochi, Kozhikode, Thiruvananthapuram, and Kollam. The state has a population of 3.5 crore and has 1.2% of India's land area. All four have some distinct indigenous industry and so could be developed into large cities.

After the state wise assessment, we have around 130 locations for developing the large cities. The current population is 132 crore, and we are likely to have 150 crore people by 2030. Each city will therefore have a little over a crore people.

It almost seems impossible to even attempt building so many large cities given that there are only around 40 cities globally with a population over 1 crore.

The magnitude of development needed to build each of these towering cities is huge. Assuming an average family size of 4, each city will need over 25 lac apartments and all cities together would need around 35 crore apartments. New York has 75% of its land under residential use. Remaining 25% is commercial and industrial. Residential areas also have some retail, but restricted largely to the ground floor. While the mix of commercial (excluding retail) and industrial will vary based on the core indigenous industries of each city, volume of retail will be the same if we are building equal cities with similar incomes levels.

Currently, around 2.5 lac housing units are being sold annually across the top seven cities. Given that over 80% of the housing development is happening in these top seven cities, a total of maybe 3 lac units is being sold across the country.

There are ~6 crore construction workers in India and around 30% (~2 crore) of them are engaged in residential and commercial building construction. India can comfortably deploy over 10 crore people to residential real estate construction if we just manage agriculture efficiently. That would increase the annual turnover of new housing units to ~15 lacs keeping other factors constant and not accounting for any scale effects. Even then we will take more than 200 years to build an apartment for everyone, assuming the population remains constant.

India's construction productivity is less than 10% of the international average[65]. India's construction industry is

---

[65] Reinventing construction: A route to higher productivity, McKinsey Global Institute in collaboration with McKinsey's Capital Projects and Infrastructure Practice, February 2017

wrought with all possible market failures. It is opaque, fragmented and fraught with misaligned incentives, which does not allow the most productive players to thrive. External factors cause unfavorable industry dynamics, which in turn cause firm level operational issues viz. inefficient design, poor planning and project management, low skilled workforce, and underinvestment in technology.

The singular focus of the entire nation towards equitable high-rise development of these 130 cities will increase the construction productivity ten-fold. Construction productivity increases over three-fold in high-rise residential and commercial development as compared to independent housing construction.

The focus will enable creation of large scale firms across the value chain, robust planning and design, high levels of standardization, and adoption of latest technologies and materials. The productivity of large construction firms is around twice that of national construction productivity level.

The massive scale of the development will automatically bring in transparency, fairness and efficiency across the development value chain. Once the nation commits to the plan, each of the selected cities will be redesigned. Smooth and fair systems will be set up for all past developments to be acquired by the large developers. The industry will come under the spotlight. Public involvement, attention and scrutiny will force the removal of bottlenecks and optimize the operations of the government and the developers. Instead of family owned and politically backed real estate firms, India's developers will be large professionally managed public enterprises. Government will work in tandem to create an enabling environment for them to thrive.

The biggest advantage of focus will be the level of standardization and the resulting productivity and quality enhancement. While each city will be designed differently, high-rise residential and commercial development automatically brings in very high levels of standardization in all core components of building construction. A mass production system based on a greater degree of standardization and modularization where bulk of the construction work takes place in factories, would lead to a five to ten fold increase in productivity.

One of the major hurdles to successfully making the transition is that, unlike manufacturing that has steady demand for a repeatable design, construction is characterized by bespoke designs and unpredictable demand. Focus on development of these 130 cities will ensure predictability of demand which is vital for companies to invest in productivity-enhancing capacity and innovations.

Focus on equitable living in these 130 cities will also help India avoid developing low quality residential buildings for low income and economically weaker sections of the society. The scale of the development and the resulting productivity and efficiency gains will be so huge that India would be able to build high quality residential real estate for everyone. If we expect people to genuinely transform into responsible citizens, they need to be treated equally. Development of equitable housing for all segments of the population will maximize productivity gains from standardization. It is another proof of the theory that equality, efficiency, quality as well as sustainability go hand in hand.

In the focussed equitable development scenario, India will build these 130 high-rise cities in 30-40 years. India already has the scale, capabilities and the influence to create an enabling environment for executing on this gigantic transformation. We have all the expertise needed for mobilizing manpower, financial engineering, urban planning and design, creating large public companies across the value chain, acquiring foreign companies and technologies, and skill development.

Given that most of the development needs to happen in the non-metros, we can assume an average cost of INR 750 per sq ft for a high-quality apartment building that includes sports infrastructure and a park. The average cost of construction for a luxury residential apartment in a high-rise building varies between INR 3000 and INR 5500 per sq ft across the top 5 cities. Real estate and development costs have a significant premium in these cities due to the wide gap in demand and supply. Once the Indian Government decides to develop the 130 cities, the public institutions are likely to eliminate all unnecessary premiums. Existing property holders would obviously be compensated based on reasonable market prices. The average cost of a 2000 sq ft apartment can therefore be assumed to be INR 15 lacs across the 130 cities.

The total capital outlay for building the residential real estate of a city would therefore be INR 3.75 lac crore (25 lac apartments multiplied by INR 15 lac) at FY21 prices. The total for the 130 cities would be ~INR 500 lac crore (FY21 prices). A simplistic assumption we have made is that cost reduction due to efficiency gains would be offset by increases in salaries. Given the current base of 3 lac units, a 10% YoY growth in construction activity over 50 years, will result in the development of the needed ~40 crore housing units. A similar growth in construction activity would be needed for the development of commercial (including retail), public and industrial infrastructure of each city. A reliable financing mechanism is critical for India to sustain this high growth in construction activity over 50 years. Government infrastructure financing institutions need to finance the development by issuing securities backed by the Indian Government. The existing institutional set up will need to be ramped up to enable smooth facilitation.

The massive development mandate will justify the creation of large enterprises and will need huge investments for the developers and construction companies to build and acquire the latest technologies and leading capabilities. India will have the business case to transition towards an import free construction and real estate industry by influencing a change in developers' mindset, real estate business practices and policy measures by the exchequer. The scale of the proposed development will significantly enhance India's leverage in trade negotiations and capability acquisition. India will be able to increase procurement of building material from domestic sources and manufacturers, through policy incentives and rebates by the Government, and incentives and subsidies on domestic procurement above a certain threshold. Long term returns will justify any short-term increase in costs and allow India to accelerate transition towards an independent industry, free from foreign capital and obligations. Eventually, a domestic procurement approach will reduce cost and enable best in class quality products to be made in India.

Government ministries and bodies are fully capable of seamlessly executing large-scale migration. India is the largest democracy and the volume of activity managed by each of its ministries is unparalleled. Indian political leaders are deeply rooted at the ground level. They listen to the masses and only act when there is consensus. India's political leadership has withered all storms and stood the test of time. They are selfless people who have sacrificed their health and lives to save the nation. They have brought India to the point where we can now spread the joy to every Indian citizen and make India sustainable. When they move towards delivering the final act, they are likely to have the complete support of the masses.

The villages, towns and smaller cities will need to be demolished, and brought under the operating entities of the Ministry of Forest, Ministry of Agriculture or the Ministry of Water (Jal Shakti), and in very select cases the Ministry of Tourism. Large organizations affiliated with these Ministries will own and manage the required operations and efficiently and sustainably produce the necessary output. While some of these settlements might swiftly migrate to live together in the new cities, others may witness a more gradual migration across various segments of the population.

The shift from villages, towns and smaller cities to these ~130 cities, will not only improve the quality of life of the migrants but will also fuel economic growth. The attractive financial compensation (land, property and enterprise buy-out) offered to the migrants will create the investment capital (savings, mutual funds, retirement plans, insurance etc.) needed for urban infrastructure and industrial development. Formal employment offered in various large public, private and PPP entities, will not only act as a strong incentive, but will also enable these organizations to gain the scale needed for indigenously and efficiently executing large scale infrastructure development and industrial production. The formalization will directly translate to economic output and increase India's economic productivity.

Once developed, each of the ~130 cities will have an economy of at least $250 billion in today's terms. Given that all the activities of the nation would be controlled through these cities, India will have a real GDP of at least $32 trillion (2020 dollars), around 16 times the current GDP.

Approximate GDP, per crore of population, of various large cities with a population greater than 1 crore is - New York ($900 bn), Seoul ($900 bn), Paris ($800 bn), Chicago ($800 bn), Los Angeles ($800 bn), London ($700 bn), Tokyo ($500 bn), Moscow ($500 bn), Osaka ($375 bn), Shenzhen ($350 bn), Guangzhou ($300 bn), Beijing ($250 bn), Shanghai ($250 bn), São Paulo ($250 bn), Chongqing ($225 bn), Istanbul ($225 bn), Mexico City ($200 bn), Buenes Aires ($200 bn), Rio de Janeiro ($200 bn), Jakarta ($200 bn), Mumbai ($150 bn), Tianjin ($150 bn), Manila ($120 bn), Bengaluru ($100 bn), Karachi ($100 bn), Delhi ($90 bn), Dhaka ($85 bn), and Cairo ($50 bn).

The leaders in the pack are alpha cities and dominate at least one industry at a global level. E.g. New York (finance), Seoul (electronics), Paris (aeronautics), Chicago (auto), LA (Hollywood), London (finance), Tokyo (finance). But all of them today have a fairly diversified economy with a large contribution of services including technology and retail. Real estate is also a large industry in each of these cities. The industrial cities of China have been built more recently and present some of the best examples of complete high-rises development. While Shenzhen's core industries are high tech, finance, logistics and culture, retail is around $80 bn and the real estate industry is ~10% ($35 bn). South American cities have no real globally competitive industry and are only partially vertical; even their consumption and services-based city economies are also greater than $200 bn.

6. Urban infrastructure

India is uniquely placed to build the best urban infrastructure for the 130 high-rise cities. We would literally be building these cities from scratch as the entire current real estate and infrastructure is grossly insufficient, poor quality and inefficient. Given how constrained we are for land, we need a strong focus on efficiency of land use. India has no case for preserving heritage buildings that are useless, inefficient and reek of a culture of inequality, injustice and extravagance. Culture can all be preserved in the clouds. It's time for us to move forward and build high quality modern infrastructure.

India stands to benefit from the significant evolution in the infrastructure and related industries. India is also now well connected with the global economy to learn best practices and leverage the capabilities and resources. The domestic infrastructure industry has also acquired capabilities to build all forms of high-quality infrastructure. Even though the Indian firms might still not own the engineering capability to indigenously produce best in class equipment and materials, they are able to deliver all forms of high-quality infrastructure.

Urban infrastructure is the underlying structural foundation of a city. Infrastructure, if intelligently designed, planned and delivered, can create an urban environment where there is perfect harmony between people, nature, structures and systems. In a high-rise city, the key pillars of urban infrastructure are the high-rise buildings, urban blue and green spaces, the mobility and sports infrastructure. They are the defining elements on a city's map and getting them right is critical for maximizing the livability, efficiency and productivity of a city.

The primary determinant of a city's layout is the urban green and blue cover. Blue cover is essential for water security and preventing the use of groundwater. Large urban agglomerations experience an urban heat island effect (UHI) i.e., an increase in temperature as compared to the surrounding non urbanized region[66]. Optimal blue and green cover is therefore also essential for a city to minimize the UHI effects. Minimizing the UHI effects and cooling the environment assume more importance and can be really effective in India's subtropical climate.

In urban landscapes, water bodies, urban parks, forests, and other green spaces are collectively referred to as urban blue green space, and all of them have significant cooling effects. Research has concluded that urban blue green space exceeding 70 % in a metropolitan area, would significantly mitigate the UHI effect[67,68].

The cooling effect of the blue-green space depends on the size, shape, connectivity, and complexity (composition and configuration) of the blue-green space, and the greenness of the green vegetation. Some researchers have proposed that landscape configuration, rather than composition, is a more important factor influencing the cooling effect of blue-green space.

On the other hand, many researchers have realized that quantifying the threshold-size of different landscape types, including the effect of landscape composition and configuration, to obtain the maximum cooling efficiency of blue-green space is essential to decision-makers and actionable climate adaptation planning. In order to most effectively alleviate the UHI effect, leading researchers have

---

[66] Water bodies an urban microclimate: A review, Centre for Study of Built Environment in the Malay World (KALAM), Faculty Built Environment, University Technology Malaysia, February 2, 2015

[67] Research on the cooling island effects of water body: A case study of Shanghai, China, School of Geographic Sciences, East China Normal University, Ecological Engineering College, Guizhou University of Engineering Science, April 25, 2016

[68] Urban green space cooling effect in cities, Escuela Técnica Superior de Arquitectura, Universidad Politécnica de Madrid-UPM, School of Engineering and Built Environment, Griffith University, Faculty of Architecture and Urbanism, University of Art, Tehran, April, 2019

proposed an idealized spatial pattern of blue-green space within a city – hierarchical hexagonal structure model[69].

Besides cooling the local environment, the urban blue or the water bodies are needed for water storage and ensuring water security at all times. So, each city needs to at least have water storage to comfortably meet the water requirements.

The annual water requirement of a city with a population of around a crore would vary between 1 to 4 cubic kilometers, the average being around 1.5 cubic kilometers. That accounts for domestic consumption (65-300 lit/capita/day), industrial and commercial (45-450 lit/capita/day), public uses (20-90 lit/capita/day), and losses & waste (45-150 lit/capita/day). A city should have stored water to meet requirements even in case of 2-3 continuous dry spells. So water bodies with a capacity of around 10 cubic kilometers would provide complete water security to a city.

The area of urban blue would therefore range from anywhere between 200 to 500 sq km. The depth of lakes in India varies from 5m to over 150m. The possible depth for a new lake would obviously depend on the geology of the region. But India should be able to build lakes with depth ranging between 20m and 50m everywhere across the country. Shivaji Sagar is the largest manmade lake in India. It has a depth of 80m and an area of ~900 sq km.

A typical lake (shallow) restoration costs around 10 crore per sq km. Most Indian cities have existing river linkages and even natural lake beds. By planning discharge from upstream dams, relocation of existing settlements, demolition of structures and cleaning up the debris, these sites can be flooded to restore the lakes in 3-5 years. Development of a

---

[69] Critical review on the cooling effect of urban blue-green space: A threshold-size perspective, Department of Geosciences and Natural Resource Management, Faculty of Science, University of Copenhagen, Key Laboratory of Urban Environment and Health, Institute of Urban Environment, Chinese Academy of Sciences Xiamen, Department of Architecture Faculty of Engineering, Sojo University, Shanghai Key Lab for Urban Ecological Processes and Eco-Restoration, Shanghai, State Key Laboratory of Urban and Regional Ecology, Research Center for Eco-Environmental Sciences, Chinese Academy of Sciences Beijing, February, 2020

large deep lake from scratch will involve several additional activities including building the river linkages and would therefore be much costlier and time-consuming. Assuming 100-500 crore per sq km as the capital requirement, an estimated investment for a lake spread over 500 sq km could be INR 50,000 - 2,50,000 crore or between $6-30 billion.

Besides fulfilling water requirements and cooling the environment, water bodies create significant additional value. A critical use would be to store renewable energy by building "pumped hydro". Pumped storage is the largest-capacity form of grid energy storage in the United States (250 GWh). The round-trip energy efficiency of pumped hydro varies between 70%–80%, with some sources claiming up to 87%.[70]

The water bodies such as lakes, canals, and ponds serve as places of recreation, alternate means of transportation, and provide a boost to the tourism industry.

Bathing, swimming, fishing, boating, camping, photography, meditation etc. are just some of the recreational possibilities that water bodies create. Water transportation is cost effective, energy efficient, environmentally friendly and more pleasing for small journeys. The aesthetic quality of water, which includes the visual, audial, tactual and psychological aspects, adds vibrancy and excitement to a space, and makes it more attractive for locals as well as tourists. The water bodies also help in the development of the town as a whole with its multiplier effects such as retail, hotel, restaurants, clubs, entertainment parlors, etc.

Apart from these benefits, the ecological benefits include supporting wildlife, controlling floods, recharging groundwater etc.

The high-rise buildings and the mobility infrastructure would need around 500 sq km. Fully high-rise districts like

---

[70] Yang, Chi-Jen (11 April 2016). Pumped Hydroelectric Storage. Duke University.

Manhattan have a population density of around 28,000 which increases to 65,000 on business days with the influx of people from surrounding areas. There are around 18 floors on average in the buildings in Manhattan. India can comfortably aim to achieve 15 floors on average. Indian cities can build more dedicated lanes for walking and cycling. We also need more tree cover on roads, walkways and cycle tracks. Even then, we can easily achieve a population density of over 25,000 in the built-up areas, given that the proportion of residential buildings would be higher than Manhattan in a 'high-rise only' model. We would therefore need ~400 sq km for residential, commercial and transportation infrastructure. The manufacturing and industrial activity would need another 10-100 sq km depending on the city.

Abundant sports infrastructure is critical and land intensive and is therefore another key structural element of urban planning. While the urban green will have urban parks for walking, jogging, running and various forms of exercise, several sports would require significant space. Sports such as golf, cricket, soccer, hockey, tennis, swimming, basketball, rugby etc. are outdoor sports and multi-level fields for these sports are not viable.

China has made rapid advances in developing its urban sports infrastructure and has achieved 1.2 square meters of venue space per capita and is aiming to reach 3 square meters by 2030[71]. Japan and the US, along with the Nordics, have the highest densities of sports infrastructure in the world. Japan has 19 square meters of venue space per capita[72].

Golf and cricket are by far the most land intensive. Both the US and Japan have a high density of golf courses. Now while the weather is not as amenable for golf in India, it is still pretty good for at least 6 months of play. It is a sport for all ages and

---

[71] Providing Sports Venues on Mainland China: Implications for Promoting Leisure-Time Physical Activity and National Fitness Policies, College of Landscape Architecture and Arts, Northwest A&F University, Yangling, Centre for Urban Research, RMIT University, Melbourne, July, 2020

[72] White Paper on Sport in Japan 2017, Sasakawa Sports Foundation, 2017

the experience of being on the course is both liberating and healthy. Achieving the same density of golf courses as in the top golf cities of the US might be a stretch. They have more than 1 golf course per 10,000 residents. For a city of 1 crore people, that would mean 600 sq km of space for just golf courses. (Each course needs 0.6 sq km or around 150 acres). To start with, India should plan for around 100 courses in a city which would need ~60 sq km of space. Once the wood stock in the urban green reaches best in class levels (very tall, thick and dense forest cover), India can possibly look at converting more urban green into golf courses.

Sports participation is mainly dependent on the availability of sports infrastructure (Deelen et al., 2016; Wicker et al., 2013). There is no reason why Indians should not play any sport, as long as they don't involve any unnecessary risks or pose a serious threat to the environment. Car and bike racing is one such category of sports that is both risky and unfriendly for the environment. Also, indulging in combat sports maybe does not make sense, but they don't require too much space.

To be best in class, India will need to allocate around 200 sq km (20 sqm multiplied by 1 crore) of land in each city towards the development of indoor and outdoor sports facilities. That would allow us to build an ample number of facilities for every sport.

To achieve an effective blue green cover of around 70%, cities will need to have an urban green spread covering 500 to 800 sq km. For a city with a deep lake and tall thick vegetation, an urban green cover at the lower end of the range would suffice.

Each city will therefore need to have a total area around 2000 sq km. The 130 cities together would then cover around 8% (2.6 lac divided by 32 lac sq km) of India's land area. Reaching a stable state with this settlement pattern over the next ~50 years would itself be a tall order.

All the chosen 130 cities will need to significantly expand to have a span of 2000 sq km. The largest Indian cities by area

(area of city proper and not metropolitan area) are Delhi (1484 sq km), Bengaluru (709), Hyderabad (650), Lucknow (631), Visakhapatnam (540), Indore (530), Amdavad (505), Surat (474), Jaipur (467), and Bhopal (463). These are figures from the 2011 census and the cities have certainly expanded since then. As per the same, there were just 22 cities with an area greater than 300 sq km as per 2011 census.

Given the current state of infrastructure, over 100 out of the 130 cities would require greenfield development and the remaining would be brownfield. In the greenfield development cities, urban planners and designers will have minimal constraints to work with. When compared with the best-in-class standards of efficiency and quality, none of the existing infrastructure would qualify for retention. In the top 9 cities and a few others, there are varying proportions of good infrastructure that should be incorporated in the new layout designs.

Lake depth, type of vegetation, industry mix and geological considerations can cause some variation in the area requirement of different cities. Existing development, water bodies, river linkages, forest cover, geology and other factors would need to be considered while deciding on the perimeter of each city. Location of water bodies and wind flow patterns would be key determinants in deciding the shape and orientation of the city's layout. The decided area should be made sacrosanct, and mechanisms need to be put in place to never let the city boundaries expand beyond the agreed upon limits.

Urban designers or planners will need to layout the urban blue green, real estate, transportation and sports infrastructure to maximize livability, efficiency and productivity. Perfect design for one city at a very granular level will enable the creation of modules and establish principles of organizing various elements. All 130 cities can then be designed using the modules and principles while adhering to the city specific nuances.

Scientific urban planning and design is critical to evaluate trade-offs between cooling effect, efficiency and productivity. While the maximum intensity of cooling is achieved with larger water bodies, higher coverage is achieved through a more spread-out pattern of small, interconnected lakes. The efficiency of various distribution networks viz. energy, transportation, water, telecommunications etc. would be highest in the case of a concentrated single block of built-up area. But that would compromise the cooling effect of the urban blue green.

Buildings, walkways, open public spaces and outdoor sports need to have the coolest environment. The direction and speed of wind are vital in spreading the cooling impact of urban water bodies. Urban streets which run downwind or a public square that is located next to a water body space acquire better thermal situations than obstructive streets. Wind flow patterns in an urban environment are influenced by the local geometry, like trees, street geometry and the distribution of building heights. Temperature is obviously lower on the leeward side of a water body space. Research proposes the vitality of open spaces close to water body sites for the distribution of the temperature in comparison to obstructive or enclosed streets. The horizontal impact of the water body on the microclimate is dependent on the density of buildings and the street's width.

In addition, the water body size and water distribution over the city has their role. Quietly huge water bodies also seem to acquire a relatively powerful cooling impact on the surroundings. A number of smaller lakes though have shown to influence bigger percentages of cities - a number of smaller normally shaped bodies of water have the highest beneficial impact when it comes to the matter of lowering extreme temperature over the course of the day.

On average, the temperature inside a park which had water was 0.4 ºC cooler than when it did not have water. In comparison to the temperatures of the residential surrounding areas nearby, the park which had water was 1.2 ºC cooler[73]. The cooling effects of rivers are significantly less than those of lakes[74].

Mixed use development maximizes the active use of space and land and minimizes carbon footprint. Not only does it increase efficiency and productivity, if designed well, it also maximizes livability. A single use low density residential neighborhood or suburban business parks are typically underutilized during long periods of time. A vibrant and sufficiently densely populated urban environment, by contrast, is well used round-the-clock, all days of the week, and during all seasons. This results from a closely knit mix of uses (e.g., offices, residences, retail etc.), with sufficient density, and which are accessible to a diversity of users (e.g., children, young, seniors, high-income, low-income, etc.). Dense mixed-use neighborhoods also allow for the effective functioning of all types of business, fitness, social, cultural activities with very low inputs of energy for transportation and logistics.

Most importantly, mixed use development brings almost everything close enough for people to just walk. Well planned neighborhoods provide the needs of daily living, within walking distance (a 500 m radius). All key destinations are accessible within a pleasant walking distance – people are able and willing to walk from home to work, to school, to shop, to recreate, and to engage in the activities of their everyday life. Longer distances are traveled through transit.

Mixed use development also includes creating ample destinations at a local level for people to congregate and feel the energy of the vibrant community. All successful cities and successful neighborhoods include vibrant places, with a

---

[73] Research on the cooling island effects of water body: A case study of Shanghai, China, School of Geographic Sciences, East China Normal University, Ecological Engineering College, Guizhou University of Engineering Science, April, 2016

[74] "Analysis of cooling effect of water bodies on land surface temperature in nearby region: A case study of Ahmedabad and Chandigarh cities in India", Malaviya National Institute of Technology Jaipur, Madanapalle Institute of Technology & Science, April 2019

strong sense of identity, which are integral to community life and the public realm: parks, plazas, courtyards, civic buildings, public streets, etc.

Reducing car-dependency is important for sustainable cities. While electric vehicles are more energy efficient, use clean energy and produce less harmful emissions, there is a long way for them to gain mass adoption. Besides, the alternative modes of transportation – namely walking, cycling, and transit will always be more energy efficient. They will result in more sustainable urban environments and will also lead to an improved quality of life. World over the best cities and neighborhoods have prioritized walking, and created desirable locations to live, work, play, and invest in.

Cities and neighborhoods need to have a robust transit infrastructure. After walking and cycling, transit is the most sustainable mode of transportation. Transportation infrastructure will need to be planned for much higher volumes of transit oriented urban patterns. High density of mobility hubs would be needed to ensure seamless transit from walking to other modes of transportation. Not only will pedestrian and mass transportation friendly planning increase the quality of life of a city, but the reduced energy consumption will also improve the economics of living and doing business in the city.

Fully high-rise development adds a whole new dimension to mobility. Mixed-use vertical cities require various forms of spatial infrastructure for seamless mobility between high-rises and the wider urban transport infrastructure. Skybridges are now a revolution in urban connectivity. Vertical urban growth promises more efficient, more sustainable higher-density cities. And now, though some obstacles remain, new structural engineering practices and transportation technologies are also putting sky-high horizontal habitat within easy reach – cities in the sky.

7. Large scale natural farming

India has the second largest agricultural industry in the world. In 2018, the global agricultural output was $3,408 billion with China, the largest producer, contributing $1,073 billion, followed by India, which contributed $399 billion (11.7%). In terms of volume as well, India is the second largest producer. Out of the 9.1 billion tonnes of total global production, India produced 1.1 billion tonnes (12%)[75]. We produced 22% of the world's rice, 20% sugarcane, 14% wheat, 12% vegetables and ~11% of the world's fruit. We are by far the largest milk producer in the world with over 22% share.

But the enormous production translates into low levels of nutrition for India's 1.3 billion people (~18% of the world's population). India's energy supply is 2,526 kcal per capita per day as compared to a global average of 2,866 and NA & Europe average of 3,501. The protein supply is 63g per capita per day as compared to the global average of 80g and NA & Europe average of 105.

The existing production is heavily unbalanced. The current research on balanced diet suggests a daily intake of 1200g of the main food groups. The recommended composition is cereals 150g (13%), vegetables 300g (25%), fruits 300g (25%), pulses 100g (8%), milk products 300g (25%), sugar 25g (2%), and oils 25g (2%)[76]. The production in India is heavily biased towards cereals and sugar. The split of current production is cereals 318m (26%) vegetables 182m (15%)

---

[75] "World Food and Agriculture - Statistical Yearbook 2020", Food and Agriculture Organization of the United Nations (FAO), Rome

[76] "Sustainable Diets: What You Need to Know in 12 Charts", Janet Ranganathan and Richard Waite, World Resources Institute, April 20, 2016; "Cereals and wholegrain foods", Better Health Channel, Victoria State Department, Department of Health, Deakin University; "Enhancing nutrition with pulses: defining a recommended serving size for adults", Christopher P F Marinangeli, Julianne Curran, Susan I Barr, Joanne Slavin, Seema Puri, Sumathi Swaminathan, Linda Tapsell, and Carol Ann Patterson, Nov 30, 2017

fruits 98m (8%) pulses 23m (2%) milk 187m (15%) sugar 376m (30%) and oil 57m (5%)[77]. Cereal production is twice and sugar is fifteen times the recommended amount, depicted clearly by the great Indian belly and the incidence of diabetes in the country. We are 40% short on required vegetables tonnage, 68% short on fruits, 75% short on pulses and 40% short on milk.

Wealth based distribution further exacerbates nutrition inequality. The market forces work fairly efficiently in India to establish prices based on demand and supply. Fruits, vegetables, pulses and milk therefore command higher prices than cereals and sugar. The rich buy more than what they actually need from the expensive food items. The food prices are literally negligible for the rich and higher middle-income segments. They even end up wasting a fair lot of it. The economically weaker sections in both rural and urban India end up with extremely unhealthy diets. The poor just cannot afford to consume sufficient fruits, nuts, seeds, vegetables, pulses, and healthy cereals. India has the highest number of undernourished people, ~20 crore (28% of world's total). The number is much higher (50-80 crore) when we consider all components of a balanced diet.

The MSP system directly or indirectly influences the pricing of the various agricultural commodities. The Central Government fixes the Minimum Support Price (MSP) of the 23 agricultural crops based on the recommendations of the Commission for Agricultural Costs and Prices (CACP). The CACP fixes the MSP after taking into consideration the production cost, the demand supply situation, international prices, and inter-crop price parity. MSP based procurement mainly happens in the alluvial plains and is effective only for major food grains that can be stored. While the procurement is less than 10% even for wheat and rice, the MSPs indirectly influence the price received by the producers through other channels i.e., local markets, Mandis, dealers and food

---

[77] Annual report 2019-2020, Ministry of Agriculture and Farmers Welfare

processors. Around 40% of the produce is sold in local markets and nearly the same amount in Mandis. Smaller farmers sell more of their produce in local markets. Local markets naturally offer a price lower than MSP. Mandis are brutal for the small farmer. Dealers and processors typically secure their requirements from a few large farmers at pre-agreed bulk prices. The MSP system has been responsible for excessive production of rice and wheat. It has resulted in severe levels of soil degradation and groundwater depletion.

India has the largest land area under cultivation (189 million hectares). The next three are the US (168 m), Russia (127 m) and China (124 m). We have one of the highest percentages (58%) of land under cultivation. The percentages are much lower for other big cultivators - US (17%), Russia (7.4%), China (12.9%), Brazil (7.6%), Canada (5.2%), Australia (6.3%).

India is ranked seventh in terms of total agricultural land - China (530 Mha), US (400 Mha), Australia (370 Mha), Brazil (280 Mha), Russia (210 Mha), Kazakhstan (210 Mha), India (200 Mha). Cultivated land is only a certain percentage of the total agricultural land in a country. Globally, around 68% of the total agricultural land is permanent meadows and pastures. India has just 10 Mha or ~5% of its agricultural land under permanent pastures.

India has a total livestock of ~550 million that includes cattle (193m), buffaloes (110m), goats (149m), sheep (74m), and pigs (9m). We also have 850 million poultry animals. We have the second largest cattle population after Brazil and have 57% of the world's buffalo.

India has the largest area of the most fertile soils in the world. The ten most fertile countries along with the percentage area under cultivation are India (58%), Bangladesh (66%), Denmark (59%), the Ukraine (58%), Moldova (64%), Hungary (51%), Rwanda (57%), Comoros (76%), Togo (49%) and Gambia (42%). India has the highest land mass of the most fertile soil types viz. Inceptisols (130 million hectares),

Entisols (92m), Alfisols (44m), and Vertisols (28m). The fertile land mass has the potential to deliver the highest productivity levels.

The wide range of fertile soils has enabled India to achieve one of the highest crop diversity in the world. The Indian gene center is among the 12 mega diversity regions of the world. Rich diversity occurs in several crops. About 25 crop species were domesticated in India. It is endowed with rich diversity of more than 18,000 species of higher plants including 160 major and minor crop species and 325 of their wild relatives. Around 1,500 wild edible plant species are widely exploited by native tribes. These include 145 species of roots and tubers, 521 of leafy vegetables/ greens, 101 of buds and flowers, 647 of fruits and 118 of seeds and nuts. In addition, nearly 9,500 plant species of ethno-botanical uses have been reported from the country, of which around 7,500 are for ethno-medicinal purposes and 3,900 are multipurpose edible species[78]. In addition, Indian agriculture has been enriched by a continuous stream of introductions of new crops and their cultivars since ancient times. The current diversity consists of indigenous plants, their wild and/ or weed relatives and well adapted introductions from practically all over the globe. Among introduced types, some good examples are cereals - wheat, barley, oats, maize; pulses - chickpea, French bean and peas; vegetables - potato, onion, cauliflower, cabbage, carrot and tomato; fruits - apple, pear, grapes, cherry, peach and apricot; oilseeds - soybean, sunflower and groundnut; fiber plants - cotton; medicinal plants - mint, liquorice, foxglove, Cinchona, Hyoscyamus (herbane) and others such as Humulus lupulus (hops). Thus, both indigenous and well adapted exotic sets of materials constitute a well-balanced matrix of crop diversity in India.

---

[78] "Indian crop diversity", N Sivaraj, SR Pandravada, V Kamala, N Sunil, K Rameash, Babu Abraham, M Elangovan & SK Chakrabarty, National Bureau of Plant Genetic Resources (NBPGR), Directorate of Sorghum Research (DSR), Hyderabad

Over the centuries, nature gifted this land with the most resilient seeds that thrived in Indian condition without the help of chemicals and fertilizers. However, the native seeds lost out to high-yielding hybrid seeds of the 1960s as part of the green revolution. India owned 1,10,000 varieties of rice till 1970. Out of these, only 6000 are surviving today. The indigenous seeds have been overshadowed by the hybrid seeds. While the indigenous seeds can be recycled and reused, the hybrid seeds can only be used once and need to be replaced every year. Indian farmers are now spending about Rs. 95,000 crore every year on the purchase of hybrid seeds from MNCs. Seeds from companies of Taiwan, Canada, China and Australia have flooded the market, despite their not being as healthy as the native varieties. The hybrid seeds need greater amounts of pesticides, fertilizers and water for irrigation. The produce from hybrid seeds is inferior in both taste and quality as compared to the native varieties. On average the hybrid seeds are ten times more costly, but the gains in yield and pressure from MNCs leave the farmer with no choice.

The desi varieties are of the highest quality in the world. The rich and diverse agro climatic environment has enabled the development of varieties that have the most superior combination of color and appearance, flavor (taste and aroma), texture, and nutritional value.

The shape, size, gloss, and vibrant color of a fruit or vegetable attract us towards picking it. Once we are attracted by the appearance, we put it into our mouths, where the aroma and taste take over. Freshness, spiciness, sweetness, and other flavor attributes are critical to our eating pleasure. Aroma refers to the smell of a fruit or vegetable product, whereas flavor includes both aroma and taste. Once the product is placed in the mouth, one can perceive the smoothness, thickness, firmness, hardness, or crispness of the fruit or vegetable material. As chewing proceeds, the perception of textural quality changes and products generally become softer. Nutritional value is an extremely important quality component that is impossible to see, taste, or feel. Nutrients are critical for the growth and long-term development of our bodies and include both micronutrients and macronutrients[79].

There are some associations between textural attributes, especially juiciness and flavor and between the color and nutritional composition of fruits and vegetables.

Genetic modifications and hybrid development results in trade-offs on one or more attributes. For example, if you increase firmness in a bid to reduce wastage and enhance storage time, the color and flavor might get sacrificed. Modified crops also require external agents to initiate chemical reactions that are critical for achieving the desired improvement. It is nearly impossible to artificially achieve the perfect balance between different attributes.

Whether it is fruits, vegetables, cereals, pulses, spices, nuts or milk, the desi Indian variety represents the best naturally evolved version. There are specific geographical regions that formed the natural habitat for the various crops to achieve their perfect forms. The natural habitats had the ideal combination of soil and climate for the perfect development of specific crop varieties.

Following is the list of produce whose highest quality varieties have naturally evolved in the Indian subcontinent:

Fruits - mangoes, bananas, oranges, apple, guava, pear, muskmelon, litchi, chikoo, grapes, peaches, plums, apricot, custard apple, strawberry, pomegranate, bael (Bengal quince) and kiwi.

Vegetables - cauliflower (gobhi), okra (bhindi), potato, cabbage, brinjal (baigan), ridge gourd (torai), calabash (lauki), apple gourd (tinda), bitter gourd (karela), pointed gourd

---

[79] "Color, Flavor, Texture, and Nutritional Quality of Fresh-Cut Fruits and Vegetables: Desirable Levels, Instrumental and Sensory Measurement, and the Effects of Processing", Diane M. Barrett, John C. Beaulieu, and Rob Shewfelt, Department of Food Science & Technology, University of California, Davis

(parval), taro (arbi), jackfruit, tomato, carrot, cucumber, radish, cucumis (kakadi), drumstick, lotus stem (kamal kakadi), sweet potato, peas, lemon, onion, beetroot, turnip, capsicum, spinach, green mustard, wild spinach, fenugreek, Indian gooseberry, Indian water chestnuts, Natal plum, Indian beans, ivy gourd, radish pods (sangri), and mouse melon (kachri).

Cereals - wheat, rice, pearl millet (bajra), sorghum (jowar), barley, maize, oat, finger millet (ragi), buckwheat (kuttu), durum, barnyard millet and amaranth.

Pulses - pigeon peas (arhar), moong beans, yellow split moong beans, black matpe (urad), red lentil (masur), split bengal gram (chana), bengal gram whole (kala chana), kidney beans (rajma), chickpeas, black eyed peas (lobhia), white peas (matar), dew gram (moth), sago (sabudana), lima beans (sem), horse gram, soybean, and dal bhat.

Spices - chillies, ginger, turmeric, pepper, cardamom, cumin, asafoetida, black cardamom, bay leaf, cinnamon, cloves, garlic, coriander, mint, curry leaves, fennel seeds, sesame, poppy, tamarind, and glueberry.

Nuts and seeds - cashew, walnut, betelnut, coconut, peanut, dates, fig, lotus seed, cudpahnut, raisin, makhana (fox nuts), pumpkin seeds, kokum, sunflower seeds, and flaxseeds.

India clearly has the potential for producing the highest quality crops of all types, and we do produce a sizable quantity of the same.

But there is also very high variation in the quality of our produce. While the variation is most evident in fruits and vegetables, it is widespread in all kinds of produce. We have an established culture of going early in the morning to the vendors to find the best quality produce. Quality usually also varies across vendors especially if they have different sourcing. It is not uncommon to find multiple varieties for the same item at the same vendor as well. There is no retail venture (offline or online) that stocks only high-quality produce.

Agriculture is the backbone of our country. The farmers have literally carried India on their shoulders. Through thick and thin, agriculture has kept us alive. It has borne the brunt of everything else that has transpired over the last few centuries. Agriculture has been our defense against all attacks. It has given us the energy and resources to build industrial and services capabilities.

Post independence, the only indigenous expertise we had was agriculture. To maintain sovereignty, we needed the numbers and control of our lands. Several land reforms were enacted to regain control and enable a more equal distribution of land. The zamindari system was abolished, and small land holdings were given to the farmers. People could be self-sufficient with the allotted land, and the government gained control through appropriate distribution.

The fertile Indian land has been merrily exploited by one and all. The excessive exploitation continued during the British era and even at the time of our independence, agricultural land percentage was already very high. The net sown area even in 1950 was 120 million hectares and has only grown to 140 million hectares (17% increase) till date. The population meanwhile has increased from 35 crore to 135 crore (285% increase). With no real restrictions on crop selection, people started growing literally everything everywhere. Buoyed by the fertility of the Indian soil, farmers planted everything they heard about and kept growing whatever grew reasonably well. It is the main reason for the vast variation in produce quality.

The government's main objective was food security for the nation, and so as long as you contributed enough to the state coffers, nobody cared what you did on your land. The population surge post-independence increased food security concerns that initiated the adoption of hybrid seeds. The

Green Revolution followed, and India achieved a food surplus status with enormous production of hybrid wheat and rice. The pressure from the burgeoning population though, was relentless, and we needed more of everything. So over time, to achieve higher yields, India witnessed the introduction and adoption of hybrids across all crop categories. The population pressure has also led us to use every possible inch of land under farming.

Agriculture is now the eldest child who has gone rogue due to increasing levels of neglect by the nation. In FY17, the government just spent 2.9% of its total budget on agriculture that employs ~58% of the country's workforce and still accounts for ~16% of the country's GDP. Agriculture, with its allied sectors, is the largest source of livelihoods in India. 70 percent of India's rural households still depend primarily on agriculture for their livelihood.

The population pressure and the hands-off nature of government involvement has created a complex set of interconnected problems. The land is now divided into economically unviable small and scattered holdings (average land holding now is 1.1 hectare). The production has become cereal centric and regionally biased. Crop rotation and other best practices for land preservation have been thrown out of the window. The lands are being constantly sowed with one crop after the other with no time for the soil to breathe or replenish. We have one of the highest cropping intensities in the world. We have blatantly used groundwater and the levels have been constantly declining. Use of fertilizers has steadily grown and has already breached hazardous levels in several high production belts. Excessive use of fertilizers and pesticides has contaminated groundwater as well as the produce. 75% of the agricultural land (~150 million hectares) now qualifies as degraded land.

The small-scale farmer is severely resource constrained leading to several inefficiencies that hamper productivity and quality. They do not generate enough income and have little access to credit to invest in their farm and literally do the bare minimum to get a decent harvest. Their incomes are further suppressed by their inability to get the right price for their produce. The primary objective for them is to feed the family and for that they grow whatever is possible on the land, putting a big dent on productivity. They simply can't afford to follow crop rotation best practices, leading to a constant decline in the soil quality. They use manual plowing, traditional equipment like wooden plows, sickles and spades, as they are unable to afford tractors and combines.

Smaller landholdings result in several redundancies that further reduce productivity. A lot of time and labor is wasted in moving seeds, manure, implements and cattle from one piece of land to another. Irrigation becomes difficult on such small and fragmented fields. Further, a lot of fertile agricultural land is wasted in providing boundaries and real estate.

The government plays the role of regulator and resource provider. The Ministry of Agriculture and Farmers' Welfare is the apex body for formulation and administration of the rules and regulations and laws related to agriculture in India. There are government departments at central and state level for different segments of agriculture. There are independent departments for different categories of produce. The Ministry of Agriculture & Farmers Welfare has been organized in three major departments:

-   Department of Agriculture Research and Education (DARE),
-   Department of Agriculture, Cooperation and Farmers Welfare (DAC&FW), and
-   Department of Animal Husbandry, Dairying and Fisheries (DAHD&F).

The sub departments are organized along:

- major crop areas viz. rice, wheat, millets, pulses, sugarcane, cotton, jute, oilseeds, fruits and nuts & spices,

- key components viz. soil, seeds, fertilizer and farm machinery, and

- all required functions viz. economics & statistics, costs & prices, plant protection, quarantine & storage, marketing & inspection, and crop forecast

The state level agencies are structured to facilitate activities between central sub departments and the districts.

Needless to say, the government bodies fully understand best practices related to all aspects of agriculture. They are also well connected with the farmer community.

The government influences the agricultural industry through regulations, direct interventions (procurement), support programs and schemes (finance, equipment, seeds, fertilizers, insurance, family welfare etc.), training (farming best practices, new technologies, quality control, soil health, post harvest management, marketing, food processing, pricing etc.) and events (trade seminars, conferences, marketing etc.).

More than influence, the industry actually runs on trust. There is a very strong bond between the government and the agricultural community. The government manages to run the agricultural operations with the lowest wage rates (INR 200-300 per day) in the country.

With no tax revenue from agriculture, the government is unable to provide any meaningful budgetary allocation. The spending is too small for the gigantic needs of the industry. It is grossly inadequate to even recover and maintain the resources (soil, tree cover and infrastructure) that are lost or are deteriorated annually.

The Government spending on new agricultural infrastructure (irrigation, warehousing, transportation etc.) are minuscule. The national irrigation scheme has an annual outlay of INR

~10,000 crore. Given the typical cost of new construction irrigation projects (~$5000/ha), that amount will irrigate ~150,000 hectares, which is 0.1% of the agricultural land that needs to be irrigated. And that assumes that the entire amount is being spent in actually building the infrastructure for a specific land parcel.

Non infrastructure spending by the government is minuscule and only directional. It usually gets exhausted in marketing or lost in the several layers of intermediaries involved across the value chain. The government has no leverage to enforce adoption of best practices by the farmers. The farmers' community is hand to mouth and practices aimed at medium to long term improvements fall on deaf ears. The suggested economic gains of various best practices are usually hypothetical. Budget does not allow for funding the targeted improvements before the farmer starts achieving the benefits. Besides, there are no assurances or certainty of realizing benefits in the heavily fragmented, informal and unprofessional industry.

To improve soil fertility, the government has created a soil health card and has even issued around 10 crore cards so far. The cards carry crop wise recommendations of nutrients and fertilizers required for the farms. It is a well-intended and smart program that should ideally influence farming practices. But like most such programs, there is no linkage to provision of the required nutrients or any incentives.

In the turbo charged political atmosphere since independence, we have never had the time to take stock of the industry at a macro level. Governments in the past have just adopted a functional improvement approach and have stayed away from any radical structural changes. They have never really had the resources or the confidence to push through major reforms. Capital formation and resulting productivity gains have therefore been only incremental in nature. The over reliance on agriculture as means of creating self-sufficient livelihoods, has brought us to the brink of disaster.

If the current momentum continues, we are literally staring down the barrel of barren lands.

But the sacrifice of the motherland and of every farmer who has worked the fields has indeed served its purpose. We have built sufficient indigenous capabilities across all industries, over-delivered on the goal of food security and have fairly and squarely won the political battle across the country. We are well integrated in all global industries and have the required scale to have a seat at almost every table.

Before agriculture starts becoming an unmanageable drag, India needs to fundamentally reform the industry. The industry needs to significantly evolve to achieve a much higher standard of living for its people and of the quality of produce.

For a sustainable and healthy India, we need to - 1) limit the cultivated (excluding fruit and nuts) land area to 100 million hectares, 2) align production with a healthy vegetarian diet, 3) produce only desi and only in their specific natural habitat and 4) eliminate usage of groundwater.

Alignment with a healthy vegetarian diet would require production of ~150 million tonnes of cereals, 275 million tonnes of vegetables, 275 million tonnes of fruit, ~100 million tonnes of pulses, 275 million tonnes of milk, ~25 million tonnes of sugar, and ~25 million tonnes of oil.

The current production is cereals (320 MT), vegetables (185 MT), fruit (60 MT), pulses (25 MT), milk (190 MT), sugar (380 MT), and oil (60 MT). Oil is also used for other purposes.

Table 7.1 - Current agricultural output and requirement for healthy diet (Metric Tonnes)

	Current output (MT)	Output needed for healthy diet (MT)
Cereals	320	150
Vegetables	185	275
Fruit	60	275
Pulses	25	100
Milk	190	275
Sugar	380	25
Oil	60	25

The current area under cultivation for each category is cereals (100 Mha), vegetables (~12 Mha), fruits (~8 Mha), pulses (30 Mha), sugar (5 Mha), and oil (~40 Mha). Cotton and jute are cultivated on ~12 million hectares.

Based on the current productivity levels, the reduction of cereal production will result in a saving of ~53 Mha of cultivated land. And along with reduction in sugar production, we will save ~55 Mha of cultivated land. If we halve the oilseed production, we will save another 20 Mha, with total saving from the three categories being ~75 Mha. The total cultivated area for these three categories after savings would be ~70 Mha.

Increased vegetable production will need 18 Mha, taking the total cultivated land to 88 Mha. Adding the 12 Mha of cotton and jute makes it 100 Mha.

Pulses already use 30 Mha of land area[80], and quadrupling the production at current productivity levels would need a total of 120 Mha. The total land under cultivation would then be 220 Mha, excluding fruits. Therefore, achieving best in class productivity in pulses becomes the top most priority for agriculture.

India's pulses productivity is in the range of 700-800 kg per hectare. Yield levels for the most productive nations are UK (3700 kg per ha), France (3650 kg per ha), Germany (3340 kg per ha), Egypt (3300 kg per ha), and USA (2000 kg per ha). India has the best possible natural habitats available for production of various pulses. By achieving the productivity of Western Europe, India can meet the production requirement of pulses without using more land area.

After pulses, increasing productivity in rice can save a significant land area. Rice production currently covers ~45 Mha and after aligning with health considerations, the area required would be 21 Mha. The productivity in rice is a little less than 3000 kg per Ha[81]. Countries with the highest rice yields are Australia (10300 kg per Ha), Egypt (9350 kg per Ha), Turkey (7900 kg per Ha), Spain (7800 kg per Ha), Greece (7700 kg per Ha), Morocco (7100 kg per Ha), Tajikistan (7000 kg per Ha), El Salvador (6900 kg per Ha), and Chile (6500 kg per Ha). The United Kingdom, Germany and France have almost zero rice production. Given its multiple river basins with high rainfall that are ideal for growing rice, India should at least double its productivity. That would save more than 10 Mha of cultivated land.

---

[80] Indian Institute of Pulses Research

[81] "A status note on Rice in India", Agriculture statistics at a glance 2015, Ministry of Agriculture and Farmers Welfare, Government of India, 2016

Wheat and other nutri cereals are currently cultivated on ~55 Mha and would need ~26 Mha after health driven reduction. Our productivity is ~3200 kg per Ha. Countries with highest wheat yield are Ireland (9500 kg per Ha), New Zealand (9200 kg per Ha), Mali (8900 kg per Ha), The Netherlands (8000 kg per Ha), UK (7900 kg per Ha), Denmark (7200 kg per Ha), Belgium (6800 kg per Ha), Egypt (6600 kg per Ha), Zambia (6600 kg per Ha), Czech Republic (6500 kg per Ha), Namibia (6300 kg per Ha), Sweden (6300 kg per Ha), Saudi Arabia (6300 kg per Ha), and Austria (6200 kg per Ha). Again, India is naturally endowed with the best habitats for the production of wheat, maize and all nutri cereals, and can at least double its productivity for these food grains. That would help save another ~13 Mha of cultivated land.

So, achieving best in class productivity in pulses and cereals will bring down the cultivated land area to 107 Mha (excluding fruits and nuts).

Increased productivity in oilseeds should be used to reduce imports (~15 MT).

Productivity enhancement in cotton production will be needed to meet the increasing demands as we transform into a developed society. We should therefore not budget for any land savings. The highest yields globally are around 1900 kg per hectare as against India's yield of ~550 kg per hectare.

Doubling the productivity in vegetables will bring down the total cultivated land area to ~100 Mha (excluding fruits, nuts and spices).

The required productivity enhancements are huge and need a fundamental change in the way we are doing agriculture.

To achieve best in class productivity levels, India needs to fully adopt modern agricultural practices. We need to optimize labor-intensive farming methods and build large scale agricultural operations.

At a very fundamental level, to achieve top tier productivity, agriculture needs large scale operations, robust infrastructure, modern equipment, cutting edge farming practices, and advanced organizational systems & processes. A very strong regulatory regime is also needed to enforce leading standards of sustainable and healthy production.

The government needs to bring about major structural reforms to enable the transformation.

First, the government needs to enable the takeover of the entire agricultural industry by large public and PPP entities.

Second, the government needs to introduce a well-crafted taxation system to build the required infrastructure, and drive productivity, sustainability and health in the industry.

To enable the takeover by large public institutions, the biggest task is to buy back the land from farmers. The acquisition needs to be a well-managed process wherein the families are well compensated and properly employed. The compensation should cover the cost of buying an apartment (at least the down payment), and relocation costs. The government should also help the farmers secure employment in one of the cities of their choice. They could be employed by companies involved in agriculture, infrastructure, manufacturing, and professional services.

There are nearly 14 crore agricultural land holders in the country. Around 10 crore have an average holding of 0.4 hectare. The minimum compensation should be sufficient even for a land holder of 0.25 hectares.

The cost of an apartment varies significantly across Indian cities but if we assume INR 20 lac as the average cost of a 2-3 BHK apartment in a high-rise, the down payment required would be INR 4 lac. So, a compensation of INR 25 lac is more than sufficient for a very small farmer to relocate his / her family to the city, and still have a fair amount of savings in the bank account.

That compensation translates to INR 1 crore per hectare in compensation cost. The land acquisition cost of NHAI was around INR 1 crore per hectare till a few years back. The land secured for national highways is usually prime land and therefore commands a premium. In case of agricultural land buy-back, the government should actually cap the compensation per hectare at 1 crore. The average compensation would then amount to around INR 0.75 crore per hectare.

The total compensation bill for buying back 150 million hectares would be $15 trillion. The Government can collect a lease rental from the public companies who farm the land. The government will need to manage the resulting inflation through appropriately structuring capital gains, incentivizing bank deposits, and price controls across some key spend categories.

On average, we would be moving 30 lac families every year to the urban centers. Over 50 years, we would have moved 15 crore families and more than 60 crore people to the cities. In the process, not only would we have modernized agriculture, but would have also fully urbanized India. By the time everyone moves to the cities, motherland would have healed considerably, and the Indian countryside would have started to show off.

The buy-back should start with the largest farms. They are better managed than the smaller farms and will help the new entities to scale up quickly. The owners of larger farms currently control the local rural / small town economies. Once onboard, they can drive the acquisition of the smaller land holdings in an efficient manner. 'Larger first' will also mitigate the risk of increasing land prices. Optimization of their operations by the new modern agriculture-oriented entities will also release farm labor (without land holding) that can be deployed in urban construction. These landless laborers will help India reach the desired level of high-rise and other urban development activity needed to settle the 30 lac or so families every year.

The modern agricultural industry will need large companies for farming, agricultural equipment, fertilizers & chemicals, storage & distribution, and food processing.

Except for farming, there are existing players for other areas that can be scaled up. The key decision is around the formation of the farming companies. Transforming the production of pulses, rice and other cereals is most critical for achieving the national objectives from agriculture. We should therefore figure out the right structure for managing the production of these three crop categories. The structure and principles that emerge can be leveraged for other crop areas as well.

To achieve the four-fold productivity enhancement, pulses need to be given the best available natural habitats. India should let 4-5 companies take over the entire production of pulses. The relevant government research and administrative bodies including The Directorate of Pulses, Indian Institute of Pulses Research, and All India Soil and Land Use Survey, need to identify the best land parcels across the country for the production of different pulses. Loamy soils in cool weather areas with low rainfall are best suited for the growth of pulses. Winter season in the alluvial belt of India is therefore ideal. The government should therefore select 30 Mha of best suited land tracts in the already irrigated areas of Punjab, Haryana, UP and Bihar. Lands being used for excess production of rice and wheat should be diverted for pulses. Currently pulses are grown in several cropping patterns mainly along with rice and wheat, and also with other cereals, oilseeds, jute, cotton, potato and tobacco. They are usually cultivated on marginal lands given the higher price assurance for major cereals. Large companies need to be regulated to prioritize the production of pulses on their farmlands and deliver increasing levels of productivity. Regulation should prevent any compromise on yield of pulses while ensuring sustainable farming. The production of other crops on these farmlands should only be done in a complimentary manner without affecting the production of pulses in any manner.

Similarly for rice, 4-5 companies should be given the mandate. In the case of rice, besides reducing production, we also need to shift towards cultivating more healthy varieties. Given that we are looking to achieve the production target from only ~20 Mha, we should restrict cultivation to areas that are naturally best suited.

Rice is a tropical plant and requires high heat and high humidity for its successful growth. The temperature should be fairly high at a mean monthly of 24°C. It should be 20°-22°C at the time of sowing, 23°-25°C during growth and 25°-30°C at the harvesting time. The average annual rainfall required by rice is 150 cm.

However, it is the temporal distribution of rainfall, rather than the total amount of annual rainfall which is more decisive. The rainfall should be fairly distributed throughout the year and no month should have less than 12 cm of rainfall. Lesser amounts of rainfall is required as the harvesting time approaches. The fields must be flooded under 10-12 cm deep water at the time of sowing and during early stages of growth. Therefore, the fields must be level and have low mud walls to retain water. This peculiar requirement of rice makes it primarily a crop of plain areas. Rice grown in well-watered lowland plain areas is called wet or lowland rice.

Rice can be grown on a variety of soils including silts, loams and gravels and can tolerate acidic as well as alkaline soils. However, deep fertile clayey or loamy soils which can be easily puddled into mud and develop cracks on drying are considered ideal for raising this crop. Such soil requirements make it an ideal crop in river valleys, flood plains, deltas and coastal plains and a dominant crop there. High-level loams and lighter soils can be used for quick maturing varieties of rice. Black lava soil is also useful for rice cultivation.

Rice is grown almost throughout the year in hot and humid regions of eastern and southern parts of India where two to three crops in a year are not uncommon.

India should find land parcels for rice in the states of West Bengal, Orissa, Andhra Pradesh, Assam, Bihar, Konkan, Goa, coastal Karnataka, Kerala and maybe some high rainfall areas in Maharashtra and Tamil Nadu.

These states also naturally produce healthier varieties of rice. The indigenous crops of India that evolved in these states include several varieties of rice such as colored rice (red rice, brown rice, black rice etc.), aromatic rice, and medicinal rice varieties. The traditional rice cultivars have higher nutrition than hybrid rice varieties. They are a good source of minerals and vitamins such as niacin, thiamine, iron, riboflavin, vitamin D, calcium, and possess higher fiber. Furthermore, these cultivars possess several health benefits such as reducing the risk of developing type II diabetes, obesity, and cardiovascular diseases by lowering the glycemic and insulin responses.

The regulatory environment in the rice industry should develop to eventually phase out all hybrid varieties. Hybrids are highly responsive to fertilizers and actually are dependent on them to deliver higher yields. They have a narrow genetic base and are therefore more vulnerable to pesticides. Hence, their growth also needs much higher amounts of pesticides. Heavy use of groundwater is needed to irrigate the hybrid varieties. Over time, the production of hybrids damages the soil, air, groundwater, the local flora and fauna, biodiversity and the health of people.

The next important crop cluster is wheat and other nutri cereals (sorghum, pearl millet, finger millet, maize and small millets viz. barnyard millet, proso millet, kodo millet and foxtail millet). Wheat is cultivated on 31 Mha and nutri cereals on 25 Mha. Out of the nutri cereals, maize is cultivated on ~10 Mha. The yield of wheat (3200 kg per Ha) and maize (2700 kg per Ha) is much higher than other nutri cereals, sorghum (900 kg per Ha), and Pearl millet (1300 kg per Ha). Wheat is cultivated on almost fully irrigated lands. The percentages of irrigated areas are wheat (94.2%), maize (27%), sorghum (10%) and Pearl millet (10%).

After health driven reduction and factoring in double productivity, we have ascertained that this cluster should be cultivated on a total area of 13-14 Mha. Based on the current split of production, wheat should be cultivated on 8 Mha, maize on 2.5 Mha, and other nutri cereals on 3.5 Mha.

Just like rice, wheat production in India is wrought with several challenges and needs to be heavily regulated and controlled. The high yielding varieties being produced have several damaging aspects for the environment. Wheat is inferior to other coarse cereals in terms of nutrition. Due to its smooth texture, one ends up eating more of it to achieve fulfillment. India does have indigenous varieties of wheat, and over time, needs to phase out all hybrid varieties. Wheat cultivation has also cannibalized the production of millets that are native to the Indian subcontinent.

Wheat has also become a staple Indian food in many forms, and it will take time for India to reduce its consumption.

India needs to limit the influence of wheat on other cereals and should therefore keep it as a separate industry. 4-5 private players can be given the 8Mha to achieve the current levels of production. The global wheat industry is extremely evolved, and these players will largely need to just adopt the best practices being followed already.

The relevant government bodies should identify the best suited lands for wheat cultivation. The temperature required for wheat during the growing season is around 15.5°C. The weather should be warm and moist during the early stage of growth and sunny and dry in the later stages. The temperature should not exceed 20°C in the growing period. A frost-free period of 100 days is usually required. The amount of rainfall required for wheat cultivation varies between 30 cm and 100 cm. The soil suitable for wheat is either light clay or heavy loam[82]. 8 Mha of ideally suited lands can most likely be found within UP, Haryana and Punjab.

Maize or corn should also be kept as an independent industry. While varieties of rice and wheat are native to the Indian subcontinent, maize is completely imported. First introduced in the middle of the 19th century, several hybrid varieties have been circulated in India to enable development in different agro climatic regimes.

It is similar to wheat in nutritional value but is very different in terms of its end uses. It has similar amounts of energy, protein and fiber, and also contains several minerals and vitamins. It is starchy food with high amounts of complex carbohydrates that are difficult to digest and provide energy for long periods. Globally as well as in India, it is mainly used as animal food. In India, ~50% is used for poultry and globally, over 60% is used as animal feed. Globally, around 20% is used for industrial purposes. Direct consumption only uses 20% of the production in India. Unlike wheat, it does not really act as a substitute for other cereals.

The low maize productivity in India is mainly because the cultivation is scattered across unfavorable agro climatic regions, is fragmented due to the nature of the industry and has increasingly been done on lands degraded by excessive rice cultivation. Consolidation and focus is critical to achieve the highest levels of productivity observed globally.

Again, 4-5 companies should be allocated the required 2.5 Mha and tasked with delivering gold standard yields by adopting global best practices. Providing the most suitable lands will bring down the use of fertilizers and pesticides.

Maize is grown in temperatures between 18°C and 27°C during the day and around 14°C during the night. But the most important factor is the 140 frost-free days. Maize is

---

[82] "Suitable Conditions Required for Wheat Cultivation (5 Conditions)", Smriti Chand

grown mostly in regions having annual rainfall between 60 cm to 110 cm. The best suitable soil for maize is deep, rich soils of the sub-tropics, where there is abundant nitrogen[83].

85% of maize cultivation in India is in the Kharif season. Rabi maize has a higher yield at 4 MT/hectare as against 2.5 MT/hectare for Kharif maize. Andhra Pradesh has achieved very high levels of productivity (~6000 kg per Ha) in maize cultivation. The highest yield in the world is 11,000 kg per Ha achieved by Chile, New Zealand, Turkey and USA.

For millets or nutri cereals, we have so far calculated a required area of 3.5 Mha. The actual area for nutri cereals needs to be significantly more. They are healthier for both the human body and the environment. Their current productivity levels are much lower than wheat and maize. They are the native crops of the Indian and African continents, and so India needs to set the yield benchmarks for the category.

Post-Green Revolution, the area under cultivation of coarse cereals decreased drastically from 37.67 million hectares in the 1950s to 25.67 million hectares[84]. Likewise, the area under cultivation of sorghum decreased from 15.57 million hectares to 5.82 million hectares and that of pearl millet decreased from 9.02 million hectares to 7.89 million hectares.

Currently, the area under different nutri cereals is Pearl millet (7.5 Mha), Sorghum (5 Mha), Finger millet (2.5 Mha), Minor millets (1.2 Mha), and Barley (0.7 Mha). The total area is ~17 Mha[85].

The productivity for millets is much lower as they are being largely cultivated on unirrigated lands. Only around 10% of

---

[83] "Maize Cultivation: Suitable Geographical Conditions Required for Maize Cultivation", Smriti Chand

[84] "The impact of the Green Revolution on indigenous crops of India", Ann Raeboline Lincy Eliazer Nelson, Kavitha Ravichandran & Usha Antony, Journal of Ethnic Foods, 2019

[85] "Production and consumption of minor millets in India - A structural break analysis", Anbukkani Perumal, Indian Agricultural Research Institute, September 13, 2018

the lands being used are irrigated. The Green revolution also pushed their cultivation to marginal lands.

India should aim to double the production of nutri cereals in the medium term. The production is beneficial both from a health and sustainability standpoint. In the increasingly urban and well-connected world, people will increasingly make smarter choices and change their cereal consumption. India should therefore maintain around 15 Mha under the cultivation of various nutri cereals. That would take the total cultivated land area to ~110 Mha.

To maximize productivity, India should find the best suited lands for each nutri cereal.

Pearl millet (Bajra) - Bajra grows well in dry and warm climatic conditions, and it is a drought tolerant crop which requires low annual rainfall ranging between 40 cm to 60 cm. The ideal temperature for Bajra cultivation is between 20 to 30 degrees. Moist weather is advantageous during its vegetative growth. Bajra thrives best in black cotton soils and sandy loam soils having good drainage. It does not prefer acidic and water logging soils. It grows successfully in soils with low pH or high salinity. Bajra can be easily grown in regions where other cereal crops like wheat or maize would not survive.

Sorghum (Jowar) - It is a tropical crop that thrives between 25 to 32 degrees. It only requires 40 cm of annual rainfall. It is an extreme drought tolerant crop, but prolonged moist or dry conditions are not ideal. It grows well in sandy loam soils having good drainage. Soil pH range of 6 to 7.5 is ideal for its cultivation and better growth[86].

Barley (Jau) - Barley requires around 12-15 degrees during growing period and around 30 degrees at maturity. The crop possesses a very high degree of tolerance to drought and sodic conditions. Sandy to moderately heavy loam soils of Indo-

---

[86] "Jowar farming information guide", Jagdish Reddy, Agri Farming

Gangetic plains having neutral to saline reaction and medium fertility are the most suitable type for barley cultivation. Acidic soils are not fit for barley cultivation, as such.

Nutri cereals should be an independent industry, again with 4-5 public / PPP players. With the size of land allocation and favorable regulation, they should be able to effectively compete with companies involved in the production of other cereals.

Oilseeds, cotton & jute, and tea & coffee should also form independent industries, each with 4-5 public / PPP companies doing the production. They have specific agro climatic requirements. They are also nonperishable so consolidation and focused production in the highest yielding regions will not pose storage and distribution challenges. Again, allocating the best suited lands for the production of each crop in these categories would significantly enhance productivity and minimize land use.

Horticulture (excluding nuts and spices) poses the perishability challenge and presents the case for a more distributed production network.

Horticulture includes vegetables, fruits (incl. plantation crops), nuts, spices, flowers, aromatic and medicinal plants. Vegetables and fruits account for over 90% of the value added by horticulture.

Vegetables are cultivated on around 12 Mha of agricultural land currently. Potatoes, onions, tomatoes, brinjal, peas, and okra, are the only vegetables that are cultivated on more than 0.5 Mha.

There is a wide variation in the yield of every vegetable measured across different states. The range of yield (measured in MT per Hectare) for different vegetables across non hilly states with a sizeable contribution is - brinjal [Jharkhand(3.2) - UP(34.4)], cabbage [Haryana(16.0) - Tamil Nadu(66.0)], cauliflower [Odisha(15.0) - J&K(31.0)], tomato [Chattisgarh(17.0) - Andhra Pradesh(44.5)], okra

[Odisha(8.9) - Andhra Pradesh(15.1)], onion [Tamil Nadu(10.6) - Madhya Pradesh(24.5)], potato [Assam(7.0) - West Bengal(29.9)], and peas [Haryana(8.7) - Jharkhand(22.1)][87].

This wide variation in yield is a reality not just for every vegetable, but for every fruit, every food grain and literally everything that is grown in India. Therefore, by limiting the production to the highest yielding regions, India can more than double the productivity. The additional efficiencies from (technology, process and infrastructure) will further increase productivity by more than 100%. The highest yielding regions usually also produce the best quality produce.

Concentrated production will result in scale efficiencies in storage and distribution. Building larger storage facilities equipped with the latest technologies would become viable. Transportation could also then be tailored to achieve the highest levels of efficiency. Bulk transportation will result in the lowest possible movement costs. Most energy efficient transportation alternatives could also be developed given the scale and certainty of operations.

So even in the case of vegetables, India needs to identify the best suited regions for each vegetable. A total of 10 Mha needs to be allocated to 4-5 large organizations to produce the required quantities of best quality vegetables. Even though vegetables are shorter duration crops and present the opportunity for 2-3 harvests every year, strong regulation is necessary to prevent over exploitation. Companies should be regulated to follow farming practices that maintain soil fertility at the highest possible levels.

Fruit trees are usually perennials and orchards act like forests. So doubling down on fruits is good for both health and environment.

---

[87] "Jowar farming information guide", Jagdish Reddy, Agri Farming

The perishability challenge is bigger for fruits as compared to vegetables. But globally, supply chains have evolved to enable seamless movement of fruits across the globe. Consumers in the developed world today have access to the best fruits grown across the world. The key enabler is the efficiency and quality of orchards that are producing the fruits.

Quality is a much bigger factor in purchase decisions for fruits as compared to vegetables. External aspects (presentation, appearance, uniformity, ripeness, and freshness) are the main components in the decision to purchase, which is usually taken when the consumer sees the product exhibited at the sales point. Internal quality (flavor, aroma, texture, nutritional value and absence of biotic and non-biotic contaminants) is linked to aspects that are not generally perceived externally but are equally important to many consumers. Appearance, taste / flavor and freshness are the most important factors in purchase decisions.

There is a marked difference between indigenous varieties of fruits grown in natural habitats and those produced in other environments with genetically modified seeds[88]. A GMO variety of strawberry grown in Haryana will never come even close to the quality of a Mahabaleshwar strawberry. Similarly, you just cannot replicate the Nagpur orange or the Kinnaur apple anywhere else. India's rich biodiversity has naturally produced or created the conditions for cultivating the best quality of almost all fruits in the world. We just have to make sure we produce them at scale only in those specific locations.

To achieve the five-fold increase in fruit production, India should allocate 25 Mha, which is around three times the current area. Nuts and plantation crops should also be a part of the fruit industry.

Aromatic and medicinal plants could be a separate industry.

---

[88] "Genetic Vulnerability of Modern Crop Cultivars: Causes, Mechanism and Remedies", Holetta Agricultural Research Center, Department of Biology, Addis Ababa University, International Center for Agricultural Research in the Dry Areas (ICARDA), 2012

Milk and egg production should have city level enterprises, maybe 2-3 players in each city. These could also eventually roll up into a few national level enterprises.

The fishing and seafood industry should also be organized with exclusive rights given to 4-5 players.

An additional consideration with the fruits & nuts and fishing industries is the sensitivity of the regions. High levels of scrutiny need to be ensured for entities operating along the border regions.

While the large public / PPP companies will get everything done that is needed, the central government will always have a very important role.

For the large players to achieve high levels of efficiency, the government needs to ensure 100% irrigation of the chosen lands, prevent floods, provide uninterrupted power supply, and build robust transportation infrastructure.

Simultaneously, the government needs to effectively and appropriately regulate each sector of agriculture. The relevant government bodies need to closely work with the large players to constantly improve the performance of the industry in terms of efficiency, quality, health and sustainability.

Through regulation, the government needs to incentivize the large enterprises to ensure food security, achieve highest levels of productivity and quality, high wage rates, benefits and good working conditions, build six sigma organizational workflows, follow sustainable farming practices, invest in using best equipment, prevent land degradation, minimize use of GMO varieties, fertilizers and pesticides, and preserve and enhance natural resources.

Government also needs regulation to control prices and manage inflation. Clear regulations would be needed around profit making, shareholding, and investor returns. Strong oversight would be needed to build healthy competitive dynamics in the industry and prevent collusion. Government needs to ensure strong operational surveillance and prevent any wrongdoings. Most of these would be multi-billion dollar organizations and would most likely get listed on Indian stock exchanges.

A well-crafted taxation system is most essential for the government to effectively support and control the industry.

The entire agricultural output needs to be taxed based on the specific infrastructure requirements. Taxation should be able to generate sufficient revenue for the government to amortize the required capital investments and operational expenditures. Tax revenues should also cover the expenses of the government organizations involved in research and administration. Tax concessions should be designed to nudge the large organizations to continuously improve their operations towards higher efficiency, quality, compensation, health and sustainability.

Concessions should encourage all capital investments that meet the key objectives. The organizations should be incentivized to use clean forms of energy at farms, facilities, offices and transportation. There should be severe penalties for any forms of pollution (soil, air or water). There should be damaging consequences for extracting natural resources viz. groundwater or minerals.

Strong control and reporting mechanisms would also be needed to prevent bureaucracy, corruption and wrongdoings at all levels of these organizations.

India has well evolved regulation and taxation for several industries that can be leveraged for agriculture. India will have the option to use the latest thinking, expertise and technology to design and enforce a highly mature system.

The practice of various forms of multiple cropping needs to be carefully addressed. We have so far estimated a total cropped area of around 110 Mha (excluding fruits and nuts) and a total of ~135 Mha. We expect this area to amply cover the volume and nutrition requirements. Fruits and nuts are usually perennials and do not involve intensive cropping. But with the rest of the production, there is always the risk of excessive multiple cropping. Currently, we have nearly 60 Mha of land that is cropped more than once.

The goal of multiple cropping should not be productivity enhancement. We will achieve productivity through focused cultivation of each crop in their natural habitats. With total cropped area at ~110 Mha, there is no dire need to reduce the cultivated land area. It would be good though if we brought the net sown area under 100 Mha or even lower. For that we will need to have ~10 Mha of land that is cropped more than once.

The goal of multiple cropping should be to improve the soil fertility for the primary crop. The research bodies need to identify the cover crops or the complementary crops that would best prepare the land for the next sowing of the primary crops. Vegetables (10 Mha)are ideally suited for multiple cropping[89]. Regulation and taxation need to drive enforcement of the recommended practices.

---

[89] "Multiple cropping systems of the world and the potential for increasing cropping intensity", August 29, 2020; 'Multi-cropping', Intercropping and Adaptation to Variable Environments in Indus South Asia - C. A. Petrie, J. Bates, Division of Archaeology and McDonald Institute for Archaeological Research, University of Cambridge, May 9, 2017; "Full length review paper on cropping systems for sustainable vegetable production", G. Rishita, K. Usha Kumari and A. Reshma, College of Horticulture, Dr. Y.S.R. Horticultural University, August 3, 2017

Table 7.2 - Total cropped and net sown area (Current and Sustainable India) in million hectares (Mha) and associated productivity enhancement

	Current (Mha)	For healthy diet output[1]	Productivity increase	Sustainable India[2] (Mha)
Rice	45	21	2x	11
Wheat	31	15	2x	8
Maize	10	5	2x	2.5
Nutri cereals[3]	15	30	2x	15
Vegetables	12	18	2x	10
Fruits	8	36	1.4	25
Pulses	30	120	4x	30
Sugar	5	3	1x	3
Oil[4]	40	20	1.6x	20
Cotton & jute[5]	12	12	2x	12
Total cropped	207	300	-	136.5
Total cropped (excl fruits)	199	264	-	111.5
Area sown more than once	~60	-	-	~11.5
Net sown (excl fruits)	~140	-	-	~100

1. To produce the output needed for a healthy diet, 2. After alignment with healthy diet requirements and productivity enhancements, 3. Output of nutri cereals estimated to double for health alignment, 4. Productivity gains used to eliminate imports (15 MT), 5. Output estimated to double with greater use as replacement for unsustainable materials / products

Large scale natural agriculture will set global standards of efficiency and quality. The model will visibly impact the environment, people's health, and living standards. The agricultural transformation would be the key enabler for India to become an advanced sustainable society. It will be the world's biggest and the most important transformation of the 21st century.

8. Sustainable consumption
Products, services and supply chains

In 1994 the Oslo symposium defined sustainable consumption as the consumption of goods and services that enhance quality of life while limiting the use of natural resources and noxious materials.

Sustainable consumption is the use of material products, energy and immaterial services to meet the present human needs as well as the needs of the future generations. Consumption refers not only to individuals and households, but also to governments, business, and other institutions. Sustainable consumption is closely related to sustainable production and sustainable lifestyles. A sustainable lifestyle minimizes ecological impacts while enabling a flourishing life for individuals, households, communities, and beyond. It is the product of individual and collective decisions about aspirations and about satisfying needs and adopting practices, which are in turn conditioned, facilitated, and constrained by societal norms, political institutions, public policies, infrastructures, markets, and culture.

People consume to satisfy their needs. In the past, early humans adapted themselves to their natural surroundings. They led a simple life and fulfilled their requirements from nature around them. With the passage of time, their needs grew. Humans settled in the fertile plains of river valleys to cultivate land. The invention of the wheel, surplus production and exchange of surplus goods or the barter system helped them to progress. The Industrial Revolution led to large scale production of goods. Means of transport and communication developed. With the passage of time and technological development, human needs underwent many changes.

The wide and enormous availability of goods has influenced human behaviors to want more and more. And once needs go beyond the point of rationality, the level of needs keeps going up. Irrational minds need new things every now and then just for mental satisfaction.

People's health is the primary driver of the needs of individuals and groups. An unhealthy person or group of people will have excessive needs. They have a weak mindset and are unable to firmly establish whether they actually want something or not. Their needs arise from the negative energy of an unstable mind and the lack of harmony they experience with the environment.

Industrial revolution in the developed world resulted in excessive production of goods.[90] Companies developed products for convenience and pleasure, and gradually people started considering those products as essential. Excessive consumption has resulted in unsustainable usage of raw materials and energy. "Modern society will find no solution to the ecological problem unless it takes a serious look at its lifestyle." - Pope John Paul II.

Irrational materialism is driving merciless exploitation of natural resources across the world. While the Middle East is hell bent on burning all the oil in the earth's crust, China is mercilessly exploiting natural resources to propel its manufacturing industry. One can argue that they are being forced to do it.

But now there is an emerging class of healthy urbanites that is adopting minimalism and sustainable consumption. This is an evolved class that is extremely careful in determining what they actually need and are smart and environmentally conscious in fulfilling the need. Urbanization coupled with the rapid evolution of science and technology, has created the

---

[90] "Industrial Revolutions and Consumption: A Common Model to the Various Periods of Industrialization", David Flacher, 2005

possibility for the world's population to still find a way of sustainable living.

High-rise urban infrastructure, consumer technology, and health consciousness are moving in tandem towards the optima of sustainable and high-quality living.

The consumption of physical products by this new evolved class is minimal and natural and is being increasingly rationalized by their use of technology. The dense urban settlement has also created the possibility of natural supply chains with no packaging.

Air

For healthy people living in a well-developed urban environment with sufficient blue and green, especially in India's subtropical climate regime, there is no need for air conditioners, heating systems or air purifiers. There is a sizable population in India that still does not use these products. Usage of such products by the entire population of India will in any case have disastrous consequences. India never invented such products and would be best served by completely avoiding this path of self-destruction. To start with, India should ban air conditioners, heating systems and air purifiers, and should stop their domestic production. The move will also encourage society to make genuine efforts towards cooling and cleaning the Indian air, as well as towards health & fitness.

Water and beverages

Water is the next most essential human need after air. Packaged drinking water and beverages (alcoholic and non-alcoholic) were invented in the First Industrial revolution and achieved global commercial dominance after the 1970s. Soda drinks gained commercial viability in the early 20th century. Before 1950, water and beverages were mainly sold in glass bottles, but once plastic bottles were invented, all hell broke loose. In 2016, more than 480 billion plastic bottles were sold.

Only 7% of these were recycled, and the rest ended up in landfills or in the ocean.

Bottled water and beverages have gained prominence in India only because we have not developed water bodies and water systems that ensure abundant supply. Soft drinks and alcoholic beverages are only the needs of unhealthy minds. Adverse health impacts of carbonated drinks and alcohol are well researched and established. Conversion of fruits into juices is known to reduce the nutritional value of fruits. Bottled juices also contain various harmful additives.

India needs to build robust water systems in its cities and bank on its wealth of natural beverages. We need to conserve our abundant sources of fresh water and build huge reservoirs for each city. That would enable assured supply in households, commercial establishments, in public places and literally everywhere we go. Bottled beverages, including juices, need to be completely phased out. Instead, we should consume the wide array of healthy sharbats and teas that are produced naturally in India. Shikanji, coconut water, aam panna, khus, brahmi, bel, nannari, kokum, buransh, chandan, and malta, are some healthy and refreshing indigenous options.

Healthy people do not need the kick of a bottled beverage. They derive more satisfaction by slowly sipping on a glass of water and other natural drinks. India should stay away from investing in the bottling industry and focus its energies on enabling fluid consumption without any packaging. Plastic bottles should be banned for all forms of beverages. The ban can be immediate given the number of bottles in circulation today. Mixes for various natural drinks should be sold in durable bottles with RFID tags to track their return and reuse. Safety mechanisms need to be built at all water release points for public consumption.

Dairy

The milk and dairy (butter, ghee, curd, shrikhand, lassi, buttermilk, flavored milk, cream and cheese) supply chain in India is split between organized players and unorganized dairy farms and households with cattle stock. With very few dairy farms within cities, the majority of the city consumption is through packaged products, which creates huge amounts of waste every day. Packaging and addition of preservatives has helped companies increase shelf life of the products, which is relevant for scattered settlements with uncertain consumption patterns. As India migrates towards urban living, the compact settlements will result in daily volume certainty. The urban environment will make it viable for companies to build a fresh, sustainable and safe supply chain for milk and dairy products. Every Indian city should have a network of large dairy farms spread across the city to minimize delivery footprint. The farms should be regulated and monitored to ensure animal friendly practices, hygienic environment and product purity. The milk and dairy products should be carried and stored in steel, aluminum, brass, earthen, ceramic or glass, across the supply chain, including at home. Milk and all the dairy products should be delivered to nearby retail (having similar containers) or directly to apartments. Niche and new innovative dairy products that have multiple variants viz. infused yogurts, flavored milk etc. will need to focus their operations on clusters of high consumption.

Given that we will take time to build our cities and the city dairy farms, India should start by completely phasing out the packaged milk and dairy products. Large companies currently engaged in the processing and packaging business should be given time to transform into a natural processing and distribution business. For the unorganized dairy vendors delivering direct to home, the Government should also implement a review system at the consumer end to prevent any malpractices. All small milk vendors (unorganized, unregistered etc.) should be mandated to be on the review platform, operated by the Government.

Food

The next essential and one of the largest consumption categories is food. Health consciousness is driving people towards fresh fruits and vegetables, natural / minimally processed staple items (food grains, legumes / lentils, and sugar) and cooking ingredients (spices, flavors etc.), foods processed minimally with healthy ingredients (sauces, pickles, dressings, bakery, confectionery, snacks, ready to eat, breakfast cereal etc.), and oils with minimal trans / saturated fat content. Processing is done to increase shelf life as well as to improve various attributes (taste, texture, appearance etc.) that attract consumers.

Food grains, legumes and spices, naturally have a long shelf life, and can easily be shifted back to a natural supply chain that does not involve any packaging. Before the packaging industry took over, they were stocked by retailers (local kiranas and wholesalers) in large containers or sacks.

Food processing in a developed economy results in around 40% of food being lost, along with generating massive amounts of packaging waste. Food is lost in processing facilities, transportation & distribution, at retail stores, and in households & restaurants. The losses stem from overproduction, excess stocking at retail outlets, and unnecessary purchases by end consumers.

Processing and packaging have dramatically reduced people's sensitivity towards fresh and high quality ingredients. The convenience of getting a standardized product has made people trade off freshness and purity.

The basic ingredients of all vegetarian processed foods are food grains, legumes, spices, vegetables, fruits, and other plants. The majority of processed foods don't spoil for long periods when stored in proper containers e.g. oil, pickles, snacks, breakfast cereal, candies etc. A compact urban set up makes it viable to shift these to natural processing and supply chain.

And given that milk and dairy have been proven to work well through a natural supply chain, there is no reason why other perishable food items can't be managed the same way. There is already an emerging retail trend wherein perishable foods are processed within the stores in front of consumers. Scale efficiencies for these products should be achieved without unnecessary processing and packaging. Every city should be able to process all food items needed for local consumption.

Cooking

Indian cooking has evolved over several centuries and produces some of the most mouth watering food in the world. Having been an agricultural society, our cooking methods include extensive use of locally available natural resources. But we have progressed rapidly in the last few decades and a significant percentage now uses gas, which is much better than burning oil or wood. But even gas is not sustainable. Most of the developed world has now installed induction cooktops in their kitchens that run on electricity. They are more efficient in their use of energy and also allow for cleaner forms of energy to power the cooking. These cooktops are now readily available in India. The Government needs to incentivize manufacturers to scale up their production, and developers and households to install them.

The other serious challenge with Indian cooking is the amount of smoke produced. The ventilator fans and chimneys do clean out smoke from the kitchen but release it into the public environment. People living in apartments are exposed to the exhaust of lower apartments for significant periods during the day.

Ductless chimneys are now in the market that clean the air using filters and releases clean air back into the kitchen. The Indian Government needs to encourage development of this technology and provide incentives for driving adoption.

High-rise urban settlement also makes it viable to operate large community kitchens where home-like food can be prepared. The large-scale preparation would be much more efficient and save energy. Households can closely monitor the kitchen and ensure the preparation of high quality, nutritious food in a clean and hygienic set up. The proximity of the community kitchens will make it easy for people to bring home the food in their own tiffins and containers.

Utensils

Another environmental nightmare linked to food and beverages, is the use of plastic and paper utensils. Paper plate was the first single use food service item, invented in 1904. Over the next century, disposable cups, utensils and plates were developed in increasingly durable—and environmentally unfriendly—materials. According to Time magazine, Americans throw away an estimated trillion disposable plates and utensils per year. Interestingly, India supplies leaves to companies in developed countries to produce paper utensils. The rapid growth of food delivery services has further accelerated the use of plastic and paper utensils and packaging boxes.

The entire culture stems from lack of self-control, and the need for instant gratification of a rushed consumer, and an irresponsible and 'do what it takes' attitude of restaurants and delivery companies. Cleaning utensils and containers takes time, effort, water and detergents. Without factoring in the environmental and health consequences, paper and plastic products appear more economical and efficient.

A healthy and conscious society treats washing dishes like any other essential work. Human hands are the most advanced and efficient machine for a variety of tasks including cleaning utensils. Cleaning utensils needs to be treated as an important task that promotes both sustainability and health. Formal employment guidelines should apply to people engaged in the profession. The durable containers, tiffins and utensils last several years, and in some cases a lifetime and even generations. The increased water use will also create viability for building large water bodies. The world has already invented safe and non-toxic detergents.

The Government simply needs to ban the use of paper and plastic utensils and packaging for delivery. The restaurants and all types of food and beverage outlets, and the delivery companies will automatically shift to the use of 'built to last' products and figure out the new normal.

Clothing

Clothing is the next most essential human need, and the clothing industry is the second largest polluter in the world after oil. The use of polyester, nylon and other synthetic materials is the main cause of pollution. Various petrochemicals are used to produce these synthetic fibers which account for ~72% of our clothing. Chemicals are also used as dyeing agents. 23% of all chemicals produced worldwide are used by the textile industry. The production of synthetic materials is energy intensive and releases massive amounts of toxic waste. 70 million oil barrels are used each year to produce polyester. Cheap synthetic fibers also emit gases like N_2O, which is 300 times more damaging than CO_2.

Excessive rearing of sheep and goats for wool has caused severe soil degradation and led to desertification in several regions across the globe. 90% of Mongolia's surface is facing the threat of desertification, mainly due to the breeding of cashmere goats. Every year, thousands of hectares of endangered and ancient forests are cut down and replaced by plantations of trees used to make wood-based fabrics such as rayon, viscose, and modal.

The environmental impact of the clothing and textiles (various household soft goods made of cloth) industry spiked after the commercialization of synthetic fabrics. Polyester became mainstream in the 1970s as it lowered the cost of production. A huge number of synthetic textile and apparel manufacturing units came up and started flooding the markets with low-cost products. A culture of fast fashion emerged where people started splurging on cheap trendy clothing. During this period, the quality of materials and dyes was compromised. The rich started filling up their households and even the middle class got into the habit of wearing new clothes every day. Today, a family in the western world throws away an average of 30 kg of clothing each year. Only 15% is recycled or donated, and the rest goes directly to the landfill or is incinerated. In the 1990s, microfibers were introduced to improve the texture of cloth products. The microfibers have caused uncontrollable environmental damage as they cannot be filtered out during recycling. Basically, to fulfill the needs of the burgeoning population, the industry took a technological shortcut whose environmental consequences are now visible. The problems have been exacerbated by the low-price, quick-turnaround segment of the market known as "fast fashion", which encourages cheap production and a throwaway mind-set.

The slow fashion industry has also progressed during this period. Several new natural and organic materials have been identified and efficient practices have been developed for their cultivation, extraction and processing. Cotton, jute, hemp, linen, bamboo, ramie, aloe vera, banana, coir (coconut fiber), corn, pineapple, seacell, lenpur, lyocell, soy silk, and nettle, are all biodegradable natural fibers.[91]

A lot of these fibers can be blended together to produce material that is superior to synthetic fibers, and that can be used for all kinds of cloth applications. Coconut fiber is a lightweight, resilient and durable fiber. Corn fiber can be used for sportswear, jackets, outer coat etc. Hemp has long fibers perfect for spinning with minimum processing and because it comes in a variety of weights and textures it can be used to produce many different articles of clothing/accessories. Hemp is an extremely durable fabric. It is also very insulating, absorbent and improves over time with washing and wearing. It reveals a new surface becoming

---

[91] "Eco-Friendly Fibers and Organic Fibers", TextileSchool, October 31, 2018

softer with every wash. It is also UV resistant, highly breathable, fast drying, hypoallergenic and non-irritating to the skin. Jute fibers are used for making carpet, apparel, composites, upholstery furnishings, and decorative color boards. Non-woven jute fabrics carry applications in medtech, agrotech, protech, geotextiles and many others. Pineapple fibers blend well with other fibers. Fabrics made from pineapple fibers also have an elegant appearance. They are heirloom textiles and are used for hometech, auto, mobitech, and geotech. Ramie is a very strong and durable fiber and is 8 times stronger than cotton and even stronger when wet. Seacell diffuses its protective and anti-inflammatory properties into the skin, stimulating the metabolism. It's like clothes are living! It contains microscopic particles of marine algae fiber that aid in cellular regeneration. Lenpur offers the comfort of silk, the touch of cashmere and the lightness of linen. Lenpur is a cut above the other cellulose fibers due to its softness, its absorption capacity and ability to release dampness, and its ability to sustain a higher thermal range — thus keeping you cooler in the summer and warmer in the winter. Soy Silk is very receptive to natural dyes due to the high protein content. Nettle is a uniquely strong, soft and naturally fire-retardant textile fiber and, when blended with pure new wool, it is the ultimate environmental upholstery solution.

The invention of low-cost synthetic dyeing brought about a color revolution in the second half of the 20th century. Flashy colorful designs gained prominence alongside the growth of complementary cultural changes in western society. Production systems using synthetic dyeing were built at scale and allowed designers to let their creativity go wild. Today, 99% of clothing is produced using synthetic colors and fabric dyeing causes one-fifth of global water pollution.

But flashy things never last, and so has been the case with clothing. Even though the consumption of synthetically dyed apparel and other soft goods is increasing in developing countries like India, sustainable clothing brands that use natural colors are gaining traction in the developed world. There is a strong resurgence of high quality plain simple clothing. Healthy people especially are looking for single colored clothing that fits well. Designers are experimenting more with shape. They are sticking to basic colors as people never get tired of wearing those. The rich, the classy, the powerful as well as the smart and talented, are very careful these days in the choice of color for their clothing. They don't like clutter and use single colored clothing as a symbol of clarity in life. You are looked down upon if you wear prints. People think you are either poor, uneducated or just dumb if you are seen in fast colorful clothing. Evolved people are opting for styles that are comfortable, timeless and resonate with one's personality, rather than something that's 'trendy' and poorly made. People are taking a hard look at their style choices and are increasingly relying on neutral-colored basics. People are getting married to the idea of buying fewer quality pieces that you will want to wear for a long time. Even high-end clothing labels are creating simple, white, black and beige clothing.[92]

The natural dyeing methods have also advanced during this period. Sources for different colors have now been clearly established. Cultivation and extraction methods have been standardized and made much more efficient. The ideal combinations of natural fabric, natural dyes and mordants are now well researched and documented.[93]

India is endowed with a rich biodiversity for producing all types of natural fabrics and colors. The clothing and the larger textile industry needs to be refocused towards the use of natural, organic, and semi synthetic fibers. Strong regulation against the use of synthetic fibers and colors is the best way

---

[92] "Earthy, boxy, boring: Do sustainable clothes have a standard look?", Jasreen Mayal Khanna, Vogue India, January 25, 2019

[93] "Sustainability of the use of natural dyes in the textile industry", K Elsahida, A M Fauzi, I Sailah, I Z Siregar, Earth and Environmental Science, 2019

forward for India. The Government needs to just enable a rapid transition of companies across the clothing value chain towards sustainable clothing. Given the amount of clothing stocked in Indian households, India can easily absorb a long supply shock in case of a complete ban on synthetic fibers and dyes. The shock will also help Indians regain clothing consciousness and build higher sensitivity towards the influence of materials and colors. The consumption will shift from buying a lot of low-cost printed clothing to buying a few high quality simple and stylish pieces.

Footwear

Footwear is also a part of the apparel industry and assumes greater significance in a health and fitness oriented society. Much like the broader apparel industry, the footwear industry also uses large quantities of synthetic materials and chemicals during production. Companies across the globe are already increasing the use of eco-friendly materials and making their production processes cleaner and greener. Sustainable brands are springing up across the developed world that are focused on developing high quality footwear with eco-friendly materials and minimal discharge of chemical and other pollutants into the environment.

Leather remains the biggest environmental adversary in the footwear industry. Leather tanneries use and release huge amounts of chemicals during the production process. The carbon footprint of leather is manifold higher than even plastics and polymers. The production environment also creates a health hazard for employees.

The footwear industry accounts for nearly 65% of the global use of leather. Several viable alternatives for leather have been developed. Cork (oak trees), pineapple leaves, mushrooms, and seaweed have been used to create durable and versatile leather. Leather footwear and other goods in any case do not have any critical application. Whether it is shoes or car upholstery, superior eco friendly alternatives are already being used commercially. There are now no sectors in which leather cannot be replaced by other materials. In the modern world, leather is purely a luxury. Digital and cloud technologies are moving the world towards a realm of operating without briefcases, office bags, wallets etc. India has already started shutting down tanneries with Uttar Pradesh leading the way. India needs to keep moving forward and impose a complete ban on the use of leather.

Apparel and textiles packaging is unnecessary and creates a large amount of waste. There is no need for packaging individual products to move them across the supply chain. Large clean containers with cloth lining would work perfectly to move products from production sites to retail stores. People can simply carry the merchandise in cloth bags.

Cleaning and personal care

Cleaning and personal care are the next most essential human need. Households need cleaning supplies for cleaning the clothes (bars, detergent powders, liquids, bleaches), the utensils (bars, liquids, powders), and the house (cleaners for floor, other surfaces, and toilet, disinfectants, repellants). Personal care includes body cleaners (soap bars, handwash, toothpaste, bodywash, shampoo, conditioner, face wash, face scrub, shaving cream), body groomers (hair oil, serum, face cream, face pack, toner, moisturizer, lip balm, body lotion, talcum powder), and beauty products (face pack, face powder, blush, foundation, sunscreen, lipstick, kajal, eye liner, mascara, eye shadow, hair color, mask, perfume, deodorant, colognes).[94]

In the developed world, personal care accounts for about 50 percent of industry sales. Soaps and detergents is the second-largest segment, contributing around 25 percent. The remaining 25 percent of sales is dispersed among many household and industrial cleaning products.

---

[94] "Industry Profiles: Soaps, Detergents, Cosmetics, And Toiletries", Encyclopaedia.com

Soap is the oldest cleaning product, whose invention happened between 2500 B.C. and 300 B.C. In the beginning, it was made naturally, with natural oils and aromatic plants that gave them pleasant smells. After the 15th century, chemical processes were developed that involved combining a fat or natural oil with an alkali (such as wood ashes or lye) under controlled conditions. Large scale production using chemicals took off during the 19th and 20th century. Hydrogenated fats were discovered in 1909. These solid, vegetable-based fats revolutionized soap by making its manufacture less dependent on animal byproducts. Shortages of fats and oils for soap during World Wars I and II also led to the discovery of synthetic detergents as a "superior" substitute for fat-based laundry soaps, household cleaners and shampoos.

Today's commercially manufactured soaps are highly specialized, lab-engineered products. Synthesized animal fats and plant-based oils and bases are combined with chemical additives, including moisturizers, conditioners, lathering agents, colors and scents, to make soaps more appealing to the senses. But they cannot fully mask the mostly foul ingredients such as the petroleum-based contents of shower gels.

The chemical prowess of consumer goods giants resulted in the invention of synthetic detergents. Alcohol sulfates were the first type of surfactants to make a significant impact in the formulation of cleaning products. Surfactants are basic ingredients in most products intended for use in washing clothes and dishes. New chemicals were discovered to enable better cleaning and frothing at low prices. The use of such chemicals expanded with the introduction of front-loading drum washing machines.

While some of the most hazardous chemicals were banned over time in Europe, US and even China, their use has continued in India. Phosphates and surfactants are amongst the strongest chemicals used in detergents. Nonylphenol is still used by most international companies in India.[95] It is a toxic chemical used as a surfactant which has a number of damaging reproductive and hormonal effects on people that are exposed to it.

Conventional detergents end up in rivers and harm the ecosystem. High phosphate concentration in a body of water creates a state where algae thrive and take over all the resources in the area, like sun and oxygen, leaving all the other marine life like fishes, bacteria, etc. to die.

The use of personal care products can also be traced to prehistoric times. Every product was originally made from natural substances. People painted their faces with reds, browns, and yellows derived from clay, mud, and arsenic. Bones and sticks were used to curl hair, and iron bands and weights used to straighten. A mineral called hematite was applied as rouge, and faces were painted with white lead. Black kohl encircled eyes. Aloe vera was known as an anti-irritant. The first perfumes were oil based.

The ancient science of cosmetology is believed to have originated in Egypt and India, but the earliest records of cosmetic substances and their application have been found in the Indus valley civilization. There is evidence of highly advanced ideas of self-beautification and a large array of various cosmetic uses both by men and women, in ancient India. In the book, 'Herbal cosmetics in ancient India with a treatise on planta cosmetica', 210 botanicals have been studied and 314 formulations are listed and described[96]. Natural formulations are provided for lip protection, skin lightening and exfoliation, dandruff removal, rejuvenation, hair removal, breast development, face pack, curing pimples, mouth freshness, curing lice and nits, hair remedies including cure for premature graying, deodorant powder etc.

---

[95] "Household Detergent Powders: How many make the grade and how much is too much?", Ministry of Consumer Affairs, July 2015

[96] "Herbal cosmetics in ancient India", Kunda B. Patkar, October 2008

In the ninth century, Arabs developed alcohol-based perfumes. Crusaders of the thirteenth century brought them to India. The perfumes developed during the sixteenth century were powders or gelatinous pastes.

The ability to create new fragrances by blending natural ingredients was developed during the seventeenth century in France. Natural perfumes were made from a variety of ingredients containing aroma. These included: essential oils, which were found in flowers, roots, fruits, rinds, or barks depending on the type of plant; resinoids, which were gums or resins that were purified with a solvent; and absolutes, which were aromas extracted with solvents existing in viscous liquid form. Natural perfumes were expensive, primarily because of the labor involved in gathering ingredients.

Chemical formulations developed during the nineteenth century began to replace expensive natural ingredients and make perfumes more widely available. Early synthetic fragrances included vanilla and violet. In the United States, Francis Despard Dodge developed citronellol and citronellal with various floral scents.

The nineteenth century also brought changes in facial makeup. Ceruse, a widely used cosmetic, was replaced by a powder made from zinc oxide. Ceruse, made from white lead, was discovered to be toxic. It was blamed for causing physical problems such as facial tremors, muscle paralysis, and even death.

Antiperspirants and deodorants were developed during the 1890s. Aluminum chloride, the original active ingredient, frequently caused skin irritation and damage to clothes. These difficulties were overcome during the 1940s when aluminum chlorohydrate was developed. Although additives were subsequently produced to improve antiperspirant activity, aluminum chlorohydrate remained the primary ingredient in antiperspirants for the remainder of the twentieth century.

Fashion trends continued to bring new innovations. Artificial skin tanning aids were developed during the late 1950s. False eyelashes became popular during the 1960s.

The 1960s also saw the introduction of "natural" products based on botanical ingredients such as carrot juice and watermelon extract. During the 1970s, the growing environmental movement in the United States brought the cosmetic and fragrance industry under the scanner.

Concerns about contaminated makeup emerged during the late 1980s. Molds, fungi, and pathogenic organisms were found in cosmetic products. Such contamination was supposed to be controlled by preservatives. Preservatives, however, proved ineffective against the microorganisms responsible for causing product contamination when they lacked stability or when a particular product was kept longer than the shelf life of its preservative system.

Cosmetics have since been polluting the environment insidiously. Microbeads and microplastics like glitter are impossible to shore out of oceans. Avobenzone in sunscreens is now proven to deplete coral reefs. Volatile organic compounds (VOCs) in fragrances and hairsprays contribute to smog and air pollution. The indiscriminate use of palm oil in 70% of cosmetics has led to massive deforestation.

Rapid industrialization post World War II fuelled the mass consumption revolution (1950-80)[97]. Cleaning and personal care products were produced at scale to reduce costs and drive mass adoption. The regulatory regime was weak in front of the manufacturers and could do little to mitigate the anticipated risks of the growing use of chemicals.

One of the most recent significant events for the soap and detergent market was the value-pricing trend. The early 1990s saw a move in this market away from premium pricing for name brands as customers became more value conscious.

---

[97] "Industrial Revolutions and Consumption: A Common Model to the Various Periods of Industrialization", David Flacher, 2005

Although exceptions existed, many soaps and detergents were seen as undifferentiated commodity items. Subsequently, big box retailers introduced their own store branded soaps, detergents, other cleaning products and toiletries, offering consumers additional opportunities to save money.

In addition to value, consumers in the early 2000s were pressed for time. As the pace of work and home life became more stressful and hectic, soap and toiletries that emphasized relaxation, but which could still be used quickly, constituted a strong category within the industry. Among these products were aromatherapy products like scented body washes, as well as other liquid and gel soaps. These were replacing bar soaps, which were declining in popularity.

Liquid and gel soaps take more energy to produce in the first place — using up to five times more energy to produce liquid soap than a solid soap bar. Studies have shown that we use liquid soap much more quickly than solid soap bars. On average we use seven times more liquid soap than solid soap. Researchers have also shown that we use more water when washing our hands with liquid soap, than solid soap bars — around 30% more.

Cleaning and personal care products also create damaging levels of packaging waste. Beauty and personal care products produced 142 billion units of packaging in 2018 alone. The problem of packaging is compounded by the use of mixed material—paper, fabric or metal fused with plastic—that makes recycling exceptionally tedious. Efficient recycling and non-toxic packaging have become basic hygiene practices expected by millennial customers. But even clean brands with better formulae and packaging aren't addressing the biggest problem—the amount of waste created. Instead of finding ways to manage the waste, the industry needs to stop creating packaging waste. Natural products significantly reduce the need for packaging and can be distributed in sustainable ways. Synthetic products need extra packaging to protect the chemical constituents.

High levels of consumer awareness are now driving a return to natural products, especially in developed nations. The rising level of internet penetration has enabled seamless knowledge dissemination. Consumers in the developed world today understand the ingredients and their impact on health and the environment. The enormous consumption over the last several decades has also made the consequences clearly evident. Regulatory regimes have become stronger and are steadily driving the move towards natural products.

Nowadays, the demand for natural and green products is high all over the world and the demand for green cleaning products has propelled the household cleaning products industry. People are willing to pay more money for natural and organic products to save the environment; thus, it has become a huge game-changer for this market. It is also predicted that the usage of harsh chemical products will lessen soon, as people are not only willing to spend hours cleaning their homes but also willing to pay more for the right kind of product.

India needs to overcome several hurdles to effectively transition towards sustainable consumption of cleaning and personal care products.

First, India needs a strong regulatory body and enforcement mechanism for cleaning and personal care products. Currently, we only have a common prescriptive standards body called BIS that sits within the Ministry of Consumer Affairs. We need an independent body for cleaning and personal care products well equipped to carry out research, formulate regulations and drive enforcement. The body needs to have airtight and foolproof systems and processes that cannot be violated by the workforce.

India needs a clear regulation on the maximum permissive limits for various chemicals in cleaning and personal care products. An environmentally superior product uses very minimal non-toxic chemical ingredients. In India, most of the synthetic detergents are not phosphate-free due to lack of mandatory legislation. Some manufacturers tend to put in liberal quantities of phosphates in detergents to increase cleaning efficacy. Common laundry detergent contains over 40 percent STPP (Sodium Tripolyphosphate), and most have STPP in the range of 8 to 35 percent. The toxicity of detergents decreases if you remove additives like perfumes, color and brightening agents. Synthetic surfactants may be replaced by non-petrochemical surfactants or vegetable oil soaps; builders like phosphates can be replaced by sodium citrate and sodium bicarbonate; dyes and fragrances can be eliminated or minimized.

Similarly, the list of toxic chemicals used in various toiletries and cosmetics need to be identified and banned. The National Institute of Occupational Safety and Health has found that one-third of the substances used in the fragrance industry are toxic. But because the chemical formulas of fragrances are considered trade secrets, companies aren't required to list their ingredients. The government needs to play an active role in testing the products and preventing their market distribution, while ensuring strong protection of trade secrets. Companies not willing to share trade secrets with the government should be banned in any case.

Products that result in inefficient use of natural resources need to be discouraged through taxation. For example, on liquid soaps, a water tax and a luxury tax should be added for excessive water and product use respectively.

The government also needs to enforce sustainable packaging for the category. The most essential product in the category is soap which can be easily packed in simple cloth or other sustainable materials. Most of the other cleaning and personal care products are discretionary. The government should therefore not be too concerned about supply chain disruptions due to a transition to sustainable packaging.

Natural semi solid, powdered and liquid products can be managed through natural supply chains. Large containers can be used for transportation and retailing, and consumers can carry them home in smaller containers of their choice.

Green certification needs to be made mandatory for all cleaning and personal care products. Currently, no detergent brand available in the market has opted for the Indian eco-label (known as Ecomark), which certifies environment friendliness of a product. The BIS has laid down the standards for eco-labelling of detergents in India. The standards suggest replacing phosphates with any other environmentally friendly substance. They also stress that the surfactants used in the manufacture of household laundry detergent powders should be readily biodegradable and the products be packed in packages made of recyclable or biodegradable materials. Standards need to be clearly specified for all cleaning and personal care products.

Natural supply chains create a challenge for labeling and certification. The risk of adulteration needs to be mitigated for products that are being transported and stocked in large containers and being dispensed loose. Adulteration during transportation can simply be prevented by sealing the containers. These containers should of course carry the green labels.

At the retail locations, a combination of licensing, random checks, complaints management and strong disincentives would be needed. Only authorized retailers should be allowed to stock and retail the products. Random checks need to be conducted by the designated quality control body. There should be a simple process for customers to inform the quality control body in case of issues. Disincentives should be strong enough for the retailers to not adulterate and to institutionalize systems and processes to prevent any wrongdoing.

Light

After cleaning, light is the most essential human need. Humans transitioned from the use of fire to the use of electric lights during the 19th century. Lighting now accounts for around 15% of electricity use. The invention of LEDs has significantly increased the efficiency and life of lighting products. The large lighting companies are now producing lighting bulbs and other forms in designs that are making luminaries redundant. Luminaires or lighting fixtures have been traditionally used to improve aesthetics but result in varying levels of energy loss. Today, the lighting source products (bulbs, tubes and other forms) themselves are elegant and stylish. Large lighting companies have evolved their product portfolio with significant research during the last few decades. There are bulbs and tubes of every possible size, shape, wattage, color and effect. Products in which you can control the illumination, color and effect are also commonplace now. The products also have inbuilt sensors and network connectivity to enable dynamic and efficient use. Luminaires, on the other hand, remains to be a heavily fragmented, non-scientific, low value industry. Small players keep creating decorative designs with really no consideration for energy efficiency. The smart and chic lighting products are now becoming a superior alternative to luminaires or lighting fixtures in residential and commercial settings. Without any luminaire, these products provide the best illumination. In the modern architectural designs, they fit in more naturally. Unlike luminaires that are usually eye-catching and distracting, the modern lighting products with simple functional designs are more appealing and timeless. Minimalistic lighting without the use of chandeliers and lampshades creates calm and classy spaces. These silently energetic spaces enable better focus and productivity.

Instead of integrating luminaires, lighting companies should focus on improving the quality and appearance of the source products. Government needs to help a few indigenous lighting companies build scale and leading capabilities, and also needs to discourage the operation of stand-alone luminaire companies.

Furniture

Furniture is a big-ticket consumer expense, and has serious environmental consequences. The developed world has adopted several strategies to prevent the damage without sacrificing consumer experience.

While wooden products still dominate the industry, strict standards are being enforced for responsible harvesting. Several forest certification schemes are now in existence with Forest Stewardship Council (FSC) certification being one of the fastest growing schemes. The certifications ensure environmentally responsible, socially beneficial and economically viable management of forests. They also help furniture companies achieve higher prices for their products. With the implementation of such schemes, the wood stock, biodiversity and the natural ecosystem of the covered forest area is preserved and enhanced. There is also a push towards using wood that is more sustainable viz. cork and bamboo.

Other sustainable alternatives are being increasingly used. Designers are working with clay, ceramics, stone dust, recycled wood, plastic and industrial waste, to reduce the carbon footprint of furniture. The production environments are being optimized for energy use and pollution, and low waste strategies are being continuously evolved.

Urban high-rises are being designed to minimize the need for furniture. Well-designed apartments typically have ample storage space. Design optimization by developers leads to the identification of ideal storage locations in each room. Kitchens have a large number of cabinets and cupboards. Living rooms and bedrooms have built-in wardrobes and some also have closets. Even the toilets are pre-fitted with cupboards. They usually also have a dedicated storeroom. High quality apartments usually have most of the storage spaces built into the apartments with concrete and other materials. The scale of the development enables the functional design of these inbuilt storage structures to cater to all kinds of requirements. Healthy and tech savvy families make judicious use of built in storage and add very minimal furniture.

Most people in the western world still buy beds, dining tables, sofas, tv cabinets, shoe rack, side tables and kids' cupboards.

But a culture of minimalism is becoming popular in urban high-rises. Minimalism as a concept evolved in Japan over centuries. It influenced Japan's architecture and interior design aesthetic, resulting in the serene and uncluttered style. The minimalist movement goes against modern consumerism, keeping life simple and uncluttered by adhering to the bare essentials.

Western interior design trends have latched onto Japanese minimalism in recent years. This style is epitomized by simplicity of form and function with open, light-filled spaces. Furniture and decorations are kept to a bare minimum, focusing only on the essentials. As a result, minimalist homes have lots of space, often with a light and airy feel.

Minimalism keeps humans closely connected to Mother Earth and also promotes fitness. People do away with expansive beds, dining tables and sofas. Instead, they just use a mattress to sleep on the floor, a low lying table to eat their meals and blocks of cushions as sofas. Bodies get fitter as people are able to stretch and cross their legs and sit in more upright postures.

India was originally a minimalist society. The two successive foreign regimes brought in a culture of excess in architecture and home interiors. Today, it is a symbol of success to have your home filled with furniture and have flashy interiors. We have created a social hierarchy where the servants are supposed to sleep and sit on the floor. The poorly designed independent houses that dominate housing in India usually have inadequate storage. People end up having scores of additional cupboards and cabinets to hoard up everything. Even as these families move to apartments, they are unable to let go and keep the apartments filled up to the brim. People continue to cling on to every possible object purchased by them or their ancestors. But there are still a large number of traditional Indian households that prefer sleeping on the floor. A lot of traditional businesses and retail shops also operate without chairs or sofas. They just sit on the floor and use low tables.

A democracy can only work well if everyone is on the same page. The low levels of education, the hand to mouth nature of our economy and excessive competition, are just leading people to literally do whatever it takes. The masses or the consumers do not have the mental makeup or the ability to think about society. But our nation operates on trust. The network of trust connects us all to the supreme leader. Only if we trust the country's leadership to make the right moves and give them a long enough reign, can we possibly get out of the rut we are in.

India needs to take a strong stance against these material aspirations that are unnecessary, divisive, unhealthy and damaging for the environment. The government needs to really step up to make India a responsible, minimalist and smart consumer of furniture. The key interventions include enforcing a system for responsible harvesting of wood, limiting the production to large scale efficient enterprises, ensuring ample built-in storage in apartments, and discouraging the production of big furniture items.

Paper

Paper creates a sizable need for storage in households as well as all types of organizations. Most of the paper documents are usually stored by people and entities to keep a record and revisit or reuse the content. Paper documents keep adding up over years and necessitate increasing amounts of storage.

The history of paper has mirrored the evolution of human society over the centuries: from the dissemination of scientific and philosophical knowledge to the spread of education right up to the creation of the kind of political and historical consciousness which gave birth to the modern nation state.

During the 19th century, paper use grew significantly as production costs reduced. The industrial manufacture of paper began in the 19th century with the expansion of mass-circulation newspapers and the first best-selling novels. With the development of new techniques for extracting fibers from trees, the price of paper fell dramatically, and paper soon became a product of mass consumption.

Once again, the history of paper and the history of humankind were closely intertwined: with the spread of cheap paper, books and newspapers became accessible to all, leading to an explosion of literacy among the middle classes. But it wasn't until the turn of the century that paper would be employed for other uses, like toilet and wrapping paper, toys and interior decoration.

Worldwide consumption of paper has risen by 400% in the past 40 years, with 35% of harvested trees being used for paper manufacture. Plantation forests, from where the majority of wood for pulping is obtained, are generally a monoculture and this raises concerns over the ecological effects of the practice. In the U.S., 36% of the annual timber harvest is used for paper and paperboard and in Canada 21% comes directly from harvested trees.

Pulp and paper mills contribute to air, water and land pollution. Discarded paper and paperboard make up roughly 26% of solid municipal waste in landfill sites. In the US, total industrial releases of toxic waste into the air were 690 million pounds (313,000 tonnes) in 2015 and pulp and paper accounted for 20%. In developed nations, the pulp and paper industry released 5-10% of the total industrial waste disposed of into water in 2015. Discarded paper and paperboard made up roughly 26% of solid municipal waste generated in 2014 and over 14% of solid municipal waste that ended up in landfills in 2014.

Worldwide, the pulp and paper industry is the fifth largest consumer of energy, accounting for four percent of the world's energy use. The pulp and paper industry uses more water to produce a ton of product than any other industry.

Paper manufacturing uses significant amounts of natural resources: between 2 and 2.5 tonnes of timber and 30-40 cubic meters of water are required to make one tonne of paper. What's more, electricity and methane gas are needed to power the industrial machines used in the various production phases and, depending on the type of paper, a host of polluting chemical additives.

For the past decade, the global paper and pulp mill industry has contracted. This is primarily due to a shift towards digital media and paperless communication across most developed economies. The demand for printing & writing and newsprint has declined due to a shift toward the application of digital media and web advertising. Factors such as the emergence of online e-commerce have increased overall demand for paperless advertisements.

Paperless operations have seeped into almost all government departments, private organizations, banks, and so on. These departments have switched to electronic data due to the convenience of improved accessibility, retrievability, speed, and safety. Such factors and trends are building grounds for a rapid decline in the global paper industry.

Rapid urbanization leading to the internet-aided conversion of media and promotional materials for advertising and Public Relations is also a driving force towards the decline in the circulation of printed media such as magazines and newspapers across developing and developed economies.

The world is converging through the internet. The web provides services of effective and cost-effective advertising, journalism and official communication. Upcoming technological advancement and its characteristic cost-effective nature have led to a significant decline in paper mills and printing houses. A few notable trends include conversion of graphic paper mills into packaging paper mills, capacity closures and declining prices.

Graphic papers (also known as Communication Papers) are used for communication purposes. They include two main paper grade types: printing & writing papers and newsprint. Printing and writing papers are used for magazines, catalogs, books, commercial printing, business forms, stationeries, copying and digital printing. Newsprint is a low-cost non-archival paper consisting mainly of wood pulp and most commonly used to print newspapers and other publications and advertising material.

Graphic paper accounts for nearly 50% of the total paper production. But only 8% of the graphic paper is recycled. The rest of the paper production is mainly for packaging.

The rapid growth of mobile and consumer applications over the last decade has now created the possibility for humans to restrict the use of paper to absolutely essential needs. For every human need that was served by paper, today, there are mobile applications. These applications seamlessly integrate with web applications and permanently store all data in the cloud. The use of mobile and web applications provides a much better experience as opposed to reading or writing on paper. Applications are becoming increasingly efficient with the use of artificial intelligence and machine learning. Instead of relying on the physical movement of paper, people can accomplish all kinds of tasks in real time. A data revolution has begun which has the potential to make every human life perfect.

India has embraced mobile and consumer internet with open arms. The Indian IT industry has also been a key driving force in advancing the development of consumer applications and driving their adoption globally. The logical Indian mind has been a key contributor in the creation of all sorts of applications spread across industries.

India has already achieved the threshold mobile and internet penetration to now make the paper industry sustainable. Besides creating incentives for further digital adoption, India needs to heavily regulate paper production. People and entities will automatically adjust and help achieve balance between natural wood and paper production.

9. Five star destinations

An 'urban only' India is not just about living in high-rise cities, but also about not living anywhere outside them. It is about managing agriculture, forestry and natural resource extraction through people living in the cities. People engaged in these occupations should simply travel to the respective locations to accomplish the tasks and then come back to their city homes. Even the defense forces need to minimize their physical footprint outside the cities and maximize their use of technology for surveillance and action.

The cities would also become the most attractive tourist destinations. They would offer a rich and eclectic mix of food, culture, and entertainment. Moving around the cities would be simple and costs would be significantly lower than those of exotic locations.

Nevertheless, people would still want to visit the Indian countryside. People will want to get away from the hustle and bustle and immerse themselves in the rich and diverse natural wealth of India. People may just want a break and enjoy the breathtaking views of a majestic mountain range or feel the sensations of a flowing river to recharge themselves.

The Indian ecosystem has one the richest and most diverse range of possibilities to explore and immerse in. The subtropical climatic regime creates four distinct weather patterns throughout the subcontinent. The Himalayas, the northeast, the western and eastern ghats, together offer a vast range of options to escape the summer heat. In winter, spring or autumn, one can literally visit any corner of the subcontinent, except for some parts of the Himalayas that become inaccessible during monsoons and peak winters.

Responsible planning and management is essential for creating high quality experiences and minimizing disruption to the natural ecosystems. Development needs to enable maximum realization of natural value and sustainable provision of essential services to create the best possible experience at any destination. A focus on the natural ecosystem of the location helps create a harmonious set of infrastructure and services that result in the most compelling experiences. A deep understanding of the local environment and landscape is essential for designing and developing the best possible experience as well as for balancing the negative effects of the development. Local traditions and architecture help in understanding what makes sense in the region.

Developing tourist destinations in a sustainable manner also maximizes the attractiveness of the destinations. Empirical results show that sustainability is a crucial determinant of the competitiveness of a tourist destination. Until recently, most travelers planned their adventures based on the most affordable and comfortable way to meet their travel goals, without giving much thought to how their choices might affect the destination. But priorities have begun to shift. On top of having a great time, travelers increasingly want to do the right thing at the places they visit.

Responsible development of tourist destinations requires significant capital and resources. The remote location of the destinations increases the cost of resources and manpower. High levels of expertise is required to design infrastructure that is harmonious with the local ecosystem. There is also a significant additional cost of following environmental norms and ensuring traveler safety. Individuals, small and medium enterprises end up making compromises on quality, sustainability and safety.

High quality sustainable development also maximizes the economic output of the destination. Low quality establishments in the form of hotels, food outlets and other retail shops create a low-price environment in the destination. Unorganized service providers for adventure, excursions, sports, relaxation, therapy etc. also offer their services at prices lower than the sustainable levels. Following environmental norms requires establishments and service providers to build additional infrastructure and processes, as well as involves greater manpower. Five-star properties engage the highest manpower per room.

Scale is essential to generate sufficient returns that adequately compensate for the high fixed and operating costs. A small hotel or a shop does not generate enough income to invest in infrastructure development or spend on quality, safety and environmental compliances. The large hotels are able to drive efficiencies in their operations and therefore are able to generate sufficient income and justify investments in ensuring quality and sustainability at their properties.

Only the large, organized players bring in tax revenue for the government to develop the overall destination in suitable ways. Tax revenue is critical for the government to build public infrastructure at destinations viz. water supply, electricity, roads, walkways, cycling tracks, bridges, cable cars, nature parks etc.

Five-star hotels provide the best holistic experience possible at any destination. They are built at the most prime location of a destination whether it is in the mountains, by the river, or at the beach. Their architecture is usually designed with a deep understanding of the landscape and weather of the location. They are equipped with an abundant range of facilities for consumption, recreation, relaxation, fitness, and work. They have large public spaces like lobbies, reception areas, lounges, gardens etc. where people can relax and socialize. They have multiple restaurants serving an eclectic mix of local and international cuisines. Some also have their own farms and orchards where sustainable agriculture and horticulture is practiced. For relaxation and exercise, they have a health club with several facilities such as a gymnasium, spa, swimming pool, and several sports facilities on grounds like tennis, squash, badminton, mini soccer, cricket etc. The larger ones also have shops for people to purchase their own groceries, fruits and vegetables. They have authentic stores to buy products produced with the naturally available resources of the region. They have the complete range of local activities for people to explore and enjoy the destination.

The five stars follow high standards of sustainability in their design and operations. Five stars are required to build eco-friendly practices like sewage treatment, rainwater harvesting, waste management, pollution control method for air, water and light, introduction of non CFC equipment for refrigeration and air conditioning, energy / water conservation (use of CFL lamps, solar energy, water saving devices/ taps), and firefighting measures / hydrants. Government regulation mandates hotels in hilly and ecologically fragile areas to incorporate creative architecture keeping in mind sustainability and energy efficiency and as far as possible in conformity with local art and architecture and with the use of local materials.

Five stars create a secure environment for people to completely let go of all worldly fears. In a five-star, parents can even let their kids roam around without supervision.

Five-star properties are a complete destination. Even today when there is a whole town or city at a location with several attractions, people rarely step out of a five star. Five-star development can literally transform any place into a tourist destination. They obviously create a high-quality sustainable experience at popular tourist spots like a mountain, beach, river, or a thick forest. But they can literally transform any landscape into a tourist destination whether it is a desert, barren land, farmland or anything else.

India had 410 five-star properties at the end of 2018. These include five-star, five-star deluxe and heritage hotels. More than half of these are located in the cities. Only about 200 five-star properties are located in tourist destinations. Kerala has the highest number (58) of five-star properties. Rajasthan has 41 five-star properties including 24 heritage hotels.

As India moves out of villages, towns and smaller cities, every abandoned location will present an opportunity to create a five-star destination. We can preserve the legacy of the 8000 odd towns by developing five-star heritage properties. Besides being the commercial center for the local region, the small cities and towns bring together everything that has evolved naturally in the region.

The eco sensitive regions have a large untapped potential for developing pure five star destinations. The Himalayan states are the most eco sensitive and the most attractive for tourists. But towns and cities even in these states define the boundaries for developing tourist destinations. Beyond these, even today, there are only small villages. Nature is extremely fragile and vulnerable beyond these towns and the terrain is also unviable for development. In Himachal Pradesh, there are 60 towns but only 4 five-star properties (2018). In Uttarakhand, there are 75 towns and only 1 five-star property. Five stars are almost non-existent in J&K and the northeast (except Sikkim).

Including some remote locations, India has around 10,000 locations to build five-star destinations. Every location should ideally have at least two five-star properties. Therefore, we will have a minimum of 20,000 five-star properties defining these destinations. Assuming 150 rooms in each property, there will be a total capacity of 30 lac rooms across these five-star destinations.

India currently has a little over 27 lac rooms across the country. The independent and unbranded segment constitutes 72 percent. Homestays and guest houses account for 15 percent. Traditional hotel chains constitute 5 percent of the total rooms, while new age hotel chains constitute 8 percent.

The industry size will increase more than five-fold once we fully transition to five-star destinations. The estimated revenue of 20,000 five stars would be INR 10 lac crore, as a five-star property on an average generates a revenue of INR

50 crore annually. The Indian hotel industry's total revenue in FY'20 stood at INR 1.82 lakh crore, out of which the organized segment generated revenue of INR 12,000 crore. Once all local activities are managed by the five stars, the average revenue will be much higher.

Five stars create significant value for the national economy both during and after development. Large capital expenditure is needed for building each property. The development cost ranges from 75 lacs to 3 crore per room for five stars. To build large properties that truly represent and define a destination, we should assume a capex of INR 2 crore per room. A 150-room property would therefore need INR 300 crore to build. 20,000 properties will need a capital expenditure of INR 60 lac crore. If we assume a growth of 10% YoY in the development of five stars over a 30-year period, capital outlay in year 1 would be ~INR 36,500 crore. With a 15% YoY growth, the year 1 capex will be ~14,000 crore. That roughly translates to financing 50 projects in the first year. The numbers will be lower if the development is planned over a 50-year period.

The development phase will generate a large demand for materials and labor, and therefore boost both manufacturing and services. Hard costs that include material and construction (including labor) account for 55-65% of the total capex. Hard costs include the finished materials, such as flooring and drywall, and basic construction materials like concrete and steel. Soft costs that are around 12% of the total cost include the architect and interior designer fees, draftsman, structural engineers, and other things like maintenance, insurance, permits, taxes, and other related costs. Furniture, fixtures and equipment are typically around 10% of the total cost, and include beds, tables, reception desks, restaurant and kitchen equipment, lights, sinks, plumbing, and furnishings like sheets, pillows, and towels. Every development project needs architects, interior designers, concrete workers, plumbers, electricians, painters, flooring installers, carpenters, HVAC technicians, structural engineers, tile installers and landscapers.

Once operational, the 20,000 five stars will also provide high quality employment to over 55 lac people (30 lac rooms multiplied by five-star average of 1.8 employees per room). There are around 40 lac people working in the hotel industry today but with a significant proportion being untrained, contractual, ad-hoc and earning low wages. Besides the 55 lac trained personnel, five stars will also drive quality enhancement in all related areas viz. construction, agriculture, horticulture, supply chain, products, and services. People engaged in low value local economies will give way to formalized high quality delivery of products and services.

The economic output and contribution to the national economy will significantly increase once the five stars take over the destination. The professionally managed set up will necessitate higher prices. The absence of low value local providers will drive the entire volume to the five stars at higher prices. Given the high level of investment made by the hotel companies, the government will also be able to enforce price caps. The government will also get tax revenue from every rupee spent at the destination.

The tax revenue will make it viable for the government to build high quality infrastructure for improving the destination experience and driving sustainability. The government will be able to build dedicated tracks for walking, running and cycling, bridges, cable cars, cable trains, hydro power plants, museums, nature parks, revamp forest and lakes and enhance structures of cultural importance.

The five stars will have the capacity to host every Indian for two days in a year. 30 lac rooms mean a total of more than 105 crore five-star days on an annual basis. Assuming an average occupancy of two people, over a hundred crore people could spend two days. Over time India can look to double the capacity after the principles of sustainability, quality and efficiency are well ingrained.

The Indian hospitality industry will then seamlessly integrate with the high-quality global tourism industry. Indian hospitality chains will be able to create meaningful partnerships with players across the globe and enable higher volume of inflow and outflow of tourists. Every Indian will become a five-star traveler and with heightened consciousness, will break barriers and remove stereotypes.

We will just need to be comfortable in witnessing the upliftment of every Indian citizen. We need to move away from the vicious hyper competitive cycle of individual benefit, hierarchy, poor quality, environmental damage, and poor economy. A healthy mind will always treat every individual as part of the global family, who deserves a high-quality life. People in their right minds will forego the urge to compete and accumulate excessive personal wealth. They would rather work together and enjoy the journey of taking everyone alongside and crossing the line together. A peaceful collaborative approach of ensuring a high-quality life for everyone is the only way we can maximize economic output as well as harmony with nature.

In an urban India, each city will become a tourist hotspot. The vibrant cities will offer an eclectic mix of local food, culture, and entertainment. The high-rise urban infrastructure would be designed and engineered to suit the local environment and would be unique for each city. The city's heritage would be reflected in the infrastructure and also preserved in various institutions. The amalgamation of green and blue spaces with the urban infrastructure will create scores of exciting and awe-inspiring destinations across the length and breadth of each city. People will have the option to gorge on local food, go berserk in the shopping districts, walk, run or cycle across the city, its lake and parks, and relax in the evening with some local music, theater and other entertainment. There will be an endless list of activities and attractions for each age group.

The stimulating and health-oriented city environment will never let your body feel guilty of indulging on a vacation.

The cities will account for a much bigger share of tourism as compared to the five-star destinations. Each of the 130 cities will have more than 50 five-star hotels each resulting in over 5,000 city five-stars. Besides being a tourist destination themselves, cities will also serve as a transit hub for the nearby five-star destinations.

City vacations would also be very affordable. The price of consumables in cities is obviously much lower than the five star destinations. Besides the five-stars, the large number of residential apartments will become equally attractive places to stay. Already being done in several cities of the world, apartment sharing offers a great affordable way for people to truly immerse themselves in a city. People can hop apartments and explore different neighborhoods. The apartments are equipped for all personal needs and help save on several costs. Plus, you form new acquaintances, who help you get the best out of the city. Living in a city resident's apartment enables you to experience the city as a resident. You truly understand all aspects of living in the city and are able to discover the local goodness that binds the residents to their city.

10. Green transportation

In an 'urban only' India, transportation needs are greatly reduced. With no human settlement in villages, towns and small cities, there is no need for transporting people and finished goods between them and the large cities. Concentrated settlement in the 130 cities would also help create efficient and sustainable transportation networks within and outside the cities. The cost of transportation and logistics in India is higher than the developed world. Transportation and logistics account for approximately 14 percent of India's GDP, as against 8-10% of the GDP for developed nations.

For mobility, people in India use private cars, private two wheelers, metro, bus, minibus, auto (personal / shared), car taxi (personal / shared), two-wheeler taxi, cycle rickshaws, bicycles and walking. In India, personalized motorized mobility, satisfied mainly by two wheelers and passenger cars, accounted for more than four-fifth of the motor vehicle population. Two-wheelers account for about 70%, followed by passenger cars at 15%. Two wheelers and cars are growing at a much faster rate than other modes, and there is a marked shift away from buses.

For logistics transportation, India uses trucks, railways and small commercial vehicles. As of 2017, India's logistics transportation share of GDP was 7% as compared to 5-6% in developed economies. Currently, freight transport in India is road-dominated—accounting for 59% of freight movement. 35% of freight demand is met by rail, 6% by waterways and less than 1% by air.[98]

The wide array of transportation modes results in chaos and inefficiency. The industry is struggling to fulfill the different

---

[98] "Goods on the Move: Efficiency & Sustainability in Indian Logistics", NITI Aayog and Rocky Mountain Institute, 2018

objectives of an unequal society. Urban mobility infrastructure these days is being built to minimize cost and travel time, as well as to maximize convenience and experience. The abysmally high income-inequality in Indian cities creates a broad spectrum of decision criteria. The sizable mass of poor and low-income workers simply chooses the cheapest mode. Small businesses that engage most of the workforce are trying to save every possible penny. The middle class is value centric and optimizes for cost and travel time. The affluent class just moves in cars for their convenience and experience. The masses can't pay for the required mobility infrastructure and the affluent are unwilling to adopt sustainable means in the messy environment. The vehicle diversity on city roads is simply mind boggling. Everyone is trying to get ahead. While the rich want to show off the power of their vehicles, the bike rider, auto wallah or a taxi driver are just not ready to be left behind. Weak regulatory regime around traffic rules and poor enforcement further exacerbates the chaos. Infrastructure is inadequate and unable to ensure smooth and safe movement of different vehicle types. The growth of vehicular traffic on roads has been far greater than the growth in the road network and as a result, the main arterial roads in the country are facing capacity saturation.

India needs to build a transportation system that is safe, sustainable, and efficient, and enables the formation of a healthy and equitable urban society. The system needs to simply connect every location in a seamless manner with no gaps.

Ensuring safety and sustainability is paramount. Life and health are more important than transportation, and so there is no justification for the use of unsafe modes that might be cheaper, faster, more convenient, or even more fuel efficient.

Speed is the biggest safety concern in transportation. An increase in average speed is directly related both to the likelihood of a crash occurring and to the severity of the consequences of the crash. For example, every 1% increase in mean speed produces a 4% increase in the fatal crash risk and a 3% increase in the serious crash risk.

Speed is the fundamental risk factor for serious accidents. Driving within safe speed limits reduces the intensity of crashes that occur due to other factors. Even if a drunk driver crashes at a safe speed, the injuries will be manageable. Most traffic violations occur due to over speeding. The use of seat belts and the functioning of airbags become irrelevant when driving at safe speeds. At low speeds, one can easily negotiate damaged roads, defects in road design, objects lying on the roads and even animals, without creating a risk for other vehicles. At low speeds, one can safely drive in darkness, and during extreme weather conditions. Braking performance is much higher at lower speeds. The ability to follow traffic rules is much higher at lower speeds. Driving at high speeds requires much higher levels of concentration. Speed induced stress and fatigue negatively impacts a driver's performance and results in exponential growth of crash risk.

Driving at safe speeds reduces the severity of injury even in the case of two wheelers. Wearing a helmet reduces the possibility of a fatal injury at safe speeds. But given that the human body is fully exposed, the risk of fatality always remains with a two-wheeler.[99]

For car occupants, wearing seatbelts and using well-designed cars generally can provide protection to a maximum of 70 km/h in frontal impacts, and 50 km/h in most side impacts. The human (pedestrian) tolerance to injury by a car will be exceeded if the vehicle is traveling at more than 30 km/h. The death risk for pedestrians hit by car fronts rises rapidly (4.5 times from 50 km/h to 65 km/h).

The problem of speeding has increased over the years since the maximum speed that new cars are capable of is, in many

---

[99] "The safety problems met by powered two-wheelers in urban traffic", P. Van Elslande, J.-Y. Fournier & C. Parraud, The French Institute of Science and Technology for Transport, Spatial Planning, Development and Networks (IFSTTAR), France, 2014

cases, double the existing speed limits on roads. Many modern cars now are easily capable of speeding, which was typically not the case when speed limits were first introduced. The development of engine technologies over the past 40 years has resulted in most cars having a top speed well in excess of maximum speed limits. Car racing has always been deeply integrated into the culture of auto companies, especially in Europe and the US. The engineering teams just kept improving the speed and power of vehicles in a bid to establish their technical supremacy on track. A grand excuse was that higher speeds would reduce the increasing congestion. Heavy safety installations were introduced to address concerns about increasing speeds. Even the governments have mindlessly supported the high-speed vehicles by creating enabling infrastructure. Significant additional resources have been deployed to build infrastructure and systems for high-speed vehicles.

India's transportation industry would be best served by reducing the maximum speeds on vehicles being produced. The maximum speed on every vehicle should be less than 100 kmph. People only need to drive at 100 kmph in case of health emergencies. Over time, vehicles should also be equipped with control systems that automatically reduce maximum speed in urban areas.

The speed capping at the production level will not only ensure safety but will also increase fuel efficiency, riding experience and the life of vehicles and parts.

The speed cap will also make domestic automakers fully capable of producing every vehicle. The need for advanced materials, parts, systems and technologies will be greatly reduced. Indian automakers will gain a significant competitive advantage over the leading global auto companies across all value seeking markets. Over time, Indian car companies will be able to deliver the best experience with the lowest use of materials and resources.

For India, sustainability of transportation is equally important. Sustainability in transportation pertains to the use of energy and materials, with energy being the most critical for India. India's commercial energy resource base is meager compared with the population; while India has a sixth (>16%) of the world's population, it accounts for only about 0.8% of total geological reserves. In 2020, the Indian transportation sector is projected to account for 21% of total final energy use and is growing at the fastest rate in the world. To ensure sustainability, India needs to power its transportation with green energy and completely phase out the use of hydrocarbons. The developed world is making rapid strides towards greener transportation, but the transformation is most critical for India. India faces the biggest crisis and therefore needs to lead the world in moving towards a completely green transportation system.

India is also constrained in the availability of key materials used in the production and operation of batteries and electric vehicles. While some proportion of battery materials can be recycled, separation of battery waste is extremely costly and inefficient. Hence the use of batteries and EVs will necessitate continuous use of resources that are limited. The entire world is constrained by these materials. The demand for copper, nickel and cobalt will exceed the currently identified global reserves, even in the most conservative adoption scenarios. At present, EVs are produced mainly using different types of Li-ion batteries (LIBs) and only to a lesser extent other battery systems like NiMH. Over the medium term, LIBs will probably continue to be the preferred energy storage technology for EVs due to their excellent technical performance. This raises the question of whether we will have enough reserves or resources of key metals such as Li, Co, Ni, Cu, Al, Mn or P required for Li-ion traction batteries. Even in other chemical combinations that might achieve commercial viability, there will always be a need for materials that are only available in finite quantities.[100]

Only renewable sources of energy can be used to make transportation truly sustainable. Solar, wind, hydro, and geothermal are the only sustainable sources of energy. Electricity generated through these sources is the best way to power sustainable transportation.

But electricity use for transportation without batteries creates a physical constraint. Significant infrastructure build up is required to enable transportation using electricity directly from the generating stations. Rail is the only transportation mode where the use of electricity has proven to be technically feasible and commercially viable. Electric rail delivers the highest energy efficiency when compared with other modes of mass transit.

Thankfully, humans have found two sustainable solutions to power other modes of transportation - Green Hydrogen and Sodium Ion.

Green Hydrogen is a completely sustainable source of energy that can be used in all types of vehicles. Hydrogen produced without the use of fossil fuels is called Green Hydrogen.

There are four main sources for the commercial production of hydrogen: natural gas, oil, coal, and electrolysis, which currently account for 48%, 30%, 18% and 4% of the world's hydrogen production respectively. Fossil fuels are therefore currently the dominant source of industrial hydrogen. Specifically, bulk hydrogen is usually produced by the steam reforming of methane or natural gas. Electrolysis is the only method where no fossil fuel is used. It just uses water, a readily available resource. The same amount of water is reproduced when hydrogen is oxidized to produce energy.

---

[100] "Manufacturers Are Struggling To Supply Electric Vehicles With Batteries", Ariel Cohen, Forbes, March 25, 2020

Electrolysis of water splits the water molecule H_2O into its components oxygen and hydrogen. When the source of energy for water splitting is renewable or low-carbon, the hydrogen produced is referred to as Green Hydrogen. Electrolysis of water is 70–80% efficient while steam reforming of natural gas has a thermal efficiency between 70–85%. The electrical efficiency of electrolysis is expected to reach 82–86% before 2030. Water electrolysis can operate between 50–80 °C, while steam methane reforming requires temperatures between 700–1100 °C.[101]

Hydrogen production and distribution is capital intensive and needs strong government commitment to make it viable. Large investments are needed by the government in the initial phases for the development of the hydrogen economy. Investment in both hydrogen production and distribution infrastructure is needed, alongside the renewable power projects required to supply carbon-neutral energy. For the moment, the scarcity of such infrastructure represents the single largest obstacle to the adoption of hydrogen technology.

Globally, the cost of hydrogen is already coming down, partly in line with the fall in the cost of renewable energy, but also due to improvements in water electrolysis.[102] The Paris-based International Energy Agency expects the cost of producing hydrogen to fall by a further 30 per cent by 2030, but the rapid reduction in the cost of recent photovoltaic solar energy projects in the Middle East could mean the local cost of commercially producing hydrogen will fall even faster.

The current areas of focus for improving the commercial viability of hydrogen are - 1) achieving a hydrogen cost target of \$1/kg H_2 by 2030 with renewable sources of energy, 2) reducing the capital cost of the electrolyzer unit and the

---

[101] "Hydrogen production: electrolysis", Hydrogen and Fuel Cells Technologies Office, Office of Energy Efficiency & Renewable Energy

[102] "Green Hydrogen cost reduction; scaling up electrolysers", Emanuel Taibi, Herib Blanco, Raul Miranda, Marcelo Carmo, International Renewable Energy Agency, 2020

balance of the system, 3) improving energy efficiency for converting electricity to hydrogen over a wide range of operating conditions, and 4) improving understanding of electrolyzer cell and stack degradation processes and developing mitigation strategies to increase operational life.

As investment in hydrogen infrastructure grows and net costs continue to fall, hydrogen will become more commercially attractive than EVs and internal combustion engines using fossil fuels. The flood gates for hydrogen economy will open as soon as the cost barrier is breached. Hydrogen will then most likely become the only fuel used in transportation (except rail).[103]

Safety is a concern, as hydrogen is flammable, but so are gasoline and lithium-ion batteries. The transportation of hydrogen for use at refueling stations poses additional safety risks — stations use sensors to monitor for leaks. There have not been serious incidents reported in California, and the industrial sector has been transporting hydrogen for decades.

Hydrogen in combination with the fuel technology presents the ultimate sustainable transportation solution. Fuel cell electric vehicles use hydrogen as a fuel to power their engines. Fuel cell is an electrochemical device which converts chemical energy to electric energy. A fuel cell vehicle (FCV) or fuel cell electric vehicle (FCEV) is an electric vehicle that uses a fuel cell, sometimes in combination with a small battery or supercapacitor, to power its onboard electric motor. Fuel cells in vehicles generate electricity generally using oxygen from the air and compressed hydrogen. Most fuel cell vehicles are classified as zero-emissions vehicles that emit only water and heat. In principle, a hydrogen fuel cell functions like a battery, producing electricity, which can run an electric motor. Instead of requiring recharging, however, the fuel cell can be refilled with hydrogen.

---

[103] "Realizing the hydrogen economy", John Bambridge, MEED for Power Technology, October 8, 2019

There are six well known fuel cells and named as Polymer Electrolyte Membrane (PEM), Alkaline (AFC), Phosphoric Acid (PAFC), Solid Oxide (SOFC) and Molten Carbonate (MCFC). In the transportation sector, generally PEM type fuel cells are preferred. The main reason for this selection is the operation temperature. All fields of transportation (trucks, cars, buses, trains, and aircraft) have already found viability with hydrogen fuel cells.

The technologies of hydrogen fuel cell vehicles have not reached maturity yet and face stiff competition from battery based electric vehicles. As with any new technology, fuel cell costs should come down if the market grows and achieves economies of scale in manufacturing and infrastructure. EV and hybrid vehicles currently have an edge in terms of overall energy efficiency. Batteries now lose only about 17 percent of the initial input of electrical energy through inefficiencies when charging and discharging, while the cycle of using electrical energy to split water into its constituent atoms and recombining hydrogen with air inside a fuel cell wastes more than 50 per cent.

The use of Iridium is another key area of technological advancement for the realization of PEM water electrolysis for large scale hydrogen production. Considering the historic and current market development of Platinum Group Metals (PGMs) indicates that the Iridium demand for PEMWE cells is a bottleneck in the realization of a mature market. A published analysis reveals that a significant proportion of global iridium mine production would be required to meet the demand for the PEMWE market alone.

Two necessary preconditions have been identified to meet the immense future iridium demand: first, the dramatic reduction of iridium catalyst loading in PEM electrolysis cells and second, the development of a recycling infrastructure for iridium catalysts with technical end-of-life recycling rates of at least 90%.[104]

But hydrogen fuel cells already have several benefits over existing technologies. The major advantage of hydrogen fuel cell vehicles over electric vehicles is that they offer a range as long as internal combustion engines. Hydrogen fuel cell vehicles also have the advantage of swift refilling just like internal combustion engines. Unlike more common battery-powered electric vehicles, fuel cell vehicles don't need to be plugged in, and all current models exceed 300 miles of range on a full tank. They're filled up with a nozzle almost as quickly as traditional gas and diesel vehicles. Other advantages of hydrogen fuel cell vehicles compared to vehicles using an internal combustion engine are that they are vibration free, do not require shifting and are quiet.

Presently, Hydrogen is more established in the commercial market. There are more than 23,000 fuel cell-powered forklifts in operation at warehouses and distribution centers across the U.S. in more than 40 states. But huge investments are underway from both automakers and energy companies to expand the infrastructure needed to drive adoption of FCEVs.

Hydrogen is the most abundant energy carrier in the world. Hydrogen is also the most abundant resource in the universe. Hydrogen energy sustainability assessments generally give positive results in all three perceptions of sustainability i.e. environmental, economic and social.[105] Therefore, a sustainable future of transportation is clearly possible with Green Hydrogen.

Sodium Ion Batteries (SIB) have emerged as another sustainable alternative for powering transportation. Sodium-ion batteries (SIB) are considered as a promising alternative

---

[104] Christine Minke, Michel Suermann et. al, Is iridium demand a potential bottleneck in the realization of large-scale PEM water electrolysis?

[105] "Sustainability Analyses for Hydrogen Fuel Cell Electric Vehicles", Hüseyin Turan Arat, Bahattin Tanç and Nevzat Özaslan, April 22, 2020

to overcome existing sustainability challenges related to Lithium-ion batteries (LIB), such as the use of critical and expensive materials with high environmental impacts.[106] Sodium batteries are much less affected by low temperatures and appear to be able to handle more charge/discharge cycles than lithium-ion batteries. The latest sodium batteries do not require scarce materials like cobalt and nickel.

Soda Ash (abundantly available in the US) is the best source to extract Sodium ion followed by sea water (available everywhere). The sources are more abundant in nature and cheaper than lithium. The sources of sodium in the form of NaCl (table salt) can be the primary source of SIB both as electrodes, doping, and electrolytes. NaCl can also be used in the form of other compounds such as Na_2CO_3 which is the most commonly applied to SIB right now.[107] Sodium extraction is minimally energy consuming.

The technology is still in a nascent stage and significant progress needs to be made especially around energy density and cathode materials for the SIBs to gain a technical as well as commercial edge over LIBs.

In March, JAC Motors, an automaker based in China, released photos of a chartreuse car that it said was the world's first vehicle built with sodium-ion batteries. The compact vehicle was fitted with a 25-kilowatt-hour battery made by another Chinese company, HiNa Battery, and a press release claimed the car's range was up to 250 kilometers (155 miles). In April, China's largest EV battery maker, CATL, announced it had developed a sodium-ion battery that it planned to release in a vehicle made by automaker Chery.[108]

The next most important factor to consider for the transportation industry is efficiency. Efficiency drives further

---

[106] Manuel Baumann, Marcel Häringer et al. Prospective Sustainability Screening of Sodium-Ion Battery Cathode Materials

[107] Nurohmah, A.R., Nisa, S.S., Stulasti, K.N.R. et al. Sodium-ion battery from sea salt: a review.

[108] Casey Crownhart, This abundant material could unlock cheaper batteries for EVs

reduction in energy and material usage, as well as enhances performance. Scale and utilization are most critical for achieving high levels of efficiency. Scale enables investment in research for identifying and developing the best materials, processes, products, and systems. Scale also results in higher levels of productivity across the transportation value chain. High levels of utilization directly and indirectly increase efficiency. Higher traffic lowers the per capita usage of infrastructure, carriers and resources, resulting in higher efficiency. High utilization also creates further opportunities for optimization and value creation.

An unshakeable focus on safety, sustainability and efficiency, will automatically lead to a system that also promotes health and equality. But at the infrastructure and system design stage itself, we need to make choices that enhance physical fitness in favor of the more convenient options. We need to refrain from building anything that is specific to an income segment. Everyone should be treated as an equal and should be able to use all the available options. Specific infrastructure, systems and carriers should only be designed for different age groups and health requirements. Stable urban settlement and large-scale production brings certainty to supply chains and minimizes the need for flexibility and agility. Agile systems are mainly needed for managing health emergencies.

The domestic transportation needs of an 'urban only' India can be clearly segregated into four buckets - 1) urban mobility and logistics, 2) inter-city travel and trade, 3) logistics between countryside and cities (produce, materials and manpower), and 4) transportation between cities and tourist destinations (people and goods).

For urban mobility, walking and cycling are the cheapest, most healthy and eco-friendly transportation options. People can walk and cycle for exercise, to go to work, to explore and have fun. Delivery of small packages can also be done on bikes. While walking and cycling cannot serve all transportation needs, its use needs to be maximized to the extent possible. High-rise cities significantly reduce distances making it possible for people to choose walking and cycling over other modes of transportation. High-rise development creates space for building dedicated walkways and cycling tracks everywhere. Concentration of shops and offices in high-rises, makes it viable to restrict all motorized traffic in shopping and business localities. Walking and cycling is also the best way to explore the green and blue spaces of a city. Cities should therefore have dedicated walking and cycling paths everywhere as a parallel alternative to other modes of transportation.

Cycle rickshaws are fully sustainable but have lost out to autos and other motorized vehicles as the Indian society got increasingly hustled. Pulling a rickshaw is a great workout as long as the compensation allows the rickshaw puller to eat well. Dedicated shopping and leisure localities should only have cycle rickshaws as the means of public transport.

The next best mode is the electric urban metro rail or simply called the Metro. Metro refers to high-frequency, high-capacity urban services which are fully separated from traffic, often underground or elevated. Urban rail provides a solution to cities impacted by congestion and air pollution. The energy consumption of urban rail is 0.12 kWh/pax-km or 432 J/m-pax that is 7x less than an average car and 3x less than an average bus in urban context. While it is extremely capital and resource intensive to build, the huge capacity, heavy utilization, long life and high energy efficiency, result in attractive returns on the large initial investments.[109]

The regions with the highest share of electric train activity are Japan (97%), Korea (90%), Russia (86%), Europe (80%), and China (75%). Passenger rail is significantly more electrified than freight in almost all regions, and regions with higher

---

[109] "The Future of Rail - Opportunities for energy and the environment, International Energy Agency (IEA), Paris, February 8, 2019

reliance on urban rail and high-speed rail are those with the largest share of passenger-kilometers served by electricity.

Because railroad infrastructure is privately owned in the U.S., railroads are unwilling to make the necessary investments for electrification. In Europe and elsewhere, railway networks are considered part of the national transport infrastructure, just like roads, highways and waterways, so are often financed by the state. Operators of the rolling stock pay fees according to rail use. This makes possible the large investments required for the technically and, in the long-term, also economically advantageous electrification.

Electric Metro trains can become fully sustainable when electricity is generated using renewable sources. Several European countries are already exploiting the potential of renewable sources to fuel their trains.

In the Netherlands (~2 crore population), every electric train running on the Dutch railway network has relied entirely on wind energy since 1 January 2017. The network uses 1.2 billion kWh of wind-generated electricity a year, roughly equivalent to the total annual domestic consumption of every household in the Dutch city of Amsterdam. The wind-powered trains carry 600,000 passengers a day. Three strokes of one of the turbines that supply it generate enough power to drive a train for 1 kilometer. Put another way, a single turbine running for an hour can power a train for 120 miles. Since 2005, its consumption of electricity per passenger kilometer has been cut by nearly 50%. Strong government intervention has been critical in preventing the use of other energy sources for supplying electricity to the network's grid. The network has secured uninterrupted power by developing a sufficiently large and diversified portfolio of wind farms.

Solar powered trains have started operating in countries like Belgium and the UK.[110] Most of these new solar train projects

---

[110] "European Trains Go Down Renewable Route", Alex Kirby, Climate News Network, February 16, 2016

are generating solar power near the tracks, stations or even on the train's roofs. While the transmission is more efficient, these distributed installations are more expensive than large scale solar farms. Solar potential also varies with location making it unviable to fully power the trains with solar. As per the current research, solar will contribute 5% to 30% of the rail energy requirements, depending on the solar potential of the region.

The best approach is to fully electrify the metro network and gradually increase the share of renewables in the national energy mix. The segregation of metro development and energy production will enable efficiency maximization at a system level.

Metro systems exist in 10 Indian cities, with about 515 km of track in operation and an additional 620 km of metro rail under construction. A further 600 km of metro lines are planned for the next few years.

In an urban only India with high-rise cities, metro will form an integral part of the infrastructure. The metro network needs to be extensive and dense to make it the preferred alternative for public transportation. Well-designed cities with mixed use development will have a well distributed traffic flow. Instead of having a city center, all urban forms will be dispersed across the developed area. A rectangular or grid network of metro will therefore be most ideal for these cities. The network layout should allow everyone to walk up to a metro station from anywhere in the city.

Cars are the most versatile transportation mode and fulfill all the remaining mobility needs of an urban society. Cars are multipurpose vehicles that can be used for daily commute, shopping, and for going anywhere in the city. They can form a private family unit as well as act as a shared mode of passenger transportation. Cars provide flexibility and door-to-door movement. They are the best means for families to bring home goods and supplies.

Cars powered by Green Hydrogen will round off a fully sustainable urban mobility system. While most cars run on fossil fuels today, hydrogen powered cars have already been introduced in the US and are fast gaining ground on electric as well as internal combustion (IC) technologies. These cars along with metros, cycling, rickshaws, and walking will cover all transportation needs of an urban society. The system will be safe, sustainable, and healthy.

But efficiency becomes extremely critical given the size of our population. India currently has around 3.5 crore cars with very low penetration (~27 per 1000). The developed nations typically have around 500 cars per 1000 population, i.e., one car for every second person. Even if we assume 1 car per 3 people, India will essentially end up needing 40-50 crore cars, in a metro plus car only urban transportation system.

Sharing models can significantly reduce the car requirement. Research suggests a replacement of 9 private cars by the introduction of one shared car. Taxis and self-drive car rentals enable high utilization of each car. Every urban taxi makes around 10-15 trips per day, essentially taking care of the daily transportation needs of at least 5 families or 20 individuals. Renting a car is also becoming more and more convenient with expansion of rental fleets, pick up / drop stations and the introduction of free-floating models. A conservative replacement rate of 5 will bring down the requirement to around 10 crore cars. If we assume one car for every 4 families (average size 4 people), the requirement comes down to 8-9 crore cars. The Metro will be essential to cater to the peak hour requirements and normalize car demand during the day.

Shared utilization makes car use cheaper, and simpler. Increased asset utilization distributes the fixed costs over a larger base of users resulting in a lower cost for every user. While increased utilization can result in higher wear and tear, shared cars undergo maintenance more regularly and professionally. When using shared car models, people don't need to maintain the car themselves. People can also get the experience of riding in different cars.

Shared car use is also safer than private cars. Taxis significantly reduce the risk of driving under stress or under the influence of alcohol. Self-drive cars are usually equipped with additional safety and speed tracking systems. People are more likely to adhere to traffic regulations when using car rentals, as it is more difficult to get away with violations and accidents.

Motorbikes, scooters, auto rickshaws, and buses are not needed in a city with a well-developed metro and car sharing system. Two wheelers are in any case unsafe and make the users completely unproductive while riding. The level of safety that a two-wheeler provides for the rider and the passenger, is compromised to an extent, as it is an open vehicle that is relatively low in weight. Hence, even minor collisions may put the riders at high risk for injuries or even death. Two wheelers do not follow the concept of lanes and violate traffic rules much more than four wheelers. Controlling two wheelers is extremely challenging - building and enforcing foolproof systems is next to impossible. Riding a two-wheeler drains energy and spoils appearance. Auto rickshaws and tempos are also an ad hoc means of transport that is wrought with issues around safety and comfort.

Buses are inefficient as compared to the metro and are much less convenient than cars. Buses are also a big nuisance on urban roads. Driving a bus in a city requires a lot of expertise, strength, and patience. Research has proven that the most common type of road on which bus crashes occur (>73%) is urban. In crashes involving buses, much more people outside get hurt and die, than those inside the bus. Car occupants (34%) are affected the most followed by pedestrians and cyclists (32%). Buses are also an indirect cause of crashes on urban roads. Harassment and crimes are also more difficult to prevent on buses.

Minibuses on the other hand fit well in an urban mobility system. They are a great form of assured transport for schools, offices, factories etc. Their limited capacity allows them to provide door to door service. Their smaller size and high maneuverability enable them to move in harmony with the car traffic. Separate bus lanes are not needed for them. Converting mini buses to hydrogen fuels can also happen much earlier than big buses. Safety becomes a concern with minibuses that offer transportation to the general public. Safety would be best ensured if their use was restricted to organizations and institutions.

An urban mobility system that only has cycles, metro, shared cars and minibuses will be seamless, uniform and equitable. People from all walks of life will move together. Traffic will move smoothly and efficiently. Roads, parking and transit infrastructure will be well defined and developed to high quality standards. Uniform and predictable traffic flows will enable focused development to minimize congestion.

For urban logistics, India uses different types of commercial vehicles and two wheelers. Two wheelers can be replaced by bicycles and efficient use of commercial vehicles. Light and medium commercial vehicles are the ideal options for transportation within the city. They provide flexibility, ease of movement in urban traffic, and ensure high utilization.

Logistics optimization is now a well-developed field. A real time database maps all the elements of the logistics supply chain network. Demand aggregation is done centrally for various logistics needs and the most efficient logistics supply chain combination is adopted.

From a safety standpoint, the use of heavy commercial vehicles (HCV) should be restricted and minimized for intra city logistics. Indian metros already have restricted timings for movement of HCV's. Ideally, HCV movement within the city perimeter should only be allowed from 11pm to 4am.

Commercial vehicles should also be made fully sustainable by transitioning to the use of Green Hydrogen.

In the ideal state, cities will only have pedestrian / cycling paths, electric metro, and shared motor vehicles (cars / minibuses / commercial) running on Green Hydrogen.

For inter-city travel as well, trains and cars are the best transportation system. They are most efficient in the use of energy and resources, offer flexibility, and a high-quality experience. With a deep urban metro network, transit to intercity trains also becomes seamless. Train technologies have rapidly advanced to deliver safe travel at speeds of more than 300 kmph. Urban taxis also offer a smooth way to catch an intercity. Cars are the best complement for intercity travel. Green Hydrogen fueled taxis and car rentals will provide a fully sustainable, flexible, private and comfortable journey experience.

Buses again lose out on fuel efficiency, comfort and travel time. Currently, buses offer more flexibility than trains due to their higher frequency. But cars are the most flexible. Buses are also the preferred alternative for people traveling between cities and towns / villages. Trains are either not available or extremely infrequent for traveling to these smaller settlements. Taxis are not affordable.

In an urban only scenario, there is really no case for buses for intercity travel. In most advanced economies, there is an intercity train almost every hour and, in some cases, more than that. Enforcement of right speed regulations will cap the average speeds of buses to 60 kmph on highways. Trains meanwhile will keep getting faster and soon reach average speeds of 200 kmph even in India. Train travel will also be cheaper and more comfortable.

Flights are currently more competitive than trains for intercity travel over 500 kms. And with the rise of high speed rail, that distance would soon be around 1000 kms. High-speed rail is best suited for journeys of 1 to 5 hours, for which the door-to-door journey time is similar as compared to flying.

High speed rail has pretty much extirpated domestic flights in Europe. The greatest asset of rail travel is that the railway stations are almost always located in the centers of towns and cities, and the slower travel speed is compensated by the fact you can board the train at any station along the line immediately, there is no loitering time at the train station (compared to airports) and the security checks, if any, are much more lenient. Also, there are usually several trains per day (or even per hour) so if you miss one, you can always take another. Moreover, railway coaches are usually more comfortable to travel in than airliner cabins.

Aircraft will take much longer to become fully sustainable. Like cars, aircraft can only become sustainable with the use of Green Hydrogen. While hydrogen cars are already close to being competitive with other fuel technologies, large passenger aircrafts are a decade away from even achieving viability with hydrogen. Getting competitive will take much longer. Governments and large aircraft manufacturers are investing heavily in the field. The good news is that hydrogen does pack a lot of energy per unit mass - three times more than conventional jet fuel. 100 seaters are expected to take off on Hydrogen by 2030.[111]

For now, flying should be discontinued for intercity distances of less than 500 km. Even in the ideal state where both trains and aircraft are running on sustainable energy sources, trains will be more competitive than flights over distances of less than 1000 km.

As India consolidates its industries in the chosen urban centers, intercity logistics will happen at a much bigger scale. Bigger enterprises across sectors would result in bigger shipments. Establishment of distinctive capabilities in various urban locations will also increase the size of

---

[111] "The hydrogen revolution in the skies", Caspar Henderson, Future Planet, BBC, April 8, 2021

shipments. Over time demand patterns will also stabilize and bring certainty to trade flows. The cities will also act as hubs for transportation of raw materials from their region to other cities.

Rail is more resource and energy efficient than trucks to move goods at scale. Economies of scale create low variable costs and intrinsically higher energy efficiencies. Rail offers the potential to move goods more efficiently and with far lower energy consumption and CO_2 emissions. Cost of freight movement by road is INR 2.58/ton-km as compared to INR 1.41/ton-km for rail. Waterways are even more efficient with freight movement costs of INR 1.06/ton-km.[112] While rail freight will keep getting faster and more efficient, truck speeds will be capped on intercity highways.

However, while rail and water perform well under certain conditions, they are not a universal solution for goods transport. They typically are only able to transport goods cost effectively on high volume corridors over long distances. Furthermore, those low-cost modes have longer transit times and are less reliable than trucks. Rail and water are inappropriate for time sensitive transport of high value goods due to the higher inventory costs. An effective mode share, therefore, is one which minimizes total transport cost while meeting the operational requirements of goods shippers.

Rail will keep eating into the trucking share of intercity logistics. Rail capacity, frequency and speeds will keep increasing. Transloading depots will keep getting more efficient. Rail freight containers will become technically equipped to handle all kinds of shipments. Rail will eventually be unbeatable for long distance intercity logistics. The fixed cost of transloading will make rail less competitive only for intercity logistics between nearby cities.

---

[112] "Goods on the Move: Efficiency & Sustainability in Indian Logistics", NITI Aayog and Rocky Mountain Institute, 2018

Rail is safer and more sustainable, and so the government should invest in making rail freight more competitive on intercity routes. Process enhancements and investments should also be made to make transloading more efficient.

Trucks are likely to retain a significant share in the near to medium term of intercity logistics. They will remain the preferred option for time sensitive shipments, those that require considerable customizations and ones with specific handling requirements. Over the long run, trucks can maintain their competitive advantage by transitioning to hydrogen. Hydrogen powered trucks have already been launched in Europe and will likely get competitive with diesel over the next decade.

Trucks and other commercial road vehicles (HCVs, MCVs, LCVs) will be the only logistics transportation mode between the countryside and nearby cities. Agriculture and horticulture produce, and extracted materials would be carried from the sites to the cities in various types of commercial vehicles via road. The distributed nature of these operations will make rail and other modes unviable.

People from the nearby cities will travel to these sites by cars and minibuses. As all these operations would be owned by public and private companies, transportation would be provided for by the companies. People will always have the option of using taxis and car rentals to travel on their own. Clearly segregated pedestrian and cycling tracks should also be built alongside all roads in the countryside.

Now lastly for traveling to tourist destinations, road transport will turn out to be more efficient in most cases. Cars, vans, minibuses and buses will cater to all types of destination travel needs. Small families and groups might prefer car rentals and taxis. Large families and groups could use minibuses and buses. The elderly might just prefer to travel by bus. Given that speed would not be a key criteria in destination travel, buses may end up being the most efficient and cost effective mode. Road transport will also serve the entire logistics requirements of most tourist destinations.

Due to low passenger and freight volumes on most of these routes, development of costly high speed rail infrastructure might not generate sufficient returns. Seasonality in tourism further reduces the viability of rail. Rail would possibly be needed in only a very few tourism hubs and certain mountainous destinations where road journeys become difficult and more strenuous. For some of the extremely remote Himalayan destinations, it might be extremely costly to maintain either road or rail infrastructure. In such cases, small aircrafts would be the best option.

11. Make it large

The Indian manufacturing industry today is black. The industry has indeed outpaced global manufacturing post liberalization. But the growth has primarily been achieved in a broad-based low-cost manner. Capital and resource constraints, and the much superior capabilities of the developed world, have forced India to become a low-cost producer. The low-cost production environment results in low levels of quality, significantly lower productivity, poor resource efficiency, high levels of untreated waste and emissions. The manufacturing industry in India, produces the highest levels of emissions and industrial waste per unit of output, in the world.

The Indian manufacturing sector's gross value added in 2019 was nearly $400 billion. Gross capital increased around $20 billion in 2019. MSME (micro, small and medium enterprises), which is essentially the informal and unorganized sector, accounts for 45% of the manufacturing output. India has the sixth largest manufacturing output in the world.

But India's manufacturing output per capita is one of the lowest in the world. We are not even in the top 100 countries. India's manufacturing output per capita is ~$310. The manufacturing GVA per capita for developed countries is more than 10 times that of India (Germany $10,000, South Korea $9,200, Austria $8,500, Denmark $7,700, Japan $7,700, Sweden $7,200, US $7,000, Italy $5,200, Norway $5,200, Israel $4,900, France $4,200, UK $3700, Spain $3,400, Australia $3,300, China $2,800).

On average, exports contribute ~30% to the GDP of developed countries. US, UK and France have a sizable trade deficit implying a further increase in the per capita domestic consumption. The trade surplus of the remaining set of developed countries is not significant enough to suggest a lower value of domestic consumption.

So, in a stable developed state, a self-sufficient India will need to have at least 10 times the current manufacturing output i.e., ~$4 trillion (2020 prices).

During FY 2015-2020, India's manufacturing GVA has grown at a CAGR of ~8%. Producer price inflation has averaged ~5% during this period. Hence, the real growth in manufacturing GVA has been 2.9%. Sustained real growth of 2.9% YoY will only get India's real manufacturing GVA to $1,670 billion in 50 years.

To reach $4 trillion, India's manufacturing output needs to grow at ~4.75% YoY for 50 years in real terms. Assuming the same levels of producer price inflation as the last five years i.e. 5%, the nominal rate of growth would need to be ~9.75%. That translates to achieving a nominal manufacturing output of ~$45 trillion in 50 years.

As India moves towards becoming a sustainable urbanized nation, manufacturing will need to rapidly transform and grow. Initial rapid transformation towards a focused and efficient manufacturing set up will be critical. It will allow India to maximize resource efficiency and build leading capabilities in the areas of focus. The domestic industry would then be delivering the highest levels of quality. At that stage, the industry would be equipped to increase production levels without making compromises on quality and sustainability. The manufacturing industry can then propel urbanization and gradually become the core of India's development and economy.

The current contribution of various manufacturing sectors is: basic metals and metal products (15.7%), chemicals and chemical products (13.6%), food products, beverages and tobacco (12.1%), textiles, leather and footwear (12.1%), transport equipment (8.6%), other non-metallic mineral products (6.4%), machinery, n.e.c. (6.4%), electrical and optical equipment (5.7%), mfg., n.e.c. and recycling (5.7%), coke, refined petroleum and nuclear fuel (5.0%), rubber and plastic products (3.6%), pulp, paper, printing and publishing (2.9%), and wood and products of wood (2.1%).

Going forward, manufacturing needs to drive urbanization while ensuring sustainability.

Urban infrastructure typically consists of residential housing (40%), transport, energy, and water infrastructure (25%), institutional and commercial buildings (20%), and industrial sites (15%).

The high-rise urban infrastructure would need building materials, structural components, machinery, equipment, sanitary fittings, fixtures (metallic, ceramic, wood etc.), electrical systems and products, and energy.

Manufacturing activity needs to be scaled up substantially in the core areas to build the high-rise cities. Materials and products need to be of high quality for the envisaged development. Given the magnitude of the development, high levels of resource and energy efficiency are extremely critical to avoid disastrous environmental consequences.

Due to the predominance of tiny enterprises and informality in the industrial sector, India has found it difficult to harness the economies of scale, adopt new technologies and regularly upgrade its capabilities. SMEs are unable to cultivate the right skills and management practices for establishing and integrating knowledge created by external partners with in-house practices and innovation processes. Given that economies of scale go hand in hand with higher productivity, the predominance of micro-enterprises has proven to be a barrier to growth.

Over 1950 to 1980, slow GDP growth was accompanied by a growth strategy dependent upon heavy industry first, combined with reservation of products for small firms with the objective of generating employment. The set of products reserved for small enterprises had grown and consisted of more than 1200 products at the beginning of reform in 1991. Over the years the number of reserved products was reduced to 500 by 2005, but it took more than fifty years to end this. This has led to the emergence of underdeveloped informal firms employing informal workers, all operating in a low-level equilibrium trap of low wages – low technology - low productivity. Additionally, labor laws for the organized or formal sector firms, made them less competitive on cost against the unorganized sector, and also reduced the demand for workers in the formal sector.

In manufacturing, scale, quality, efficiency, productivity, innovation, and sustainability have a strong positive correlation with each other. Focus on the domestic market and indigenous production is critical for the Indian manufacturing industry to become an advanced industrial economy. Essentially, domestic focus, indigenous production, scale, quality, efficiency, productivity, innovation and sustainability, are all interdependent. An analysis of each sector would help understand the interlinkages and figure out the best path for the Indian manufacturing industry to successfully transform itself.

Aggregates, cement, iron & steel and aluminum form the biggest components in the construction of buildings and other infrastructure. Basic metals viz. iron and aluminum are also the largest constituents in the production of automobiles and capital goods.

Aggregates

In 2020 the global anthropogenic (created by humans) mass outweighed all of Earth's living biomass.[113] Sand, gravel, and crushed rock, together referred to as construction aggregates, constitute the largest share of the anthropogenic mass and are the most extracted solid materials by mass.

---

[113] "Sustainability of the global sand system in the Anthropocene", Aurora Torres, Mark U.Simoni, Jakob K. Keiding, Daniel B. Müller, Sophus O.S.E. zu Ermgassen, Jianguo Liu, Jochen A.G. Jaeger, Marten Winter, Eric F. Lambin, May 21, 2021

Aggregates are the most basic material used in construction. They constitute around 80% of the concrete mix (high-rises and bridges) and over 90% of an asphalt mix (road surface, pavement, embankment etc.).

On average, 38,000 tons of aggregates are necessary to construct one lane mile of interstate highway. Construction of the average home requires 400 tons of aggregate, while the average size of a school or hospital requires 15,000 tons. The density of aggregates varies from 1400 kg/m3 to 1700 kg/m3.

The residential high-rises of each (~30 lac apartments) will need ~750 million cubic meters or over 1 billion metric tons of aggregates. This assumes 250 cubic meters or 375 tons per high-rise apartment.

The total aggregate requirement for each city would therefore be ~2.5 billion tonnes or around 2 billion cubic meters (assuming residential to be 40% of the total infrastructure). The total requirement for the 130 plus Indian cities would be around 325 billion tonnes.

The current estimated annual output of aggregates in India is around 3.4 billion tonnes.[114]

The 500 sq km lake planned for each city would provide much more than the aggregates required for building the city. The volume of each lake with an average depth of 20m will be 10 billion cubic meters. The material that is dug up will largely have the composition of aggregate. The total tonnage generated would be around 15 billion tonnes, more than 5 times the amount of aggregate required for the city's development.

Aggregate sourcing from the planned lake will create positive value for nature and humanity. It will resolve the biggest concerns with the aggregates industry - the ecosystem

---

[114] "Overview of Indian aggregate industry", Sanjay Nikam, Indian Cement Review, Construction World, November 1, 2020

damage, and the energy spent in transportation. Distributed aggregate sourcing by small players causes extensive damage to the local ecosystems. Sand and gravel resources are easy to extract but have a high ecological value and provide essential ecosystem services such as flood protection, food production, and groundwater storage and filtering. Ecosystem degradation associated with mining harms species and ecosystems such as wetlands, rivers, coastal dunes, and seagrass meadows. Ecological restoration of mining sites requires scientific planning, which is an extremely resource intensive and lengthy process. The transportation of bulky aggregates leaves a huge carbon dent on the environment. Sourcing aggregates within the city perimeter would therefore lead to huge energy savings.

The huge scale of these lake sites will also help consolidate the aggregate industry and make it efficient and sustainable.

The proportion of electricity used in quarrying and processing would be significantly enhanced. Cities will be able to provide direct access to uninterrupted power supply throughout the area of excavation, where quarrying and refining is done.

Consolidation will enable the companies to maximize energy efficiency. The industry is highly energy intensive, and the usage of advanced equipment is most critical for reducing energy use. Once the city blueprints and the lake boundaries are decided upon, it will make sense to award the excavation contract to one or maybe two players. The massive scale of these contracts will enable the players to procure the best equipment and technology. The expensive equipment would need to be imported from foreign companies such as Terex, KEMCO (Japan), BHS (Germany), and CDE (Ireland), among others.

After the government restricts quarrying to only these city lake locations, the heavily fragmented and unorganized industry will transform into a large-scale organized industry. Most ideal would be to have a few national players who can build and deploy leading global capabilities and drive maximum scale efficiencies. The well capitalized large players will also be able to follow environmental, health and safety regulations. The need for scale has been increasing already and the industry is consolidating with more and more organized players coming in. Increasing competition for land, higher quality requirements, and stricter regulations, have been increasing both capital and operational costs.

The aggregates industry will need to work in close coordination with city and lake development authorities and infrastructure developers. There will also be a case for vertical integration between infrastructure developers and aggregate producers.

Managing the construction waste would be critical in an urban development context. Operating within city perimeters, the excavation companies will need to follow guidelines to control dust.

The huge amounts of excess aggregate will enable several forms of large-scale development. At a national level, the excess aggregate could be used to reclaim land in the coastal areas, revive barren lands and restore damaged landscapes and ecosystems. Cities will need to have clear plans for deploying the materials for various purposes viz. development and restoration of mountains and landscapes, processing for other minerals, development of materials etc.

The development of high-rise infrastructure will also necessitate demolition of existing low-rise infrastructure in cities, towns and villages. Professional capabilities are essential to maximize reuse of the demolition waste for urban infrastructure development. Demolition companies also need to have the capabilities to fully process the waste generated and clear out the land parcels.

Cities need comprehensive assessment and quantification of construction and demolition waste generation, to plan adequate infrastructure and systems for treatment and management. Characterization of the C&D waste is necessary for the management plan, including collection, transportation and storage, processing techniques and technologies used, and products to be manufactured out of recycled waste.[115] The method for quantification has to consider the new-age construction materials.

Cement

Cement is the other important constituent of the concrete mix which is the most extensively used building material. There is no real threat of substitutes for cement, as it is already replacing bitumen – a widely used alternative. Cement also remains to be the primary constituent of ultra high-performance concrete (UHPC) that is being increasingly used in high-rise construction.

India's production of cement in 2018-19 stood at 337 million tonnes. India is the world's second largest cement producer with a cumulative production capacity of 540 million tonnes per annum ('MTPA') in 2020.[116]

The total cement required to build the cities and other public infrastructure would be around 50-70 billion tonnes. Typically, a concrete mix is about 10 to 15 percent cement, 60 to 75 percent aggregate and 15 to 20 percent water. Therefore for 325 billion tonnes of aggregate, around 60 billion tonnes of cement would be required.

Around 100 billion tonnes of limestone would produce the required quantity of cement. Typically, about 1.65 tonnes of limestone and 0.4 tonnes of clay are quarried for each tonne of cement produced. 75% of the limestone is currently used for manufacturing cement.

Cement raw materials, especially limestone, are geologically widespread and (luckily) abundant. India's total reserves of

---

[115] "Another brick off the wall: Improving Construction and Demolition Waste Management in Indian Cities", Avikal Somvanshi, Center for Science and Environment, August 25, 2020

[116] Indian minerals yearbook 2017, Indian Bureau of Mines

limestone of all categories and grades have been estimated at ~200 billion tonnes.

The availability of raw materials is the key determining factor in the location of cement plants. They are normally located in close proximity to limestone deposits and ideally close to other major raw materials (clay and gypsum).

There are 7 cement clusters in India. They are Satna (Madhya Pradesh), Chandrapur (North Andhra Pradesh and Maharashtra), Gulbarga (North Karnataka and East AP), Chanderia (South Rajasthan + Jawad & Neemuch in MP), Bilaspur (Chattisgarh), Yerraguntla (South AP), and Nalgonda (Central AP).

The cement industry has been going through a phase of consolidation with large Indian cement players preying on smaller ones and foreign cement majors acquiring controlling stake in Indian majors. The consolidation is enabling extended reach and increased revenues, better economies of scale and technology upgradation. ~95% of the installed capacity is accounted for by large producers, around 40 in number. The top 20 companies control 90% of the market. 40% of the market is controlled by two groups. With the adoption of modern production methods and assimilation of state-of-the-art technology, the large Indian cement plants are today fairly good in both energy and material efficiency and produce consistent high-quality cement.[117]

But cement is one of the most energy and freight intensive industries and is a big carbon emitter. The energy consumption is estimated at approximately 2% of world total, and 5% of industry total. The fuel mix in the industry is carbon intensive, and the calcination process itself produces CO_2, so that in total the cement industry contributes ~7% of the global CO_2 emissions. In a modern cement plant, 60% of

---

[117] "Energy and Material Efficiency in Cement Industry India", Business Bliss Consultants FZE, December 10, 2019

the CO2 emitted by a cement plant results from the calcinations of limestone, 30% from combustion of fuels in the kiln and 10% from other downstream activities.

Carbon capture and electric kilns could make cement manufacturing almost completely green. Technology has been developed and proven for both but needs strong policy interventions for the economics to work.

Post-combustion CO2 capture technologies are the preferred option to retrofit existing facilities, as the CO2 is captured from the exhaust gas of the cement plant, thus not affecting the existing cement production process.[118] Among the available post-combustion technologies, chemical absorption with liquid solvents is the most mature technology: to date, it has reached the largest demonstration scale at cement plants, and provides the least risky pathway for the retrofitting of existing facilities. Moreover, solvent and process development are expected to lead to further cost reductions as the technology deploys in the cement sector, as has previously occurred in the power sector. In fact, this is the technology selected by two of the commercial scale projects in the pipeline. On the other hand, although with a lesser technology readiness level, solid sorbents based post-combustion CO2 capture processes also show great promise.

Even the large players find it unviable to invest in carbon capture, use and storage.[119] The installation costs of capture technologies run into hundreds of millions of dollars, and there is a significant variable cost, currently in the range of $50-100 per ton of CO2. The cement cost shoots up manifold making them uncompetitive in the global market.

The Indian government needs to simply finance these investments through Green Funds. Central Government

---

[118] "CO2 Capture, Use, and Storage in the Cement Industry: State of the Art and Expectations", Marta G. Plaza, Sergio Martínez and Fernando Rubiera, Instituto de Ciencia y Tecnología del Carbono, October 30, 2020

[119] "Cement's CO2 Emissions Are Solved Technically, But Not Economically", Michael Barnard, November 26, 2019

agencies need to finance these Green Funds by issuing Government backed securities (equity and debt) to investors. Financing should be secured as loans / investments / contributions from the RBI, domestic banks and financial institutions, international bodies and large global corporations.

The second important area is the adoption of electric kilns. There are ongoing efforts to change the plants' fuel mix towards alternative fuels that leave a lower carbon footprint. But the best path is using electricity from the grid, and letting the grid take care of the fuel mix. Currently, the use of coal and other fossil fuels is much cheaper than the use of electricity. Hence, the electric kiln technology, although technically feasible, has not gained commercial success.

India should plan a transition to electric kilns in sync with the planned renewable increase in grids across the country. The transition should be initiated in plants that are located in regions with the highest expected additions of renewable capacity. Viability gap funding should be provided from the central pool of green funds, until the use of fossil fuels is significantly cheaper than electricity.

Going forward, industry consolidation and capacity additions should also be done to facilitate the shift to carbon neutral cement production.

Iron & Steel

Iron and Steel is the next most essential industry for urbanization and infrastructure development. The use of iron and steel across various industries further boosts sustainability as the products are built to last, avoid waste creation and can be recycled.

But India faces a huge shortage of iron ore. India has around 5-8 billion tons of reserves of iron ore (Hematite mainly) whose mining is technically and commercially feasible without damaging the environment.[120] The total iron ore resources of India have been estimated at around 28.5 billion tonnes.

India will need around 10 billion tonnes of iron ore just for the residential high-rises. Around 7.5 kg of steel is needed per sq ft in high-rise residential real estate, which translates to 15,000 kg of steel per 2000 sq ft apartment. 40 crore apartments would require roughly 6 billion metric tonnes of iron / steel. Given that 1.6 tonnes of iron ore produces a tonne of pure iron, India roughly needs 10 billion tonnes of iron ore.

Commercial and industrial real estate and public infrastructure (roads, railways, bridges, airports etc.) would need at least 15 billion tonnes of iron ore. Residential real estate is around 40% of the total infrastructure in a developed scenario, and iron & steel is more heavily used than in residential real estate.

Besides infrastructure, steel would always be needed to make heavy equipment, automobiles, household products, appliances, electrical equipment etc. All these other categories together consume as much steel today as is consumed by overall infrastructure.

The rational approach would be to import as much as possible, out of the total 20-25 billion tonnes needed for the one-time infrastructure build up. Over the next 25-30 years, India will need to import around a billion tonnes of iron ore annually. China is currently importing around a billion tonnes every year. There are multiple countries (Australia, Brazil) that have a significant surplus. India will need to collaborate with China to ensure supply continuity and keep the prices in check.

India is currently the second largest steel producer after China. In the last few years, we have been producing a little over 100 MT of crude steel and around 135 MT of finished

---

[120] "Chapter 2: Indian iron ore resources and exploitation", Iron & Steel Vision 2020, Indian Bureau of Mines

steel. The total production capacity for crude steel is ~140 MT. The industry is planning to achieve a cumulative capacity of 300 MTPA by 2031 and become self-sufficient in manufacturing several specialized grades. The planned capacity expansion is expected to require Rs 10 lakh crore incremental capital investments by 2030–2031.[121]

To fulfill the urbanization requirement, India will need to ramp up capacity to around a billion tonnes in 10-15 years. China grew its crude steel production from ~100 MT in 2000 to over a billion tonnes in 2020. It reached 500 MT in 2007. The industry has evolved over the last two decades and capacity build is likely to be much more efficient now. A clear mandate can help India seamlessly build up the needed capacity.

India should also leverage the excess steel production capacity in the developed world (especially South Korea, Japan and Russia) and China.

The large Indian steel companies are ready to scale up in an efficient and sustainable manner. The private sector accounts for over 85% of the production of crude and finished steel. There are around 10 large companies including public sector enterprises. Each of these has integrated steel plants and understand the advanced technologies needed to ensure high levels of efficiency and low carbon footprint.

Some of the Best Available Technologies (BAT) have been adopted by the Indian steel industry for improving energy efficiency & mitigation of GHG emissions.[122] These include power generation from the waste heat and blast furnace exhaust gasses, improving blast furnace productivity, improving coal efficiency, cleaning the gasses produced in the furnace, energy monitoring and management systems, reusing heat for steel rolling, eliminating the need to reheat

---

[121] Annual reports, Ministry of Steel, Government of India

[122] "Efficiency in the Indian iron and steel industry - an application of data envelopment analysis", Roma Mitra Debnath, V.J. Sebastian, Indian Institute of Public Administration, April 2014

materials and furnaces, energy efficient technologies for hot strip and casting mills etc.

Scale of production facility is a key determinant in maximizing energy and material efficiency. Integrated steel plants with a capacity of more than 5 MT are able to afford the high fixed costs needed for higher efficiency. Currently, around 50 per cent of the production is done by small and medium private manufacturing units that are technically as well as scale inefficient.[123] Restricting production to only large integrated facilities will also help optimize the supply chain networks and build scale efficient transportation systems that minimize energy and resources.

Energy consumption, even in most of the integrated steel plants in India, is generally high at 6-6.5 Giga Calorie per tonne of crude steel as compared to 4.5-5.0 in steel plants abroad. The higher rate of energy consumption is mainly due to obsolete technologies including problems in retrofitting modern technologies in old plants, old shop floor & operating practices, poor quality of raw material viz. high ash coal/coke, high alumina iron ore etc. The energy consumption in steel plants is, however, gradually reducing because of technological upgradation, utilization of waste heats, use of better quality inputs, etc.

Material value productivity in India is still very low. In Japan and Korea, less than 1.1 tonnes (and in several developed countries 1.05 tonnes) of crude steel is required to produce a tonne of saleable steel. In India, the average is still high at 1.2 tonnes.

The lack of modern technological and capital inputs and weak infrastructural facilities lead to a more time consuming and expensive process of steel making and yield an inferior quality of steel. The country depends on imports for high value-added (HVA) steel because of a lack of sufficient scale

---

[123] Indian minerals yearbook Iron Ore 57th edition, Indian Bureau of Mines, Ministry of Mines, Government of India, March 2019

for domestic production for such steel grades. In India, HVA steel comprises about 8 percent of the finished steel production compared with the world average of about 20 percent and South Korea achieving 35 percent share of HVA steel in finished steel production. The industry needs to invest in technical capabilities to fulfill the HVA steel demand from the capital goods and automotive sectors.

India has the opportunity to become a global leader in the steel industry. During this phase of expansion, the domestic steel industry can build and acquire leading capabilities. If planned well, in the long run, the Indian steel industry can be fully self-sufficient, one of the most technologically advanced, and be part of the elite group that drives the global industry.

The ten-fold scale up will necessitate massive investments. The large capital will allow Indian companies to acquire the latest technologies for delivering the highest levels of efficiency (material and energy) and quality and minimizing their carbon footprint.

During this growth phase, India can get at par with global peers on all fronts. A comparison of Indian steel producers with global best-in-class peers highlights an 80 percent lag in R&D spending (as a percent of revenue), a 30 percent lag in CO_2 emissions (per ton of crude steel), a 25 percent lag in energy intensity (per ton of crude steel), a 4 percent lag in yield, and a 6 percent lag in capacity utilization.[124] Both greenfield and brownfield expansion projects should enable the adoption of latest technologies for higher blast furnace productivity, reduced emissions, water conservation, and digitalization.

India will need to build domestic capabilities for producing the highest quality steel and steel products. After India reaches the developed stage, steel requirement for

---

[124] "Rewriting the growth story for India's steel industry", Rahul Mishra, Nishant Nishchal, Manish Mathur, Mahak Gupta, Kearney, January 21, 2021

infrastructure will reduce significantly. But high-quality steel will always be needed for consumer-oriented industries viz. appliances, containers, utensils, automobiles etc. Therefore, to build sustainable competitive advantage globally, India needs to get integrated with the global centers of excellence. Over time, India should be equipped to design and manufacture the highest quality steel products, without needing to import steel, technology or equipment.

Now given that, today India is heavily dependent on the world for material, energy, coal and technology, it will have to follow the global standards of sustainability. The world today is more conscious than ever about climate change and the damaging repercussions of unsustainable growth are apparent to everyone. Every ton of steel produced in 2018 emitted on average 1.85 tons of carbon dioxide, equating to about 5-8% (varying estimates) of global carbon dioxide emissions.[125] The world can simply not afford for India to fulfill its steel demand with current production methods.

Unless India fully commits to the highest standards of sustainability, efficiency and quality, India will not be able to garner global support. Besides, adopting the latest technologies for maximizing energy and material efficiency, carbon capture & storage, and minimizing coal use, is critical for India to get competitive in an increasingly regulated global steel industry. The massive scale of the required expansion will make it viable for the Indian steel players to acquire even the most expensive technologies for reducing GHGs and increasing energy efficiency.

To support the massive expansion, there will also be a need to accelerate the purchase of captive coking coal mines globally. India's steel industry depends on imports for coking coal, a key raw material in steel manufacturing. Eighty-five percent of the coking coal that Indian steel plants require is imported compared with countries such as China and South Korea,

---

[125] Steel production and environmental impact, Greenspec

where the share of coking coal imports required is 15 percent and 11 percent respectively.

In a well-planned expansion, the industry will be able to increase the share of EAF (electric arc furnaces) production which is more energy efficient and produces lower emissions than the blast and induction furnaces. The demolition waste from the cities and towns will provide a huge volume of iron and steel scrap. Recycled steel is a key input needed for all steel making process routes. EAFs can be charged with up to 100% of recycled steel and basic oxygen furnaces with approximately 30%. Use of scrap metal leads to significant energy and raw material savings: over 1,400 kg of iron ore, 740 kg of coal, and 120 kg of limestone are saved for every 1,000 kg of steel scrap made into new steel.[126]

India should also invest heavily in the usage of biomass. CO2 emissions are unavoidable, but they could be reduced by means of biomass-derived fuels and reductants applications. Biomass can replace fossil fuels in sintering or pelletizing, substitute coke as a reducing agent and fuel in the blast furnace, substitute pulverized coal injected (PCI) as a fuel in the blast furnace; substitute coal-based char utilized for recarburizing the steel and can be used for reducing pre-reduced feeds.

India should act as the world's laboratory for achieving zero CO2 emission levels. Several technologies are currently being developed and are in different stages of technical and commercial readiness. Top gas recycling blast furnace (TGRBF), carbon capture and storage (CCS), substitution of pulverized coal injection (PCI) with biomass, steelmaking process with hydrogen direct reduction of iron ore (H-DR) and using biomass in EAF, are the current technologies that will result in maximum CO2 reduction.

---

[126] "Decarbonization challenge for steel", Christian Hoffman, Benedikt Zeumer, Michel Van Hoey, McKinsey, June 3, 2020

The deployment of carbon capture and storage (CCS) in a steel plant can reduce carbon dioxide emissions from existing plants without major modifications. A full-scale deployment of the TGR and CCS technologies is now possible. The potential for CO2 reduction is around 5–10% from TGR alone, 50–60% with TGR technology combined with carbon storage (TGRBF + CCS), and over 80% with TGR with biomass-based BF and carbon storage (TGRBF + CCS / biomass). While the capital cost of TGRBF + CCS / biomass is around 50% more, the operating cost is only around 5% more than conventional BF/BOF.[127]

Aluminum

Aluminum is the most abundant metal in the earth's crust (8.23% by mass), almost twice as abundant as iron. Aluminum is widely regarded as the building material for the modern age. In high-rise construction, it is widely used for windows, roofing, facades, cladding, curtain walling and structural glazing, prefabricated buildings, architectural hardware, H&V, shop fitting and partitions.[128] Aluminum is also used extensively in plant, ladders and scaffolding. Aluminum enables every possible architectural concept to be realized – regardless of whether it is a new build or a modernization.

Aluminum is the second most widely specified metal in building after steel and is used in all sectors from commercial building to domestic dwelling.[129] One of Aluminum's primary appeals to specifiers is its exceptional strength to weight ratio. It is also far less susceptible to brittle fractures. The material's low modulus of elasticity enables temperature induced stresses to be accommodated.

---

[127] "Pathways for Low-Carbon Transition of the Steel Industry - A Swedish Case Study", Alla Toktarova, Ida Karlsson, Johan Rootzén, Lisa Göransson, Mikael Odenberger and Filip Johnsson, Department of Space, Earth and Environment, Chalmers University of Technology, Department of Economics, University of Gothenburg, July 27, 2020

[128] "Use of Aluminium In Building Construction", engineeringcivil.com

[129] "Aluminum: A Building Material", Howard Precision Metals Inc.

Aluminum is also gaining prominence as it makes buildings more energy efficient.[130] It is much more heat reflective than other metals which prevents the interiors from getting hot. An aluminum roof will reflect the light from the sun and never get hot in the first place, which can decrease inside temperatures as much as 15 degrees Fahrenheit when compared to steel. This is especially critical on the Indian subcontinent. Other metals such as galvanized steel absorb more heat and energy, and also lose more of their reflectivity as they weather. In conjunction with heat reflectivity, aluminum is also less emissive than other metals, and so becomes useful in efficient heating. Due to these energy saving properties, aluminum qualifies under LEED (Leadership in Energy and Environmental Design) standards.

Besides construction (25%), other major uses for aluminum metal are in transportation (23%), consumer durables (air conditioners, refrigerators and utensils), electronics and electrical equipment, machinery and equipment (processing equipment, pipes and tools), furniture and packaging.

Aluminum is 100% recyclable and can be recycled infinitely without losing any of its properties.

The global per capita stock of aluminum in use in society (i.e. in cars, buildings, electronics, etc.) is 80 kg. The developed countries have 350–500 kg per capita and less-developed ones have 35 kg per capita.

A population of 150 crore in India would need around 500 million tonnes of Aluminum, which requires more than 2 billion tonnes of bauxite. The annual bauxite mining output in India is currently around 25 MT.[131]

The developed countries and China continue to use the bauxite reserves of Africa and Asia. Bauxite is the principal

---

[130] "Technological Advances and Trends in Modern High-Rise Buildings", Jerzy Szolomicki, and Hanna Golasz-Szolomicka, Faculty of Civil Engineering and Faculty of Architecture, Wroclaw University of Science and Technology, August 26, 2019

[131] Aluminum and Alumina, Indian Minerals Yearbook 2017 56th edition, Indian Bureau of Mines, Ministry of Mines, Government of India, March 2018

aluminum-containing ore for the commercial production of aluminum metal. Bauxite is processed and transformed using the Bayer process into alumina, which is then smelted using the Hall–Héroult process, resulting in the final aluminum metal.

India has so far discovered 660 million tonnes of viable reserves and an additional 2.9 billion tonnes of remaining resources (economically unviable currently). Importing from countries with large surplus reserves (Guinea, Australia, Vietnam, Brazil, Jamaica) will enable India to meet its requirements during the development phase.

India is a significant producer of primary aluminum and is a net exporter currently. The current annual production is around 3 million tonnes. The total global production is around 100 MT out of which 2/3rds is primary production from the ore and 1/3rd is secondary production from scrap. China accounts for over 55% of the global production. As of 2019, the world's largest smelters of aluminum are located in China, India, Russia, Canada, and the UAE.

The second stage of primary aluminum production comprises the electrolytic reduction of aluminum oxide to aluminum. The electrolytic process, known as the Hall-Héroult process, is carried out in smelting plants. This is the most energy-intensive stage in the aluminum production chain requiring massive amounts of electricity. The producers tend to locate smelters in places where electric power is both plentiful and inexpensive.

Aluminum smelting requires large amounts of electricity, typically around 14-15 MWh per tonne of metal produced. Indirect emissions from electricity generation consumed during the smelting process account for 61% of the total GHG emissions in the aluminum sector worldwide (mining to semi-finished products). The secondary route of aluminum production, i.e. from recycling, reduces energy consumption by 95%, as compared to the primary route. Expanding secondary production through better scrap collection and sorting will be important to raise energy efficiency and decarbonize the aluminum industry.

The energy mix of the grid or the source of captive power plants therefore has a major impact on primary aluminum's carbon footprint. aluminum smelting plants are usually placed in locations different from the mine sites; logistics and access to electricity at favorable terms are the main factors determining the plant's position. Over 90% of European production used non-fossil sources of electricity in 2019. Hydropower is the primary source of electricity for aluminum smelters in Europe. Coal and oil have been progressively phased out from the energy sources to power European smelters. However, in China, which accounts for more than half of global supply, electricity used by aluminum smelters is typically generated by coal-fired plants (88%). The aluminum industry can assist with grid decarbonization by providing flexibility services that would help integrate a higher portion of variable renewables. Electricity producers can assist by offering electricity pricing incentives to aluminum producers using demand management systems.

Interestingly, Chinese smelters now have a much lower total energy consumption compared to the world average since 2005, driven by a far more efficient electrolysis process on average. Chinese smelters' lower process energy intensity reflects the installation of new capacity with the best available technology over the last years, in combination with the closure of older, less efficient facilities. India should follow China's lead in adopting the latest technologies for existing and new smelters.

Carbon capture, utilization and storage (CCUS) and the use of inert anodes have the potential to make aluminum completely green.[132] The world's leading aluminum

---

[132] "Sustainability aspects of Bauxite and Aluminium", Joint Research Center, European Commission, July 2021

producers are likely to commercialize carbon free smelting by 2024.

The Indian aluminum industry is well consolidated amongst 1 public and 4-5 private players. The entire value chain of bauxite mining, production of alumina and aluminum production is controlled by these companies. There are a total of around 10 facilities with varying degrees of integration. Most of these also have captive coal mines and coal based power generation.

Heavy engineering

In the metals and mining industries, the most critical gap that India needs to plug is in core engineering capability. India needs to build domestic enterprises that possess end to end capabilities for building efficient and sustainable manufacturing facilities. India currently relies almost completely on foreign engineering companies to provide technology and equipment for new plant installations. There are several multinational companies involved in metals and mining engineering and technology, with most of them headquartered in Europe, US, or Japan.

Danieli (revenue ~$3 billion), is an Italian multinational company with product lines that cover blast furnaces, DR plants, seamless and welded pipe mills. They cover the whole spectrum of ironmaking and steelmaking plants, from iron ore to any steel finished products. The main business units of Danieli are ironmaking and steelmaking (direct reduction, scrap processing, melting, refining and recovery plants), flat products (casting, rolling, processing and finishing lines), and long products (casting, rolling, tube, pipes, extrusion, forging and finishing lines).

SMS Group (revenue around $3.5 billion), headquartered in Germany, is a plant supplier to the metallurgical industry for steel, aluminum, copper and metals. It provides plant construction and mechanical engineering services. The Company offers plants and machinery solutions for casting, cold rolling, forging, hot rolling, metallurgy, mini mills, and tube and pipe making services.

Paul Wurth (turnover around $500 million) is a Luxembourg based international engineering company and an established technology provider for the global ironmaking industry. Its portfolio includes design and construction of complete blast furnace and coke oven plants, direct reduction plants, environmental protection technologies, and waste treatment and recycling facilities. It also provides products and services in engineering, project management, site supervision, commissioning assistance, operator consulting and after-sales, with a special focus on digital solutions.

Metso Outotec (~$1.5 billion revenue), is a company Finnish company and frontrunner in sustainable minerals processing technologies, end-to-end solutions and services globally. The company helps aggregates, mining, metals refining and recycling customers improve efficiency, productivity and reduce risks.

Sarralle, a Spanish multinational, is a leader in EPC Projects for Steel Melting Plants, Rolling Mills and Finishing Lines. Its business lines are steel melting plant (designs, manufactures and provides broad line of products and complete turnkey solutions for steel works), rolling mill (engineering, procurement & construction projects for the processing of semi-products needed in a diverse range of end products), processing lines (design, construction, installation and commissioning of lines for the processing of entire range of metal coils), environment & energy, and workshop storage systems (design, manufacture and commercialization of products for storage and optimization of working spaces).

Primetals Technologies is part of Mitsubishi Heavy Industries (MHI), a Japanese conglomerate, with $37 billion in revenues. It is a worldwide leading engineering, plant-building and lifecycle services partner for the metals industry offering a complete technology, product and service portfolio. It was created in 2015 for MHI to closely collaborate with Siemens, in the field of metals machinery and develop an enterprise that would be renowned for its technical and business excellence.

The original equipment manufacturer (OEM) landscape includes a few other large enterprises such as Siemens, Rockwell Automation, ABB, Honeywell etc. They are technology giants and offer solutions for almost all industries. They have evolved from having their own manufacturing operations to being a solution provider. They own the core technologies (design, research and IP) and operate through a tightly held network of subcontractors. These subcontractors produce systems, components and parts usually for a part of the production process.

India simply cannot rely on imports for its heavy engineering needs. Based on estimates, for doubling the installed capacity of crude steel to 300 million tonnes (in 10 years), India will need capital goods worth $136 billion. For ramping up the capacity to a billion tonnes, the requirement will be more than $500 billion. The ramp up across all sectors of metals and mining will necessitate investments of more than $2 trillion. India might actually be able to afford the capex but will find it very difficult to afford the on-going maintenance and replacement costs. Besides, India would then have completely lost the opportunity to build domestic capabilities. The core engineering companies across the world are tightly held operations where foreigners are simply not allowed. People from the developing world are still kept at bay from working in manufacturing units, especially in original equipment manufacturers. They are usually given administrative jobs and not allowed to build a full understanding of the research, design and production value chain. Even if India gains some experience while working in multinationals that set up facilities in India, it would be of no use, as there would be little market opportunity left for India to have a viable business case for developing its own enterprises. India cannot expect to be the OEM for the development of Africa. The case is right now to serve your own needs.

Only if we stand up to fulfill our own needs, can we expect to fulfill the needs of others across the globe. Core engineering capabilities are essential for India to be a strong independent nation. Unless Indians build these technologies on their own, India will always be dependent on the developed nations and will keep paying a premium. In doing so, India will sacrifice its natural resources, lose the opportunity to create meaningful employment and reduce inequality, and will essentially end up staying a slave colony. Indians will remain spineless. If we take a shortcut to development, India will simply become a puppet in the hands of the large global corporations. We have over-produced and so we are responsible for building an ecosystem that can sustain that population. Every leading technology company became big only because they built technologies for their countries' needs. In serving their own nation, they did everything with their own hands.

Building domestic heavy engineering capabilities is also the best financial alternative and strategy. First, it will save us the premium we need to pay for engineering technology, equipment, maintenance, and upgrades. Second, once we start building domestic capabilities, we will have a better understanding of the technology requirements and landscape. We will therefore have a better understanding of value and will have greater leverage in dealing with foreign players. Right now, we are only able to create leverage by comparing the different solutions and alternatives presented by the various technology companies. Third, building domestic capabilities requires investment by Indian financial institutions, whereas, purchasing technology from foreign players will necessitate raising foreign capital and dilution of Indian equity in some form or the other. Fourth, acquisitions will actually become cheaper when India decides against purchasing engineering technology and equipment.

OEMs across the world are facing a slowdown and will become unviable especially if India decides to stop buying from them. The developed nations have already built the capacity they need, and China is doing everything on its own. The biggest heavy engineering players are now focussed on providing sustainable technologies for mining and metal processing industries. Their older portfolio of plant construction and machinery is available at a much lower cost these days. Developing countries such as India with weak environmental regulations continue to buy these cheap technologies. Instead, India needs to buy out some of these OEMs to create end to end domestic capabilities in efficient production. In parallel, India needs to invest in research in frontier technologies viz. automation, carbon capture etc. Small agile Indian companies can be given the mandate to evolve frontier technologies alongside the deployment of efficient technologies. These companies should simply collaborate and learn from the current centers of excellence for frontier technologies but should again do the actual development in India with Indian resources. India should also look to acquire niche companies focused on frontier technologies.

Indian heavy engineering players are essentially marketing and EPC companies that procure equipment from foreign companies and execute projects in India. The key players in the Indian heavy engineering industry are BHEL, HEG, IGSEC, and L&T. None of them have the capabilities to manufacture industrial equipment on their own. They are able to produce some basic components and parts, but even there, they are faced with serious competition from China. All of these are public sector entities where capability building would be slow even if investments were made.

Acquisitions, along with a strong focus on domestic engineering research and product development, is the best path forward for India. Acquisitions will not only be cheaper than spending trillions of dollars India in continuously purchasing equipment but will also be cheaper than developing these technologies domestically from scratch.

India will possibly need an outlay of $100-200 billion to acquire technology companies for the metals and mining industries, and maybe a total of over $500 billion for securing OEM capabilities across all manufacturing sectors. India will need to acquire 3-4 large engineering companies to cover all capabilities across all manufacturing sectors. Alongside, India will also need to acquire several small engineering companies for each industry. Most large engineering firms secure the equipment from these smaller companies. India will also need to acquire small companies involved with the development of frontier technologies.

In 2012, ArcelorMittal sold its 48.1% stake in Paul Wurth to SMS Group for $362 million. SMS Group recently bought the remaining stake. These shares were previously held by the Luxembourg state and state-owned banking organizations. SMS has now become the sole owner of Paul Wurth's plant engineering business, strengthening its competence in metallurgy and hydrogen technology. Edwin Eichler, Chairman of SMS group GmbH, said: "In the coming decades, decarbonizing technologies will replace the traditional blast furnaces and coking plants in integrated steel plants. Therefore, the energy balance at the steel plant will have to be reconsidered and reorganized. Our customers will require fully integrated solutions to bring about this change. Alongside the decarbonization roadmap, efforts will continue in developing digital solutions to establish self-learning processes. This disruption in the global steelmaking market means the time is right for Paul Wurth and SMS Metallurgy to form a single solution provider."

Acquisitions will only help if India is able to manage them well and fully disseminate the technologies within the Indian ecosystem. India needs to heavily invest in encouraging engineers (students and working professionals) to build every possible technology. Strong collaboration is needed between the government bodies, existing companies (heavy engineering and manufacturing), and the universities. The government will need to finance the entire R&D effort, as the existing companies do not have the financial buffer.

India is currently spending around INR 25,000 crore annually on research through the various science departments and the recently created National Research Foundation. The funding is grossly inadequate and does not directly serve the technology objectives of the companies in the field. Currently, the research grants flow from the science departments to the educational institutes. The faculty and students in these institutes identify projects to work on, based on specific gap areas identified by companies and general direction of scientific evolution. Most of these projects are weakly funded and involve minimal real-world interaction with the companies. Individual engineers usually work on very small pieces of technology, and hand over their work to faculty. Very rarely do research projects in Indian institutes achieve commercial deployment. Most patents in India are filed by multinational companies that have adequate R&D budgets. Research productivity of Indian companies and educational institutions is low due to lack of funding and focus.[133] The top patent filers in India in 2018-19 were Qualcomm (1,559), Samsung (1,320), Huawei (968), Ericsson (650), IITs combined (557), and Oppo (498). Some other notable India filers were TCS (239), CSIR (202) and BHEL (173).

The government's research funding needs to flow directly to Indian companies for technical capabilities they need to get more competitive than the multinationals. Instead of creating labs and workshops in universities, government research funds should be used to finance the operation of R&D centers, centers of excellence and product development, within the existing companies. Both public and private

---

[133] "Patents crucial for India to bridge tech gap with US and China", G Seetharaman, The Economic Times, October 6, 2019

companies should be able to seek research funds by presenting a clear business case. The business case also needs to clearly outline the structure of repayment (royalty, equity, revenue share etc.) to the Government. Every project should provide a positive return to the government. Instead of being a cost, R&D investments will at least become neutral if not an earner, and hence will lead to the opening of the flood gates of government research funding.

The mini project organizations within existing companies will most likely deliver against plans and failures would only identify the next scientific or real-world roadblock that needs to be removed. The project organizations would be staffed with people from the company, working professionals (engineers, experts, consultants etc.) hired from outside, and university students. The projects would vary depending on the technological needs of the company and / or the industry. Acquisition of engineering companies could also be financed through this route. After achieving technical and / or commercial success, these organizations could either stay within the company, or even grow into independent companies, depending on what makes sense for broader market adoption. Mechanisms should be set up for financial institutions (banks, insurance companies etc.) and Indian venture capitalists / private equity to invest along with the government.

Ceramics

The next important material for households and commercial establishments is ceramics. In the building & construction industry, ceramics are majorly used for producing tiles, bricks & pipes, and sanitary wares. Ceramic is the most-preferred material due to its properties such as toughness, hardness, electrical resistance, and chemical inertness.

The Indian ceramics industry is worth nearly $7 billion USD. Tiles is the biggest segment with 78% share followed by sanitaryware (12%), tableware (8%) and technical ceramics (2%). The ceramic tile industry can be broadly categorized into wall tile (20%), floor tile (23%), vitrified tile (50%) and industrial tile (7%) segments. In 2019, exports accounted for 28% of domestic production. India is ranked 3rd in the world in terms of production.[134]

The size of the global ceramics market is around $150 billion, which is split across tiles (45%), bricks & pipes (25%), abrasives (10%), sanitary ware (7%), pottery (6%) and others (7%).

The ceramic industry in India is about 100 years old. Ceramic products are manufactured both by large and small enterprises with wide variance in type, size and standards. Though ceramic manufacturing units are spread across India, most of the units are concentrated in Morbi, Surendranagar and Khurja. Morbi (Gujarat) accounts for around 90% of the ceramic production in India. Only a few units have state-of-the-art technology and manufacturing facilities. The major ceramic cluster Morbi also uses obsolete technologies for production and printing, except for a few organized players. The overall production in India is therefore largely low quality and inefficient. European ceramic manufacturers continue to export significant quantities of ceramic tiles and kitchen ware due to their high product quality. Over the years, the industry has been gradually modernizing through new innovations in product profile, quality and design to become more competitive globally.

The organized / national sector consists of 14 major players and their share of production is 40 %. The unorganized/regional sector consists of approximately 200 units (70% based in Gujarat) and their share of production is 60%. The unorganized small players have a substantial share of the production across all sub-segments - tiles, sanitary ware, tableware, and ornamental ware. The plant capacities vary from 1.6 to 54 million square meters (MSM) and the average

---

[134] "Status Quo and Outlook 2022: Indian Ceramics Industry", Messe Muenchen India & EAC International Consulting, March 2018

capacity utilization of the major players in the ceramic industry is about 75%.

The potential is huge considering the present per capita consumption (0.50 square meters per person) of ceramic tiles in India in comparison to over 2 square meters per person for countries like China, Brazil and Malaysia. During the period of developing the high-rise cities, the consumption levels will be significantly higher.

Soda ash, kaolin, clay, silica, and sand are key raw materials used in manufacturing of traditional ceramics. Feldspar and quartz are rare minerals that are critical in the manufacturing of ceramic tiles and sanitary ware. The global demand for these rare minerals has been growing forcing the domestic industries to rely heavily on imports of these inputs. The export of both raw materials has gone up substantially and hence the Board of Indian Council of Ceramic Tiles and Sanitary ware (ICCTAS) has already appealed to the government for a ban on export of these raw materials.

Raw materials (22%) and energy (21%) are the two largest elements in the cost structure of ceramics manufacturing process. Labor and overhead costs constitute 16% and 13%, respectively.

Plant size has a significant impact on levels of energy efficiency and GHG emissions.[135] Small plants consume twice the amount of energy as compared to medium / large sized plants, due to the quality of kiln and the nature of raw materials. The consumption of higher energy indirectly contributes to environmental pollution. Ozone depletion and eutrophication are also much higher in case of small plants.[136]

Health and environment are completely compromised in smaller operations. To stay competitive with the scale

---

[135] "Widening the coverage of PAT Scheme Sectoral Manual - Ceramic industry", Shakti Sustainable Energy Foundation, The Energy and Resources Institute (TERI), 2012

[136] "The environmental impact caused by the ceramic industries and assessment methodologies", Muthiah Muthukannan, Aruna Sankar, Chithambar Ganesh, October 12, 2018

efficient larger players, smaller players have to keep their costs low. The size of their earnings does not even allow them to spend on installing environment and health friendly systems, technologies and processes. Workers in the ceramic industry are highly prone to silicosis and silico tuberculosis during their working life span. Ideally every worker should have the right gear to prevent any form of exposure. They should also be given a health insurance policy that provides for full body check-ups every month or so. Plants need to be fully equipped with decarbonization technologies.

The Indian government continues to encourage MSME participation in the industry. It keeps launching schemes to provide financial assistance, technical support and market access / expansion opportunities for MSMEs. Even though scale efficiencies are significant in the industry, all energy efficiency initiatives are aimed at improving the energy efficiency of small and medium enterprises.

Like many other industries, the Indian ceramics industry is being forced to manufacture at low-cost. China, which has emerged as the leading ceramic manufacturer as well, keeps dumping cheap Vitrified tiles at 25% below normal value.[137] India can simply ban imports from all countries that do not fully enforce environment, health and safety standards.

To do so, India first needs to enforce the highest standards of health, environmental and safety in its own backyard. India simply needs to shut down all the small scale and medium scale enterprises. India needs to focus its resources on 3-4 players that can build and deploy the most efficient manufacturing facilities and produce highest quality products. A sustainable and healthy regulatory regime can be effectively evolved with these large players. They will have the capability, market security and capital availability to

---

[137] "Widening the coverage of PAT Scheme Sectoral Manual - Ceramic industry", Shakti Sustainable Energy Foundation, The Energy and Resources Institute (TERI), 2012

invest in improving workforce compensation, health and safety standards, and decarbonization technologies.

Structural gains in industrial productivity and efficiency levels have already been achieved in the industry. In 1980, ceramic industry technology took off, thanks to the introduction of the mono roller layer furnace, which meant that the baking process, which until then was discontinuous, became continuous, allowing a considerable increase in productivity, as well as, having a significant impact on energy consumption. In the 1990s, production processes were automated and optimized to achieve maximum line flexibility. There has already been extensive development of new products, ceramic types, new colors and designs. From the 90s, a great technological effort has been made in ceramic pastes and enamels for the various classes and ranges of final products as well as the porcelain stoneware research. The number of formats for each type of product is now huge. This great variety of sizes and designs has been made possible by the technological advancements of the presses and printing systems.

The global ceramic sector has now reached its minimum in relation to the cost of manufacturing and its maximum in terms of product quality.[138] It is very difficult to overcome the quality of the product with the technology currently available. Although new ways of improving production are constantly being investigated, in the short and medium term it will be difficult for new technologies to replace the current ones and be implemented on a large scale. The improvements that we are likely to see in the coming years will focus more on the outside of the production plants, such as the optimization of logistics focused on a global market.

Like most other industries, the world has developed efficient and sustainable manufacturing technologies for producing ceramics. India has also developed sufficient capability to

---

[138] "Challenges of Ceramic Industry", Vicente Javier Romero Romero, 2019

now use the frontier technologies for its big urban move. Indians fully understand all the latest technologies and can get everything built domestically. We have a clear understanding of the demand and the type of products that are essential for sustainable urban development. The huge market opportunity creates a viable business case for making the investments needed to scale up.

Sanitaryware, the second largest segment of the ceramics industry, is an important growth segment from an urbanization standpoint. It includes ceramic plumbing fixtures like sinks, basins, toilet bowls, lavatories, etc. Bathroom fittings, also a part of the broader sanitaryware industry, include taps, drains, soap dishes, shower heads, electrical appliances, etc. The larger chunk of the market (almost 40 per cent) still remains unorganized. Moreover, around 69 per cent of the rural households and 19 per cent of the urban households still lack access to safe sanitation which indicates the latent opportunity in the country's sanitary ware market. The size of the sanitaryware and bathroom fittings market would be around $2 billion today. In terms of market share, the organized sector has dominated the industry, whereas, in terms of volume, the unorganized players ruled the industry.

The Indian sanitary ware market accounts for 8 per cent of the total global production and ranks second in terms of volume in the Asia- Pacific Region. Presently, the Asian market is dominated by China in terms of production of sanitary ware and India comes second, followed by Thailand. This growth is also led by the presence of international sanitary ware companies in India because of the low-cost of production and availability of cheap labor have been an attraction for foreign companies to operate in India. Currently, only 60 per cent of the Indian sanitary ware market is organized. The major organized players in the field include a mix of Indian (Cera, Hindware, Jaquar, Parryware, Asian Granito etc.) and foreign (Kohler, Grohe, Toto, Duravit etc.) companies. On the other hand, the unorganized sector (40 per cent) consists of companies which produce substandard quality products that damage the industry's organized sector. The premium segment is estimated to be 10-12% of the current total market. A lot of the growth in the industry is being driven by the premium segment with people looking for luxury products, complete bathroom solutions, eco-friendly products (high-efficiency flushing system, sensor taps etc.).[139] India needs to strike the optima by just focusing on essential functionalities and building solid and efficient sanitaryware. India should ideally stay away from automated products, as in the long run they are detrimental from both a health and material use standpoint. A sensor tap needs more materials and resources to build and is also more fragile and would therefore need to be replaced more frequently. The sensors easily get damaged, and the hands unnecessarily lose out on doing an essential task. Products that are simple and have basic functionalities require the least use of materials and resources, are most efficient, last the longest and do not get damaged easily. For example, there is simply no point in creating shower heads with different flow type options. People end up using only one, so it is best to just design the flow type that is best. People can always change the pressure levels in any case. Companies need to strive to remain on the most efficient frontier that maximizes resource efficiency and product effectiveness.

Glass

Glass has become an integral part of modern urban society. While the glass requirement is much higher in cold countries, even sub-tropical countries like India need a fair amount of glass for high-rises. Glass manufacturing accounted for 1% of total industrial (manufacturing, mining, agriculture and construction) energy use and around 0.33% of total global energy use. The glass industry energy consumption per unit of output ratio is similar to that of other energy-intensive

---

[139] "Changing Trends in Indian Sanitary Ware Industry", Vinay Jain, August 26, 2019

industries.¹⁴⁰ However, because glass has a low volume of shipments compared to other energy-intensive industries, the share of total industrial energy use is lower for glass.

The global glass industry is worth more than $200 billion with flat glass accounting for around $120 billion. In terms of output, the global flat glass production capacity is nearly 100 million tonnes.¹⁴¹

Flat glass is used in buildings (windows and facades) and automotive industries. Flat glass is also used in solar-energy applications as well as in urban and domestic furniture, appliances, mirrors and greenhouses. Construction of high-rises requires significant quantities of glass, and forms the biggest segment of glass consumption. Two thirds of flat glass production is used in architecture.

Almost all flat glass is made by means of the float process. Plant construction is capital intensive, needs appropriate expertise and has traditionally been limited to a few major players.

China broke through the "old guard" and in just over two decades. started leading the global float production.¹⁴² China's flat glass production capacity grew rapidly since the 1990s; in 2019 capacity exceeded 60% of the global total. While many of the "old guard" manufacturers—AGC, Guardian, NSG and Saint-Gobain—continued to expand their presence geographically, the majority of new plants that popped up were built by smaller, regional manufacturers. Of China's 64 plants, only 10 are operated by one of the four global float leaders. And seven of those 10 are joint-venture operations with local manufacturers. New entrants especially from China made technology more widely available and significantly reduced the barriers to entry. Previously float

---

[140] Glass industry energy consumption and emissions data, Energy Information Association US

[141] "Towards an international year of glass in 2022", International Commission on Glass

[142] "How shifting markets and new players are transforming the float glass industry", Katy Devlin, National Glass Association, February 14, 2016

glass production was reserved with the global giants, who had mastered the technology and had the financial means to carry on the capital-intensive business.[143] The introduction of turnkey technology enabled new players to rapidly build end to end capabilities and produce the complete range of glass products. But many of the float plants built by local, mid-sized glass manufacturers were not designed to meet Western production or environmental standards. The economic downturn and increasing environmental pressures over the last decade have made China rationalize its production capacity. China's environmental protection and capacity replacement policies have been tightened, restricting new production capacity. On the demand side, China's fast-growing building and transportation industries are fundamentally changing to energy-saving, safe and lightweight products. Green building is adding 1.6-2 billion m2 annually to 60 billion m2 existing floor area, 90% of which is in high-energy-consumption buildings that urgently need transformation.[144] So the processing of energy-saving insulating glass, tempered vacuum glass, electrochromic glass, flameproof glass and other products is expanding rapidly.[145]

India will need over 200 million tonnes of flat glass just for residential high-rises. This is basis 20-25 sq m of wall area to be built with glass per apartment and architectural glass thickness of 10 mm. Each apartment would therefore need ~600 kg of glass (10 mm glass weighs 25 kg per sq m). The total requirement for 35 crore apartments would be a little over 200 million tonnes.

The total glass requirement for all forms of infrastructure will be more than 500 million tonnes. Commercial high-rises

---

[143] Glass Alliance Europe; Glass Association of North America

[144] "Strengthening sustainability in the glass industry", Peter Kamicha Kamau, Marek Stec, Li Tu, Sabine Schlorke, IFC, World Bank Group, July 2021

[145] "Flat glass consumption on a meteoric rise in the 'green construction' industry", Shikha Sinha, May 14, 2019

need at least double the quantity of glass per unit of construction. Even though they might represent less than half of the residential development, commercial buildings use much higher quantities of glass to improve energy efficiency and enhance aesthetics. Also, the glass used in commercial high-rises is of higher quality and thickness. Additionally institutional buildings and public infrastructure such as stations, airports etc will also need significant quantities of glass. Glass is essential for making the high-rises energy efficient even in a subtropical country like India. Commercial and residential buildings can simultaneously control the entry of heat and reduce the use of artificial lights by using glazed glass. Solar control coatings restrict heat from the sun entering inside.

India currently manufactures around 2.5 million tonnes of float / flat glass out of which nearly 75% is consumed domestically. Saint Gobain (50%) and Asahi (16%) have around two thirds of the total float capacity in India.[146] Gold Plus Glass, Hindustan National Glass and Sejal Float Glass are the only pure play Indian companies with a significant float production. But these companies have limited technology capabilities and do not have the resources to invest in research and product development. HNG Float tied up with Toledo Engineering Co (TECO), USA for the design, engineering, installation and commissioning of the float plant and sourced ancillary machinery from global players like CNUD and Bottero. The Indian industry is also facing serious competition from China and Indonesia.[147]

India needs to scale up 3-4 domestic players with each having significant production capacity (more than at least 2 million tonnes). India is largely self-reliant in materials for glass making - silica (sand, 75 per cent), soda (around 15 per cent)

---

[146] "Widening the coverage of PAT scheme, sectoral manual - glass industry", Shakti Sustainable Energy Foundation, The energy and resources institute (TERI), 2012

[147] "Indian float glass industry review", Sunder Singh, AIGMF, Glass worldwide, 2010

and calcium compound (lime, 10 per cent).[148] Building domestic companies that are competitive with the global giants would need strong focus. India will need to consolidate the domestic industry, eliminate imports and make huge investments to acquire capabilities across the value chain. The chosen players need to be provided significant resources and support to invest in research, develop all types of flat glass products, and meet the highest standards of product quality and operational efficiency. Acquisitions will enable these to rapidly control the entire value chain. Given that Indians are well entrenched in all types of companies and have gained sufficient experience, India can also bring together the experts. There is no dearth of young engineering talent who will deliver with the right guidance.

While flat glass is highly durable, it does have a limited life, around 30 to 50 years. Hence, glass will need to be replaced over time. As India grows the glass industry, it also needs to build an ecosystem that enables efficient recycling.

Currently, flat glass cullets can only be reused to a limited degree and quality demands are high. Flat glass cullet arrives at recycling companies in a variety of forms depending on the application but is rarely just float or cast glass: the cullet can have thermal insulation or sight protection coating attached to it, be printed with ceramic inks, be part of laminated units or wired glass. All of this complicates the preparation process and reduces the number of ways in which the cullet can be reused. Moreover, laminate glasses with specific functions will be used much more often in the future, with the challenges growing as a result.

Flat glass from façade glass or window elements places increasingly high demands on recycling companies. Laminate glasses contain a huge variety of materials, ranging from PVB foils and liquid crystal layers all the way up to metals. At the same time, there are very few systems that

---

[148] "Indian flat glass revival on the cards", Sunder Singh, Glass Worldwide, 2016

allow these glass products to be collected and prepared in a traceable manner. According to the latest figures, cullet makes up 26% of the raw materials used to manufacture flat glass in Europe. It is currently estimated that technical, infrastructural and economic framework conditions in Europe limit the existing potential to a maximum of 37% cullet use.[149]

The Netherlands has a nationwide collection system. Following an initiative to set up a recycling system in 2000, Vlakglas Recycling Nederland was founded in 2002. The organization collects all types of flat glass – including wire glass and laminate glass – and processes them to create recycled material. The foundation for this is a network of collection points for glass manufacturers or processors, in waste management centers and in on-site container collections used by demolition firms.

The system is financed through a mandatory recycling fee calculated on the basis of the area of the manufactured or imported glass. But only 7.5% of glass was fed back to the flat glass manufacturing process. The majority went to the container glass industry and glass wool production. In the long term, however, the organization aims to raise the share of waste flat glass fed back to flat glass production to 20%.

High costs usually prevent recycling companies from processing building elements containing glass. Separating the material from other construction waste is an early hurdle, while dismantling the building elements poses an even greater challenge. The amount of work and personnel expenditure for separating the building elements, the space requirements and the transport costs are just some of the factors that need to be taken into account. Unfortunately, in many countries including India, it is still possible to dispose of glass waste at a landfill site together with other materials as an inert material. In doing so, an important raw material is

---

[149] "Recycling flat glass – circular economy with potential", Gesine Bergmann, The Glass Technology Forum, Verband Deutscher Maschinen und Anlagenbau (VDMA), December 17, 2020

lost. In the future, laminate glass will contain much more material that is to be recovered.

In order to do this in a cost-effective manner, it is necessary to enhance or develop completely new separation technologies – a task that mechanical engineering and research must overcome together. An end-of-life strategy is absolutely necessary before a manufacturer launches a new product on the market. Sustainability begins with product development.

The glass container industry is a second major force in the marketplace with global sales near $70 billion, split between beverages, cosmetics, food, pharmaceuticals and others.

Used every day by billions of people, glass containers present countless advantages for both consumers and the environment. Being 100% recyclable, container glass can be melted down and reformed an infinite number of times. The container glass industry is potentially a perfect example of a circular economy in action. Europe boasts glass recycling rates as high as 90%.

Glass containers are enabling a healthy and sustainable shift away from plastics. Glass does not contain any of the potentially harmful chemicals which some plastic bottles do. Plastic is continually downcycled until it is rendered completely useless for recycling. After that, in most cases, it winds up in a landfill, where it slowly breaks down into microplastics and emits methane. Unlike fully recyclable materials like glass or aluminum, plastic doesn't decompose, biodegrade, or become something else over time. Once it has been turned into plastic, it remains plastic forever. It just gets tinier. These dangerous beads of microplastic can become ingested by animals and humans through our water supply.

While the demand for flat glass has tapered down in the developed world, container glass consumption continues to increase.

The per capita consumption of container glass in India is at 2.5 kg; much lower compared to other nations (China 10, USA

28, Germany 50, France 64, South Korea 90). For a healthy urban society, the optimal level of container glass consumption should land somewhere between 20 to 30 kg per capita. Currently, the liquor segment accounts for 57% of total glass container demand in India. Glass beer bottles constitute 62% of all U.S. glass container shipments.

The glass bottles and containers market is highly competitive with a dozen large and mid-sized players accounting for over 80% of the capacity.[150] Long tail of small producers accounts for the rest. The top three, Hindustan National Glass, Piramal Glass and AGI Glaspac, have 70% of the capacity.

The Indian glass container industry involves a dozen mid-scale producers besides these three. HNG is in the process of stabilizing its capacity following massive additions at its existing Nasik unit and commissioning of the greenfield project at Naidupet, Andhra Pradesh. Of the other players, Piramal and Janta Glass have added capacity and modernized their production facilities. Two small glass container units belonging to liquor manufacturers Mohan Meakins and Khoday Glass faced closure due to their operations becoming uncompetitive.

Apart from a few major manufacturers, there are more than 1000 medium and small manufacturers. The majority of the glass manufacturing units are located in Firozabad, Baroda, Ahmedabad, Mumbai, Kolkata, Bengaluru and Hyderabad. In industry clusters such as Firozabad, Baroda and Kolkata, the glass industry has evolved from cottage industry to the level of organized industry.

Indian MSMEs continue to deploy primitive means of technologies and suffer low energy efficiency due to two primary reasons - poor furnace design because of the unbalance between capital cost and operational cost and short-term views and compromises to keep the costs low.

---

[150] "Indian glass industry set for brisk action", Sunder Singh, Glass Worldwide, 2014

Even the large Indian players are tiny when compared with the leading global players. Each of the three largest container glass manufacturers has revenues in excess of $5 billion. HNG's revenue is around $0.25 billion.

The global players have acquired a large portfolio of manufacturing plants spread across several countries, with each having more than 50 plants.[151] Stricter environmental norms in developed countries, especially Western Europe, have driven these companies to shift capacity to developing nations.

The scale of these organizations enables them to invest in research to maximize the efficiency of their operations. Research and development (R&D) is done centrally in these organizations, usually at the headquarters. Relevant technologies are implemented at various plant locations based on the local market conditions.

OI Glass (Owens Illinois), the third largest container glass maker, is currently focused on advancements in the areas of product innovation, manufacturing process control, melting technology, automatic inspection, light-weighting and further automation of manufacturing activities. Recently, the company increased its focus on advancing melting technology with investments in modular glass melting furnaces. The company's investments in this new technology seek to reduce the amount of capital required to install, rebuild and operate its furnaces. This new melting technology is also focused on the ability of these assets to be more easily turned on and off or adjusted based on seasonality and customer demands.

The glass container industrial plants have high fixed costs and low marginal costs. The melting process is the dominant energy consumer. Depending on the glass product, 50–85% of the required energy is utilized for melting in the furnace. For industrial purposes, only continuously operated melting

---

[151] Annual report 2018, Owens Illinois

furnaces are of importance. Discontinuous pot furnaces and semi-continuous day tanks are small and extremely inefficient. After construction and start-up, a melting furnace is operated continuously throughout the entire year. It is vital to note that the energy supply of the glass melting furnace must not fail for a longer time interval, because that would lead to solidification of the glass melt and thus to the destruction of the melting furnace.

Approximately 75% of global container glass companies use regenerative EP furnaces. Furnace melting capacities range from 30 to 500 TPD, with a typical container furnace size of 300 TPD.

SP furnaces constitute almost 90% of melting furnaces installed worldwide in the flat glass industry. The average melting capacity of an SP furnace is 600 TPD with a maximum melting capacity of 1200 TPD.

Electric furnaces have emerged as the most sustainable and efficient melting option.[152] The thermal efficiency of an electric furnace is 85% as against 45% of a regenerative end-fired furnace. Furthermore, electric melting furnaces have lower investment costs. As smaller furnace volumes are utilized, regenerators are not necessary, and expensive high-temperature crowns are not required. In addition, combustion-induced gaseous emissions, e.g., CO_2, NO_x, and dusting are strongly reduced, so that the investment costs for filter systems and the operating costs for cleaning are diminished. There is less volatilization resulting in lower raw material costs, and repair costs are lower. Additionally, efficiency does not depend as strongly on furnace size and capacity as with fossil-fired furnaces.

---

[152] "A review of decarbonization options for the glass industry", Michael Zier, Peter Stenzel, Leander Kotzur, Detle Stolten, Jülich-Aachen Research Alliance, JARA-Energy, Institute of Techno-economic Systems Analysis (IEK-3), Chair for Fuel Cells, RWTH Aachen University, May 23, 2021

Currently, maximum EM (electric melting) capacities of 250 TPD are possible. EM can be used for 80% of the glass produced worldwide including container and flat glass.

India currently relies on foreign companies for almost all equipment and parts. In 2013, a HNG started a new production facility with a 650 TPD furnace, the largest in India. HNGIL bought the equipment and technology for this furnace from HORN Glass, SORG GmbH, Zippe, Emhart, Mysac, and Sipac.

Manufacturing technology for glass, like most heavy industries, is owned by European technology companies. A few other leading technology companies are Linde, Nienburger, Rexam, TNO, and Optimum. Large glass producers had initially built these in-house. These technology operations involve heavy research and development and have extremely high fixed costs. The glass manufacturers eventually carved out and divested these businesses. These standalone technology companies have grown large either by building end-to-end expertise for an industry (glass in this case) or by focusing on a specific technology or part of the production process. Some of the largest equipment technology companies have built solutions for multiple industries.

Another valuable product in construction is glass fiber, particularly for reinforced plastics and insulation; the global market currently is approaching $10 billion in annual sales. A key application is pipework for transmission of water and other strategic liquids; storage tanks and baths for water are also important. In the future glass fiber products are expected to displace steel, aluminum, wood, PVC and other traditional materials. Building, transportation and electronics industries in particular have enormous potential for using glass fibers.

Fiberglass production is similar to flat and container glass till the melting stage. Melted glass is formed into fibers or a woven blanket using a process called pultrusion. The fibers are then used with other materials to form different types of composites.

Domestic glass comprises the manufacturing of glass tableware, cookware and decorative items such as drinking glasses, bowls, plates, vases and ornaments. The growth of this segment is essential as urban societies move away from the use of paper and plastics.

Special glass has a high added value linked to its intense technological content. This sector includes a large range of products such as lighting glass, glass tubes, laboratory glassware, glass ceramics, heat-resistant glass, optical and ophthalmic glass, extra thin glass for the electronics industry such as liquid crystal display (LCD) panels, photovoltaic and radiation protection glasses.

A high-rise urban India will need a lot of glass during the development phase as well as on an on-going basis. India has gained sufficient understanding of products and technologies to fully own the value chain for serving the domestic demand. India possesses knowledge of best practices, latest technologies and processes and the engineering horsepower, to produce everything related to glass indigenously. With a clear understanding of our long-term demands, India simply needs to extend the planning horizon to 30-40 years. We need to consolidate the industry into large domestic enterprises as well as invest heavily to be self-sufficient on the technology front. Even if India has to make acquisitions outside, it can only be done by really large domestic players. On the technology front as well, we will keep paying a huge premium unless we build it ourselves. India has already the threshold level of capability and a full understanding of the sustainable technology frontier as well as the path to get there.

We just need to protect and back our domestic players for a period of around 10-20 years. This is when we consolidate to form the large domestic enterprises and invest heavily in research and development. As outlined earlier, the government needs to directly finance the R&D of existing domestic players to help them develop and acquire end-to-end technologies for manufacturing. China files 50% of global patents these days and more than double the patents filed by the US. India files less than 1% and 2/3rd of its patents are filed by multinational companies operating in India. India needs dedicated effort from its domestic players to bridge the technology gap in industries such as glass. India needs to build domestic glass technology companies that can help achieve global standards of efficiency, quality, and sustainability. They should be able to produce the most cutting-edge machinery and equipment in India. That will enable the large Indian players to get into a position to not only defend the domestic market but also compete effectively in global markets. Once the technology capabilities reach the level of fulfilling our functional requirements in a sustainable manner, India will be truly self-sufficient.

The Indian cities of an urban only India will help achieve the highest levels of sustainability in the glass industry. Every city will have the raw materials and stable local demand for scale efficient plants to operate. Cost would be minimized for transportation of both raw materials and finished products. Electricity will be available at lowest possible costs for EM furnaces to be viable. High recycling rates would be achieved with established rules, regulations, and organizations. High quality talent will be available for research and development.

Pipes

Pipes form an essential component of any human settlement. They are the veins through which water and blood flow. The Indian pipe industry is fully controlled by domestic enterprises and produces all different types of pipes - plastic (PVC, UPVC, HDPE), iron, concrete, clay, etc. PVC pipes today account for the majority of the pipes being produced in the country. The pipe industry overlaps the material industries i.e., iron & steel, concrete and plastics. Most of the pipe manufacturers are vertically integrated producers of various products from their core material. Iron & steel companies have integrated forward to produce different finished products and so on.

The share of the top-5 pipe producers has risen from 22% in FY12 to ~37% in FY21. The share of organized players in the piping industry has increased from ~50% in FY10 to ~67% in FY21. Over FY15-FY20, organized players have topped industry growth as they continued to gain market share from unorganized manufacturers and few larger regional organized players facing B/S challenges. By consistently investing in branding and BTL activities, organized players have increased plumber/ consumer awareness over importance of quality and adherence to BIS standards in pipes, particularly for residential real estate. Organized segment growth has further been aided by increased focus on value added products and fittings, as well as product portfolio expansion offered to channel partners; in this manner, organized players have become one-stop solution providers for plumbing applications. Organized players will continue to gain market share while unorganized players will reel under operating challenges amid volatility in imported raw materials and stricter tax compliance. With tax compliance becoming more stringent due to e-invoicing/GST regulations and stricter adherence to BIS standards, unorganized manufacturers continue to be impacted.

The plastic pipes industry was estimated at Rs 400bn-420bn or ~$5.3 billion in FY21 and saw a ~10% CAGR over FY16-FY21; growth was driven by rising demand from irrigation and WSS (water supply + sanitation) sectors, and metal pipe replacement demand from residential real estate.

Raw materials form 65-70% of sales for the plastic pipes industry and their prices are directly linked to crude oil, changes in global demand-supply conditions and import-export regulations. Key raw materials for the plastic pipe industry are PE (polyethylene), PVC (polyvinyl chloride), CPVC (chlorinated polyvinyl chloride) and PPR (made from

Polypropylene Random Copolymer plastic). Most of the industry's RMs are supplied either from domestic petrochemical companies or imported. India currently relies completely on imports to meet its CPVC requirements from Korea, Japan, China and Europe. For PVC, 45-50% of requirements are met indigenously while the balance from Taiwan, Japan, South Korea and China (collectively over 70% of India's imports). In the case of PP, indigenous production satisfies 90% of the domestic requirement. For HDPE, 40-45% of domestic requirement is met through imports from the UAE, Saudi Arabia, Qatar, Singapore and the US (collectively over 80% of India's imports).

Anti-dumping Duty (ADD) imposed on CPVC imports by some countries from Aug '19 and the pandemic-induced supply chain disruptions have affected business models of many regional/unorganized players, even as they are likely to come back once things normalize.

Information was reviewed on the cradle-to-grave impacts of five commonly specified pipe materials: ductile iron, polyvinyl chloride (PVC), high density polyethylene (HDPE), reinforced concrete, and vitrified clay.[153] Data was examined that compared the impacts of each pipe material in six life phases: Resource Extraction, Manufacturing, Transportation, Installation, Use, and End-of-Use Fate. Sustainability was defined as one, contributing the least amount of greenhouse gases throughout the lifetime of the material; and two, minimizing toxicity impacts. End-of-Use-Fate was eliminated as there is little evidence that buried pipe is recycled in meaningful quantities or that it would markedly lower global warming potential.

The Production phase (Resource Extraction and Manufacturing) accounts for 92-99 percent of the total global warming impact of the first three phases (including Transportation). The Installation and Transportation Phases

---

[153] "Selecting Sustainable Pipe Materials", Capt. Steven Bosiljevac, Capt. Luke Schulte, Lt. Cdr. Julia Kane, USPHS, The Military Engineer, August 2018

are minor contributors to global warming potential when compared to the Production and Use Phases. In addition, considering the first three phases (Production, Transport, and Installation), concrete pipe shows the least global warming potential while ductile iron shows the greatest.

Within each material, differences exist at varying diameters. Iron pipe has the highest global warming potential at diameters less than 24-in. PVC has the highest for diameters greater than 30-in. This anomaly is created by the schedule of pipe thickness associated with different pipe material.

Small diameter pipe sizes have lower global warming potential from production, transport, and installation; however, the energy consumed to convey a quantity of water/wastewater is increased.

As India urbanizes, pipe requirements will change from smaller low-quality pipes to high quality durable pipes with larger diameters. Production as well as use of the bigger and better pipes is more sustainable. The small diameter low quality pipe industry has flourished in India due to the explosion of unplanned low-quality infrastructure, mainly the independent / low-income housing. As India plans and builds its urban cities, efficient water and sanitation systems have to be designed connecting the water sources (lakes, rivers), high-rises, industrial parks, the cleaning / treatment centers, and discharge areas (farmlands etc.). The network has to be designed at scale with no unaccounted and individual water extraction or disposal.

Paint

Paint is another important industry both for urbanization and industrialization. The global paints and coatings industry generates revenue of ~$160 billion and the Indian paint industry is valued at ~$7.1 billion (FY20). Asia Pacific (APAC) accounts for 45% of the global market share, because of high demand and tighter environmental norms forcing multinationals to shift capacity to developing countries.

The Indian market is dominated by the decorative segment with ~75% market share. This is unlike the global and APAC markets' structure where the decorative segment (architectural) contributes less than 40%. Industrial paints account for 60% of the demand globally and even at an APAC level. Over the years, the decorative paint segment has grown at a CAGR of 11.4% against the industrial segment, which has grown at a CAGR of 7.9%.[154]

Industrial paint's lower contribution in India's overall paint market is mainly attributable to lower industrial and infrastructure development compared to other matured countries and developing countries like China. Higher technical know-how is required in the industrial paint segment, which also creates a barrier for India's unorganized players.

The Indian paint market is an oligopolistic market with the top 4 players controlling a little less than 70% market share of the overall domestic paint industry. In the unorganized sector (~30% market share) there are about 2000 units manufacturing various categories of paints. The total volume of the market is about 5 million tonnes.

The country's per capita consumption of paints of ~4 kg, is lesser as compared to per capita consumption of 15-25 kg in the developed countries. Given the huge income inequality and a sizable poor population, the per capita consumption is actually not that bad. The key reasons for the high consumption of decorative paint in India are the poor quality of coatings and the annual ritual of getting the house painted before Diwali. Re-painting cycle in India has reduced significantly from 7-8 years till early 2010s to 4-5 years now and is unlikely to reduce any further in the medium term. Increase in rental housing and increasing efficiency of repainting services have led to the major reduction. Demand in smaller cities and towns has been growing at a faster pace

---

[154] "Paint sector update", Nirmal Bang, September 2020

than in metro and tier I cities. A high-rise urban settlement will have lower paint consumption due to the cleaner lifestyles and rational thinking. In a high-rise urban and well-developed industrial scenario, the consumption will therefore be 15-20 kg per capita.

Crude oil and its derivatives form over 50% of the industry's raw materials. Over 50% of raw materials like phthalic anhydride, pentaerythritol, methyl methacrylate, aromatics, etc, which act as resins, solvents and additives, are derivatives of crude oil. Titanium dioxide pigment, derived from ilmenite, comprises ~20-25% of the total content of paint. Around 70% of India's domestic demand for TiO_2 is met through import deliveries and China is the leading exporter of TiO_2 to India. Imports from China for Asian Paints and Berger Paints vary between 8% and 10% of total raw material cost.

The Indian market, much like global markets, has been moving towards more eco-friendly water-based paints from the solvent-based ones.[155] Gross margins are also better in water-based paints compared to solvent-based due to the lesser dependence on crude. Even consumers have been increasing preference for water-based coatings on account of their superior aesthetics, durability and washability.

Only 10% of the environmental footprint of coatings is created during formulation, with some 50% generated upstream by the raw material manufacturing industries, and 40% created downstream in use and disposal. Changing raw materials and waste management are therefore the key imperative for the industry from a sustainability standpoint.

Through its choice of ingredients, the industry can impact the footprint of the whole supply chain. The coatings industry needs to ensure that the ingredients only contain materials that will not harm the environment or society either in

---

[155] "Technical EIA guidance manual for integrated paint industry", IL&FS Ecosmart Limited, The Ministry of Environment and Forests, Government of India, September 2010

application or recycle. The petrochemical, plastics and chemical industries provide the majority of the materials used by the coatings industry and represent a key element of the coatings environmental footprint. Novel chemistry has an important part to play in environmental footprint reduction. Some recent examples include 1) The development of an additive for internal decorative wood coatings that reacts with formaldehyde and blocks its release (Dow), 2) Acrylic grafting on to alkyds to change their morphology to avoid the need for both solvents and surfactants (Arkema), and 3) Partial replacements for titanium dioxide such as Dow's precomposition polymer technologies and Solvay's calcium carbonate product range.

The field that has the highest potential for reducing the carbon footprint is the replacement of chemicals with bio-renewables.[156] Bio-renewable technologies have been known for many years and are receiving increasing attention of late as sustainability increases in priority. AkzoNobel14 has committed itself to doubling the renewable component of its raw material purchasing slate by 2020. The use of bio-renewables cannot only reduce the environmental footprint of downstream products but also extend the diversity of supply sources of formulation ingredients. Some bio-renewables have demonstrated the potential to offer improved property profiles due to their often more complex structure than the materials they are replacing.

Bio-based coatings are an emerging market with approximately 5 % market share in Scandinavia and Western Europe.[157]

Netherlands implemented a sustainable procurement catalog for public tenders in July 2016 which states: "The higher the proportion of bio-based raw materials and/or recycled raw materials in the products supplied, the higher the value of the

---

[156] "Bio-based coatings overview: Increasing activities", Jan Gesthuizen, European Coatings, August 20, 2020

[157] "Bright future for bio-based coatings", Damir Gagro, European Coatings, April 8, 2021

tender." This makes it easier for bio-based solutions to be considered. The catalog applies to a large variety of projects, from road building, marine projects, landscaping, construction and much more.

In Switzerland, a label called Umweltetikette encourages paints and varnishes made of renewable raw materials. To achieve the highest environmental label, paints and varnishes must contain 95 % renewable raw materials. The label is also awarded to adhesives, wood preservatives, plasters and fillers. The high level of acceptance among users is also likely to be ensured by the fact that the label also sets minimum performance requirements, such as wet abrasion resistance or contrast ratio.

The most potential for bio-based paints is in decorative applications such as wall paints. Here the bio-based resin is an essential part of the product, while it becomes only a relatively smart part when the coating is used as part of a final product like furniture or a car. The lower the technical hurdles are, the more likely you are to find bio-based feedstocks directly usable for your application. The bright opportunities for bio-based coatings are in high-value applications and value chains driven by downstream players, such as brand owners with strong sustainability policies, like the automotive, furniture and packaging industries.

While there are a relatively small number of bio-based paints and coatings within the current market, further research and development will allow greater understanding of bio-based materials and their performance. As the market for these coatings is still rather small and as their production – as well as the production of the respective raw materials – is more complex and costlier than that of conventional products, they are still more expensive.

The industry is already working on a second generation of biomass, derived from biowaste and cellulose. Both materials are available in huge quantities. This will further broaden the portfolio of bio-based materials.

Akzo Nobel recently announced a bio-based innovation - a completely new technology that's able to cure chemicals for paints. The breakthrough technology uses bio-based monomers and requires just UV light, oxygen and renewable raw materials, for the production of resins. By 2040 or 2050, the company expects to only use bio-based monomers in their resin production.

In 2017, PPG launched a bio-based wall paint for the professional and consumer market.[158] The paint is made using bio-based resins, which is a key raw material in paint formulation. The resin has been made from renewable resources such as sugars, natural oils, and starch from corn and agricultural waste. These natural materials replaced for a large part the fossil ingredients that traditionally constitute the binder resin of both solvent borne and waterborne paints.

Some examples of key bio-renewables of interest to the coatings industry are 1) Corbion Purac supplies lactide building block chemicals made by the fermentation of sugars that can enable polyester resin producers to create modified resins with improved property profiles in their final application, 2) North Dakota University has developed bio-based polyvinyl ether copolymers from soya bean oil and menthol, which provide product enhancements ideal for alkyd coatings, 3) Eindhoven University of Technology, Holland and Imperial College, London, UK have recently reported discoveries of innovative catalyst systems that make possible the polymerization of a range of resins incorporating carbon dioxide, without the help of enzymes. Some of the resins produced by these mechanisms "are promising as binders in industrial paint formulations", 4) Bayer has developed tailor-made polyether carbonate polyols from propylene oxide and carbon dioxide, 5) Brown University has made a breakthrough in the manufacture of acrylates using ethylene and carbon dioxide with nickel as a promoter, and 6) With carbon dioxide as one of the products generated by the

---

[158] "PPG Launches New Bio-based Wall Paint", Coatings World, March 10, 2017

decomposition and incineration of coatings, the regenerative circular economy can be exemplified by its re-incorporation in resins and binders.[159]

Waste generated at paint manufacturing facilities include equipment cleaning wastes, spills and area washdowns, off-specification paint, bags and packages, air emissions, filter cartridges, obsolete products and customer returns. Non-wastewater generation at paint manufacturing plants ranges from 300 to 450 tonnes per 1,000 tonnes of paint produced. Paint recycling, solvent recovery and re-use, improved cleaning efficiency etc. are some of the key steps taken by manufacturers to make the paint formulation process cleaner.

The downstream impact of the paint industry can be best minimized through waste paint recycling, recycling coated substrates, and enhancing the lifetime and functionality of coatings.[160] Programs have been launched, in Canada, the United States, France, U.K. and the Netherlands to collect waste paint, and reconstitute and blend them ready for resale and use. Downstream sectors such as the packaging, automotive and furniture industries have built businesses around the recycling of used parts. Coatings manufacturers need to support downstream industries by ensuring that there are no toxic chemicals or intermediates created in the recycle loop that prevent safe processing of the substrate into its new form. Improvements in paint performance (both industrial and decorative) can have a significant impact on the sustainability of the entire life cycle. In the context of industrial coatings in which substrates such as metals and wood are protected, enhanced lifetime of the coating is a major benefit. Enhanced functionality can bring significant improvements to the sustainability of downstream

---

[159] "Environmental Performance - Coatings companies from around the globe have realized the environmental benefits of being more environmentally conscious", Tom Williams, Coatings World, September 8, 2005

[160] "Sustainability in the Coatings Industry - What Lies Beyond 'Business as Usual' Improvements?", Tony Mash, Paint & Coatings Industry, April 1, 2015

industries, particularly in areas where energy reduction is a valued goal. Examples are coatings that deliver the desired results with a reduced number of coats, decorative paints that better reflect light, internal and external roof coatings that reflect heat away from houses during hot seasons and keep warmth in during the winter, coatings that generate useable electricity, coatings that are scratch resistant in automotive applications, coatings that remove impurities from the air, and low-emission paints to protect indoor air quality.

Electrical and electronics

The electrical and electronics industry has assumed critical importance enabling humans to harness different forms of energy for almost every imaginable task. Electrical and electronic products have become essential for an efficient urban society.

Electrical devices convert the electrical energy into the other form of energy like heat, light, sound, etc. whereas the electronic device controls the flow of electrons for performing the particular task. The main difference between electrical and electronic circuits is that electrical circuits have no decision making (processing) capability, whilst electronic circuits do. An electric circuit simply powers machines with electricity. However, an electronic circuit can interpret a signal or an instruction and perform a task to suit the circumstance. For example, a microwave oven often beeps when it has finished cooking, to inform the user that his or her meal is ready.

Most modern appliances use a combination of electronic and electrical circuitry. A washing machine has an electrical circuit comprising a plug socket, fuse, on/off switch, heater and motor, which rotates the drum. The desired wash cycle and temperature are inputted by the user via the control panel. These instructions are interpreted by electronic circuits, which have been designed and programmed to understand what the user would like based on what buttons have been pressed. When the electronic circuit has interpreted these commands, it sends signals to the electrical circuit to operate the heater and motor, to heat and rotate the drum, for the time required.

Most electronic components are very small and require small direct current (DC) voltages. A single microprocessor, which will fit on the end of your finger, may contain hundreds or thousands of tiny components, some of which are only a few atoms wide. Electrical components tend to be larger and use alternating current (AC) voltages. Whilst most electronic components operate on 3-12 volts DC, electrical appliances require 230 volts AC. In factories and power stations, however, components may require up to 11,000 volts. Some products, such as computers, have far more electronic components than electrical components. Large industrial sites such as factories or power stations, however, have far more electrical components.

The link between electronic and electrical circuits is typically provided by relays or transistors. These are essentially switches but, rather than being pushed manually like a light switch, are operated by a small current from an electronic circuit. Therefore, a small circuit - often with many tiny components -can be used to operate much larger electrical equipment. This makes using household and industrial products safer, and means they are smaller and more energy efficient.

Relays are mechanical devices which, when a small current is applied from an electronic circuit, a metal contactor closes the electrical circuit, allowing a much larger current to pass. Relays were however large and unreliable, and tended to require a lot of current. After repeated use, the moving parts become worn and stop functioning correctly. Transistors, however, can be made much smaller and require tiny amounts of current, and have no moving parts. The transistor was invented in 1948 and is arguably the most important invention of the last 100 years.

Electrical equipment

The electrical equipment industry consists of electric lighting equipment, household appliances, power generation, transmission and control equipment, batteries, and wires and cables. Key sub segments include general lighting, automotive lighting, back lighting, small electrical appliance, household cooking appliance, household refrigerator and home freezer, household laundry equipment, other major household appliance, transformer, electric motor and generator, switchgear and switchboard apparatus, relay and industrial controls, secondary batteries, primary batteries, other cables, coaxial cables, and fiber optical cable.

The global electrical equipment market is expected to grow from $1180 billion in 2020 to $1271 billion in 2021 at a compound annual growth rate (CAGR) of 7.7%.[161]

This sector is fragmented both globally and in India. But there are a few global companies that account for a substantial portion of the market. The large players are integrated manufacturers of electrical and electronic products.

Operating structures involve high fixed costs. Copper, aluminum and steel are essential raw materials used in the manufacture of products. Fluctuations in commodities prices can have an impact on a company's earnings performance. Operating efficiency is crucial for these companies to succeed. For the most part, the industry's operating margin ranges from 10% to 20%. Some leaders achieve margins in the 30s and 40s. Popular efficiency and cost-reduction methods include Six Sigma, Lean Manufacturing, Best Practices and common production platforms. Effective hedging strategies can bring volatile commodity prices under control.

In most cases, research and development expenses are less than 5% of sales. Nonetheless, R&D outlays are important to

---

[161] "Electrical Equipment Industry Sees Consistently Increasing Demand With Rapid Innovations In Technology", TBRC Business Research, April 26, 2021

the industry. Innovation allows a company to improve its competitive position. Managements work to keep up with shrinking product life cycles and attain standardization to maintain cohesiveness and save money.

Generally, net margins are close to 10%. For equipment makers with little or no debt, net margins match operating margins. Those with significant debt obligations often have net margins in the single digits. Companies tap the equity and debt markets, and use cash, for expansion and acquisitions, depending on the comparative cost of capital and their tolerance for risk.

The industry has a history of substantial merger and acquisition activity. Scale is important to profitability. Emerging nations have provided an impetus for growth and low-cost labor, production and land. Asia Pacific is the largest region in the global electrical equipment market, accounting for 45% of the market in 2020. Major companies in the electrical industry include Panasonic Corporation, Samsung Electronics Co Ltd, ABB Ltd, Sumitomo Electric Industries Ltd, and Toshiba Corporation.

Electronics

The Electronics industry, valued at USD 1.75 trillion, is the largest and fastest growing industry in the world. The industry is segmented into communication electronics ($640 bn), computers ($500 bn), automotive ($215 bn), consumer ($180 bn), military ($160 bn), industrial ($155 bn), and medical electronics ($115 bn).

The Electronics industry is driven by innovation and a lot of money and effort goes into research and development to design and make improved parts and products, as well as improve manufacturing processes.

Companies in the electronics industry are always in tough competition to implement innovative ideas and introduce the newest technology in the market first. This puts a lot of pressure on design and engineering teams to develop and create innovative products and services faster and cheaper. Sales and marketing teams are also under pressure to drive sales and ensure that profit margins remain way above production and operational costs.

Companies are also specializing in specific niches to guarantee sustainability and maintain profitability. Many electronics manufacturing companies are outsourcing manufacturing and production of parts or products. The rise of Electronics Manufacturing Services (EMS) and Contract Electronics Manufacturing (CEM) companies is a testament to that. These are companies that are contracted to manufacture parts or products for other companies, and also provide a variety of value-added services.

Technology has been and will continue to be a determining factor in how sustainable and profitable a company in the electronics industry will be. Companies will have to invest more in R&D, restructure, and become more service-oriented by leveraging such technological advancements as the Internet of Things (IoT). Electronic equipment manufacturers will have to make use of robotics and automation to improve both efficiency and productivity. Some companies have already integrated different sensor technologies in their manufacturing processes to gather substantial data that can provide timely insights to drive growth and profits.

Today, three defined models of the electronic industry can be distinguished[162]: US-Japanese-Korean, European, and Chinese. It is important to note that the main scientific groundwork in electronics today is concentrated in the USA, Japan and Korea. Serious research bases have been created in these countries, and production sites have been sufficiently developed. All this was created over many years and contributed to the fact that to date, complete production chains have been formed in the above countries, which

---

[162] "Modern challenges in the electronics industry", Gavlovskaya Galina V, Khakimov Azat N., May 14, 2020

characterizes the first of three models of functioning of companies in the electronics industry.

A number of countries in Western Europe also conduct their own developments in the field of electronics (mostly in the field of telecommunications and automotive electronics), but they do not have large production capabilities, which forces them to send their developments to the production capacities of other countries, as a rule, China and countries of the Southeast Asia. The European model for the formation of the electronic industry is also characterized by the development of those areas of the electronic industry that are closely related to priority areas of the economy.

The Chinese model is characterized by the fact that contract production has been actively developing in the country for many years. At industrial sites in China, products are manufactured according to the developments of European, North American and other countries of the world. In particular, the vast majority of all components of the global electronic industry (namely, radio components, computer components, etc.) are made in China. Developments of such world-famous brands as HP, Apple, Dell are sent to Chinese manufacturers. However, it should be noted that in recent years the country has clearly seen a tendency to increase the number of its own national developments, which are able in some segments of the electronics to compete with American or Japanese products. In China, design centers have been actively developing in recent years, which carry out the design of scientific developments in the field of radio electronics. In the last two decades, China has been a leader in the export of office and telecommunications equipment.

Semiconductors form the core of the electronics industry. Their end-to-end production is arguably one of the most critical capabilities in today's technology driven world. The US controls IP, design and technology. Japan makes silicon wafers on which chip circuitry is etched. The Netherlands produces lithography machines that etch circuitry onto wafers. Taiwan Semiconductor Manufacturing Company (TSMC) has the biggest and most sophisticated fabs that make chips on order for anyone. South Korea, led by Samsung, also has advanced fabs.

On the other end is China, the largest chip buyer, consuming 60% of all chips produced globally. Its annual chip import bill exceeds $300 billion. China's plan to develop a local semiconductor industry has alarmed the US. In the last two decades, China succeeded in making low-end chips, not a mean feat. But it failed to make advanced chips. To acquire such technology, around 2015, it tried buying firms in the US, Europe and Asia. But alert host governments blocked all such efforts.

China got a breakthrough when Huawei developed a chip for use in the 5G equipment. But, Huawei, like most others, had to rely on US firms for chip design. Acting quickly, the US, using export control laws in 2019, stopped its firms from helping Huawei. The US soon forced TSMC, Samsung, and other foreign suppliers to stop selling to Huawei to continue using US designs, equipment and tools. The US monopoly in the IP and chip design made the threat credible.

Fabs need significant annual investments. You make an oil refinery, and it functions for 50 years with the same technology. Not for fabs. Intel, Samsung, TSMC and everyone else – each spends over $20 billion in R&D, process improvement and new fabrication machinery every year. Fab technology is complex with very high failure rates. China is a case in point that even significant investments are no guarantee of success. Just a square inch of a chip contains billions of transistors. Distance between two transistors is measured in nanometer (nm), which is one-billionth of a meter. The lower the distance, more the transistors in a small area, and more powerful the chip.

Currently, Apple's iPhone 13 uses a 5-nm chip, the most advanced chip on a phone. Apple's iPad may soon be the first product to use a 3-nm chip. Compared to a 5-nm chip, the 3-

nm chip is 15% faster and consumes 25% less power. Contrast this with the most advanced chip made in China. Despite two decades of lavish government support, China could make only a 14-nm chip. This is at least two generations behind the 5-nm chip.

The world will soon have surplus fab capacity. The US-China rivalry has spurred large investment in new fabs. The US government will spend $50 billion on chip manufacturing. Intel is building two fabs in Arizona for $20 billion. TSMC will spend $100 billion on new fabs. Many other proposals are being discussed.

The electrical and electronics industry is already past the point of rational use and optimal maturity. Structural efficiency gains have already been achieved with the development of high quality electrical and electronics equipment. Whether it is mobiles, computers, television, home appliances, lighting equipment, switches, wires or any electrical or electronic device, the world has already developed products that deliver very high levels of efficiency.

Over the last two decades, the developed nations have been blindly replacing mechanical functionality with electronics. While these replacements provide improved consumer experience, there is significant resource consumption associated with these products. The overall societal value or the net value to humanity of the new age electronic products is increasingly becoming negative. The total societal value or the net value to humanity needs to factor in energy consumption, material consumption, carbon footprint, health impact, and waste generated.

Over the last two decades, technology companies have simply been adding layers of electronic circuitry and materials, in a bid to develop new products and to keep growing. The Internet of Things is a case in point where companies are building connected products by putting a wifi chip in them, with little regard to material, energy and health implications. The human body has the best electronic circuitry and there are serious physical and mental health consequences in making it redundant.

Automotive electronics is also a glaring example of the overuse of electronics. Electronics account for 40% of the car cost today for some of the latest cars. The electronic circuitry is fragile and extremely expensive to replace. Most people do not even use the wide range of electronic functions available in their car. Automation and electrification are driving a surge in the demand for automotive electronics, especially sensors. Automation is an unnecessary attempt at replacing the driver - safety would be better achieved with speed controls. And electrification is also not sustainable given the paucity of battery materials.

The use of electronics has to be limited to essential tasks that create significant value for society. Enhancements should focus on improving the quality and efficiency of such products. Human involvement or mechanical functionalities should only be replaced if the net value to humanity is positive.

One of the most important challenges the global electronic industry faces nowadays is a global slowdown in the pace of innovation. The innovation in the electronics industry is becoming more and more incremental, with less improvement coming each year, clearly suggesting that the industry has reached an innovation plateau. Smartphones, tablets, laptops and desktops, they've largely plateaued in terms of advancements. Every new version is mostly about slightly faster processors, a wee bit more storage, better camera. Form factors for all of them are well, squares or rectangles. A triangular smartphone or tablet doesn't make much sense after all, so they may get a bit thinner or thicker even, but that's about it.

The material burden (production and waste) of incremental product launches is massive. Every such product launch creates aspirations for society at large. Products remain under-utilized and a huge amount of non-biodegradable waste is generated. The second-hand markets (online platforms and gray market) only work well for the most essential, popular and high-quality products.

Hardware becomes ubiquitous over time. Rational and stable businesses understand that dynamic, while others stubbornly focus on iterating hardware in a bid to drive growth. Consumer technology today isn't solving real customer issues. Startups and companies are focusing too much on products that we (society) don't truly need.

The main reason for the shift of manufacturing of electronics to Asia is the availability of key natural resources. The world has limited reserves of a number of rare-earth metals that are actively used in the production of electronics (cobalt and nickel), and a major volume of these resources are located in the Asian Region.

The industry needs to become much more responsible in creating new products. Experts suggest that most of these critical reserves might not even last for more than 20-30 years. The whole electronics industry needs to be severely regulated to only produce the most essential goods. The semiconductor industry is at the heart of creating non-essential products. Once microchips were created that could combine human intelligence with different functionalities, people started creating products for every task that humans were doing. There has been little consideration to the health impact of not doing those tasks and the unnecessary material / resource consumption.

Now, India is pretty much at ground zero when it comes to the electronics and semiconductor industry. We have nothing on the semiconductor front - design or manufacturing and are therefore fully dependent on foreign companies. The developed world has built capabilities that seem almost insurmountable for a country like India.

Importing or allowing foreign companies to manufacture in India, creates a huge pressure on India's natural resources.

We simply have to sell our natural wealth to buy technology. Not only does that lead to exploitation of the natural resources, but also prevents India from improving the quality of life of its citizens. A considerable proportion of the jobs associated across the industry value chain are lost. To compensate for the lost value creation within the economy, we end up making compromises on various aspects of quality of life that are essential. Unless we produce everything ourselves, we will never be able to engage everyone meaningfully and fruitfully.

There simply cannot be any difference between domestic consumption and production in any industry. Electronics production (~$100 billion) in India accounts for ~25% of the total electronics market size (~$400 billion).[163] The gap creates a huge burden on the economy and the country's natural resources. To balance consumption and production, not only does India need to significantly ramp up domestic capability and production, but also needs to ban the consumption of foreign made goods. The only case for buying the latest technologies is for defense, and even that case becomes weak if India is simply focused on sustainability. Besides, true defense capability will only be built when we build everything ourselves and own the secrets. Buying defense equipment from the developed world is just an endless money game where nations just keep spending more and more on defense instead of building the nation. Restricting human settlement to the ~130 cities will in any case solve most of the defense issues and accelerate capability development across all industries.

Not just electronics and technology, which are huge, highly valuable, critical and futuristic industries, India simply cannot rely on foreign assistance for any of its industries. Electronic products and electronic components are the largest non-oil imports of India as in FY 2019. 70-80% of electronic components are imported into India. South Korean

---

[163] "Electronics Industry in India", Deepti Ahuja, Amit Singh, Nexdigm, SKP Group, June 2017

and Chinese players dominate the consumer electronics segment in India. The only case for reliance is in the import of materials and energy, which in any case creates a huge deficit for India.

India has now developed sufficient technology and engineering capabilities to produce anything end to end. We have already conquered the most complex industries and produce some of the best engineers in the world. The talent pool is huge and hungry to get anything done. We just need to channelize our energies in the right direction.

India will need to adopt protectionist policies across industries and especially electronics and technology, for domestic capabilities to be built. As long as the purpose of domestic capability building is sustainability, the global powerhouses will be fine with the stance. Having built these industries from the ground up, they of course understand the importance of doing so in improving the quality of life of the masses and preventing systemic compromises in the exploitation of natural resources. As long as India is fully transparent and clearly communicates the rationale for fully owning and executing the complete industry value chain, India will have global support.

To start with, India needs to focus on the core and the essentials. India simply needs to focus on quality and efficiency and should completely stay away from flashy products that cannot stand the test of time.

Electrical components and semiconductors form the core of the electrical equipment and electronics industry. The production in India is around $10 billion which represents a very small fraction of the domestic market requirement. The Electronic Component market in India is mainly led by electromechanical components, such as PCBs and connectors, followed by resistors and capacitors which make up passive components. Moreover, active components like ICs, diodes, etc. are likely to witness higher demand in the coming years. Currently, the demand for Electronic

Components is largely met through imports from China, Taiwan, South Korea, and Japan. Highly specialized and precision components like ICs, chip components, PCBs, and LEDs are primarily imported due to their low production in India.

The electronics industry is constantly undergoing changes due to disruptive innovation, thereby increasing pressure on the value chain to continuously upgrade. The sourcing and contractual interdependencies between OEMs and suppliers is now more complex due to the high technological nature of components, number of components required for a single finished product, level of aggregation or assembly required, and the need to adapt to changes in product design. The Indian ecosystem for Electronic Components is still evolving and has a long way to go. India is steadily developing the value chain and ecosystem for Electronic Component manufacturing and conducting feasibility studies for semiconductor manufacturing. Many organizations like Xiaomi, Foxconn, Wistron, and Lion Circuits have planned facilities to make PCBs in India. Some of the major international players that currently control and are investing in the Indian market are Bosch, Mitsubishi, Haier, Panasonic, and Huawei.

India needs to fully take charge of the semiconductor industry and only have domestic players producing all electronic components for the Indian market. It is a highly capital-intensive industry with low availability of raw materials. The electronics industry is primarily dependent on the number and competency of domestic chip fabrication centers (Fab centers) present in the market. Fab centers require a dedicated ecosystem, which includes investment, know-how of chip fabrication, raw material supply, continuity of demand, and unit upgradation competency. Given the current scenario, India lacks most of the necessary ammunition for development of domestic chip fabrication units. India will need to create 3-4 giant organizations to fully build domestic semiconductor capabilities. Strong political will is essential to bring together domestic enterprises (from related segments) and Indians with relevant expertise, experience and the right mindset, to lay the foundation of these iconic national entities. The research backlog is gigantic, and these Indian companies will have to be heavily funded to carry out the necessary research to develop high quality and high performance semiconductors. India should again refrain from driving the research for such a critical industry only through certain educational institutes.

The essential segments where India should fully own the industry value chain are lighting, power generation, transmission and control, batteries, wires & cables, household appliances (cooking, mixing, refrigeration, ventilation, fans and coolers), television, mobiles, computers, wearables, music, monitoring and surveillance, medical, industrial and military equipment. India should simply stay away from non-sustainable electronic goods such as air conditioners, heaters, dish washers etc. and non-essential ultra smart products.

India needs to have 3-4 large companies controlling each of these segments or a combination of these. Even the smallest of these segments is highly complex, capital intensive and extremely evolved. High quality efficiency products can only be produced at scale, so there's really no case of encouraging MSMEs anywhere in these industries.

Instead of building Electronics Manufacturing clusters and hubs, India simply needs to pick a handful of companies, and provide them all the support needed. India needs to discontinue the operation of small enterprises and only stick to these handpicked players. These companies will need substantial financial assistance and resource allocation to rapidly build capabilities and produce for the nation. Policies will need to be formulated across the board to enable these companies in terms of manpower, resources, and market control.

India also needs to completely shut down the operation of foreign players on Indian soil and refrain from introducing any policy or support for enabling foreign players to set up shop in India. India has learnt enough and now needs to independently produce for at least its own consumption. Only once India takes that responsible stance, the world will provide real assistance in terms of technology transfers.

India should actually refrain from becoming a low-cost manufacturing hub for companies across the globe. Being a low-cost competitor results in poor domestic capability building, depressed income levels, lower levels of efficiency, and poor standards of health, safety and environment. A focus on sustainability and building manufacturing capabilities for products that align with sustainable living, will also make it easy for India to judiciously use its resources and regain market control. India will need a strong sustainability monitoring mechanism for the entire electronics industry. All products and technologies should pass rigorous sustainability standards and clearly demonstrate a positive net value for the society. India should also limit the unnecessary use of electronics in segments such as automotive, home appliances, lighting etc. as electronics are fragile as compared to the mechanical systems, significantly reduce product life and increase maintenance requirements.

India needs to have a single-minded focus on developing its indigenous industry and making it fully independent. Given the size of the domestic market opportunity, Indian companies will have a viable business case to acquire leading companies across value chain and industry segments.

Electronics is the biggest uphill battle for India, given its size and the current state of affairs. Most key segments within the electronics industry have been almost fully captured by foreign players. The share of mobile handsets industry in the total electronics segment in India is estimated to be nearly 35% by production, making this industry the largest electronics segment. The production of the broad communication and broadcasting segment is currently around $25 billion with mobile and its components accounting for a majority share of the same. 120 manufacturing units of mobile handsets have been set up in India over the last three years with nearly all global smartphone players now present in India. Samsung, Apple, Xiaomi, OnePlus, OPPO, and Vivo are key players. While it almost seems impossible to compete against these, India is now fully capable to fully regain complete control in around 10 years. We already have marketing companies (Micromax, Lava, Karbonn, Spice) that have a full understanding of the value chain and all the required components. India is a powerhouse now when it comes to software and design. We just need to equip and protect the domestic companies to gradually build every component themselves. These are critical domestic enterprises and cannot be allowed to operate like startups. Serious government involvement and support is essential to scale up these enterprises and make them fully capable of meeting the complete domestic demand. These enterprises can also not be driven by individuals - they need strong professional management, distributed shareholding, collective decision making and rigorous processes. India has a more than sufficient talent pool today to perform each and every function required in these organizations.

While the imports across major electronics segments are in the 10-50% range, most of the domestic production is also being done by international companies. A whole host of international companies such as LG, Samsung, Panasonic, Sony, Phillips, Haier, Blue Star, Daikin, Onida, Videocon, Hitachi, and Whirlpool control India's essential home appliances segment. Eventually, India needs to buy back the foreign operations and fully control its domestic industry. In the home appliances segment, India does have some domestic enterprises for various product segments. They are slightly inferior to the international companies in terms of quality but are good enough now to be scaled up. Only when the domestic enterprises are given protection and allowed to scale up and cater up to the entire Indian market, will they be able to invest and build leading world class capabilities. India is now in a state where it can smoothly manage this transition from foreign production to domestic enterprises, with minimal supply shocks and consumer outcry.

Industrial electronics is the next key segment whose current production is again around $10 billion. The production of Power electronics, process control and automation equipment with built-in software, and analytical instruments, accounts for nearly 85% of the total production of Industrial Electronics. BHEL, Honeywell, BlueStar, and Siemens are the key players. India needs to carve out 3-4 domestic companies from BHEL to fully take over this segment.

The next segment is computers where India has literally no capabilities. The current domestic production is around $4 billion. India will literally need to build this segment ground up. Again, while it may seem complex, the industry is fairly standardized in terms of the components used. India has a huge after sales ecosystem that has developed a deep understanding of all the requirements and possesses the engineering capabilities needed for production. India just needs to bring everything together.

LED is another essential segment, and the only electronics segment where Indian companies have the majority market share.

Furniture

Global furniture market is estimated at USD 1.1 Trillion out of which the Indian market size is less than 5%. India Furniture Market was US$ 17.77 Billion in 2020. While the size of the industry is already pretty large, significant transformation is needed to make it sustainable.

The global furniture market can be broadly categorized into four categories - domestic furniture, office/corporate furniture, hotel furniture and furniture parts. Globally, domestic furniture accounts for 65 per cent of the production value, whilst corporate/office furniture represents 15 per cent, hotel furniture 15 per cent and furniture parts 5 per cent.

Globally, the furniture industry is known to be essentially an assembly industry employing various raw materials including wood-based panels, metal, aluminum, plastics, fabrics, leather and glass, as well as mechanical and ICT components. Wood and wood-based panels represent a substantial share of raw materials. Labor costs also constitute a relatively important component of the final cost structure. Being a resource and labor-intensive industry, entry barriers are rather low.

Adequate machinery endowment is widely recognised as a crucial factor in the production process, as it delivers efficiency and productivity gains.[164] This applies to all the furniture segments, but in particular in case of assembly-line manufacturing operation, when production is in big series. Standardization of production goes hand-in-hand with minimization of costs, and in this process, technology (both in production and logistics) has a decisive role. Capital investments in plant and machinery also have an impact on reducing waste and increasing safety.

In general, tangible investments in the furniture sector concern the automation of the production process. To automate the production process, firms usually introduce Computer Assisted Manufacturing (CAM) solutions and Computer Numerical Control (CNC) machines. Important investments are made in this area by medium and large sized enterprises to optimize production, to create synergy between different lines or sites of production and to achieve

---

[164] "Furniture manufacturing challenges on the world market: the Bulgarian case", Rossitsa Chobanova, Radostina Popova, October 2015

scale economies. In particular, German and Italian wood furniture manufacturers are at the forefront in terms of woodworking machinery technology and are considered world leaders.

Design, R&D and innovation are crucial factors to maintain market positions. Design is widely recognized as offering furniture manufacturers a competitive advantage. This is made necessary by the changing needs of consumers and market pressure. Present trends are towards customizations, ergonomics, and functionality. Eco-issues are also becoming increasingly important globally and require significant R&D and innovation. Innovation in materials and technologies is a critical driver of competitiveness in today's industry. Nanomaterials and nanotechnologies is a promising field of innovation in today's industry. Process innovation is another source of competitive advantage for manufacturers. European manufacturers make significant investments in developing newer production methods that help save energy. For instance, the furniture production line can be equipped with an environmentally friendly wood-chip burner that recycles all the waste wood and chippings and uses it as fuel.

Being an unorganized sector (85% unorganized) merely focusing on hand-made furniture, the furniture sector in India is grossly inefficient.

Various types of raw materials are used for furniture making in India. The key raw materials include wood, metal and plastic, with bamboo and cane also being used in some cases. Wood accounts for nearly 65 per cent of all furniture made in India.[165] This includes several types of indigenous wood, as well as imported wood. India imports wood from various Southeast Asian countries such as Indonesia, Malaysia and Myanmar. MDF boards are imported from Europe, soft and hard wood are imported from Russia and other Southeast Asian countries. Veneered panels are becoming increasingly

---

[165] "Furniture market and opportunities", KPMG, IBEF

popular in India and are imported from the European Union and USA.

Popular wood types used in India include Walnut, Sandalwood, Teak, Sheesham, Deodar, Ebony, Redwood, Rosewood, Red Cedar and Sal. Teak accounts for almost 50 per cent of the total wooden furniture produced, Sal and Deodar account for about 20 percent and the balance includes Mahogany, Cedar and other tree types. Bamboo Material Boards (BMB) are increasingly being used in place of plywood. India also has abundant rubber wood supply. Natural rubber plantations cover 520,000 hectares with an additional 6,000 hectares being replanted almost every year since 1994. The southern state of Kerala produces 95 per cent of the total supply of rubber wood in India.

Indian states well known for woodwork include Gujarat, Jammu & Kashmir, Punjab, Uttar Pradesh and Kerala. India is one of the largest consumers of wood in Southeast Asia. The country has sufficient availability of tropical wood. However, growing concerns about the environment and the need for conservation of forests have led to a reduction in the supply of wood over the last few years.

Furniture produced in India falls into two broad categories, depending on the end user - domestic furniture meant for home use and commercial furniture meant for the office and hospitality sectors. Domestic furniture represents almost two-thirds of the total output. The key success factors for each category vary. Manufacturers in the domestic sector typically try to differentiate on the basis of design variety and price, while in the commercial space, having a strong and reliable brand is important.

Furniture imports in India have been growing at nearly 64 per cent CAGR, over the 5-year period from 2001 to 2006. A key driver is the increasing demand for furniture, fuelled by the boom in housing and commercial construction. Increasing income levels and influence of global lifestyle trends have also led to many urban, affluent Indians, moving towards imported furniture. European furniture manufacturing companies have been the first entrants, with their premium products (mainly veneered) in India. They were led by the K K Birla joint venture, Gautier, with Groupe Seribo of France. Furniture imports from other Asian countries have come in much later. Barring a few, such as Renaissance Home, Interior Espania, Pinnacle Saporiti and Gautier, most of the imported furniture dealers sell their products either under their own brand name or without any branding. In recent times, import of cheaper furniture from Southeast Asian countries has been increasing.

Small scale entrepreneurs in developing countries like India fall short of exploiting the full potential of current technological means. Thus, increasing the efficiency in production assumes greater significance in attaining potential output at the industry level. However, it is an undeniable fact that the majority of small scale entrepreneurs are characterized by poor economic status due to inefficient utilization of available resources.

For an evolved urban society, furniture requirements are minimal, and India is completely capable of fulfilling that demand. There is no case for the presence of foreign companies in the furniture industry. A minimalist urban India will need extremely functional, high quality and highly efficient furniture. Furniture products are likely to be different from what the Indian society has gotten used to. Per capita demand for furniture will be much lower as compared to the per capita consumption seen in the higher middle class and above income segments of India. Variability in the consumption should also decrease and standardized high-quality products should achieve mass adoption.

India needs to consolidate the industry and achieve high degrees of efficiency and quality in the production. All the MSMEs need to be merged into 3-5 national level players. The manufacturing locations for these companies should be restricted to cities to make the operations efficient, produce high quality products and enforce regulations. Material use and product development for these large furniture companies needs to be heavily regulated.

Product complexity and portfolio diversity have a negative impact on operational performance and result in non linear increases of material, effort and energy. Product development in the furniture industry needs to be restricted to essential items and should evolve to drive the adoption of a minimalist lifestyle. Furniture design should aim to drive the adoption of low-lying tables, cushion only sofas etc. Mattresses, pillows and cushions should replace bulky furniture viz. beds, sofas, chairs etc. Simple and efficient products need to be produced at scale to drive high levels of material and resource efficiency. The government also needs to lay down guidelines for urban high-rises to design interiors that support a high-quality minimalist lifestyle and minimize unnecessary use of furniture.

The use of plastics, synthetic materials and precious rocks (marble, granite etc.) needs to be completely phased out. Some fabrics and blends require heavy use of chemicals, which can lead to hazardous waste and excessive contamination. Furniture manufacturers must also minimize the use of such materials. Wood will continue to be the mainstay of the furniture industry, along with metals. The government needs to determine the types of wood that can be sustainably used for manufacturing. The government needs to enforce stringent regulation to ensure responsible harvesting of different types of wood. Only responsibly sourced wood and other sustainable materials should be used for production. The entire operations of the large manufacturers should be made fully transparent. Each and every product should be certified after stringent verification by a government body. While the developed economies are also encouraging green certifications, these do not make a real impact as only a handful of consumers are willing to pay the sustainability premium. Unless each and every product is mandated to be sustainable, the industry at large will not change.

There are a large number of Scandinavian, American and Japanese furniture retailers today that can serve as a guiding light for the Indian furniture industry. Some of the leading minimalist furniture companies include Ikea (low-cost, functional), AYTM (minimalist Danish design - sophisticated and sleek), Menu (Scandinavian, simple and beautiful), Muji (a one-stop shop for minimalist products), Ferm living (Scandinavian, sleek, modern), Blu Dot (American, sleek, elegant, and simple), Umbra (original, modern, functional, and casual) etc. Companies driving sustainability include Sabai (FSC certified wood and recycled fabrics), Made Trade (responsible sourcing and fair compensation), Savvy Rest (responsible and natural sourcing), Thuma (modern, minimalistic, recycling), Simbly (FSC certified wood), Medley (FSC, organic, natural), EcoBalanza (certifications - FSC, Global Organic Textile Standard, and Greenguard), Vermont Wood Studios (responsible wood sourcing, fair wages) etc. Both these sets of companies are leading the charge on sustainability by combining design, material innovation, and sourcing. They are working towards the creation of a minimalist urban society that seeks functionality, efficiency, quality, health and everlasting beauty.

Although most of them are just retailers and aggregate / source their products / materials from different suppliers, they are driving sustainability across the value chain and minimalism in the society. Indian industry should have a few vertically integrated enterprises and maybe a few large enterprises that specialize in a particular segment of the value chain e.g. wood production, dye production, logistics etc.

Textiles

The textile industry serves one of the most basic requirements of a community and is a key determinant of the quality of life. The global textile market size was valued at $961.5 billion in 2019. The market is fragmented due to the presence of several small- and medium-scale manufacturers, especially in countries such as China and India.

Textile is a flexible material that is formed using numerous processes, including knitting, weaving, crocheting, or felting. These materials are extensively used to manufacture a wide range of finished goods, such as upholstery, kitchen, transportation, bedding, construction, medical, protective equipment, apparel, handbags, and clothing accessories.

On the basis of application, the market has been segmented into household (bedding, kitchen products, upholstery, and towels), technical (construction, transportation, medical, and protective equipment), fashion and clothing, and others. Fashion and clothing is the largest consumer of textiles. In terms of volume, the fashion sector holds a considerable share of over 70.0% of the total market. Apparel, ties and clothing accessories, and handbags are the key areas that significantly consume textiles.

Based on raw material, the market is segmented into cotton, chemical, wool, silk, and others. Cotton is the largest raw material segment, accounting for a market share of ~40%. Favorable properties of cotton include high absorbency and strength, and color retention. China, India, and the U.S. are the major cotton producers in the world.

The industry is further segmented into natural fibers, polyesters, nylon, and others. Natural fibers dominate the market and include cotton, linen, flax, silk, hemp, and wool. They are considered to be biodegradable and renewable and are hence eco-friendly. Polyester fiber is characterized by high strength, quick-drying, and high chemical and wrinkle-resistant properties. These advantages have made polyester one of the most widely used products in the textile industry. Polyester finds application in a variety of end-use products such as carpets, curtains, nets, and ropes. Nylon is widely used in the synthetic textile category. It exhibits properties such as high resilience, elasticity, luster, and low moisture absorbency, and hence finds application in several industries including apparel and home furnishing. Others include polyethylene (PE), polypropylene (PP), aramid, and polyamide. Polypropylene is a synthetic fiber that has high strength and water-resistant properties. Similarly, polyamide is known for its high strength and durability.

The current global apparel market is estimated at $1.7 trillion. EU and USA were the largest apparel market in 2017-18 accounting for 41% share while they are home to just 11% of the world population. The per capita spending on apparel is therefore around $1000 for the developed nations. The market size of India's apparel industry is around $70 billion, which translates into per capita apparel spending of ~$50.[166]

The global textiles and apparels trade is worth around $900 billion. Amongst the major exporters of Textile & Apparels (T&A) globally, the top 10 exporting countries enjoy a share of 72% in global T&A exports with China and Hong Kong maintaining the top position with 37% share, followed by India with a share of 5% in 2017. It is then followed by Bangladesh, Germany, Italy, Vietnam and Turkey each having a share of 4%.[167]

Therefore, the best path for India is to create a high value textile and apparel industry serving the domestic market. Even if the global textiles and apparel trade increases to $2 trillion and Indian achieves a 20% market share (a fairly aggressive scenario), the size of the Indian industry (export plus domestic) would be $500-600 billion. But if India elevates the domestic industry and increases the apparel spending tenfold (which would still be half the spending levels of the developed nations), the domestic industry itself would become larger than $700 billion. The choice of building a high value domestic industry has minimal

---

[166] Annual Report 2018-19, Ministry of Textiles, Government of India

[167] "Five ways for Indian textiles to get a bigger global market share", Kearney, Forbes, November 24, 2020

uncertainties and is fully controllable and executable without any external dependencies.

The industry would also become efficient, high quality and sustainable. While the industry will lose out on the share of global trade in the near to medium term, in the long run, India will gain significant competitive advantage. Sustainability concerns are already starting to take away production from China, Bangladesh, Indonesia, Malaysia etc. Given that the smaller countries like Bangladesh, Indonesia, Malaysia, Vietnam etc. will always be highly dependent on the world for material, resources, technology and talent across various industries. They will have no option therefore but to remain a low-cost outsourcing alternative for textiles and apparel manufacturing. US, China, India and possibly Brazil / Mexico will emerge as fully developed sustainable industries with capabilities across the entire value chain. The US, China and India also have the distinct advantage of being self-sufficient in the production of natural fibers.

The Indian industry has already achieved the capability levels to now transform into a self-sufficient high value industry. The domestic textiles and apparels industry peaked at $106 billion in FY2020.[168] The Indian textile industry is one of the largest in the world with a large unmatched raw material base and manufacturing strength across the value chain. With huge investments, persistence innovations, latest product mix and planned marketing, today, India has come out as a flourishing outsourcing center for textiles and apparel industry. Exports, which account for a third of the industry, meet the most stringent quality criteria.

India will need to consolidate the entire industry within 8-10 companies. India already has more than 10 well developed companies (Arvind, Vardhman, Welspun, Raymond, Trident, K P R, Page, Nitin Spinners, Rupa, Himatsingka etc.) that can be made to take over the entire industry. While these

---

[168] The Textile Magazine

companies have acquired technical production capabilities, the scale of the required consolidation is massive and might almost seem impossible.

The industry currently includes an extreme variety of both hand-spun and hand-woven textiles sectors and the capital-intensive sophisticated mills sector. The decentralized power looms/ hosiery and knitting sector forms the largest component in the textiles sector. More than 90% of textile units are unorganized. Traditional sectors contribute to more than 75% of total textiles production in the country. There are no labor rules, labor unions, and no social security regulations for the workers. The workers of these unorganized units are getting less wage as compared to other sectors, so these people are socially insecure and deprived of the basic medical health and education facilities. The small-scale units and the cottage industry continue to operate on the ancient principles of making every family a self-sustaining business operation. With the advent of technology, the industry has become increasingly capital intensive and rapidly moved towards production efficiency and quality. Indian garment units operate at 40-45 per cent efficiency level, which is lower than their counterparts in countries like China and Turkey which operate at 60-65 percent efficiency, etc. Beyond a handful of organized players, the textile and apparel industry majorly comprises of fragmented entities that lack the financial and managerial bandwidth to identify, analyze and rectify productivity related challenges. Fragmented nature of industry, management mindset, lack of best practices & technical knowhow and higher attrition rate are some key challenges that plague the Indian industry.

In an apparel factory, productivity improvement can be achieved by focusing on all entities of a manufacturing ecosystem- manpower, machine & material and capital. The key components of what is referred to as 'Factory re-engineering program' are production planning & control, systems and processes at shop floor, workforce training, factory layout planning and use of work aids. At a country level, presence of efficient firms would help India increase productivity, resource efficiency, quality and wages.

Consolidation of all the small and medium units into these 8-10 large national players will significantly increase efficiency and quality across the value chain. Consolidation will prevent price undercutting and enable these national enterprises to adopt best practices. These companies will be able to invest in research and development of materials, design and manufacturing. The government will be able to fully enforce quality, health and environmental standards on these large organizations. Without the need to keep costs low, every employee will be compensated to lead a good quality life. The government will also be able to drive policies around minimum wages and benefits.

The larger organizations will be better equipped to unlock the true potential of Indian cultural heritage and local traditions. They will be able to carry out the necessary research, develop high quality designs, and use high quality materials, to produce apparel products that bring out the various Indian flavors in a classy manner and make them appealing for everyone.

Creating Indian apparel brands is essential for Indian companies to create and capture the entire value potential of the domestic industry. The large Indian textile companies have so far simply adopted foreign brands and sell them in both domestic and foreign markets. Indian companies will need to create their own brands and will need some protectionist policies to help the Indian brands grab the entire domestic apparel consumption pie. A limited number of brands from each of these large national companies will help bring clarity in the domestic apparel industry.

Brands will also be essential for the Indian companies to achieve high levels of efficiencies. Brands help companies create products with a uniform characteristic quality and features, which is known as standardization. Standardization of a product allows an enterprise to sell its product in large quantities and drive scale efficiencies across the value chain. The business benefits from the economics of buying products in bulk, selling products in large quantities, and reduced costs in terms of advertisement. A business that supplies a standardized product has a high potential for producing good quality products since the production operations concentrate on one product. The business also has the opportunity to research techniques to input on the product to increase its quality standards and improve the consumer base. Standardization or SKU reduction enables companies to create more effective products that most efficiently serve the functional needs of customers. The complexity of business operations would reduce significantly in terms of production, inventory, storage and distribution. Indians and eventually people across the globe will eventually be able to relate to each of these brands. Apparel purchase will become a much simpler and enjoyable experience, as the brand promise gets deeply ingrained. A relentless focus on quality by these large Indian enterprises will also remove the menace of fast fashion that has taken over the industry over the last few decades.

The large Indian companies will be able to invest in the latest technologies and achieve the highest levels of efficiencies. While the Indian textiles players are behind the curve on automation, larger scale will enable them to invest in digitizing the entire value chain. With their own brands, they will have the case for using AI-enabled analytics to design high quality collections. Manufacturing will be able to leverage solutions such as IoT-based real-time performance monitoring, predictive maintenance, robotic process automation admin operations, and automatic guiding vehicles for moving materials. Sales and customer engagement will be able to invest in AI-based predictive lead scoring, smart B2B sales management tools for generating and managing leads and digital showrooms, virtual 3D sampling, and participation on digital B2B platforms for customer engagement and transactions.

The large companies will also be able to phase out the use of synthetic materials and dyes. This is especially critical for India to reduce dependence on oil and make the industry sustainable. Besides, India has been a pioneer in the production and use of natural fibers and dyes. Large scale natural clothing operations will be able to aggregate and produce the mix of materials and colors that is needed to produce clothing that is genuinely superior to synthetic clothing. The large companies will have the resources and market influence to ensure proper management of sources of natural fibers and dyes, efficient use of technology, commercial availability of natural fibers and dyes, high awareness levels amongst different end user segments, and institutionalization of standards for quality and eco-friendly certification.

Indian players can create a differentiated value proposition, by focusing on quality rather than quantity, having more functional and innovative designs, and ensuring sustainability and traceability along the value chain. Currently, India has low competitiveness in the high volume-low value addition parts of the market given high interest rates and a more challenging industrial relations environment. To gain market share, Indian should ideally target smaller volume segments with higher value addition, higher service level and wider customization requirements. In the long run, Indian players will also be able to build a sustainable competitive advantage against other textile manufacturing hubs and attract global retailers and customers if they pivot their operations and marketing campaigns around sustainability. With product authenticity and traceability becoming key differentiators, companies need to make investments in advanced tracking solutions for real-time order updates across the value chain as well as in robust state-of-the-art traceability solutions that help prove a product's origin.

FMCG

Global fast-moving consumer goods (FMCG) market size was valued at ~$10 trillion in 2017. FMCG can be defined as packaged goods that are consumed or sold at regular and small intervals. Food and Beverage is the largest segment followed by Personal Care, Home Care and Health Care.

Major global consumer product companies (such as Unilever, P&G, Colgate, Nestle, Heinz) have a lion's share of the global market. These companies have been established for a very long time and possess a clutch of strong brands with proprietary technology. Most of these companies are cash rich and well managed. Their brands generate strong cash flows and allow them to reinvest in strengthening their brand equity further, with continued promotions/ advertisements. They also have the financial clout to acquire small local brands to strengthen their position in the category. These companies also make considerable investment in R&D to sharpen and maintain their edge in the business.

Most of the global majors have their origins in Europe or the USA. They find their home markets saturated and are banking on the third world for future growth. These companies are setting up shop and are aggressively expanding their base in these countries. They also look out for opportunities to acquire local brands to push start or consolidate their position in these markets.

FMCG companies globally have embarked upon major restructuring / cost-cutting exercises as the business has become fiercely competitive. Also, several innovations in packaging media have taken place.

In the last few years, the process of adapting to local conditions has accelerated. MNCs are adapting their products, process and marketing communication to the local conditions. They alter the manufacturing process to maximize use of local raw materials and suit their products to the taste and requirements of local consumers. This process has been necessitated by the imperative to be cost effective and be competitive vis-a-vis strong local players.

The role of packaging has increased significantly in recent times, partly due to improvement in packaging technology. Traditionally, packaging was expected to serve the purpose of protection and economy. Then, packaging was expected to fulfill the objective of convenience. Today, packaging is used as an effective tool for promotion. Besides, new packaging technology has enabled most FMCG companies to significantly reduce their packaging costs.

Across the globe, we're seeing a resurgence of the home-delivery model—with a twist. Consumers aren't just picking up the phone to order; increasingly, they're pulling up the retailer's webpage or using their mobile app. One-quarter of global respondents are already ordering grocery products online for home delivery, and more than half (55%) are willing to use it in the future.[169] The milkman is back, but this time he's gone digital.

Online shopping has a number of benefits, but physical stores also have strong key advantages over e-commerce—especially for fast-moving consumer goods. Aside from the obvious in-store benefit of fulfilling immediate shopping needs without paying shipping fees, there are powerful sensory experiences—smelling freshly baked bread and seeing and feeling the vibrant color and texture of perfectly ripe strawberries - that is virtually impossible to replicate online. It's also difficult to match the power of human interaction and the thrill of unplanned discovery that physical stores can provide. Just as important, for many consumers, grocery shopping can be a fun activity that generates positive feelings. In fact, the majority of global respondents (61%) believe going to the grocery store is an

---

[169] "The future of grocery - E commerce, digital technology and changing shopping preferences around the world", Nielsen, April 2015

enjoyable and engaging experience. A similar percentage (57%) thinks grocery shopping in a retail store is a fun day out for the family. In mixed use urban societies, people find it best to go down to the stores and get things themselves. The habit of getting the essentials yourself adds a healthy routine to daily life. People are also a lot more conscious of what and how much they are buying. Getting groceries and other items yourself also makes it possible to avoid unnecessary packaging.

Technology, in any case, will never be a substitute for the basic elements of a great shopping experience that is mainly determined by innovative store design, ample selection, execution excellence and exceptional service.

Across the globe, we're seeing the rise of proximity retailing. In the eyes of global shoppers, small and simple is beautiful right now. While there is some growth for large stores, the real winners are mini markets, small supermarkets and convenience stores. And digital is taking proximity/convenience retailing to a new level of customer centricity. There is nothing more convenient than a store in your pocket or in your handbag.

Globally, the trade channel mix is becoming more fragmented as consumers shift toward smaller store formats. On a value basis, large supermarkets and hypermarkets account for just over half (51%) of global sales, but smaller formats such as traditional, drug and convenience stores are growing at a faster rate. In fact, year-over-year sales growth in drug stores, small supermarkets and traditional stores, doubled, or more than doubled, that of large supermarkets and hypermarkets.

Until the 19th century, you would have likely purchased your food at a public market, where you could see and touch produce, smell combinations of the foods and spices for sale, and speak to sellers and other customers. In this multisensory environment, you would have discerned the quality of foods through their appearance, smell, and texture, and through communication.

Beginning in the 1920s, large grocery stores began absorbing neighborhood stores in cities like New York. By the mid twentieth century, you would be shopping in grocery stores similar to what you'd be familiar with today. Stores that carried everything you needed—butcher, baker, produce, and packaged items. Bright lights and colorful displays, aisles and aisles of options, carefully displayed and enthusiastically marketed.

This change in our sensory experience involved a shift in the entire food chain from producers to distributors and retailers since the late nineteenth century.[170] The United States was then at the forefront of the industrialization of agriculture and food processing, the emergence of the food-coloring business, and the growth of a modern food retailing system. The US initiated mass production and mass marketing that also made it conducive to drive greater standardization of food colors. With rapid industrialization and market expansion in the United States from the 1870s on, agricultural producers and food processors sought to streamline production, emphasizing efficiency, consistency, and standardization.

Through this shift many consumers attained an unprecedented variety of foods. Mass production, long-distance transportation systems, and refrigeration technology meant a wider variety of both agricultural and processed products reached a broader population. But sensory experiences became increasingly uniform and predictable. A bag of apples, a box of breakfast cereal, and a tub of margarine invariably offered consumers from Los Angeles to New York the same color and the same flavor.

---

[170] "How Sight—Not Taste, Smell, or Touch—Became the Sense of the Supermarket", Ai Hisano, October 19, 2020

Prioritizing our visual experience was essential for this shift. Color turned out to be easier to control, reproduce, and commoditize than other sensory factors. The smell of food, for example, was difficult to convey in print or other media. Color served as a powerful communication tool for the food industry not only to appeal to the eyes of consumers but also to stimulate gustatory, olfactory, and tactile sensations.

Farmers, food processors, dye manufacturers, government officials, and intermediate suppliers began devoting enormous resources to determine and create the "right" color of foods, which many consumers would recognize and, in time, take for granted.

Seeking to create uniform, bright colors as the sign of succulent fruits and vegetables, growers and packers tended to prioritize the appearance of their produce over the actual taste. Several studies conducted in the 1920s and 1930s suggested that produce artificially ripened with ethylene gas (a gas that helped speed up the ripening process of fruits and vegetables) did not develop full flavor due to a lower sugar content than those ripened on the plant. One study, for instance, showed that tomatoes ripened by ethylene remained solid for a longer period than did vine-ripened fruits. The firm fruit was easy to transport and looked good, but it came at the expense of flavor and texture.

This creation of visual hegemony in our food systems has had multifaceted consequences. The emphasis on vision, as well as the standardization of color, expanded the portfolio of items that people could access and consume. For example, scientific engineering at the turn of the twentieth century made canned foods available to both lower- and upper-class consumers as an alternative to "fresh" foods throughout the year—canners even argued that canned foods were fresher than "the fresh articles." The introduction of synthetic dyes enabled citrus growers to provide bright orange oranges as a product of nature with wider consumers than before.

This "democratization," however, engendered inequalities in health risks. Cheaper food products, including low-grade canned foods, at the time were more likely to contain cheap, sometimes poisonous, coloring substances. Consumers who could not afford expensive and reliable foods were more exposed to the risk of health hazards.

A luscious, uniform look of fruits and vegetables on a supermarket shelf also came with environmental implications. Seeking a uniform look, fruit shipping companies, such as United Fruit, began mass-producing one banana variety, leading to a monoculture system that devastated the land, as well as the health of workers.

The emphasis on appearance in selling food, among other reasons, contributes to substantial food waste. Every year, 40 percent of food is wasted in the United States. That includes 20 billion pounds of produce that is not even harvested, left on farms because it doesn't meet grade standards, including shape and color.

Fast forward to New York and the alpha cities of today, and we will witness a resurgence of natural, fresh, minimally processed and packaging free retailing. The cities are moving towards a future where food service companies, cosmetics brands, and groceries stores provide consumers with reusable containers "designed to be returned to the seller, washed, reused.

Sustainability oriented stores are popping up everywhere promoting the use of refillable shampoos, conditioners, and body washes, which use cleaner ingredients than the mass retail brands.

Packaging-free shopping is both the newest and the oldest trend in the book. New because modern shops opening in the trendy neighborhoods of cities around the world are propagating sustainable ways to stock up essentials. Old because it's not all that long ago when there was a shorter name for packaging-free shopping: Shopping. There simply was no other way to shop.

Our grandparents went to the local grocery store, the market or straight to the farmer, where cereals and grains were sold from giant barrels or sacks, fruit out of a wooden crate, milk straight from a churn. Not until the middle of the past century did pre-packaged goods on supermarket shelves slowly begin to displace this old way of shopping (which still remains the norm in some less developed regions).

For decades, the convenience, range of products available and long shelf life made possible by packaging were considered progressive. Today, consumers are increasingly aware of the environmental impact of waste, much of it unnecessary, and are striving to shop more sustainably. The revival of packaging-free shopping is well on its way.

What really sets this new breed of sustainable shops apart from regular supermarkets has little to do with size. Instead, it's all about style, conscientiousness and community. Packaging-free shops look good as their design sits easily with current trends towards minimalism. In an urban environment, they give you the opportunity to ground yourself in nature.

The Indian FMCG sector has a market size of ~$60 billion. The industry is still in its nascent stages in India and has a potential to reach a size of more than a trillion dollars as consumption gets increasingly organized. Given that much of the development is yet to happen, India has the opportunity to learn from the evolution of the global FMCG industry and adopt the most optimal and sustainable path.

The industry is segmented into Food & Beverage (45%), Personal Care (23%), Home Care (11%) and others (20%).[171] The Indian FMCG Industry is characterized by high

---

[171] "Current trends in FMCG sector in Indian market context", Prof. Mudasir Ahamed Khan N, Prof. Kavya C., Prof. Abrar Hussain, Department of MBA, Sri Sri Shivakumara Mahaswamy College of Engineering, Bangalore, R.R. Institute of Advanced Studies Bangalore, 2020

competitive intensity with the presence of a large number of vertically integrated companies that have made huge investments in setting up distribution networks and promoting brands. There is a strong presence of leading multinational companies, high competition between organized and unorganized players and low operational costs.

The barriers to entry for foreign players have reduced and it has become easier to import materials and technology. With more MNCs entering the country, the industry is highly fragmented. Advertising expenditure continues to grow and marketing budgets as well as strategies are becoming more aggressive. Private label offerings by retailers are growing as they offer a discount to mainframe brands and have superior quality to smaller and weaker brands. Rural consumption growth has outpaced urban consumption with the increase in percentage in monthly per capita expenditure in rural markets surpassing its urban counterparts.

India is a food surplus nation and has the most evolved food processing capabilities in the world. India also has a sufficient number of domestic FMCG companies that have acquired efficient product development, production and distribution capabilities. As the industry moves towards realizing the trillion-dollar domestic potential, India should now start phasing out the multinationals. India should gradually increase the cost of doing business for multinationals and enable the domestic players to buy out the Indian operations of multinationals. India will need to make key acquisitions in personal care and home essentials, as the multinationals have highly evolved product lines in these categories.

Being an agricultural economy, Indians still want the touch and feel experience before committing to any purchase. So culturally, we are extremely inclined to just do away with all forms of packaging. The high density of population in our cities leads to high levels of consumption, providing certainty to production.

India's FMCG industry has the opportunity to lead the charge on sustainability. FMCG companies will need to significantly change their operating models to drive sustainability. The new high-rise urban India presents an ideal ecosystem to make packaging free or open retailing a reality. While open retailing will significantly simplify the FMCG value chain, it will necessitate leaner, more agile and optimal supply chains.

Storage and placement for open retailing will require adopting the age-old methods and operating structures of Kiranas (grocery retailers), Aaratiyas (wholesalers) and Mandis. A focus on quality will help make these operations suitable for the new urban India. Supply chains and logistics will need to be nimble and have evolved container technologies to minimize spoilage and waste. The FMCG companies themselves will need to forward integrate into retail or develop efficient models to work with the open retail establishments.

FMCG manufacturing units will need to be simplified towards making the product, packaging and supply chains healthy and sustainable. Usage of chemicals and preservatives would need to be significantly reduced with precise and stringent regulations across various product categories. Indian FMCGs also need to moderate the use of complex carbohydrates, sugar, spices and oils in food products e.g. Indian sweets, biscuits, cakes and chocolates with less sugar and higher protein (lentils) content. There is significant scope for research and product development to evolve healthy Indian foods. Foreign FMCGs have introduced a plethora of unnecessary processed foods that need to be discarded. The industry needs to encourage consumption of products (e.g. fruits, vegetables and milk) in their natural and pure form. India has a wealth of natural formulations for every FMCG product category and needs to enable their commercial large-scale production. Patanjali is a case in point for giving the global FMCGs a run for their money with mass production of Indian formulations. Domestic Indian enterprises need to invest significantly in research and product development for personal care and home essentials to make high quality and natural products. Elimination of packaging will necessitate adoption of large containers suitable for large scale inventory and logistics. Companies and retailers will also need to have appropriate large containers at the retail outlets for efficient storage, placement and dispensing.

Processing will move closer to retail. For an urban only India, it would be most optimal to locate the processing and distribution centers within the identified 130 cities. The city locations are ideally suited to efficiently process products from local produce. Processing in the city will allow efficient shipping to other cities using the rail / truck freight and minimize spoilage. Integrated processing and retailing operations (live retailing) will replace the package retailing for several FMCG categories. Live retailing will manifest in several forms such as neighborhood stores simply retailing one or more FMCG product categories without packaging, standalone live retailing shops offering minimally processed products (beverages etc.) or freshly cooked foods ideally meant for immediate consumption, a big warehouse surrounded by retail outlets (fruits & vegetables, cereals, pulses, spices etc.), a big processing center surrounded by related retail outlets (namkeens, sweets, bakery, confectionery, sauces, pickles, dairy products, soaps, creams, perfumes, cleaning liquids etc.), and several other forms.

Open retailing will be more manpower intensive. Making products naturally, handling natural supply chains and managing open retail operations, would all need more people.

The industry will evolve such that large national and regional players (with processing, warehousing, distribution and retailing in each city) will control each FMCG category. There would possibly be 5-10 large players that control product groups with greatest synergies and adjacencies across the value chain. Narrow product clusters with greater vertical integration across the supply chain.

Each company might have multiple brands for one product category. In all, there would likely be 30-50 large FMCG companies in India. While these would account for over 70% of the market, they would be complemented by city level and standalone open retail operations.

This domestic trillion-dollar industry will not only serve as the model for the world, but will also produce globally differentiated high quality products. Unlike most other industries, consumer goods is an everlasting industry. Nations will increasingly become self-sufficient in industries such as energy and engineering technology, but the produce of the Indian subcontinent will always be differentiated. The quality and diversity of the produce of the Indian subcontinent is unmatched and gives India a source of timeless competitive advantage. We just need to believe in the fundamentals, keep things simple and sustainable, and this industry alone will take care of all possible trade deficits.

Pharmaceuticals

The global pharmaceuticals industry is worth around $1.2 trillion. European and American companies remain the leaders. In 2019, Roche had the largest pharmaceutical revenue of the order of $48.3 billion and highest research and development (R&D) spend of $10.3 billion. Novartis had sales of $46.09 billion and an R&D spending of $8.39 billion. Pfizer had pharmaceutical sales of $43.66 billion and spent $7.99 billion on R&D, with its products being available in more than 125 countries. Other large companies from the US are Merck & Co. ($40.90 billion), Bristol-Myers Squibb ($40.69 billion) and Johnson & Johnson ($40.08 billion). In Europe, Roche and Novartis in Switzerland, Sanofi in France, GSK and AstraZeneca in the UK, were the leaders. Most of today's major pharmaceutical companies were founded in the late 19th and early 20th centuries. Key discoveries of the 1920s and 1930s, such as insulin and penicillin, became mass-manufactured and distributed.

The largest share of pharmaceutical revenue corresponds to branded and patented medicines. Amongst therapeutic drugs, oncologic, antidiabetic, respiratory, autoimmune disease, and antibiotic and vaccine drugs are the top pharmaceuticals generating approximately $100 billion, $79 billion, $61 billion, $54 billion and $41 billion, respectively, in 2018.

Global pharmaceutical market is highly dynamic and is characterized by greater levels of R&D expenditure and extensive regulation of its products. Amongst all industries, the pharmaceutical industry has the largest investment in R&D. Such spending involves identification and development of compounds for new drugs, and it is increasing throughout the world over time. Worldwide, the largest number of new compounds and pharmaceuticals between 2013 and 2017 was generated by the US pharmaceutical industry, followed by that of Europe.

Growth performance and competitive advantages of countries go together with their activities of technological innovation and imitation. Technological development measured by patent and R&D expenditures have a significant impact on the trade performance of the countries. In the pharmaceutical industry, which is one of the most technology-intensive industries, the extent and nature of innovation is crucial for countries to prolong their productivity growth and competitiveness in the long run. In broad terms the process of technological change can occur through improvements in the products, production process, raw material and intermediate inputs, and through enhancements in the efficiency of the management system.

The modern pharmaceutical industry can trace its origin to two main sources: companies such as Merck, Eli Lilly and Roche that had previously supplied natural products such as morphine, quinine and strychnine, moved into large-scale production of drugs in the middle of the 19th century, whilst newly established dyestuff and chemical companies, such as Bayer, ICI, Pfizer & Sandoz, established research labs and discovered medical applications for their products. Nevertheless, growth was relatively modest and at the start of the 1930s most medicines were still sold without a prescription. Almost half of them were compounded locally by pharmacists and in many cases physicians themselves dispensed medicines directly to their patients.

However, a number of major advances were made in the early part of the 20th century. Salicylic acid, a natural constituent of willow bark, had been recorded by Hippocrates as having analgesic properties. In 1897, scientists at Bayer demonstrated that a chemically modified version of salicylic acid had much improved efficacy and the product, aspirin, is still in widespread use today. In the 1920s and 1930s both penicillin and insulin were identified and manufactured, albeit at a modest scale. The Second World War provided a major stimulus to the developing industry, with requirements for the large-scale manufacture of analgesics and antibiotics and increasing demands from governments to undertake research to identify treatments for a wide range of conditions. After the war, the implementation of state healthcare systems in Europe, such as the UK's National Health Service (NHS), created a much more stable market, both for the prescription of drugs and, much more importantly, their reimbursement. This produced a major incentive for further commercial investment in research, development and manufacture. This greater role for the state was paralleled on both sides of the Atlantic, with increasing government regulation of medicine production.

The post-war period from the 1950s to the 1990s saw major advances in drug development with the introduction of new antibiotics, new analgesics, such as acetaminophen and ibuprofen, and completely new classes of pharmaceuticals such as oral contraceptives, beta blockers, ACE inhibitors, benzodiazepines and a wide range of novel anti-cancer medicines.

The thalidomide scandal of 1961 triggered a complete reassessment of state controls on the industry. New regulations now demanded proof of efficacy, purity and safety, with the latter leading to a massive increase in the requirements and costs of research and development, particularly in the clinical testing of new drugs. As the barriers to entry in drug production were raised, a great deal of consolidation occurred in the industry. Likewise, the processes of globalization, which had begun before the war, increased. This resulted in new drug development being dominated by a small number of very large multinational companies and the beginning of the era of the "blockbuster" drug.

In 1977, Tagamet, an ulcer medication, became the first ever blockbuster pharmaceutical, earning its manufacturers, GSK, more than US$ 1 billion a year and its creators the Nobel Prize. This was followed by a succession of products, each seemingly more successful than its predecessors. Prozac, the first selective serotonin reuptake inhibitor (SSRI) was launched by Eli Lilly in 1987 and omeprazole, the first proton pump inhibitor (PPI), was introduced by Astra in 1989. Atorvastatin, marketed as Lipitor in 1996, became the world's best-selling drug of all time, with more than US$ 125 billion in sales over approximately 15 years.

This was probably the golden age for the industry, with research producing an apparently endless stream of increasingly successful and profitable products; since then, the industry has been beset by a series of major problems, many of which have yet to be solved.

The pharmaceutical industry in some ways resembles an iceberg. These very well-known companies, which are loosely defined as research-based pharma companies, represent 40% of the market in terms of revenue; however, they correspond to only a small fraction of the industry as a whole, with >90%

of pharmaceutical companies, known as generic companies, being largely invisible to the general public. In turn, these generic companies produce the vast majority of all pharmaceuticals sold.

Generic pharmaceutical companies are low-cost, low-margin and low-risk businesses. Generic companies do not need to incur any research and development costs, although some of the larger companies do undertake process-orientated R&D in order to introduce more efficient, and lower cost, manufacturing. Although manufacturing in the industry is highly regulated, product volumes are small and manufacturing costs are relatively low. Marketing costs are also very low since the products are already well established in the marketplace and the demand is well understood. In many ways, generic pharmaceutical companies are in commodity markets where competitive differentiation is based on cost of goods and profitability is determined by market share.

The research pharmaceutical companies operate under a completely different business model. It is these innovative companies that bring the new pharmaceuticals to the market. This is very expensive, time-consuming, and involves extremely high risks. Research and development in the pharmaceutical industry is very expensive, but it is the development activity that dominates the costs, particularly in the clinical trials which follow the preclinical development.

Since patent life is one of the key determinants of the income that can be generated from a product it is not surprising that research companies try to extend patent life as much as possible. This "patent evergreening" can sometimes be done simply by patenting the manufacturing process or the drug formulation or, in some cases, the drug delivery system, all of which can be implemented much closer to the launch date. Generic companies, on the other hand, endeavor to have patents set aside or to find ingenious ways to get around the patents. There has also been an increase in recent years in "pay for delay" agreements between patent holders and generic manufacturers.

The pharmaceutical industry is in a state of flux. Besides a dwindling drug pipeline and patent expiries across the world, one of the biggest concerns for the industry are the spiraling costs of research and development, necessary for new drug discoveries. Plus, the end customers of the pharma sector, including governments, patients, and insurance companies, are becoming increasingly reluctant to pay the escalating prices for new medicines. They are demanding more value for lower prices.

The global pharmaceutical industry is a prime example of the negative consequences of creating nation states. Nations across the world are pretty much at the mercy of the European and American drug companies for life itself. There is simply no logic for patent protection in medicine. If the intention is the well-being of everyone in this world, medicine technology should be open for everyone. In a world where we treat every global citizen as an equal, technology and resources should be made available for everyone, with controls to ensure efficient, healthy and sustainable use.

The distributed operations of the global pharmaceutical companies across different regulatory regimes is the core problem of the pharmaceutical industry. Due to the varying nature of political, economic and legislative progress across developed and emerging economies, ethical guidelines have not been adopted in a uniform manner worldwide.[172] This has paved the way for ethics dumping as we know it today. The term 'ethics dumping' was coined in 2013 by the European Commission (EC) to describe the act of doing research deemed unethical in a scientist's home country in a foreign setting with more lax regulations.[173] Ethics dumping requires

---

[172] "Book review: 'Bottle of Lies' explores Ranbaxy and the unethical underbelly of Indian pharma", Suhit Kelkar, May 4, 2020

[173] "Medical research is conducted in developing countries to avoid ethics legislation", Sophie Perryer, June 10, 2019

strong ethics legislation and compliance mechanisms in one setting (high income) and the lack thereof in another setting (low or middle income). This legislative and compliance gap is then used to undertake research abroad that would be prohibited or severely restricted at home. As such, ethics dumping should not be conflated with unethical domestic research practices but understood as the act of traveling abroad to evade ethical guidelines. Over the past 50 or so years, many prominent pharmaceutical companies and prestigious research organizations have been known to engage in ethics dumping, particularly as part of clinical trials.[174]

India in particular has become something of a hotspot for ethics dumping. A clinical trial comes at a huge cost, so bringing that down is a key consideration for a lot of research organizations. By relocating to countries such as India, where costs are lower, companies can cut their overheads. India also has a large and varied population, so that's also part of the reason why trials are being conducted in this part of the world. The country became an even more attractive environment for medical research in 2005, when ethics laws were relaxed in a bid to strengthen India's position as a key player on the global pharmaceutical stage.

Ethics dumping of this nature flouts basic rules of consent, both within the field of medical research and as a human right. The inequitable power dynamic between research organizations and unwitting test subjects also makes it very difficult for the latter to claim any kind of recourse if they do suffer ill effects as a result of a trial.

The main objective of ethics dumping is profit making. Conducting trials in low-income countries is much cheaper and enables companies to substantially increase their profits. Ethics dumping directly brings out the disastrous consequences of outsourcing.

---

[174] "The ethics of global clinical trials", Katrin Weigmann, April 7, 2015

But outsourcing in general creates a negative loop for emerging and low-income economies. In a bid to increase profits, large companies typically outsourced low value or commoditized tasks. Manufacturing commoditized items (API manufacturing in case of pharmaceuticals), low value research, software development, customer support, and several functional processes have been outsourced over the last few decades by large corporations. Lower income or emerging economies perform these tasks at much lower costs. The costs are lower because the regulatory regime is compromised on all fronts whether it is health, quality, education, pension, safety or environment). To increase competitiveness against other low income and emerging economies, these countries have no option but to turn a blind eye.

Outsourcing low value manufacturing / services to lower income countries is flawed on many fronts. Manufacturing consumes significant resources and energy and generates heavy emissions. The developed world (North America, Europe and Japan) has smartly outsourced all possible manufacturing to Asian countries. Even though China has created a large economy by becoming a global manufacturing hub, inequality (Gini coefficient) is still one of the highest in the world. Low-cost manufacturing has created a huge base of low wage workers. In their bid to manufacture at low-cost, emerging nations compromise critical aspects such as health, education, environment, pension, safety etc. Concentrated production in LCCs significantly increases cross-border transportation requirements that are extremely energy intensive.[175] Worldwide transportation of goods is a significant source of carbon emissions and energy use throughout the entire supply chain. Sourcing products from suppliers who lack a commitment to sustainable business practices (largely true for most suppliers in Asia) leads to an increased environmental impact. Approximately 80% of the

---

[175] "Increasing Sustainability in Global Supply Chains", Daniel Stuesse, Washington University, 2017

world's merchandise trade by volume is carried over water. Marine vessels are a key source of freight energy consumption globally, accounting for around a third of the total freight energy consumption. Because of globalized supply chains, maritime shipments of non-energy commodities, such as manufactured goods, agricultural products, and minerals have grown much faster than global GDP. Global supply chains have also increased the use of heavy trucks, which again account for a third of the freight energy consumption globally. Global supply chains also result in much higher packaging requirements. Sustainability means using resources to meet the needs of the present without compromising the ability of future generations to meet their own needs. Low-cost manufacturing hubs such China, India, Vietnam, Indonesia, Malaysia, Bangladesh etc., are fast consuming their resources to meet the needs of the developed world and leaving little for their own future generations. Besides consuming limited natural resources such as minerals, the excessive use of agricultural produce creates a huge unsustainable carbon footprint.

While outsourcing does allow for capability development, most countries (especially small and medium sized countries) are simply unable to use that capability for creating a self-sufficient domestic industry over the long term. The outsourcing industry actually disincentivizes and makes it more difficult for emerging countries to develop end-to-end industrial capabilities. In an equitable global society, outsourcing should only happen for things that simply cannot be done in the home country. And global industrial leaders need to enable the creation of end-to-end capabilities and self-sufficient industries wherever possible. Countries that have the scale (sizable domestic demand) should aim to become self-sufficient and move forward towards full scale capability development. A protectionist stance might result in losses in the short term but is the only way to build a high-quality self-sufficient industry. If a nation has to prosper economically, it can only do so by having fully developed indigenous industries. Any unnecessary dependence on other nation states results in suppression of income, development and living standards. People working in the outsourcing industry or low-cost manufacturing units are inherently considered inferior to the countries they serve and operate with much lower standards in all aspects. The purpose of minimizing cost for a foreign company is not even fulfilling for employees over the long run.

The dependence of outsourcing industries increases income inequality in the low-income country and also prevents the low income countries from bridging the gap against the developed nations. Smaller countries do not have the option to become fully self-sufficient, but countries such as India that have sufficient material resources and people (talent and demand), have the opportunity to become independent. India has smartly leveraged the outsourcing industry to build indigenous capabilities but needs to move forward and control the entire value chain of various industries. India has broad self-sufficiency on materials, will soon be independent on energy and has sufficient technology capabilities across industries. The Indian manufacturing industry needs to simply focus on serving the Indian market. The domestic demand is huge, making an inward focus economically attractive as well. Serving other markets puts unnecessary stress on the already thin resource and energy stock of the country. India needs to start phasing out its export oriented low-cost manufacturing industry.

Pharmaceutical manufacturing evolved significantly during the late 20th century. Technology has advanced in large-scale manufacturing environments to deliver higher outputs. The pharma industry has witnessed the introduction of sophisticated machines and automated lines that require less human intervention whilst producing greater volumes with consistency and reliability. Sterile products have benefited from novel innovations with a transition from glass containers to plastics and the evolution of technologies such as blow-fill-seal (BFS), prefilled syringe (PFS) and prefilled pens (PFP). A growing number of oncology and other potent molecules have been enabled owing to the introduction of containment systems such as isolators, RABS (Restricted Access Barrier Systems) and PPE (Personal Protective Equipment). Machines have become smarter with the use of PLC and PC systems with process control, data acquisition, data storage and trend analysis. The use of SCADA systems has enabled data security, recipe management and access control. The introduction of sophisticated instruments in quality control (QC), such as high-pressure liquid chromatography (HPLC), gas chromatography, nuclear magnetic resonance (NMR) and X-ray diffraction (XRD) have helped with both precision during analysis and facilitated the discovery and development of new drugs and formulations. Throughout the last century, as new chemical entities were being discovered, the industry consolidated the large-scale production of these chemical moieties and their subsequent generics. For large emerging economies, it is mainly a case of replicating the capabilities already built in the developed world.

We now know that pharmaceuticals can enter the environment in three different ways: in effluents discharged from manufacturing sites, from the disposal of unused and life-expired medicines, and via excretion from patients undergoing treatment.[176] Detailed quantification for any individual pharmaceutical is difficult, but there is general agreement that the latter source dominates the global environmental input, with effluent discharges and the disposal of unused medicines making relatively small contributions. Relatively high local concentrations can occur adjacent to discharges from industry, particularly in developing countries and from hospitals. Most scientists, in

---

[176] "The Pharmaceutical Industry and the Future of Drug Development", David Taylor, Pharmaceuticals in the Environment, 2015

academia, governments, regulatory bodies and industry, who have evaluated the published data, have concluded that there appear to be no appreciable effects on aquatic life due to pharmaceuticals in the environment. In other words, short-term immediate damage to the environment is very unlikely.

The pharmaceutical industry has found a cure for all major diseases, with only a very few rare diseases remaining that are still incurable. Advancements will continue to improve efficacy levels and patient experience. The manufacture and production of drugs with chemical entities as active pharma ingredients (APIs), both patented and generic, will continue for a long time. However, the number of patented chemical drugs is dwindling, and this will lead to a reduction in generics in the future.

Biotechnology has gained prominence over the last two decades and is gradually increasing its share of the pharmaceutical industry. Biologics have had a profound impact on many medical fields, primarily rheumatology and oncology, but also cardiology, dermatology, gastroenterology, neurology, and others. In most of these disciplines, biologics have added major therapeutic options for the treatment of many diseases, including some for which no effective therapies were available, and others where previously existing therapies were clearly inadequate. However, the advent of biologic therapeutics has also raised complex regulatory issues, and significant pharmacoeconomic concerns, because the cost for biologic therapies has been dramatically higher than for conventional (pharmacological) medications. The pharma industry has now invested in developing biologics and biosimilars and, for the past two decades, we've seen remarkable growth in this area. Currently, there are more than 300 patented biologics, half of which are likely to go off-patent in the next few years, which will lead to a rise in new biosimilars.

The age-old adage of "prevention is better than cure" assumes great significance in today's world. Prevention is the biggest driver of longevity. While with cure, we attempt to save 5-10 years of our lives, with prevention, humanity can increase lifespans by more than 50 years. Preventing our bodies from diseases and unhealthy conditions is the best path towards both the longest possible and the most fulfilling life. Now given that the global pharmaceutical industry has found a cure for most known diseases, the focus needs to be on keeping the bodies healthy for as long as possible. Growing health awareness has encouraged people to become more oriented toward preventing health problems and diseases.

There are several factors that can influence the health of an individual, but preventive healthcare can play a significant role in keeping a person healthy. Preventive healthcare pretty much encompasses every aspect of life - what, when and how. Preventive medication and foods is a key segment of the massive preventive healthcare ecosystem.

The potential size of the preventive healthcare market is much larger than the entire healthcare industry today. The estimated market size of the preventive healthcare technologies and services market today is ~$200 billion.[177] On the technology front, the market is fragmented into Early Detection and Screening Technologies, Vaccines, Chronic Disease Management Technologies, and Advanced Technologies to Reduce Errors.[178] Besides equipment, there is a huge potential market for preventive medicine, foods and services.

Some sectors are already eyeing the value of this market. Food companies such as Nestlé and PepsiCo are refocusing their brands around health and wellness. Mobile health has the potential to move us as a society from treating disease to preventing disease. Companies such as GE, Google, Samsung and Apple are investing in wearable technology and devices that can monitor health — from heart rate and blood pressure

---

[177] "Preventive Medicine, the Future State", Subhro Malik, Infosys Insights

[178] "Focus on pharma: Creating a market for disease prevention", Elvira Thissen, GreenBiz, December 5, 2014

to blood sugar and cholesterol. Google is partnering with pharma company Novartis to develop and market "smart contact lenses" that can help measure glucose levels. The launch of the Apple Watch, with a big focus on health monitoring, is a significant step towards mainstream technologies that could enhance healthcare. Pharma companies have also started focusing on prevention with programs aimed at major chronic diseases. The International Federation of Pharmaceutical Manufacturers & Associations and the International Federation of Red Cross and Red Crescent Societies have announced a partnership on NCD prevention to design a behavioral change-based toolkit.

But the general view in the sector is that prevention lacks a strong business case and is not a revenue generator. The current roadblock to the growth of the preventive healthcare market is the lack of coverage by the payors (insurance companies). Insurance coverage will create the market - enable spending and R&D required for the development of drugs, equipment, services and technologies.

Insurance coverage for prevention is central to creating a robust preventive ecosystem. It will bring together a whole host of stakeholders, especially when it comes to primary prevention to achieve behavior changes such as quitting smoking or changing diets. To encourage lifestyle changes, potential partners in the private sector may include food companies, retailers, education services and tech companies. Insurance, pharmaceuticals, well-being and food will increasingly overlap to enable a healthy lifestyle.

At the time of independence in 1947, India's pharmaceutical market was dominated by Western MNCs that controlled between 80 and 90 percent of the market primarily through importation. Approximately 99 percent of all pharmaceutical products under patent in India at the time were held by foreign companies and domestic Indian drug prices were among the highest in the world.

The Indian pharmaceutical industry has made rapid strides during the last few decades and is now fully equipped to help its people lead healthy lives.

Today, India is the largest provider of generic drugs globally. Indian pharmaceutical sector supplies over 50% of global demand for various vaccines, 40% of generic demand in the US and 25% of all medicine in the UK. Globally, India ranks 3rd in terms of pharmaceutical production by volume and 14th by value. The domestic pharmaceutical industry includes a network of 3,000 drug companies and ~10,500 manufacturing units. India is 3rd largest market for APIs globally, 8% share in Global API Industry, 500+ different APIs are manufactured in India, and it contributes 57% of APIs to the WHO prequalified list.

India has considerable manufacturing expertise; Indian companies are among the world leaders in the production of generics and vaccines. Indian companies have also started entering into the realm of R&D; some of the leading local producers have now started conducting original research. Needless to say, we have deep experience in conducting clinical trials.

In its bid to grab a greater share of the global pharmaceutical trade, India is looking to reach a market size of ~$130 billion by 2030. In 2020, the size of the Indian pharmaceutical industry was ~40 billion with a 50-50 split between domestic industry and exports. The Indian pharma industry has grown at a compounded growth rate of (CAGR) of ~11% in the domestic market and ~16% in exports over the last two decades. While the domestic market has grown at a similar pace to the gross domestic product (GDP), the overall growth has been driven by the industry's leadership in supplying generic formulations to markets across the globe.

On the domestic front, the current ambition translates into a growth rate of 10-11% over the coming decade. On the export side, we are looking to increase our share of global trade from 2.5% to 6-7%. The global pharmaceutical trade is expected to reach a size of US$1-1.3 trillion by 2030, translating into a ~$73 billion Indian pharmaceutical export industry.

The per capita health spending in India is abysmally low at ~$75. Developed nations spend more than 40 times on each individual (US ~$10,700, Switzerland ~$9,900, Norway ~$8,200, Denmark $6,200, Sweden ~$6,000, Germany $5,500, Netherlands $5,300, Canada $5,000, France $4,700, UK ~$4,400, Japan ~4,300, Italy ~3,000, Spain ~$2,800). Even other large emerging economies spend 5-10 times more than India (Brazil $850, China $500).

So simply increasing the domestic per capita spending by a factor of 10 (by say 2030) will make the pharmaceutical industry worth ~$200 billion (excluding exports). Not only is this much higher than the market size we are targeting to reach with an export-oriented industry, but it will also truly make Indian companies self-sufficient and most importantly result in a higher quality of life for Indians. Over the next 20-30 years, India should aim to achieve a health spend of over ~$2,000 per capita with a 30-40% spend on pharmaceuticals, including preventive medicine. That would translate to a pharmaceutical industry size of $900 billion to $1.2 trillion.

To propel the domestic pharmaceutical industry and make it self-sufficient, India needs to enable much higher levels of health spending and scale up domestic players to fully control and capture the spend.

India needs to gradually mandate robust insurance coverage across various industries and professions. The expansion needs to be planned and executed along with consolidation across industries and formalization and organization of the services sector. Income levels have to be increased across the board, especially for the lowest income bracket to maintain their consumption levels. India will also need to plan for the loss of cost competitiveness and the resulting reduction of exports. Maintaining the optimal value of the Indian currency would be needed for securing critical imports.

Scaling up domestic enterprises is fundamental for India to have a self-sufficient pharmaceutical industry. A few large publicly listed enterprises will be able to carry out cutting edge research, institutionalize efficient and safe systems and processes, achieve top tier efficiency across the value chain, consistently create high quality products, and provide a much higher standard of living for the employees. Once we stop competing in international markets, we gain price control which encourages the companies to follow all best practices. Decoupling from international markets will also give India the opportunity to rapidly move towards a most advanced regulatory regime. Companies will be able to simply increase prices to accommodate the increasing costs of compliance - complete insurance coverage will shield people from any adverse impacts of price increases. Indian companies will no longer need to follow unethical practices to minimize costs.

The industry is currently heavily fragmented with around 3,000 manufacturers and around 10,500 manufacturing units. The entire industry has been built as a low-cost manufacturer of generics for the developed markets. The top ten pharma companies in India are Abbot, Cipla, Ranbaxy, GSK, Sun, Zydus Cadila, Mankind, Alkem, Pfizer and Lupin. The industry is very fragmented where the largest company has only 8.5% market share, the second and third ranked companies have 6.2% and 4.6% market share respectively. The top 17 companies have 51% share and top 44 companies have 80%. The market is even more fragmented in the below 50 Ranked companies. There is huge pricing pressure in the industry due to this fragmented nature. The major market share is with Indian pharma companies, with multinational companies (MNCs) having less than 20 per cent by value.

Enforcing regulations becomes a nightmare in a heavily fragmented industry. Pricing pressure from global markets and MNCs forces Indian regulators to introduce price controls. To serve the poor of the country, the government keeps on extending a minimal cost, low quality infrastructure of pharmacies and other healthcare delivery systems. This creates a negative cycle for the domestic players as they are unable to generate profits and invest in building leading capabilities.

India needs to consolidate the pharmaceutical industry (including AYUSH) into 5-10 large companies. The consolidation should be accompanied by increasing standards of operations across all aspects of drug discovery, development, production and distribution. The government needs to enable the consolidation and sanction all resources to fast track the same. The regulatory body should work in tandem with the identified national entities (that will eventually control the entire Indian market) to enforce higher standards of quality, safety, health, compensation, retirement benefits etc. The nodal agency should achieve full transparency into the operations of the big Indian pharma companies. Support mechanisms need to be created for companies to carry out R&D without making compromises. Financial security needs to be provided to these companies to encourage adherence to best practices. Bonuses and variable compensation should be capped / minimized to discourage poor decision making. The industry should also be gradually protected against foreign participation.

India also has a huge opportunity to become a leader in research, development and production of preventive medicine. India needs to fully regulate the various forms of traditional medicine (AYUSH). Scientific research needs to govern each and every formulation and efficacies need to be clearly proven. R&D, production and distribution of these traditional medicines should also be restricted to a few large organizations. No unproven, ad-hoc formulation should be allowed on the market. India also needs to regulate the production of over-the-counter medicines, nutrition supplements and food items. Insurance needs to evolve to encourage spending on preventive medicine (AYUSH) and nutrition supplements.

Exercise is one of the best preventive medicines. Sports and various forms of workouts are therefore an essential need of a healthy and sustainable society. Manufacturing of sports goods assumes great importance for people's well-being. Sports participation is essential, not winning. People should engage in sports for the sole purpose of keeping themselves fit and healthy, and not for competing with others. Sports become risky when you are simply looking to win. Sports are the best form of cardio and should be treated that way. To get better at a sport, the body needs to get better in terms of strength, stamina and flexibility. Sports gear and equipment play a very important role in helping and encouraging us to improve our bodies.

Sports

The global sports equipment, apparel and footwear industry is worth $400-$500 billion. The largest share of the global market is for sportswear (45-55%), then for equipment (35-45%), and followed by sports footwear (15-25%).

The global sports goods industry has been termed as a 'fringed global oligopoly'.[179] A handful of transnational corporations (Nike, Adidas, New Balance etc.) cover a major share of the world market for various sports goods. In each developed country, a number of competing small and medium-sized enterprises take over the remaining 'fringe' of the local domestic market. Global sporting goods manufacturers, e.g., Nike and Adidas, have built a large number of overseas affiliate companies in emerging economies to seek cheaper labor forces and lower operation costs over their home country. Sporting goods manufacturers in emerging economies face limited financial resources, lack of skilled labor forces and machinery, and lack of overseas market information. Affiliate companies of global sporting goods manufacturers in developing countries are able to

---

[179] "The sport industry in growing economies: critical issues and challenges", James J. Zhang, Euisoo Kim, Brandom Mastromartino, Tyreal Yizhou Kian, John Nauright, International Journal of Sports Marketing and Sponsorship, March 2018

provide resources for local companies to gain production skills, managerial knowledge, and technological advancement. The global giants manage subcontractors in emerging economies by providing substantial knowledge on production, including training of unskilled workers, assisting equipment replacement, and supervising quality controls that allow subcontractors to meet the industrial specifications and quality standard. Nike manufactures over 90% of its shoes in Asia. Based on the acquired knowledge and skills from the principal corporation, some of the subcontractors were able to build their own local sporting goods brands successfully. For instance, Hwaseung, a South Korean athlete shoe maker, produced shoes for Nike from 1978 to 1986 as an original equipment manufacturer. With the accumulated technology and skills on athlete shoe making, the company dismissed the contract as a subcontractor with Nike in 1986 and successfully launched its own sporting goods brand, Lecaf, and has served the Korean and overseas markets ever since. Japan, Korea and China, have all become self-sufficient with domestic companies having a significant share of the home market. While most Japanese companies have grown organically since their inception in the early 1900s, China and Korea have adopted several strategies and inorganic means to build domestic capabilities and enterprises.

The oligopolistic nature of the industry explains why price is not the major strategic lever used by companies to keep or increase their market share. In an oligopoly, a price war might have a disastrous outcome, such as bankruptcy (possibly leading to a duopoly or monopoly). Competition in the oligopolistic sports industry is based on product quality, cost reduction and innovation rather than on pricing.[180] This results in higher profit levels and enables each oligopolist to invest a substantial share of its revenues in research and development (R&D), in product design and in cost-saving

---

[180] "The sports goods industry - Handbook on the economics of sport", Wladimir Andreff, January 2006

processes. Price variations are supplemented with marketing strategies based on product differentiation and the reputation of the firm. These strategies include associating the company's product with the image and wins of a champion and suggesting the high quality of the product through sponsorship of a leading sporting event (Olympics, World Cup) or a famous club or national team. Nike's 'just do it' slogan or "tick" have become world symbols of a way of life (valuing winners, energy, health and wealth) even more than the label of a range of products. The oligopolists adopt all the usual practices to create barriers to entry (restricting distribution, order cancellation, technological patents, economies of scale and scope etc.). Adidas, Nike, Reebok, and Puma have actually been sued, found guilty and fined for unduly restricting competitors in sports shoe distribution.

As Sports was never considered a strategic industry, most developing nations have taken a liberal stance to foreign participation. In a comparatively short period of time, lucrative foreign direct investment completely altered the global sports good industry. The industry rapidly moved towards global supply chains, enabling international sporting goods corporations to take advantage of cheap and abundant labor and raw material in developing countries. They provided impoverished countries with much-needed capital, direct employment, advanced technology, and access to international markets. The developing countries eventually copy the product portfolio of the global giants and introduce their own versions through the domestic enterprises. The lack of trademark enforcement and loopholes in copyrights protection in developing countries results in long drawn legal battles around copyright infringement, piracy, and squatting, which are further complicated by language barriers and cultural differences.

India has a tiny sports goods industry with an annual turnover of ~$250 million. Around 60% of the sports goods made in the country are exported, suggesting a domestic market size of ~$100 million. The domestic market is highly unorganized. The industry comprises mainly small-scale units employing around 5,00,000 people. Meerut and Jalandhar account for the majority of production.

Sports equipment researchers continuously improve the performance of sports equipment by improving the design of sports equipment, using high-tech materials, and innovating technical means.[181] Scientific design is the necessary condition to effectively improve the function of sports equipment. More and more hightech materials are used in the field of sports equipment manufacturing, which makes the performance of sports equipment get unprecedented improvement. Carbon fiber materials have now become the norm across various sports segments due to their light weight, high strength, corrosion resistance and easy processing.

While the Indian industry faces a huge capability gap against the large transnational corporations, the potential market size offers the opportunity to create domestic sports giants. Nike revenues are ~$40 billion, Adidas is ~$25 billion, Under Armor and Puma are both around $5 billion. The potential size of the Indian sports goods industry is more than ~$100 billion. But the industry growth will largely be linked to the pace of urbanization and the development of sports infrastructure. So as the spending ramps up to serious levels, India should focus on consolidating the industry into 4-5 domestic enterprises. These should be protected from foreign investments / ownership. Even with the current market size, these select companies will be able to significantly enhance the quality of their products and build an exhaustive portfolio of sports goods. These large companies will have the resources to invest in product development, production efficiencies, distribution, and marketing. The government will have a key role to play in the initial phases of consolidation, to essentially get the various entities to merge

---

[181] "The Influence of the Design and Manufacture of Sports Equipment on Sports", Zhenyu Qiu, 2020

and get organized. These large entities will also need easy access to capital to invest in building leading capabilities across the whole spectrum of sports goods and value chain. These companies should also be able to make certain niche acquisitions in developed markets. These large Indian enterprises will have several competitive advantages against the global giants in the Indian market. They will be able to control the market dynamics and drive its evolution.

In parallel with the consolidation, the government needs to work with the large Indian companies to introduce regulations around quality, safety, working conditions, compensation, benefits and environment. Regulations will further accelerate consolidation. The regulatory changes need to be introduced simultaneously across industries and along with the introduction of broader social security to maintain people's ability to spend responsibly on their wellbeing. The Indian legal system will also need to enable the large domestic players to freely develop products without being restricted by the intellectual property developed in other markets.

Increased regulation will reduce cost competitiveness of Indian sports goods in global markets. But given the much smaller size of the export industry as compared to the domestic market potential, India should willingly make that trade-off in the short term. Over the long run, India should aim to export only those products where it can command a significant premium.

Transnationals and other foreign companies should also be simultaneously phased out from the Indian market with a gradual ramp up of protectionist policies (import tariffs, foreign company taxation, FDI limits, ban on direct retailing etc.). Phasing out should be carefully planned to minimize supply disruptions for the end consumers. Once the domestic companies have built sufficient capability to serve the domestic demand, protectionism could be accelerated.

Toys

Toys have become a basic component of family childcare. Toys keep children engaged and help them develop critical skills - cognitive, motor, sensory, communication, emotional, social and creative. They enable higher development of a child's brain and help maximize its potential. Kids love toys and always have. The earliest toys date back to 4000 B.C. and were made of natural materials like sticks, rocks, and stone. Some children even played with animal bones. Throughout the centuries and decades, children's toys have evolved. Natural materials gave way to plastic. In recent years, the market has been influenced by varying consumer tastes, with children opting for more sophisticated video games and electronic toys. The invention of talking toys, video game consoles, and tablets brought technology to the forefront of the toy industry and forever changed the way children play. A walk down the aisle of a mass-market toy store will demonstrate how classic toys for children have given way to an abundance of high-tech toys.

Pediatricians suggest that electronic toys impede a child's development. Electronic toys reduce physical activity and provide much less opportunity to interact with others and the broader physical environment. That also hampers the development of language and communication, cognitive and emotional skills. With physical toys, children engage actively, develop spatial orientation and a real understanding of physical elements around them. Play and exploration is one of the most powerful ways very young children learn about how the world works. It helps them work out how to control their bodies and how to interact with people. It helps them learn about the impact their actions can have on objects and people in their environment and about how to produce the desired effect. When children play alone with digital toys, the negative effects of electronic devices on their development are intensified.

What happens in the environment of infants and toddlers influences the quality of their play. For instance, play with constant adults contributes to the attachment process, and the level of attachment between infants and adults is positively correlated with quality of play. This effect is attributed in part to the level of responsive feedback to their actions that babies get from their environment. There is also a positive relationship between the amount of quality play – often characterized in the literature as 'mature play,' where children are working near the ceiling of their level of development – and later abilities at such skills as problem-solving.

High-tech toys can be very seductive. They are marketed in ways that exploit adults' desire to choose toys that will enhance their children's learning. They grab adults' and babies' attention with movements, sounds, and lights. They do exciting and magical things that only the designers understand. And they promise to teach skills and prepare children for the future with such phrases as 'early learning activities designed to develop minds,' 'friendly voice introduces six vocabulary words,' 'musical and light responses teach concepts of cause-and-effect,' and 'bright colors and flashing lights create visual interest.' Many of these kinds of toys are made by familiar and trusted toy companies (such as Fisher Price), or are branded with familiar cartoon figures (from public television shows like Sesame Street or Disney movies like Winnie the Pooh). This fact further contributes to an image of developmental appropriateness and the lure to buy.

Many studies have suggested that playing with too many toys could affect the concentration level of kids and even hamper creativity, life skills, social interactions, imagination, mental health, and team spirit. Having too many toys results in an attitude of taking things for granted, wasteful behavior, tendency to easily get bored, lesser interest in building, reading, writing, art and physical activities, an attitude of selfishness and possessiveness, and territorial behavior. Children with too many toys are unable to comprehend the purpose of different objects and the underlying need for various things. They usually grow up as unorganized and lost individuals.

Too many toys is usually a consequence of some weakness on the part of parents. Parents' busy schedules and lack of interest in childcare are common reasons for them to stock up on toys. Instead of spending quality time with their children and making them internalize good habits, they bribe their kids with toys to get things done. To some parents, getting expensive and more toys gives a sense of luxury, opulence and status.

The size of the global toy industry is around $100 billion. The industry is characterized as a low concentration market resulting in high levels of competition. Entry barriers seem to be low. Although manufacturing requires capital investment, the size of the investment seems to be limited, implying that there are no sizable sunk costs involved in toy production. Lack of entry barriers adds to the competitive pressure in the toy production sector. Compliance with the Toy Safety Directive (TSD) diminishes sector profitability but doesn't necessarily prevent entry. However, if these costs turn out to be excessive over a longer period of time, small companies may decide to exit the market, reducing competitive pressure.

Vertical integration between toy producers and wholesalers/retailers (downstream integration) or resource suppliers (upstream integration) has not been observed much, although some major toy manufacturing companies have in-house warehousing capacity. Since toy manufacturing is a labor-intensive process that usually requires manual assembling, outsourcing to low labor cost countries is a common strategy in order to reduce the production costs.

Global toys and games market is mainly influenced by large global enterprises, which enjoy considerable economies of scale, as a result reduce their costs and enhance profit margins. With regard to power-asymmetry, the toy market players usually follow the major players such as Mattel, Hasbro, and Lego. In practice, smaller manufacturers are restricted by higher manufacturing costs and struggle to successfully bring their products through mainstream channels.

Traditional toys and games account for around 80% of the total production, and are steadily losing market share to electronic toys, video games, tablets and smartphones. Traditional toys and games include products such as dolls, infant and preschool toys, construction toys, outdoor and sports toys, board games and puzzles and arts and crafts toys.

Traditional toys and games are dominated by global brands such as LEGO, Hasbro and Mattel. These three are followed by two Japanese companies Bandai Namco and Takara Tomy. While Mattel is the leading company in the world in terms of sales, in China it ranks 4th with a 0.8% share. Likewise, Hasbro represents about 0.8% of the Chinese market but does not rank in the top 5.

The toy market is characterized by wide-ranging product differentiation that serves to weaken the degree of rivalry amongst manufacturing units to a great extent, and also deteriorate buyer power. Due to the high degree of product differentiation, the toys and games market requires infinite inputs, some of which are technology intensive, like electronic components, processors, etc.

Producers face cost and price competition to a significant extent. This competition on costs is reflected in the production strategy of producers, with many producers outsourcing production to China to reduce costs. In toy production, margins in the entire sector are under pressure with long-term profit margins around 6% for the top 100 firms in terms of size. The margins are lower for small and medium sized (SME) firms than for large firms. Also, the profit margin for retail is lower than for manufacturing of toys.

The short product life cycle of toys drives the need for innovation and research and development (R&D). Innovation is widely acknowledged in the sector as essential to maintaining a competitive position. In addition, it allows manufacturers to experience (temporarily) reduced price competition for innovative toys.

The need to escape cost competition also shows itself in the importance of marketing strategies. Traditional advertising still plays an important role and significant investments are undertaken with respect to this marketing channel. However, the landscape is changing, and digital product offering is becoming more important.

In terms of product segments, construction toys and outdoor and sports toys show the highest growth forecast among traditional toys. Board games and puzzles show stable market share forecasts, as they face most direct competition from video games, tablets and smartphone applications. The market for plush toys appears to have low growth forecasts.

India's share in the global toy market is less than 1% and is worth $700 - 800 million.[182] The Indian toy industry comprises a large number of indigenous manufacturers and a few leading global companies. The toy industry is mainly based in the small and cottage sectors, with about 4000 manufacturers. Funskool is the largest toy manufacturer in India with 30% share, followed by Mattel (20%), Hasbro (9%), Bandai (4%) and Lego (4%) and Leap Frog (3%) and the others accounts for about 30%.

The inflow of cheap mechanical toys that started flowing into the country with the liberalization of the Indian economy surpassed the traditional toy market in a matter of years,

---

[182] "An Overview of Indian Toys Industry", ILO Consulting, October 14, 2020

overrunning the market with low-quality Chinese imports. As a result, many toy factories closed in the past 30 years as they couldn't compete with China-made toys, especially the electric ones.

At present, the toy industry in India, is facing severe competition from the Chinese toy imports since China is arguably the largest exporter of toys in the world.[183] Nearly 2000 SMEs have closed so far in the last 4-5 years and about 20% of the toy industries are on the verge of closure with the rise in imports from China and Italy.

There are two broad segments of toys - educational and recreational. Under Educational toys, various toys & games made out of plastics and cardboard materials are under prominence, while recreational toys primarily include electronic toys such as remote controls, video games, battery operated toys, cars, plastic toys, dolls, soft toys and mechanical pull back toys. However, out of all of these toys, the electronic toys & games as well as the battery-operated toys are not being manufactured in India. But as far as most other categories are concerned, these are being manufactured in India as well as being imported.

India's import of toys in 2018-2019 stood at $1.4 billion (around INR 10,000 crore). Almost 85% of the toys sold in India are imported, with China being the top source, followed by Sri Lanka, Malaysia, Germany, Hong Kong and the US. The export value of toys and games is almost insignificant, resulting in an unnecessary trade deficit.

Toy making is, by nature, labor intensive. The life of a toy is limited. For instance, a Transformer Toy sells well when the movie releases but the off-take dies down soon after. Therefore, the demand for a product changes rapidly leading to high product diversity and innovation. These factors not only rule out mechanization, but also call for flexible staffing.

---

[183] "Research study on productivity & competitiveness of toy manufacturing sector in India", Economic Services Group, National Productivity Council, New Delhi, September 2017

Indian laws do not permit recruitment or retrenchment based on demand if the organization grows beyond a certain size in terms of employee strength. Hence, most units in the toy sector are very small and no major corporations have forayed into the industry despite the low capital investment needs. China, on the other hand, built huge factories, some employing as many as 30,000 workers. In most cases, the workers were provided accommodation at the factory and paid on an hourly or per piece basis. This meant that they could generate huge volumes, which significantly reduced the cost of production.

There are a large variety of innovative toys available in the Indian market at present. Toys are domestically produced by small, midsized, and large manufacturers and those that are produced from renowned international brands. Each toy category has inexpensive and high-end versions.

The government has made toy quality certification mandatory to revive the indigenous industry. India began enforcing quality control for imported toys from September 1, 2020, to ensure that only products conforming to standards enter the country. The Quality Council of India found in a December 2019 survey that 67% of imported toys were unfit and dangerous for kids.

The government is planning a Phased Manufacturing Programme (PMP) for toys with an aim to build a robust indigenous manufacturing ecosystem. India's domestic toy industry comprises ~4,000 micro, small and medium enterprises (MSMEs) and is primarily in the unorganized sector—a key area of focus for the government. The plan is to set up big toy units with a number of peripheral smaller toy component manufacturers. The smaller ancillary units will feed components to larger companies, as per design and advice of the larger company. The central company can source costly technologies from overseas in a WTO compatible environment. This will lead to multiple trades in technology wherein the central company seeks technology from a technology provider in the developed country and also provides technology in parts to its vendors/supplier companies.

The government is contemplating incentives for components and accessories, along with a license regime, for imported toys. International companies are being incentivized to make India their export base. The program will make local assembly of toys cheaper than imports since the benefits are in line with the PMP for mobile phones that was introduced in 2015. The government has offered tax relief and differential tariffs among other incentives on components and accessories used in the production of mobile phones to provide a push to local manufacturing and reduce India's dependence on imports under the PMP. The Department for Promotion of Industry and Internal Trade (DPIIT) is reaching out to large-scale global manufacturers in a round table for investments in the Indian toy industry. India has also invited top global toy makers to invest and a round table with major manufacturers is being planned to discuss Indian-themed toys.

The government is gradually introducing a new norm in the minds of consumers to purchase safe and good-quality 'Made in India' toys as against cheap and poor-quality imported toys. Adverts are also being gradually designed in a manner to target children and parents as influencers in building the Made in India brand loyalty, similar to the marketing campaigns of Amul and Maggi.

Though the toy industry is mainly driven by designs and marketability, technology remains the backbone for converting designs into viable and marketable products. Outright purchase of technology or licensing arrangements for the toy industry does not appear to be viable. The internationally available technologies are very costly and are beyond the reach of toy manufacturers from the SMEs. Under the WTO scenario, institutional back up can help solve issues of costly technologies, obsolete designs, market intelligence and better tooling. Methods of reverse engineering will not be available henceforth to the toy manufacturing companies. As a result, these companies may have to invest in their own design and development. Modern prototype development techniques, better tool room facilities would be more useful to the toy units. The industry needs to be sensitized and upgraded regularly based on WTO provisions and related opportunities. The toy industry has to develop a culture of innovations and market intelligence.

India finds itself in a position to swiftly transition to a toy industry that best serves the purpose of child development and engagement, delivers quality, consistency and equality, and is fully controlled by domestic enterprises. The industry is not complex in any case and India has all the capabilities needed to produce high quality traditional toys and games. We have not ventured into electronic toys and don't need to do so, given the negative effects on child health and development. Besides, electronic toys present unnecessary concerns related to safety and sustainability.[184] Technical complexity is also much higher in case of electronic toys.

Instead of incentivizing global players to increase their production in India, we simply need to ramp-up 4-5 domestic companies. All the existing SMEs need to be consolidated into these large enterprises that should have full-fledged capabilities in material sourcing, product development, production, distribution and marketing.

Delinking from the global toy industry is the best strategy for India. The regulatory bodies need to closely work with the identified large enterprises to consolidate the industry and steadily phase out foreign companies. The industry needs to transform from a low-cost low quality toy producer to a high-quality high wage industry. The premium Indian consumer will need to be prepared for a period of unavailability of products from the leading global companies. This revenue

---

[184] "The Increasing Role of Electronic Toys in the Lives of Infants and Toddlers: should we be concerned?", Diane E. Levin, Barbara Rosenquest, Jan 2001

shift towards domestic enterprises will be essential for them to build leading capabilities.

It is the only way in which we can ensure that every child in India has equal access to toys. If we build an outsourcing industry, there will always be a huge variation in quality and prices. But with these select large domestic enterprises, India can produce quality toys at scale. India has a wealth of cultural heritage to build a robust portfolio of toy products appropriate for various stages of child development. Besides, India today also possesses unparalleled engineering and product development talent.

A well protected domestic market focused Indian toy industry can cross $20 billion in turnover in 10-20 years, depending on the pace of reform across other industries. With the current approach, the Indian toy industry will find it difficult to even cross $5 billion in 20 years. Focus on ramping up 4-5 enterprises will be much simpler as compared to growing the SMEs. Government intervention and support will yield the desired results, instead of being ineffective and inconsistent. These companies will also need legal protection to build high quality products and production technologies.

With consolidation, the industry will also become a lot more stable. Large and diverse product portfolios and vertical integration of these enterprises will enable them to manage demand fluctuations and short product life cycles.[185] These companies will gain significant efficiencies across the value chain. With protection from foreign competition, companies will be able to build a quality working environment with high wages and benefits. Wages and product pricing would then simply grow with the growth of the Indian economy and average income levels.

---

[185] "Study on the competitiveness of the toy industry", ECSIP Consortium, August 2013

Automotive

Automotive has been central to the growth of developed economies and has enabled them to gain supremacy over the rest of the world. In the economy of developed countries, growth in the automotive industry by 1% causes a GDP growth of 1.5%.[186] Indirect impact of the automotive industry on GDP is strengthened through related industries that are suppliers to the automotive industry. The automotive industry in the developed countries is the leading branch of machine building. There is not a single large economy that does not have a large automotive industry on its territory. The share of the automobile industry in the GDP of developed countries ranges from 5 to 10%.

The share of the automotive industry in the machine-building production of Germany is 14%, Japan-12%, South Korea-10%. One dollar invested in the automotive industry increases the gross domestic product by $3 (average multiplier). According to this indicator, the automotive industry has no equal among other sectors. Thus, the automotive industry represents one of the key branches of the economy, providing development of other industries and the country as a whole. The successful work of the auto-building complex determines the well-being and fate of millions of inhabitants, and also to a large extent the country's defense capability. The automotive industry in countries such as the US, Japan, Germany, and South Korea is a vivid example of the formation of a global "super-industry." The more developed the automobile industry in the country, the higher the share of GDP of this country in world production.

It is important to note that the level of development of the country's economy is characterized, in particular, by the size and structure of exports and imports. In the industrial structure of the US, Germany, Japan, and South Korea, the

---

[186] "The role of the automobile industry in the economy of developed countries", Behzad Saberi, Peoples' Friendship University of Russia, May 17, 2018

share of engineering (including automotive) ranges from 25 to 40%. In developing countries, this figure is less than 10%. The more effective the economy, the greater the share in world exports, and the export structure has more high-tech products and less raw materials. In terms of exports of goods per capita, these countries are among the top 10 exporting countries. The structure of exports of these countries includes cars and aircraft, machinery and equipment, computers and other electronics, sophisticated household appliances, etc. However, most of the exports from these countries is made up of cars, vehicles, parts and accessories. Cars are one of the largest export products surpassing even oil. It is the volume of machinery and equipment exported from these countries that is considered to be the most important indicator of the level of technological advancement of the nation, and the trends in this sector characterize the effectiveness of a nation's performance. The automotive industry has a developed and complex infrastructure located all over the world.

The turnover of the automobile manufacturing industry was around $3 trillion in 2018. The industry produced over 70 million cars and 25 million commercial vehicles (cars, vans, trucks and buses) in 2018.[187] Automotive is a capital-intensive and knowledge-intensive industry. The industry is also a major innovator investing more than $100 billion in R&D. It is worth noting that tax revenue from car manufacturers in 26 industrialized countries is more than $500 billion per year.

The auto industry consumes steel, iron, aluminum, plastic, glass, carpeting, textiles, computer chips, rubber and much more. According to statistics, about half of the world consumption of oil, rubber, about 1/4 of the glass output, and 1/6 of the steel output is accounted for by the automobile industry. The industry is the second after aircraft

---

[187] "Global automotive market overview", Crescendo Worldwide, 2019; "Economic and Market Report", European Automobile Manufacturers Association, EU Automotive Industry 2018, 2019

construction in terms of the volume of consumed products of other industries.

Two primary components of the industry value chain are assembly and components manufacturing. The global auto industry comprises assemblers, global mega suppliers, first-tier suppliers, second-tier suppliers, third-tier suppliers and aftermarket.[188] The assembler-supplier relationship has significantly evolved over the last few decades. First, there has been a shift in design activities from assemblers to suppliers. Second, there has been a shift towards supply of complete functions (systems, sub-assemblies and modules) rather than individual components. A first-tier supplier becomes responsible not only for the assembly of parts into complete units (dashboards, brake-axle-suspension, seats, cockpit assemblies and so on), but also for the management of second-tier suppliers. Third, the assemblers became more involved in the specification of the production and quality systems of their suppliers. With the increasing importance of just-in-time (JIT) production systems and the imposition of quality-at-source, even simple tasks became more critical for the overall efficiency of the operations.

Economies of scale are significant in assembly as well as component manufacturing. To achieve scale efficiencies, the assemblers have standardized platforms and models across their constituent companies and divisions. Component manufacturers have also grown by expanding vertically rather than horizontally.

The auto industry is often thought of as one of the most global of all industries. Its products have spread around the world, and it is dominated by a small number of companies with worldwide recognition. Globally, the auto industry remains concentrated, with around 10 companies accounting for over 85% of the production and sales. While there were some new

---

[188] "The global automotive industry value chain: what prospects for upgrading by developing countries", John Humphrey and Olga Memedovic, United Nations Industrial Development Organization, September 2, 2003

entrants to the assembly sector (Hyundai in the Republic of Korea and Proton in Malaysia), the East Asian crisis undermined the prospects of other challengers. Competition between the Triad (North America, the European Union and Japan) producers has led to further concentration.

While other economies attempted to develop self-sufficient automotive industries, none of them (except China) could sustain the efforts. From the 1950s onwards, various developing countries used import-substitution industrialization policies to promote the development of their domestic auto industries. By the early 1990s, there were substantial self-contained vehicle industries in Latin America, the ASEAN region, India and China. But trade liberalization began to change this situation in the 1990s. Quantitative restrictions were phased out and tariffs reduced, while Trade-Related Investment Measures (TRIMs) like local content requirements and foreign exchange balancing came under increasing attack. After the wave of liberalization in the 1990s, component manufacturing was substituted by exports wherever possible.

The leading global automakers adopted several strategies to control markets across the globe. They formed a complex network of regional production systems that prevented emerging countries from developing end to end capabilities. A division of labor was created between different countries in a region to restrict capability development to specific components, modules or sub-assemblies. The global players carved out their own component manufacturing companies enabling them to become suppliers for all automakers present in a particular market. They also adopted a follow sourcing strategy limiting the possibilities for local component producers. The preference for using the same supplier in many different locations is known as follow sourcing. In lieu of setting up assembly and component manufacturing units, large companies of the Triad negotiated market access and eventually acquired a dominant or complete market share.

Only China, Russia and India have been able to develop domestic enterprises capable of competing with the large global players, at least in the home market. They are also the only ones to have built some level of capabilities across the value chain. Smaller economies in Central Europe, Eastern Europe, South America and Southeast Asia, could never build end to end capabilities.

The global automotive revenues are expected to double to ~$6 trillion in 2030 and will mainly originate from disruptive business models such as mobility as a service (MaaS) or data-enabled services. At the same time, profit pools are expected to shift towards new technologies and services, with more than 80 percent of the industry profit pool originating from autonomous, connected, electric and shared (ACES) technologies and new business models.

In the US, data-rich tech giants are building a technology driven landscape for the future of mobility. Given their high valuation at capital markets, they are freely developing new models without the need to be immediately profitable. In China, on the other hand, state-backed companies clearly follow the top-down direction supported by policy makers.

The current push towards autonomous, connected and electric technologies[189] is creating an unsustainable resource burden for the planet. Autonomous vehicles (AV) could increase urban sprawl and out-compete public transport, causing increased traffic and less productive cities. Electric vehicles depend on limited reserves of battery materials. And all these technological enhancements significantly increase the consumption of precious semiconductor materials.

The market size of the auto industry in India is around $105 billion, which includes ~$15 billion of imports. Component

---

[189] "Race 2050 - a vision for the European Automotive Industry", Mckinsey center for future mobility, January 2019

makers account for more than half at ~$60 billion. India is in a unique position to become the first large economy with a self-sufficient and sustainable automotive industry. The transition can be achieved in 5-10 years, much faster than one would expect from such a large and strategic industry. Due to the high capital-intensive nature of the business, the industry is already consolidated on the assembly front, with India also having its own large automakers for each segment. India has smartly balanced protectionism and liberalization to get within striking distance of complete self-sufficiency. In transforming towards a fully independent domestic industry, India should double down on shared mobility to keep the passenger vehicle demand in check and avoid the unsustainable push towards electronics.

Until about the mid-1980s, the Indian automotive industry was protected by high import tariffs and production catered to the demands of local automobile manufacturers. Manufacturing was licensed and the market was restricted, with quantitative restrictions on imports of automobiles and auto components and a high tariff structure. The early 1980s saw the entry of Japanese manufacturers - a JV between the Indian government (Maruti Udyog) and Japanese Suzuki came into being as Maruti Suzuki. The company developed a very strong ancillary network around it. A number of JV collaborations with foreign partners enabled Indian companies to benefit from technology transfers and improve quality. Companies first outsourced manufacturing to local players, gradually moving from imports to local production. Beginning in the middle of 1991, the Indian automobile industry and passenger vehicles segment in particular, witnessed liberalization. By the end of the decade, many major MNCs including Daewoo, Peugeot, General Motors, Mercedes-Benz, Honda, Hyundai, Toyota, Mitsubishi, Suzuki, Volvo, Ford and Fiat, were operating at a significant scale in the market. By the turn of the century, India was well on its way to becoming a low-cost small car making hub for domestic and international markets.

Indian automakers today are fairly self-sufficient on the assembly front for all vehicle categories. Currently, the contribution of Indian owned manufacturers (primarily Tata and Mahindra) in passenger vehicles is around 15%. Maruti Suzuki accounts for around 50% of the passenger vehicle market.[190] In two wheelers and commercial vehicles, Indian owned manufacturers (Hero Motocorp, TVS Motor, Bajaj Auto, Tata Motors, Ashok Leyland etc.) hold the lion's share. Indian manufacturers have developed a full range of passenger and commercial vehicles needed to efficiently serve the domestic market. Their vehicles cover the entire spectrum of mobility requirements and are some of the most fuel and cost efficient in the world. Given the safety concerns related to two wheelers, India should ideally sell its two-wheeler companies to other developing and under-developed economies and then gradually phase out these companies from the Indian market. From an urban mobility and health standpoint, India needs a few focused players that can produce high quality bicycles and other non-motorized vehicles.

64% of Indian component companies are solely owned by Indian business houses although they contribute only 32% of the industry's revenue.[191] Remaining 36% of the companies are either JVs or foreign owned and account for 68% of the revenue. Most of the homegrown companies also have technical alliances with foreign firms.

Even though the Indian manufacturers and component makers account for only a small percentage of the domestic market, on a standalone basis, India now has end to end capabilities in the automotive industry. Indian lead firms have made significant efforts toward upgrading over the years, including the use of advanced modular platforms, new materials, and platform sharing in India. The concept of upgrading refers to the capacity of firms to make better

---

[190] "Indian automobile industry report", IBEF, 2022

[191] "Who owns the Indian Component Industry", Nabeel A Khan, ETAuto Originals, July 2, 2021

products, more efficiently, and move into more skilled activities. The improvement in the breadth and depth of local capabilities in India was aided through foreign acquisitions undertaken by local firms. But when compared with the large global players, Indian firms are still fairly behind on quality, design and technology. Indian firms are still heavily dependent on foreign companies for design, development and R&D.[192] The contribution of overseas design and development is highest in passenger vehicles, while local development is higher in case of two wheelers and commercial vehicles.

In the current scenario, the dependence on foreign JV partners is higher in the case of electrical and electronics, a segment where 9 percent of the component makers in India work. With the growing adoption of autonomous, connected and electric mobility, the market share of foreign owned firms or JVs with international technical partners will grow. A sustainable move away from electronics can help India significantly reduce its foreign dependence. Engineering and transmission, which constitutes 37% of the total autoparts makers in India, is another area where JVs and technical alliances are pivotal. Mahindra and Tata have both evolved their R&D capabilities to a level where they are able to independently produce high quality engines.[193] Introduction of regulation to limit vehicle speeds to 100 kmph will significantly reduce the technology dependency of Indian players in several segments (engine, transmission, body etc.) In metal working, forging and casting and precision components, Indian owned components tend to operate independently even today.

India can become fully self-sufficient if it dissociates itself from the global markets and production systems. The integration with the global value chain forces Indian

---

[192] "Update on Auto Components Industry", Care Ratings, March 2021

[193] "Mahindra XUV300 to get 130PS mStallion turbo-petrol across all variants", Tuhin Guha, Overdrive, September 16, 2021

automakers and component manufacturers to compete on cost with other production centers, leaving them with little margin to invest in R&D. They have to keep the prices low to effectively compete with the foreign players. Given that the Indian companies have a higher cost of raw materials, price competition further impedes their ability to invest.

Delinking from global markets will accelerate indigenous R&D and help India become independent in technology. Global automakers and mega suppliers largely govern the quantum and focus of investments by the Indian firms. Dissociation will help Indian component makers to develop a full spectrum of capabilities. Once we let go of the exports, foreign companies will have little leverage to seek royalty from Indian manufacturers. Autoparts makers shell out as much as 5 percent of their revenue towards royalty. Indian automakers will also be able to accelerate design and product development as they will not be limited by the intellectual property of global car and component makers.

Creation of a fully independent automotive industry will help India capture a much larger market size. Currently, a 20% share in assembly (~$45 billion) and around 50% share in components (~$60 billion) gives India a revenue of ~$35 billion. This includes ~$20 billion of exports. Now, if Indian companies get 100% share of the domestic market, stop all exports, and substitute the imports with domestic production (worth around $15 billion), Indian companies can earn a revenue of ~$85 billion ($105 minus $20 billion).

Sustainability, safety and self-sufficiency are interdependent for the Indian automotive industry. Sustainability suggests limiting the use of electronics and moving towards Green Hydrogen. The use of electronics and high-tech components is the key dependency of the Indian automotive industry on global auto and component makers. The cost of electronics is around 40% of a new car cost these days and nearly 60% of the labor costs to repair a collision vehicle result from the electronics.[194] Even low-end vehicles are quickly approaching 100 ECUs and 100 million lines of code as more features that were once considered luxury options, are becoming standard. Around half of the ECUs are dedicated towards safety systems. The burden of electronics and high-tech features almost vanishes if the cars are manufactured for a maximum speed of 100 kmph.

The growing number of functionalities using advanced electronic systems significantly reduces scale efficiencies in production. Managing the huge quantum of wiring requires sizable manual effort. The increased number of electronic component-based features drives a multifold increase in the number of car variants, which creates a huge additional burden for development, testing and production. India would be well advised to develop strong control on the use of electronic components in vehicles.

Mechanical systems trump the use of electronics on sustainability, safety, quality and efficiency. Mechanical systems are solid and durable, as against fragile electronic systems. They are built to last and are much less resource intensive in production as well as over the long term. Well-designed mechanical systems are also most efficient and are less liable to failure as compared to electronic systems. Indian automakers have conquered the mechanical engineering front of the automotive industry and should not get distracted by this unsustainable wave of electronics. They should simply focus on improving the efficiency and quality of mechanical systems.

From an automotive materials standpoint, India would not be dependent on imports, if it minimizes the use of electronics and semiconductors. It is just that other developing countries such as Vietnam, Malaysia, Indonesia etc. sell materials such as rubber at lower prices. India can keep importing materials but should avoid the export of materials.

---

[194] "How software is eating the car", Robert N. Charette, IEEE Spectrum, June 7, 2021

On the assembly front for both passenger and commercial vehicles, we already have large Indian companies that can serve the domestic market if the foreign players are swiftly phased out. India needs to simply follow the Chinese model and gradually increase ownership restrictions in both the assembly and component sectors to drive out foreign players from the Indian market. India will possibly need 2-3 more indigenous enterprises in the passenger vehicles segment and maybe another couple of large enterprises in the commercial segment. India can also simply buy out the Indian entities of the global automakers. The larger Indian companies will also have the resources to invest in technologies that drive sustainability in vehicles and their manufacturing.

Consolidation is most critical in the components industry to make India self-sufficient. While we do have a couple of large Indian players (Motherson Sumi and Bharat Forge), the industry is highly fragmented with most firms being Indian businesses and relatively lower number of foreign firms and JVs operating in the segment. Of the 400 odd players present in the market, only 30 record revenues higher than Rs 150 crore. Two third of the industry players have annual revenues less than 50 crore. Indian suppliers are small and medium enterprises (SMEs) which do not have many opportunities or resources to upgrade. The major challenges faced by the indigenous component manufacturers are high cost of capital, nonavailability of skilled labor, and higher operational cost. Stiff competition from China and other Asian countries on the price front also restricts their ability to invest.

Consolidation of the component industry into 10 or so players will help India take control of technology across all component and value chain segments. These large players should be organized to build specialization in related component segments from amongst engine, transmission, steering, suspension, braking, wheels, electrical parts, body (sheet metal), glass, interiors etc. Indian companies have already gained sufficient experience and capabilities in each of these segments. Consolidation will allow the pockets of expertise to come together and build end-to-end capabilities. The large enterprises will be able to increase R&D intensity and become fully independent even in more complex areas such as precision instruments and manufacturing equipment. The restructuring will lead to a natural exit from JVs and technical alliances with foreign firms. Indian component makers are currently heavily dependent on foreign companies to get technology and are either working with them as joint venture partners or have formed technical alliances. Some Indian component makers work with a multitude of collaborators across the globe. The convenience of adapting to the changing technology faster, low volume in some high-cost technology has also made the industry opt for joint ventures and technical alliances. All these JVs and alliances will become redundant as the Indian companies organize themselves, logically aggregate capabilities and start focusing on the domestic market. The Indian technology operations of international companies like Bosch, BorgWarner, Denso and Magneti Marelli should ideally be bought out by the Indian players.

The gradual move away from being a cost competitor in the global markets will help India introduce best practice regulation. The large Indian players can steadily increase compensation, benefits (health, education, housing, pension), and working conditions. The regulatory body will be able to ensure a continuous improvement in quality, safety & emission standards, resource efficiency and waste management.

In the stable state, the self-sufficient and sustainable Indian automotive industry will be worth $300-$400 billion. We estimated earlier that a population of 150 crore people would need around 10 crore passenger cars in a shared mobility scenario. The replacement rate in the global automotive industry is around 20%. A conservative estimate of annual replacement rate would be 10%, resulting in annual passenger car sales of 1 crore units, around 4 times the current sales volume. Hence, broadly the stable state industry size (passenger and commercial vehicles) would be four times the current size of the domestic industry. The current domestic market size (excluding two wheelers) is $70 billion. The shift from being a cost competitor to a high value regulated industry would increase the production costs by 20-50%.

Rolling stock

The global train and components market, also referred to as the rolling stock industry, was worth $150-200 billion in 2020. The major players are the vehicle OEMs (25% share) and suppliers of components and parts (~50% share).[195] In addition, railway operators and third-party service shops are predominantly responsible for maintenance of the vehicles (remaining 25% of the industry revenue).

The OEMs' vehicle portfolio is large and includes locomotives (electric, diesel and shunting), passenger vehicles (electric multiple units, diesel multiple units, high speed trains, very high-speed trains, coaches, light rail vehicles, metro vehicles, automated systems), freight wagons (open, covered, tank, platform / intermodal, hopper / bulk), and special vehicles (tamping machines, grinding machines, track laying machines, ballast profiling machines). Rolling stock manufacturing today requires high level facilities and technologies. Locomotives, EMUs and DMUs have computer systems, advanced control units supported by software etc.

Complex local requirements and certification standards often result in small product series, sometimes with fewer than 100 vehicles in the same series. This often leads to high complexity in the production process as well as to challenges

---

[195] "Global market of rolling stock manufacturing: Present situation and future potential", Yoshihiko Sato, January 31, 2006

for maintenance in terms of always having the right capabilities and spare parts at hand. Additionally, product data management remains an ongoing challenge because of the high degree of individuality of each vehicle.

The rolling stock industry is facing heavy consolidation pressure due to large global overcapacity. The top 10 OEMs increased their market share from 53 percent in 2010 to 71 percent in 2015. The 2015 merger of the two Chinese rolling stock OEMs, CNR and CSR, created CRRC. The new company is the market leader across almost all market segments, with revenue of ~$35 billion (2018). CRRC is now the global leader for high-speed trains, electric locomotives, and metro cars. Hitachi acquired Italian rolling stock manufacturer Ansaldo Breda, strengthening its footprint especially in Europe.

This phase of significant consolidation includes both horizontal as well as vertical integration moves. Small and medium-sized incumbents face increasing pressure and are often either taken over or exit the market. The underutilization of production facilities in all geographies may force additional consolidation, with an estimated unused capacity of around 40 percent in factories in North America, 40 percent in Europe, and 60 percent in Asia.

Tier-1 suppliers are capturing the lion's share of the rolling stock value chain: currently around 65 percent of the value chain in the new vehicles business is covered by suppliers. Suppliers achieve profit levels of ~10 percent and above, while OEMs' EBIT margin remains around 3 to 4 percent. First of all, this is due to suppliers' clear USP and limited competition among suppliers resulting from the fact that there are only a few specialized players in each subsystem (e.g., braking systems). Moreover, high R&D expenditure is required to sustain a fast development pace in high technology.

High-level decomposition analysis suggests that some components will likely remain OEM in-house parts: control, diagnosis, safety, and propulsion systems, for example, as well as core engineering. While some components are already largely outsourced today, such as wheel sets, braking systems, and the interior, suppliers are likely to increasingly take on additional components such as the body, connectivity systems, and potentially application engineering.[196]

Suppliers have limited attractiveness as M&A targets for OEMs. OEMs would preferentially buy from other suppliers rather than from a competitor owned supplier. This would result in a heavy decline in revenues and profits for the acquired supplier.

In mature markets, infrastructure investments are driving higher asset utilization, such as double tracking, longer loops and yards to allow an increase in maximum train length and tonnage as well as velocity increases due to improved infrastructure and better transport scheduling. Even if the volumes transported grow globally, the demand for new rolling stock will remain more or less constant in these regions.

As costs increase considerably by shipping rolling stock over long distances, production close to the local market offers great advantages. Most developed markets have had their local rolling stock manufacturers to build the country's railways infrastructure. Chinese CRRC was propelled into a position of global leadership purely by serving the huge domestic demand.

Sustainable urbanization will drive massive growth in the rolling stock industry. Reduction in car ownership and creation of car free zones will accelerate development of a robust urban rail transit network. Bans on short haul flights and increasing speeds will make intercity train travel the most preferred mode. Replacement of the diesel locomotive with renewable powered electric and hydrogen trains presents a massive upgrade opportunity.

---

[196] "Huge value pool shifts ahead – how rolling stock manufacturers can lay track for profitable growth", Arnt-Philipp Hein, Anselm Ott, Mckinsey, 2016

An urban only India needs urban metro, intercity passenger and freight trains. India is already fully self-sufficient to cater to the demand across all three segments. For all three categories, indigenous Indian manufacturers have already crossed the threshold speed limits. BEML has already produced high quality urban trains that deliver speeds of 80-95 kmph.[197] For intercity passenger, Vande Bharat, manufactured by ICF Chennai, is capable of delivering speeds upto 180 kmph. In a recent test of freight speeds, Indian built freight trains delivered speeds of 100 kmph. Average speeds across the rail networks in India are low because of outdated rolling stock, track congestion and track design. Moreover, the development of faster and lighter trains also poses important challenges in terms of energy efficiency.

With rail at the center of urban mobility and intercity transportation, the rolling stock opportunity in India is much larger than China. India is therefore well advised to stick to its indigenous companies for taking India forward. Our four large companies (Indian Coach Factory, Modern Coach Factory, Rail Coach Factory, and BEML) are fully capable of manufacturing the required rolling stock and building the rail infrastructure.

The overall case for technical collaborations with foreign companies is also weak. Given the massive size of the opportunity, indigenous Indian companies will have ample opportunity and resources to continuously upgrade their technology and achieve faster speeds and efficiency levels. Besides, Indian design is likely to be more optimal and sustainable, given the value mindset of Indian manufacturers. They are likely to stay away from luxury and avoid features that result in unnecessary consumption of energy and other limited resources.

India should only seek technology partnerships for acquisition of sustainable technologies. Partnerships can

---

[197] "Rail & Metro Product Brochure", Bharat Earth Movers Limited (BEML), October 2019

accelerate the development and rollout of green technologies such as renewable electricity generation & transmission, hydrogen fuel cell, use of natural gas instead of diesel, solar power, hybrid traction, aerodynamics, lighter materials, mechatronics and environmental instrumental control and monitoring.

Railways are fundamental to efficient transportation and equitable living. The railway network needs to enable the same across the envisioned ~130 equal cities. Railways infrastructure development should play a key role in facilitating the formation of these ~130 equal cities.

Designing the stable state railway infrastructure is paramount for the success of the Indian rolling stock industry. It is important to develop the rail infrastructure in sync with the development of our ~130 cities and the transformation of our industries and the economy. Once the stable state network requirements are established for an urban-only India, the planning horizon gets significantly extended. Planning for the stable state will help remove certain segments such as suburban and long distance rail from the development charter. Most importantly, India will realize that there is no value in accelerating the development in select clusters or corridors. Instead of the current approach of removing current bottlenecks and targeting rapid development, India will be able to plan and execute broad based delivery of a high quality sustainable network in a phased manner. Instead of having to compete for fast track development of high priority projects, Indian companies will be able to independently deliver with their current capabilities. They will also be able to continuously evolve their own capabilities without getting hustled by the large existing global players.

India will also be able to independently generate the capital needed to finance the massive development. The full roadmap will clearly specify the capital requirements during the different stages of development. The linkages with economic and industrial development will determine demand / revenue and expected returns on capital as well as help identify the potential sources of capital. Clarity on the end state will significantly increase the bankability of the sector. Besides banks, other financial institutions such as insurance companies (will earn revenue in perpetuity from railway projects) and pension funds that grow in India with the broader economic development, could become ideal sources of capital. The government itself will have more appetite to provide upfront capital, given the attractive returns expected in the long run. The government could also use railway investments as a lever to increase the size of the economy.

Shipbuilding

The global shipbuilding industry is worth around $150 billion. Shipbuilding industry has always been dominated by maritime nations like Britain, France, Germany, USA, Japan, Korea, and China. Shipbuilding has two main segments - commercial segment and naval. Presently commercial shipbuilding sectors are dominated by China, Japan, Korea, and European Countries (EC); whereas the naval shipbuilding sector is dominated by USA, China, EC, Russia, Japan, India. Shipbuilding is considered to be one of the most strategic, oldest, most open and highly competitive markets in the world. As shipbuilding is a highly capital-intensive industry so strong government support and political stability is prerequisite to survive this industry. The ship and shipbuilding industry is low-tech compared with industries such as aviation, automotive and technology.

The shipbuilding industry is responsible for the design and construction of oceangoing vessels all around the world. Most of the global ship production today is concentrated in Asian countries such as China, Japan and South Korea, though large shipyards also exist in many other countries. The shipbuilding industry is involved in the construction and modification of ships and these operations are carried out in specialized facilities called shipyards. Commercial ships or vessels can be broadly segmented into segments that include tankers, bulkers, LNG carriers, LPG carriers, containers and others. Ships are custom built on a made to order basis. The shipbuilding process starts with inquiries from customers, followed by completion of various processes until the vessel is completed. It takes at least 2 years to complete the manufacturing of a ship.

Some of the noteworthy recent trends are green shipbuilding technology, automation, modular shipbuilding technique, advanced outfitting, ship launching airbag, LNG/LPG fueled engines and solar and wind powered ships.[198] The global shipbuilding industry will be most affected by increased competition, environmental regulations, enhanced globalization and political and financial instability. In response to the decarbonization trend, the development of next-generation ships is gaining momentum worldwide. These ships use ammonia or hydrogen as fuel to reduce greenhouse gas emissions.

Historically, shipbuilding has played a key role in the industrial development of the developed nations. Nations have invested heavily in the domestic shipbuilding industry as shipyards offer a wide range of technologies, employ a significant number of workers and generate significant income. Global controls are minimal in the industry. After World War II, Japan used shipbuilding in the 1950s and 1960s to rebuild its industrial structure; Again South Korea started to make shipbuilding a strategic industry in the 1970s, and China is now in the process of repeating these models with large state-supported investments in this industry. Conversely, Croatia, Brazil, Philippine, Myanmar, Vietnam are privatizing its shipbuilding industry. Shipbuilding has gone into decline in high labor cost countries as state subsidies have been removed and domestic

---

[198] "A Study on Global Shipbuilding Growth, Trend and Future Forecast", Khandakar Akhter Hossaina, N.M.Golam Zakaria, Bangladesh University of Engineering and Technology, August 2017

industrial policies do not provide support anymore. The British shipbuilding industry is a prime example of this with its industries suffering badly since the 1960s.

China is now the world's largest shipbuilder with around 45% of the world's total orders, and its quality and technology have improved significantly. At present, Korea is the world's second largest shipbuilding country with a global market share of about 30%. South Korea leads in the production of large vessels such as Super tanker, cruise liner, LNG and LPG Carrier, drill ship, offshore structure (FSPO, FPO) and large container ship. South Korea's shipyards are highly efficient, with the world's largest shipyard in Ulsan operated by Hyundai Heavy Industries slipping a newly built, $80 million vessel into the water every four working days. South Korea's "big three" shipbuilders, Hyundai Heavy Industries, Samsung Heavy Industries and Daewoo Shipbuilding and Marine Engineering, dominate global shipbuilding, with STX Shipbuilding, Hyundai Samho Heavy Industries, Hanjin Heavy Industries and Sungdong Shipbuilding and Marine Engineering, also ranking among the top ten shipbuilders in the world. While evaluating the trend of the global shipbuilding industry, it is found that Japan had been the dominant ship building country from the 1960s through to the end of 1990s but gradually lost its competitive advantage to the emerging industry in South Korea which had the advantages of much cheaper wages, strong government backing and a cheaper currency.

The split of the world fleet by vessel type is dry bulk carriers (43%), oil tankers (30%), container ships (13%), general cargo (4%) and others (10%). The share of oil tankers has declined (~50% in 1980) due to an increase in the usage of other sources of energy other than crude. The percentage share in dead-weight tonnage of Dry bulk carriers has increased from 27.2% in 1980. The percentage share in dead-weight tonnage of General cargo ships has declined rapidly from 17% in 1980 due to the rise in containerization. The percentage share in dead-weight tonnage of Container ships has grown consistently from 1.6% in 1980. The unitization of cargo and growth of container handling equipment facilitated the growth of container trade. The rest of the fleet consists of various other types of specialized cargo carriers such as LPG/LNG carriers, chemical tankers, reefer vessels, project cargo carriers etc.

The shipbuilding industry witnessed a period of unprecedented growth riding on the stimulus of global demand in the early 2000s. Many Indian shipyards buoyed by possible business opportunities made significant capital investments to scale up their infrastructure. The market share of Indian yards in terms of global orders grew from 0.2 per cent in 2002 to 1.2 per cent in 2007, which was projected to go up to 7.5 per cent by 2017.[199] However, these projections went awry due to the global recession in 2008 and fall in oil prices. The consequent low demands for ships, led to large scale cancellation of export orders. This accompanied with withdrawal of government subsidy in 2007 and relatively low competitiveness of our shipyards, compounded the challenges of the fledgling industry. These market dynamics resulted in poor cash flows and created serious capital debt servicing challenges for the yards, plunging the market share of Indian shipyards to 0.01 per cent by 2013. Today, Indian registered ships carry just about 0.9 per cent of the global shipping stock while ships constructed in India carry even less. The revival of the Indian shipbuilding industry through global export orders appears unlikely in the near future.

The majority of shipbuilding orders to the shipyards in current times, are primarily from the Indian Navy and Coast Guard. In wake of the Indian Navy's vision of indigenous defense production, warship construction has witnessed an unprecedented growth. The Indian Coast Guard is also engaged in a massive expansion plan and is in the process of

---

[199] "Shipbuilding market developments Q2 2018", OECD Directorate for Science Technology and Innovation, 2018

acquiring various craft to strengthen the maritime boundaries of the country.

The ability of the Indian shipbuilding industry in efficiently meeting the demands of the Navy is restricted by inferior technology capabilities. The industrial base for India's naval defense remains limited - infrastructure is inadequate as are the in-house R&D facilities. The main reason for the limited development of the industrial base is the low volume of ships being constructed for the Indian Navy which limits the standardization.[200]

The performance of the DPSU and PSU shipyards is poor due to high burden of debt, high working capital costs, poor cash flows, poor productivity/ efficiency and poor project management. The industry performance for the Indian Coast Guard requirements has been much better in terms of project completion mainly attributable to less complex weapons and sensors, leading to timely completion of the project.

For a country that is predominantly peninsular with an extensive coastline and about 1200 islands, India's shipbuilding capabilities have not kept pace with its economic development, market demand and human resource potential. This offers huge scope for the development of the shipbuilding sector considering that the country's potential in the sector has not been exploited fully. The shipping industry in India is an untapped market with huge potential which can give windfall gains with minimal effort. The shipbuilding industry has not received the required attention and focus, amongst competing priorities, uncertainties and lack of assurance on short term returns.

Increased defense spending, growing foreign trade and development of inland water transportation are strong tailwinds for the growth of the industry in the short term, medium term and long term respectively. Excessive foreign

---

[200] "Shipbuilding, a large national perspective", Rear Admiral G K Harish VSM and Commander Prashant Singh, Vivekananda International Foundation, January 2020

trade is unsustainable and in the long run needs to be restricted to only cover material shortfalls and the export of highly differentiated products. The transition to renewable energy sources will continue to reduce demand for oil tankers. Transition to more sustainable fleets is a strong tailwind and creates a huge opportunity for growth in the Indian shipping and shipbuilding industry. Being the world's poorest super-emitter, India needs to take a lead in driving sustainability across the board.

For India, security concerns at the strategic level dictate maritime defense in the Persian Gulf, Gulf of Aden and the entire Indian Ocean Region. Further, a shipbuilding industrial base, catering to naval vessel acquisition and freight carriage through domestically owned merchant ships is strategically significant for national security. A strong domestic shipping industry provides greater leverage for national security, contingency response, the enforcement of safety norms, monitoring of environment compliance, control over immigrant and refugee movement and labor issues. However, India has traditionally neglected the importance of a strong merchant marine and the same is evident in the share of cargo movement by Indian flag vessels.

Inland water transportation infrastructure is a huge opportunity for India in the long run. A sustainable India will have a robust network of over 300 interconnected rivers and around 150 massive city lakes. These water bodies will stimulate sustainable development of passenger and freight transportation, power generation, hospitality, fishing, watersports etc. The Indian shipbuilding industry will need to significantly broaden its product portfolio to cover this new demand segment. The government has already taken initiatives to develop the inland waterways to tap into the low operating cost of water transport. A strong indigenous commercial shipbuilding industry can help in promoting inland waterways as a cost-effective mode of transport.

The shipbuilding industry will also have a major role to play in harnessing ocean energy (tidal, wave). Shipbuilding companies will need to partner with energy companies to advance India's engineering and scientific capabilities and execute these massive projects.

The growth of the Indian shipbuilding industry will be a boost for several ancillary industries and employment generation. The shipbuilding industry has an immense direct and indirect positive impact on almost all other leading industries such as steel, aluminum, electrical machinery and equipment etc., besides its huge dependence on the infrastructure and service sectors in an economy. About 65 percent of the value addition in a ship under construction comes from manufacturers of shipboard material, equipment and systems. The shipyard, by itself only adds 35 percent of value, by putting together these materials and integrating equipment/ systems. It has been established that for the same turnover, the shipbuilding industry generates at least three times the employment generated by the heavy engineering industry. The shipbuilding industry offers avenues for large scale employment generation for both skilled and unskilled manpower.

Consolidation is essential to galvanize the Indian shipbuilding industry. The Indian industry has the capacity and expertise but is functioning below its capacity and capability levels. At present, there are 28 major shipyards in India which include 6 shipyards owned by the Central Government, 2 by the State Government and the remaining by the private sector. The majority of the shipyards in the country are under a huge debt burden and not earning any profits. Consolidation of the industry into 3-4 players will solve the financial problems, enhance the capabilities and increase performance. Without cost pressures from smaller players and secure demand from the domestic market, these large national enterprises will perform at much higher levels. Production of higher volumes will help increase standardization and provide efficiency gains across the production value chain. The larger enterprises will also have the resources to invest in R&D.

India has the threshold level of capabilities in shipbuilding to move forward without any foreign assistance. While increasing the strength of our Naval and Coast Guard is important, there is no urgency for doing so. India can do it at its own pace. An indigenous industry helps India capture the full value of shipbuilding and the related demand & supply side industries. Unless we produce everything ourselves, there will always be technology and process gaps. Even small gaps can create capability deficits at a system level. Engineering capabilities in manufacturing are not restricted to a single industry. Development of engineering capabilities in one industry directly impacts capabilities across other industries where similar systems and components are used. Indigenous development is therefore essential to gain true self sufficiency in broader manufacturing as well as for India to extract the full commercial potential of various industries. In the case of defense, indigenous production significantly increases the competitive advantage.

India only needs perspective on the possibilities and will be best served by developing its shipbuilding industry indigenously. By importing, India stands to lose employment, true capability building as well as the opportunity to find its own optima. Foreign companies have minimized labor intensity and use excessive amounts of energy in their production facilities. India should go through the productivity evolution itself and find the optimal levels of manpower needed across industries. Indigenous production is critical for India to transform from being an overpopulated dependent country to an advanced industrial economy. The effort of building the various industries will help the Indian workforce get organized into meaningful organizations that enable efficient and sustainable living. Instead of living a poor life under the guise of natural entitlement, Indians will become responsible and build systems that lift the quality of life for everyone. For India to strike the right balance between population and productivity, it is most essential to start controlling each and every activity across the manufacturing value chain. Performing every task ourselves will help us evolve into a truly responsible society.

Aerospace and Defense

The global Aerospace and Defense (A&D) industry was worth $838 bn in 2017. The indirect impact of the aircraft industry is estimated to be as much as three times its direct size, considering its linkages with other sectors of the economy. The key industry segments are defense ($265 bn) and commercial ($240 bn) aircraft manufacturing. Aircraft & Engine OEMs represented 28% ($235 bn), Civil & Military MRO & Upgrades 27% ($226 bn), Aircraft Systems & Component Manufacturing 26% ($218 bn), Satellites & Space 7% ($59 bn), Missiles & UAVs 5% ($42 bn) and other activity, including flight simulators, defense electronics, public research accounted for 7% ($59 bn).[201] The commercial aircraft manufacturing industry is largely a duopoly between Boeing ($93 bn) and Airbus ($74 bn).

Aircraft manufacturing involves the manufacturing of the aircraft body along with the software and components required for the functioning of aircraft. For the construction of an aircraft, companies need a variety of raw materials like steel plates or plastic parts. These can be purchased from many suppliers on the world market. In addition, the aircraft companies need a lot of parts they can only get from a small number of manufacturers like plane tires (Goodyear, Bridgestone, Michelin) or high-tech components (Siemens, Honeywell). The last and most important group are the suppliers that deliver components that have to do with the plane's efficiency and nevertheless with its security. These are parts like the hull and the engines (Rolls-Royce, General

---

[201] "Chapter - The contours of global aircraft manufacturing industry", The Global Commercial Aviation Industry, Daniel Vertesy, 2015

Electric). The aircraft manufacturers normally develop new planes together with these suppliers and therefore form long-term strategic alliances. The aircraft manufacturers themselves perform all the steps from the R&D, production, and pilot training to the even sales for new aircraft.

The global commercial aircraft industry remains one of the last industries overwhelmingly concentrated in Europe and North America, and to the US in particular. Emerging economies have hardly gained a 10% global share in the output of aircraft, aircraft parts and components and maintenance and repair works. "Global" supply chains are still concentrated in a handful of countries, mainly Canada, the United Kingdom, France, Japan and Germany. The industry produces around 1500 aircraft annually for the commercial sector.

The top 20 companies accounted for over $500 billion of revenue and include Boeing (US), Airbus (France), Lockheed Martin (US), General Dynamics (US), United Technologies (US), GE Aviation (US), Northrop Grumman (US), BAE System (UK), Raytheon (US), Safran (France), Thales Group (France), Leonardo (Italy), Rolls-Royce (UK), Honeywell Aerospace (US), L3 Technologies (US), Textron (US), Bombardier Aerospace (Canada), Mitsubishi Heavy Industries Aerospace (Japan), Harris Corp. (US), and Huntington Ingalls Industries (US).[202]

High market concentration characterizes the aircraft industry not only globally, but also within countries. The largest American and European aerospace and defense companies match and even exceed the size of entire countries' aerospace industries, both in terms of turnover as well as in terms of labor force. Boeing or EADS, with all their activities in the aeronautics (commercial and military) and space segments around the world combined, generate more annual sales and employ more persons than important

---

[202] "On a solid profitable growth path, 2018 Global Aerospace and Defense industry outlook", Robin S. Lineberger, Aijaz Hussain, Deloitte, 2018

aerospace producer countries such France, Germany or the UK. This degree of concentration is the result of a consolidation process of several decades ending in the late 1990s, through which the global industry underwent dramatic mergers and acquisitions and the formation of vast transnational corporations that integrate a large variety of aerospace and defense production activities and services.

Among the largest aerospace producing companies one finds not only those whose main activity is to design, manufacture or sell aircraft such as Boeing, EADS, Lockheed Martin, Bombardier or Embraer, but also engine producers United Technologies Corporation, General Electric, Safran or Rolls-Royce, or avionics and other component and system suppliers, such as Honeywell or Thales. Many firms have heterogeneous activities, acting as both system integrators as well as parts designers; some are active in both the fixed wing and the rotary wing markets. Much of the sales of the top 20 companies are military oriented, a few of the top companies (Lockheed Martin, General Dynamics or Northrop Grumman) are not active at all in the civilian aircraft market. For the other companies, the share of commercial sales (at least for those that report it) varies hugely, from about a quarter or less (BAe Systems or Finmeccanica) to around two-thirds (Boeing, EADS, Dassault), to a 100% (as in the case of Bombardier Aerospace).

With higher production requirements for both aircraft and defense equipment in the future, it is critical for A&D companies to invest in new and advanced technologies. This will help the companies be at the forefront of manufacturing, enhancing productivity and efficiency.

In terms of geographical distribution, most of the companies have their headquarters in the USA (Boeing, Lockheed Martin, General Dynamics, Northrop Grumman, United Technologies, Raytheon, General Electric, to mention a few) or in Europe (e.g., EADS, BAe Systems, Finmeccanica, Thales, Safran), however, a growing share of their activities are more globally spread. At the same time, it is very telling for the type of internationalization of the global aerospace industry that Embraer, the fourth largest commercial aircraft producer, represents the only company in the list with its headquarters located in an emerging economy (Brazil). In a more extended list of the global top 100 aerospace companies, there are only a few companies originating from outside Europe or North America, that include AVIC of China, Hindustan Aerospace (HAL) of India, ST Aero of Singapore and Korean Aerospace Industries (KAI). These companies are parts and components suppliers as well as producers of defense products for local air forces.

Technology complexity, capital intensity, and the long lead time of product development continue to pose significant barriers of entry to this industry. Company size is important in the sector because only the largest players can raise sufficient capital (often in joint ventures) to finance the development of new projects with new technology.

Even so, China and Russia are steadily moving towards becoming self-sufficient in manufacturing commercial aircrafts. For Commercial Aircraft Corporation of China (COMAC), the majority of its customers are Chinese airlines and leasing companies. Nevertheless, to compete with the existing duopoly, these new entrants will face several challenges to establish a track record of safe and reliable operations. These challenges include procurement of orders from global carriers, risk of cost and schedule overruns and certification from US and European regulators.

The A&D industry is likely to continue to experience increased M&A globally driven by Original Equipment Manufacturers (OEMs) continued pressure on suppliers to reduce costs and boost production rates. Large prime contractors are expected to consider acquiring small to midsize companies to gain access to new technologies and markets. Pricing pressure from aircraft OEMs and their expansion of high margin aftermarket services has pushed suppliers to consolidate for scale and cost effectiveness. The European defense industry is unlikely to see large M&A deals.

Valuations of A&D companies have been on the rise, with P/E ratio being 30% higher than 5 years ago. The S&P A&D index experienced a 400 percent improvement over the last 12 years compared to a ~100 percent improvement in the S&P 500 index.

Around 2.4% of global CO2 emissions come from aviation. Together with other gases and the water vapor trails produced by aircraft, the industry is responsible for around 5% of global warming. The industry is achieving fuel efficiency improvements of the order of 1% per year, and flights are increasing 6%, resulting in a rapid rise in total emissions. Mile for mile, flying is the most damaging way to travel for the climate.[203] Based on data from Britain, a single passenger traveling on domestic flight leads to a climate impact equivalent to 254g of CO2 for every km, but on a long-haul flight the impact is 102g of CO2 for every km as there is a huge amount of emission during take-off and landing. An intercity train releases the equivalent of just 41g for every passenger km. Traveling by coach releases even less – the equivalent of just 28g of CO2.

India has been focused on manufacturing military aircrafts. India's state-run company Hindustan Aeronautics Limited (HAL) manufactures its own Military technology aircrafts. For commercial aviation, India still operates on planes built by foreign manufacturers.

Both commercial and defense aviation sectors are experiencing robust growth. Since 2015, the government has taken several initiatives to attract foreign investment in the A&D industry - including increasing international engagement, a revamped FDI policy, and a new defense procurement procedure with amendments in offset

---

[203] "Should we give up flying for the sake of the climate?", Jocelyn Timperley, Smart Guide to Climate Change, BBC, February 19, 2020

regulations, and the announcement of the strategic partnership model. The Indian government eased norms for the Defense sector in June 2016, permitting foreign companies to own 100 percent of domestic ventures with the approval of the government. In 2017, the government announced the strategic partnership model for defense manufacturing policy, under which Indian firms will be allowed to enter into strategic partnerships with non-Indian OEMs in key defense sub sectors such as fighter aircrafts, submarines, helicopters and armored fighting vehicles. In the commercial aircraft sector, India is expected to witness an 8% YoY growth over the next two decades. India is forecast to have a demand for a record 2100 new aircraft worth more than $290 billion over the next 20 years. The demand will primarily support the growth of low-cost carriers (LCC), which already account for more than 60% of the total flights in the country. In 2021, the share of LCC has supposedly crossed 80%.

The significant advancements in communication technologies in the 21st century has made commercial aviation non-essential. The case for air freight also holds only for transporting fresh produce over distances larger than at least 500 km given the current state of other modes in India. The world is still at least 20 years away from developing fully sustainable aircraft. Till that time, allowing growth in civil aviation will create a massive energy and resource burden on India, and leave a humongous carbon footprint. India should therefore start with an instant ban on short haul flights. India should start with 500 km as a minimum distance for domestic flights and gradually increase the same as the Indian rail industry evolves. Hauling fresh produce from remote Himalayan destinations would be the only other valid case for commercial aviation.

For manufacturing aircrafts and components for the long-haul flights (domestic and international), India should develop 2-3 large vertically integrated OEMs. All domestic commercial aviation purchases should be made by these select enterprises, giving them the scale to ramp up capabilities. These companies should also get at the forefront of developing fully sustainable technologies for commercial aviation. Only once that is done, should India consider flying over smaller distances. To build these domestic OEMs, the best path for India is to make several acquisitions across key segments of aircraft manufacturing. In parallel, these companies will need to form JVs and technical alliances with Boeing, Airbus, and other tier I and tier II suppliers.

India does have full scale aircraft manufacturing capability except for turbine engines. Given the complexities and challenges associated with the aviation industry, India has done very well in this specialized area of engineering and manufacturing. HAL now builds military trainer aircraft and has proposed some brand-new fighter jet designs. It has also built helicopters, agricultural aircraft and has one of the largest maintenance depots and engineering services in the world. India has already developed a well-established ecosystem of component suppliers for the global aircraft manufacturers. Tata Advanced Systems Limited, Mahindra Aerospace and Bharat Forge are close to reaching the threshold scale for becoming an aircraft manufacturer. Consolidating the various smaller component manufacturers and technology developers into 2-3 larger entities will provide a significant capability jump. Post consolidation, India should be able to build a safe and reliable commercial airliner in about 10-15 years.

A single-minded focus on fully owning the domestic market will help the Indian companies to avoid the competition (cost, quality, market) with global OEMs and suppliers. Purchase restrictions on Indian airlines would be key for making the domestic companies viable. Attempting to build domestic companies while competing with Boeing, Airbus, Bombardier and Embraer would be a high-risk venture with no guarantee of profitability. Given that even domestic long haul is non-essential, India should be ready for a complete walk away by global companies.

Strong regulatory stance and significant investment will be needed from the Indian government to fund the organic and inorganic capability building. A fully protected domestic market with minimal price linkages with the global markets will allow the domestic industry to flourish and the government to recoup its massive R&D focused investments over the long term. In a protected scenario, the viability threshold for an indigenous airline reduces significantly as we would not be competing with the latest design or technologies of Boeing and Airbus. The protection will also make it viable for banks and financial institutions to fund the sizable investments needed for R&D needed to continuously innovate for efficiency and sustainability. Clearly establishing the impact of domestic industrial development in driving sustainable consumption will help India tackle the heat it is likely to face at global platforms for trying to protect its industries.

In the case of defense air capabilities, India will need to over-invest over the medium term to become self-sufficient over the long term. This is the only critical area where India needs to compromise sustainability and indigenous production. We clearly need the most advanced air capabilities today and are far from developing those ourselves.

The best path would be for India to have two other private domestic players besides HAL. While HAL should be made completely indigenous without any foreign dependence, the two private players should acquire defense systems from global leaders. They should enter into JVs and technical alliances, as well as make acquisitions. Reliance Defense has already made a foray along the suggested lines. India just needs to be careful in ensuring a majority public ownership of these companies of national importance and diluting any sort of family control.

India also needs to phase out, significantly reduce the size or fundamentally transform certain key industries. These include leather, chemicals, wood products (furniture, panels & plywood, paper), plastics and jewelry.

Leather

The total turnover of the Indian leather industry is ~$18 billion with exports contributing ~$6 billion.

The production of leather hurts animals, the environment, and the workers who manufacture it. Animal-derived leather has almost three times the negative environmental impact as its synthetic counterparts. Although some leather makers deceptively tout their products as "eco-friendly," turning skin into leather also requires massive amounts of energy and dangerous chemicals, including mineral salts, formaldehyde, coal-tar derivatives, and various oils, dyes, and finishes, some of them cyanide-based. Most leather produced in the U.S. is chrome-tanned, and all wastes containing chromium are considered hazardous by the EPA. Tannery effluent contains large amounts of pollutants, such as salt, lime sludge, sulfides, and acids. People who work in and live near tanneries suffer, too. Many die of cancer possibly caused by exposure to toxic chemicals used to process and dye leather. Arsenic, a common tannery chemical, has long been associated with lung cancer in workers who are exposed to it on a regular basis.

The developed world has smartly outsourced leather production with developing countries now producing over 60% of the leather.

India needs to restrict leather production to critical industrial and professional applications. India should start with a ban on consumer applications of leather such as furniture, shoes, bags, belts, clothing etc. There are viable substitutes available in the market for each of these consumer products. India should then phase out leather from non-critical industrial applications such as vehicle interiors. Eventually, the use of leather should be restricted to mission critical applications such as the production of defense equipment.

Chemicals

The global chemical industry had total revenues of just over $4 trillion in 2019. The breakdown of the global chemical industry across key segments is as follows: Basic Chemicals (32.6%); Plastic in Primary Forms and Synthetic Rubber (21.0%); Photochemicals, Explosives and Other Chemicals (16.1%); Household Cleaning and Personal Care Products (10.2%); Fertilizers and Nitrogen Compounds (6.7%); Paints and Varnishes (6.7%); Man-Made Fibers (3.6%); and Pesticides and Other Agrochemical Products (3.1%).[204] This composition involves a trend towards faster growth of specialty / value-added chemicals such as photochemicals, pesticides and fertilizers and nitrogen compounds, which are gaining ground against basic chemicals.

The global chemicals industry consumes more than 10% of fossil fuels produced and emits an estimated 3.3 gigatons of greenhouse gas emissions a year, more than India's annual emissions.[205] The chemicals sector is the largest industrial user of oil and gas, and it has the third-largest carbon footprint – behind steel and cement. About half of the fossil fuels that the industry consumes are burned for their energy. The rest is used as feedstock for products such as plastics with the emissions released only when these products reach the end of their lives, for example, when waste plastic packaging or an old mattress is incinerated.

The chemicals industry is deeply ingrained into various end user industries. Lowering the industry's emissions is possible but technically daunting. Plus, this large, complex industry, which supports millions of jobs worldwide, has a significant political and economic clout. Chemicals are also used to

---

[204] "Value chain analysis of the chemical industry in Jordan", Trade for Employment Project, Ministry of Industry Trade and Supply, Deutsche Zusammenarbeit, GIZ, Kingdom of the Netherlands, Kingdom of Jordan, 2019

[205] "How the chemicals industry's pollution slipped under the radar", The Guardian, Nov 2021

minimize carbon footprint e.g., providing coatings for solar panels, lightweight plastics to reduce vehicles' energy consumption and insulating materials for buildings.

Improving the efficiency of chemical plants and switching to renewable sources of energy will have the highest impact, given that around half of the carbon footprint of the industry is in the form of emissions.[206] Improvements in energy efficiency had leveled off in the developed world even before the turn of the century. The gains were made through aggressive energy management, housekeeping improvements, use of cogeneration or direct generation of electricity and improvements in process and equipment design. Improvements in waste heat recovery (fired heaters and steam account for 75% of process energy use) have been made in the 21st century.[207] Europe is well on its way to electrifying its chemical plants and increasing the share of renewables on the grid.

Substitution of chemical ingredients and chemical waste management is extremely difficult and results in a similar downstream impact on the environment in most cases. Various avenues are being explored to replace chemicals and materials with plants. For example, there is significant work being done in making bioplastics with plant materials such as sugar, corn or seaweed. Efforts are also being made to turn waste products into raw materials for the chemical industry. Chemists have been using agricultural waste or waste plastics, even the ultimate waste material, carbon dioxide, as feedstock. But all these ideas, especially those involving a shift in feedstock, are very hard to implement. Technologies to turn agricultural or plastic waste into new chemicals are still unproven on a large scale and using carbon dioxide as a raw material will require vast amounts of zero-carbon energy.

---

[206] "Energy efficiency and use in the chemical industry", Tracy Carole, Paul Scheihing, Lou Sousa, American Council for an Energy Efficient Economy (AICEEE), 2001

[207] "Economic Analysis of the Impacts of the Chemicals Strategy for Sustainability", Report for the European Chemicals Industry Council (Cefic), Becca Johansen, Brais Louro, Inge Kukla, Graham Pattle, Jodie Denmark, Chris Hughes, Daniela Jeronimo Roque, November 18, 2021

Manufacturers making products with plants rather than fossil fuels need to ensure that they do not create new problems through deforestation, destroying wildlife habitat, raising food prices or increasing the use of water or pesticides. With renewable feedstock, you will need to reestablish new supply chains.

India's chemical industry generated revenue of ~$180 billion in 2018-19. India exports 50% of its total production. The sector is highly diversified with a low Herfindahl index (highly competitive) and has deep linkages with the agriculture and manufacturing industries.[208] Majority of the Indian chemical sector still comprises small to midsize businesses that cannot afford to spend on world class technologies. The technology being used by bigger medium to large businesses are coming from overseas. Indian chemical companies spend only 1% on R&D whereas the global benchmark is 5%.[209]

India needs to minimize the carbon footprint of the chemical industry by restricting the production for essential end user applications. In parallel, India needs to consolidate the industry into 3-4 large players. These larger players should be driven towards high levels of energy and resource efficiency and the adoption of best-in-class waste management practices.

The simplest and the best way to cut emissions from the chemical sector is to simply use and produce fewer chemicals. The first step for India is to phase out the use of chemicals from clothing, toys, household cleaning and cosmetics. Regulatory bodies of the respective industries need to plan a rapid transition towards the use of natural alternatives. In the paints and agriculture industry, the usage needs to be minimized, again through a combination of using natural substitutes and shifting to natural farming methods. In

---

[208] "Indian Chemical Industry Analysis", Indian Brand Equity Foundation (IBEF), 2022

[209] "Sector Analysis Chemical Industry", Anand Logesh R R, Breasha Gupta, Divika Agarwal, Rasika Joshi, 2020

pharmaceuticals, industrial & automotive (lubricants), and mining & construction, increasing plant efficiency (energy and resources) and effective waste management, would be the logical way forward.

The regulatory body for the chemical industry needs to drive scientific and smart elimination of harmful chemicals from different industries. E.g., PFAS, also known as "forever chemicals", that cause cancer, are being eliminated from their "nice-to-have" applications such as nonstick cookware, long-lasting mascara, or water-repellent surfer shorts that don't need the level of high performance that "forever chemicals" confer. The researchers recommend that "forever chemicals" be used only in really important products, such as protective gear or medical devices that save lives. The same philosophy could be applied to identify and eliminate other chemicals that have been unnecessarily formulated in products, such as adding antimicrobials to soaps that can already kill germs. Simplifying the chemical ingredients in products has an added benefit: they are easier to take apart or recycle when they are no longer useful.

The Indian Plastics industry, a subset of the chemical industry, generates a turnover of ~$25 billion. The Indian Plastics industry is highly fragmented. Entry barriers are low, with low capital intensity, no technological barriers, and supportive government schemes. The industry comprises ~30,000 processing units, 85-90% of which are small and medium enterprises, employing ~4m people. The share of organized players has increased from ~45% in 2015 to ~60% in 2020.

There are four main components of the Plastics industry: Pipes (pipes, systems, fittings, tanks etc.), Consumer Products (furniture, house wares), Packaging, and Industrial Products (auto interiors, components, material handling equipment etc.).

Packaging (~$21 billion) accounts for ~83% of the market, followed by Pipes (~$4 billion).[210]

Plastic packaging not only creates hazardous waste (chemical waste during production and non-biodegradable after use), but also results in several indirect adverse consequences. Plastic packaging encourages excessive food processing, transportation and consumption. It prevents people from purchasing products in their natural and fresh forms. Natural supply chains are disrupted, and manpower involvement is significantly reduced. In a compact mixed use urban environment, there is no food item that needs to be sold with plastic packaging.

To start phasing out the use of plastics from packaging, India should:

1. Introduce a negative list of items that cannot be sold with plastic packaging. The list could start with dry food commodities and beverages and eventually cover all consumer goods.

2. Levy a green tax for products packed in plastics; this should encourage the shift towards no packaging or other sustainable forms of packaging.

3. Restrict the production to biodegradable plastic only.

4. Formulate and enforce best practices for sustainable production and waste management methods.

5. Shut down all small and medium sized operations and restrict production to 3-4 companies.

The use of plastics in the pipe industry should be minimized. Given the sizable share of plastic pipes currently and their growing need for urbanization, the phase out needs to be planned with a well-planned shift towards concrete, steel and other more sustainable materials. A green tax should be

---

[210] "The Big Leap to a Formal Economy", Motilal Oswal, June 2018

levied to make plastic pipe products less competitive and accelerate the shift.

Wood products

The main wood products manufactured in India are wooden furniture (~$20 billion), wood panels (~$4 billion) and paper (~$8 billion).

The paper industry has been fully displaced by technology. The transition towards a paperless economy should be planned alongside the indigenization of production of mobiles and computers. Responsible raw material sourcing should be enforced immediately for the sector. A green tax needs to be included for paper purchases (consumer as well as commercial). The resulting increase in paper prices will further encourage judicious use of paper. Lastly, the industry should be consolidated into 3-4 large enterprises that provide full transparency of their operations to the regulatory body. The Indian market is highly fragmented with the top 3 players accounting for only 9% market share compared with 68% in the USA. There are currently around 900 paper mills in the country.

Wooden furniture is unhealthy, unsustainable and promotes social inequality. Its use needs to be significantly reduced to make production sustainable. India needs to promote the use of minimalist furniture at home, office, hotels, hospitals, educational institutes, retail, restaurant, public places etc. To start with, a heavy tax needs to be introduced on the purchase of non-essential wooden furniture items such as tables, chairs, beds etc. Clear guidelines need to be formulated for tax exemption of wooden furniture items based on the quantity or percentage of wood used. Furniture imports should be banned as they create unnecessary cost pressure on the domestic market, forcing the local players to adopt unsustainable practices. Responsible sourcing should be enforced immediately with strong penalties for defaulters. Simultaneously, the industry needs to be consolidated into a few large enterprises. These should be heavily regulated to ensure responsible sourcing, minimalist product development, and efficient operations.

The wood panel industry includes plywood sheets (~70% of the market), engineered wood panels (MDF [Medium Density Fiberboards], furniture board and particle board) and decorative surface products such as laminates.[211] New construction activities drive most of the demand (85-90%) in the wood panel industry while the balance comes from renovation and replacement. The plywood industry is highly fragmented with ~75% of the market share controlled by the unorganized sector. Unorganized players compete with organized players on prices due to the tax advantage. MDF segment is fully organized given the high capital requirements.

India simply cannot avoid using wood panels in urban construction but should make the use sustainable. First, the use should be restricted to functional uses in construction where wooden panels work well as against other alternatives e.g. doors. Usage for non-essential and luxury applications should be absolutely stopped. Manufacturing of wooden interior products should be banned. Second, the sustainability (including a complete life cycle assessment) of engineered wooden panels needs to be carefully evaluated. A holistic comparison needs to be done against natural plywood to determine the usage. Third, responsible sourcing needs to be enforced. Fourth, a green tax needs to be levied to cover the additional effort of responsible sourcing and other sustainable practices. Fifth, the industry should be consolidated into a few large players, whose operations are fully streamlined and regulated. Strong licensing requirements need to be introduced to only allow highly capable (process and technical capabilities) and well capitalized companies to operate in this sector. Gradually,

---

[211] "India Timber supply and demand 2010-2030", Dr. Pramode Kant and Raman Nautiyal, International Tropical Timber Organization (ITTO), 2020

regulations around wages, working environment, safety, and health should be introduced.

India should stop both imports and exports of wood and wood products. Imports create cost pressure on the domestic industry as well as encourage unnecessary demand. Exports add to the resource burden on the already resource constrained landmass.

The stable state manufacturing output for making India sustainable would be $3.5 to $4 trillion (2020 terms).

The total output of the sectors for building and maintaining the urban infrastructure would be $1.0 to $1.5 trillion. These include aggregates ($50 bn), cement ($135 bn), steel ($500 bn), aluminum ($50 bn), other metals / minerals ($50 bn), metal consumer ($50 bn), heavy engineering ($125 bn), ceramics ($25 bn), wood panels ($75 bn), glass ($50 bn), pipes ($25 bn), paint ($25 bn) and electrical & electronics ($500 bn).

The total output needed from the core construction sectors is 100-200 times the current capacity. Therefore, the stable state industry size can be estimated as 5-10 times the current size of the respective industry. Scaling up the output to reach the stable state size would need 15-20 years. Urban infrastructure development can be completed in another 20-30 years once the industry reaches stable state production capacity. Even after the urban infrastructure build-out, the output of these segments will stay close to the stable state levels to maintain and upgrade the infrastructure.

The stable state output of sectors driving sustainable consumption would be around $2.5 trillion. These include electrical & electronics ($500 bn - major), furniture ($100 bn), textiles ($700 bn), FMCG ($1000 bn), pharma ($200 bn), sports ($100 bn), and toys ($20 bn). Electrical and electronics industry will cater to both urban infrastructure development and sustainable consumption.

The output of sectors enabling green transportation would be a little over $500 billion. These will primarily include automotive ($400 bn), rolling stock ($25 bn), shipbuilding ($10 bn) and aerospace ($100 bn).

Steady state output of deprioritized sectors would be around $100 billion. These include chemicals, leather, plastics, and paper.

Table 11.1 - Industry size ($ bn) and employment (MM) - Current (FY21) and Sustainable India (FY72)

Sector	Size FY21 ($ bn)	Size FY72 ($ bn)	Employed FY21 (MM)	Employed FY72 (MM)
Aggregates	2	50	0.2	3.0
Cement	15	135	0.8	3.0
Steel	45	500	0.8	3.0
Aluminum	10	50	0.2	0.7
Other metals / minerals	5	50	0.2	0.7
Metal consumer products	5	50	0.5	1.0
Heavy engineering	10	125	1.2	1.5
Ceramics	7	25	0.6	1.0
Glass	4	50	1.5	2.5
Pipes	5.5	25	0.3	1.0
Paint	7	25	0.3	0.6
Electrical & electronics	30	500	1.0	5.0
Furniture	18	50	0.5	1.0
Textiles	40	350	3.0	2.5
FMCG	60	500	3.5	5.0

Pharma	40	300	0.7	1.5
Sports	0.25	75	0.5	2.5
Toys	1	15	0.5	2.0
Automotive	70	500	1.0	2.0
Rolling stock	1	25	0.2	1.0
Shipbuilding	0.5	10	0.1	0.5
Aerospace & Defense	2.5	100	0.2	1.0
Leather	18	5	0.4	0.1
Chemical	50	50	0.2	0.5
Plastics	25	10	0.5	0.1
Wood panels	4	75	0.1	0.5
Paper	8	5	0.4	0.2
Manufacturing - total	**~480**	**~3,700**	**20.5**	**43.3**

Consolidation will be the biggest enabler for various manufacturing sectors to scale up to steady state production capacities. It will enable domestic enterprises to bring together capabilities across the value chain, invest in building leading capabilities both through R&D and acquisitions, increase efficiency and quality, reduce price competition & increase profit margins, and become more financially attractive. It will also give domestic enterprises the scale to buyout the India operations of various MNCs.

Regulation and consolidation will reinforce each other. An increase in licensing and compliance requirements, wage levels and standards of health, safety and environment will drive consolidation and vice versa.

The steady state manufacturing industry will employ around 5 crore (50 million) people in the long run. Currently, the industry formally employs around 2 crore (20 million) people, with informal employment also being significant (possibly another 3-4 crore). In the stable state, the production will be ten times the current production but the scale up will lead to significant efficiency and productivity gains that lead to optimization of the manufacturing workforce. In the long run, in say 50 years, manufacturing employment should stabilize around 2-3x of current formal employment. The expansion of the formal workforce will create sufficient room to absorb the adhoc manpower employed in the highly fragmented manufacturing sectors.

The government needs to be at the forefront of driving the consolidation. The government needs to build national consensus on the importance of consolidation and introduce policies and mechanisms (valuation, new employment etc.) that encourage SMEs to voluntarily sell-out. The integration of the SMEs into the larger enterprises should be planned and executed carefully. All consequences should be planned for, and proactive steps need to be taken to mitigate risks of unemployment, distress, revolt etc. The government will need to influence banking and financial institutions to provide financial back-up to the chosen enterprises.

Consolidation will make the Indian enterprises self-sufficient and give them a competitive advantage over MNCs in the Indian market. A self-sufficient domestic focused manufacturing industry is fundamental for making India sustainable. Sustainability will continue to be compromised as long as India remains a low-cost competitor in global markets. Imports obviously generate unnecessary pressure on the already constrained natural resources, but exports are even more dangerous. They force the domestic industry to operate at the lowest possible costs, resulting in minimal R&D, low wages, and poor standards of health, safety & environment. Even the operation of multinational corporations in the Indian market is not sustainable. The MNCs have an unfair advantage in terms of financial and technical muscle, forcing the domestic players to operate in the lower cost and quality segment.

Scaling up domestic enterprises and phasing out foreign companies and imports while still maintaining material and financial linkages with the world will be extremely challenging. Moving from being a low-cost competitor to becoming a high value producer, would require steady improvements in various functional areas such as R&D investments, labor laws, safety, health, environment. Given the interlinkages between different manufacturing segments, the functional improvements across sectors would need to be well coordinated.

The scale up across the various manufacturing segments should largely happen in parallel. The manufacturing ecosystem has complex interdependencies. Manufacturing for urban construction will fuel the growth in sustainable consumption. Growth of construction related manufacturing in turn depends on the evolution of core engineering capabilities. Also, several engineering systems and technologies cut across multiple manufacturing industries. Even operational efficiency and quality standards cut across. Moving from a low-cost competitor to a high value producer would result in price increases in the domestic market. Therefore income levels have to be gradually increased across all manufacturing and services sectors to maintain the purchasing power. Regulations also need to be slowly and carefully introduced in parallel to avoid sectoral cost spikes.

As long as India maintains an unwavering focus on becoming sustainable and has no ambitions to conquer global markets, it will have the support of the developed world. Nobody will stop India from getting its house in order, especially when the mess it is creating is already becoming a nuisance for the world. The MNCs will happily leave the Indian market and global manufacturing and engineering companies will willingly provide assistance, if India is genuinely moving on the path of sustainability.

12. Sustainable energy balance

For mother earth, the Indian energy sector is a big fat filthy child. Unless the industry rapidly transforms into being fully sustainable, the child will develop into a monster that will destroy its own and the world's natural resources.

India is heavily dependent on imports for fulfilling its current energy demand. The total primary energy supply was 889 MToE (million tonnes of oil equivalent), equal to ~37 Exajoules[212] and also equal to ~10,337 TWh.[213] Imports accounted for 47% of India's total primary energy supply in 2020-21. Crude oil (49% of total imports) was the biggest import, followed by coal (33%), oil products (10%) and natural gas (7%).[214]

India's energy profile is completely dominated by fossil fuel-based sources (97% of the primary energy supply). The primary source is coal (65%), followed by crude oil (26%), and natural gas (6%).

India has the fifth largest reserves of coal in the world. As per the global energy industry information, India has ~101 billion tonnes of proven reserves of coal that would last for around 130 years based on current levels of production. Proven reserves are quantities that can be recovered with reasonable certainty in the future from known reservoirs as per existing geological and engineering information under existing economic and operating conditions.

The Government of India has estimated the total coal reserves to be ~352 billion tonnes, out of which 50% are proven (~176 billion tonnes), 42% are indicated and 8% are inferred. India produced 716 million tonnes of coal in 2020-21 was, a slight

---

[212] "Conversion factors and unit abbreviations", Key world energy statistics

[213] "India 2020 energy policy review", International Energy Agency, January 10, 2020

[214] "Power sector at a glance All India", Ministry of Power, Government of India, 2021

decrease from 731 million tonnes produced in 2019-20 (Covid impact).[215]

India's reserves of crude oil (~587 million tonnes) will not even last 20 years at the current rate of annual domestic production (~30 million tonnes). The total quantity of crude oil in the primary energy supply is ~235 million tonnes, which gives India a 2.5-year reserve in case of external supply shocks.

The natural gas reserves are also limited at 1373 BCM. India produced 29 BCM and imported 30 BCM in 2020-21.

India is already the third-largest energy consumer in the world after China and the United States. The total primary consumption (primary energy supply minus exports) for India was ~32 Exajoules in 2020. China's primary consumption was 145 Exajoules and the US was ~88 Exajoules.[216] India's Total Final Consumption (Primary Energy Supply minus energy spent in production and distribution) was ~23 Exajoules (equivalent to 554 MToE or 6,442 TWh) 2020-21.

The total consumption will increase manifold if India follows the energy consumption practices of the developed world. The annual per capita primary energy consumption in India is currently ~23 Gigajoules / GJ. It is small as compared to the consumption of other developed economies - the US (265 GJ), Germany (145 GJ), Japan (135 GJ), France (133 GJ), Spain (106 GJ), the UK (102 GJ) and Italy (97 GJ). Fossil fuel rich economies are even a notch higher - Qatar (594 GJ), UAE (424 GJ), Canada (361 GJ), Kuwait (353 GJ), Saudi Arabia (303 GJ), Oman (268 GJ), Australia (218 GJ), and Russia (194 GJ). The Nordic countries also consume very high levels of energy per capita due to the cold climate.

---

[215] "Energy statistics India 2022", Ministry of Statistics and Program Implementation, National Statistical Office, Government of India, 2022

[216] "BP statistical review of world energy", 2019

Industry accounts for the bulk of the energy consumption in India at 56%, and including agriculture, the industrial share is 60%. Residential consumption is 22%, followed by transportation (9%) and commercial (7%).[217] For the US, the split is industrial (34%), transportation (26%), residential (23%) and commercial (17%).[218]

For India to achieve energy sustainability, we first need to establish the energy consumption required by a sustainable India. Then we can figure out if renewables can help strike a sustainable energy balance.

The industrial output of a sustainable India will be ~10 times the current output in terms of value - estimated to go from $400 billion to $4 trillion. But the overall industrial energy consumption will go up ~7 times at the current levels of energy efficiency across industries due to three main reasons. First, the most energy intensive industries (iron & steel, aluminum, cement, aggregates, glass and ceramics) will need to scale around 5 times the current size to meet the development needs of a sustainable India. Second, the size of chemicals, leather, paper and fertilizers industries that are energy intensive and non-sustainable would be minimized, leading to gains in overall industrial energy efficiency. Third, industries that are estimated to scale up the most (~20x expansion estimated) viz. FMCG, textiles, would mainly expand in terms of value while volume is likely to remain constant and might actually decrease with higher quality and optimal levels of consumption. A sustainable transformation of these industries will reduce the energy intensity per unit volume of output - natural retailing will minimize the energy spent in packaging and processing.

India's industrial energy intensity (energy consumption per unit of output) is around 60% more than the leading

---

[217] "An Overview of Energy Sector in India", Nagaraju Kaja, School of Planning and Architecture, Vijayawada, 2015
[218] "Use of energy explained", US Energy Information Administration (EIA)

industrial nations.[219] India's industrial energy intensity is ~100 ktoe/$ bn of output (PPP adjusted).[220] The industrial energy intensity of other large nations with a fully developed and diversified industrial sector are UK 49 ktoe/$ bn, Germany 57 ktoe/$ bn, France 60 ktoe/$ bn, Japan 61 ktoe/$ bn, and the US 80 ktoe/$ bn.[221]

Energy consumption per unit of production in the manufacturing of steel, aluminum, cement, paper, textile, etc. is much higher in India, even in comparison with other developing countries.[222] The Indian steel industry consumes nearly 7.2 - 8.2 million Kcal per tonne of steel, as compared to 5 million kcal used in developed countries.[223] The electrical and thermal energy intensity in the Indian paper industry is 1092 kWh/ton and 4.32 MKcal/ton, as compared to 650 kWh/ton and 2.9 Mkcal/ton, respectively in developed countries.[224]

Fragmentation is the biggest driver of low energy efficiency across various industries in India. The large Indian companies have achieved 80-90% of the efficiency levels of the developed countries. But the energy intensity of smaller Indian firms that account for the majority of production in most Indian industries is more than four times the large firms.[225] Small and medium sized firms do not have the capital to invest in the most efficient equipment and

---

[219] "Energy Efficiency Potential in India', Indo German Energy Forum

[220] "Industry (including construction), value added (% of GDP)", World Bank

[221] "International approaches to industrial energy efficiency: a comparison of countries", Meegan Kelly, American Council for an Energy Efficient Economy, 2016; "The 2014 International Energy Efficiency Scorecard", American Council for an Energy-Efficient Economy (ACEEE), July 17, 2014

[222] "Intensity and Use of Energy in Indian Industries and the Contribution of Energy to Growth", Bishwanath Goldar, Suresh Chand Aggarwal, Pilu Chandra Das, Fifth World KLEMS Conference, Harvard University, June 2018

[223] "Understanding industrial energy use: Physical energy intensity changes in Indian manufacturing sector", Binay Kumar Ray and B. Sudhakara Reddy, Indira Gandhi Institute of Development Research, Mumbai, June 2008

[224] "Understanding industrial energy use: Physical energy intensity changes in the Indian manufacturing sector", Binay Kumar Ray and B. Sudhakara Reddy, Indira Gandhi Institute of Development Research, Mumbai, June 2008

[225] Bureau of Energy Efficiency Annual Report 2019-20

methods. Indian firms also have lower energy efficiency due to inadequate research expenditure. Indian companies tend to be more labor intensive - energy intensity increases significantly with labor intensity. Energy efficiency also tends to get higher with the age of the company[226]further proof that consolidating Indian manufacturing would result in significant energy savings.

Over the next 20-30 years, India can achieve energy efficiency standards of the leading industrial nations. While the developed nations have outsourced some of the most energy intensive industries, India can match their overall energy efficiency by minimizing the size of certain energy intensive industries viz. Chemicals, pulp and paper, fertilizers, leather etc.

Therefore, the total final consumption (TFC) of a sustainable Indian industry would be around 16,500 TWh, as against the current industrial TFC of ~3,600 TWh. This is based on a 7x expansion in energy consumption (existing efficiency) and a ~60% gain in industrial energy efficiency.

Agriculture consumed ~225 TWh of energy in India in 2020. The average energy consumption in India is around half that of the developed nations.[227] Hence, we can expect the agricultural energy consumption to double (~500 TWh) as India starts using more machinery for large scale natural farming.

The residential sector represents ~22% of the current primary energy consumption, amounting to around 1,400 TWh. There is huge variation in the energy consumption profile of households in the country. While basic functional households consume less than 100 units (kWh) per month,

---

[226] "Determinants of Energy Intensity in Indian Manufacturing: An Econometric Analysis", Santosh Kumar Sahu & K. Narayanan, 2011
[227] "Agri-environmental indicator - energy use", Eurostat, Aug 2021

households equipped with all modern appliances consume more than 500 units per month.[228]

Air conditioners would result in a huge energy demand if they became commonplace in every Indian household. Their use can add anywhere between 200 to 1500 units per month of electricity requirement, depending on the extent of use. A household running 20 hours of AC (1.5 ton) per day for 5 months in a year, will need 350-400 units of additional electricity per month.

A functional urban household needs around 100 units of electricity per month, without AC, heating, dish washing and cooking. This includes the use of an efficient refrigerator and responsible use of washing machines. In a basic functional household, ~60% of the energy is consumed in cooking.[229] A sustainable India should switch to electric only cooking - electric energy efficiency is 74% as compared to natural gas which has an efficiency of 40%.[230] Electric cooking also results in minimal emissions. Factoring in the efficiency gains of electric cooking, a functional urban electric household would need 190-200 units of electricity per month.

The total final consumption of ~40 crore such urban households would be around 1,000 TWh.

Energy consumption of the commercial sector is around 75% of the residential sector in the US. If India follows the principles of sustainability in its commercial establishments as well, the ratio is likely to be similar. Hence, commercial India would need energy equivalent to around 750 TWh of electricity.

---

[228] "Electricity Consumption Patterns", Aditya Chunekar, Abhiram Sahasrabudhe, Shweta Kulkarni, Prayas Energy Group, Pune, August 7, 2019

[229] "Plugging in: A collection of insights on electricity use in Indian homes", Radhika Khosla, University of Oxford, December 2017

[230] "Cooktop Comparison: Gas, Electric and Induction", Abhishek Jain, Bijli Bachao, April 22, 2016

For transportation in a sustainable India, passengers would need urban metro, intercity passenger rail, shared cars, long haul flights and destination buses, and freight will move with rail, commercial vehicles (including trucks), flights and shipping.

Every city will need ~1 TWh of electricity to power its urban metro network. Beijing (~2 crore) metro consumed 1.6 TWh in 2015 with 12 M daily pax.[231] Indian cities with a population in the range of 1-1.5 crore will need similar amounts of energy even if the urban metro network density is higher. ~130 cities will need around 130 TWh of electricity to power their urban metro network.

Intercity passenger rail will need around 200 TWh of electricity. In 2018-19, Indian Railways recorded 1,011 bn non-suburban passenger kms (PKM). These represent the passenger movement outside the urban areas. While 89% passengers in 2018-19 traveled by road, the share of road passenger movement is likely to stabilize around 20% in sustainable India. Shared cars are expected to be the main non-urban mode of passenger transportation on roads. Intercity rail will then carry ~7350 bn PKM annually in a sustainable India, assuming the overall travel intensity remains the same. Indian Railways has one of the lowest rail energy consumption per PKM at 75 kJ/PKM.[232] China is even lower at 65 kJ/PKM but Japan is 135 kJ/PKM, Europe is 400 kJ/PKM and the US is 700 kJ/PKM. High utilization, minimal amenities and absence of air conditioning are the primary drivers of the low rail energy consumption in India. The consumption in a sustainable India should then be around 100 kJ/PKM with better facilities and higher energy efficiency (traction and non-traction). Hence, the total intercity rail energy consumption would be around 200 TWh (7350 bn

---

[231] "Energy-saving operation approaches for urban rail transit systems", Ziyou GAO, Lixing YANG, 2019

[232] "Moving towards a low carbon transport future, increasing rail share in freight transport in India", The Energy and Resources Institute (TERI), Shakti sustainable energy foundation, 2019

PKM X 100 kJ/PKM X 0.277778). (1 Petajoule equals 0.277778 TWh)

Rail freight movement will need around 220 TWh of electricity. Indian Railways carried 658 billion NTKM (net tonne kms - only includes the weight of goods being transported). Coal is the biggest commodity carried by rail with 263 billion NTKM transported in 2017-18. Railways transport 60% of the total coal in India. We can remove the coal freight quantities from the freight estimation for sustainable India. Currently, rail freight accounts for 20% of the total freight movement in the country, but the share will likely be 50-50 in the stable state. The overall freight quantity will also increase by a factor of around 7 due to the expansion in the industrial output. Concentrated and localized production in the 130 cities should result in at least a 20% reduction in freight requirements. The total freight requirement for a sustainable India would therefore be around 8,000 billion NTKM. The freight energy consumption per unit is low in India at ~100 kJ / NTKM. Using the same, the total energy requirement for rail freight in sustainable India would be ~220 TWh.

Freight transportation by road will need energy equivalent to ~550 TWh of electricity. The total road freight in sustainable India (50% share of total freight) will be ~8,000 billion NTKM. The blended (HMV and MCV) energy use for road transportation is 250 kJ / NTKM. Multiplying the two and using the relevant conversion factors for changing joules to TWh, the total energy consumption for freight transportation by road will be ~550 TWh. Switching commercial vehicles to the use of green hydrogen will reduce the energy requirement by ~30%.

Shared cars (ride sharing and self-drive rentals) will need ~1,000 TWh of electricity. Sustainable India will need around 10 crore shared cars (refer Green Transportation). The average distance traveled annually by a taxi is 70,000 km. Hydrogen fuel cell cars have breached the 250 km mark per kg of hydrogen.[233] Toyota Mirai recently entered the Guinness Book of World Records for traveling 260 kms per kg of hydrogen.[234] Currently, the most efficient production facilities need 50 kWh of electricity to produce 1 kg of hydrogen. By 2050, the requirement is likely to come down to 45 kWh per kg of hydrogen.[235] System efficiency is also likely to improve by more than 20% during the next couple of decades with better anodes, cathodes, electrolytes etc.[236]

Long haul air travel will need an energy equivalent of ~550 TWh of electricity. Kolkata airport mainly operates long haul flights (> 1,000 km) in India and has an annual domestic pax of ~2 crore.[237] While the population of Kolkata metro region is around 1.5 crore, the total population served by the airport would be around 5 crore. A sustainable Indian city will have a population of 1.0 - 1.5 crore and will likely have a higher frequency of air travel per capita. Assuming both these factors cancel out each other, we can use the Kolkata pax as a reference for a sustainable Indian city airport. The average long-haul distance for domestic flights will be around 1,200 km.[238] An average of 3 liters of jet fuel is needed per pax per 100 km.[239] The energy density of jet fuel is 35 MJ/L. Jet fuel production efficiency is around 80%. Multiplying the total pax km with fuel per pax km gives us the total fuel requirement. Multiplying the fuel requirement with energy density gives us total energy requirement for passenger air travel. For 130 cities with only long-haul air travel, the energy

---

[233] "Research on Hydrogen Consumption and Driving Range of Hydrogen Fuel Cell Vehicle under the CLTC-P Condition", Zhijie Duan, Nan Mei, Lili Feng, Shuguang Yu, Zengyou Jiang, Dongfang Chen, Xiaoming Xu, and Jichao Hong, December 2021

[234] "THIS car comes with highest mileage, runs 260 km in 1 liter fuel - Toyota Mirai", Zee Media Bureau, October 25, 2021

[235] "Comparative life cycle assessment of hydrogen-fuelled passenger cars", Daniele Candelaresi, Antonio Valente, Diego Iribarren, Javier Dufour, Giuseppe Spazzafumo, 2021

[236] "Recent Developments on Hydrogen Production Technologies: State-of-the-Art Review with a Focus on Green-Electrolysis", Leonardo Vidas, Rui Castro, University of Lisbon, December 1, 2021

[237] Kolkattainternationalairport.com

[238] "Annual report 2018-19", Ministry of Civil Aviation, Government of India

[239] "How much fuel per passenger an aircraft is consuming?", Laia and Pierre-Selim, July 31, 2018

requirement would be around 570 TWh. This does not include the energy use for air freight and destination flights, which are not likely to be significant in comparison.

We can safely assume that shipping would require less than 100 TWh of energy, even if India fully exploits the shipping potential of its river networks and the Indian Ocean.

Buses, which would largely be restricted to destination and event travel, should also have a relatively small energy requirement. We assume that the requirement would be less than 50 TWh.

In total, the transportation energy requirement of sustainable India would be the sum of energy requirements of all these modes - Urban metro (130 TWh), intercity passenger rail (200 TWh), rail freight (220 TWh), road freight (550 TWh), shared cars (1,000 TWh), air (570 TWh), shipping (100 TWh) and buses (50 TWh). These add up to an energy requirement equivalent to ~2,800 TWh of electricity.

The total final consumption of energy of a sustainable India will be ~22,000 TWh - sum of industrial (~16,500 TWh), agriculture (~500 TWh), residential (~1,000 TWh), commercial (~750 TWh), and transportation (2,800 TWh). This is 2.5 times the total final consumption recorded in 2020. Industrial consumption would account for over 70% of the total final consumption.

Table 12.1 - Total Final Energy Consumption - Current (FY21 / 2020) and Sustainable India (FY72)

Segment	Unit	Current (FY21 / 2020)	Sustainable India (FY72 base case)
Industrial	TWh	3,800	16,500
Residential	TWh	1,400	1000
Commercial	TWh	500	700
Transport	TWh	600	2,800
Agriculture	TWh	200	500
Construction	TWh	*	500
India - total	**TWh**	**6,500**	**22,000**

*Included in Industrial

Coal stock can shoulder 65% (current share of the total supply) of this energy requirement for ~50 years, based on international estimates of India's coal reserve, and for 150-200 years, as per India's own estimates.

The emission intensity of coal is the highest amongst the various fossil fuels. Based on the life cycle assessment of various fossil fuels, coal has an emissions intensity of ~1000 g CO_2 / kWh, oil 955 g CO_2 / kWh, and natural gas ~600 g CO_2 / kWh.[240] These represent the amount of CO_2 emitted for each unit of electricity produced with the respective source. The emission factor for generating 1 MJ of heat energy by coal is 88 g CO_2 / MJ, oil 73 g CO_2 / MJ, and natural gas 51 g CO_2 / MJ.

To become fully sustainable, India needs to meet its energy requirements with renewable sources - solar, wind (onshore and offshore), hydro, ocean thermal energy and bioenergy.

Nuclear energy is neither sustainable nor safe and creates the risk of irreversible mass scale destruction. It should simply

---

[240] "Emissions intensity", Wikipedia

not be developed in any form or harnessed for any purpose. The main fuels (Uranium, Plutonium, Thorium) for fission are available only in finite quantities. The current estimate of recoverable global reserves of Uranium are just 4 times the amount of fuel produced already. Thorium is three to four times more abundant in nature than uranium but has no isotopes that readily fission to produce energy. Thorium has to be converted to uranium in a reactor to become useful as a nuclear fuel.

Fusion technologies have long been touted to provide a clean and sustainable source of energy but are a classic case of creating venetian blinds.[241] Since the 1940s, viable energy production through fusion has been 10-20 years away. This target has kept moving as new roadblocks, sometimes much bigger than the previous ones, keep emerging.

We're basically trying to make stars on Earth. The fusion of two hydrogen atoms to make helium is the main process that powers the sun and other stars. When such light atomic nuclei combine, they release an immense amount of energy. But because these nuclei have positive electrical charges, they repel one another, and it takes tremendous pressures and temperatures to overcome that electrostatic barrier and get them to merge. If scientists can contain the fuel for fusion—a plasma mixture of deuterium and tritium, two heavy isotopes of hydrogen—the energy released in the reaction can make it self-sustaining. But how do you bottle a plasma at a temperature of around 100 million kelvins, several times hotter than the center of the sun?[242] A reasonable mind would have simply decided against venturing further, but scientists continued to find encouragement from the rich economies.

No known material can withstand such extreme conditions; they would melt even extremely heat-resistant metals such as tungsten in an instant. The answer long favored for reactor

---

[241] Michael Mankins and Richard Steele, Turning Great Strategy into Great Performance

[242] Philip Ball, "What Is the Future of Fusion Energy?", Scientific American, June 1, 2023

design is magnetic confinement: holding the electrically charged plasma in a "magnetic bottle" formed by strong magnetic fields so it never touches the walls of the fusion chamber. The most popular design, called a tokamak and proposed in the 1950s by Soviet scientists, uses a toroidal (or doughnut-shaped) container.

The process requires exquisite control. The furiously hot plasma won't stay still: it tends to develop large temperature gradients, which generate strong convection currents that make the plasma turbulent and hard to manage. Such instabilities, akin to miniature solar flares, can bring the plasma into contact with the walls, damaging them. Other plasma instabilities can produce beams of high-energy electrons that bore holes in the reaction-chamber cladding. Suppressing or managing these fluctuations has been one of the key challenges for tokamak designers. "The big success of the past 10 years has been in understanding this turbulence in quantitative detail," says Steven Cowley, who directs the Princeton Plasma Physics Laboratory.

One of the biggest obstacles to magnetic-confinement fusion is the need for materials that can withstand the tough treatment they'll receive from the fusing plasma. In particular, deuterium-tritium fusion makes an intense flux of high-energy neutrons, which collide with the nuclei of atoms in the metal walls and cladding, causing tiny spots of melting. The metal then recrystallizes but is weakened, with atoms shifted from their initial positions. In the cladding of a typical fusion reactor, each atom might be displaced about 100 times over the reactor's lifetime.

The consequences of such intense neutron bombardment aren't well understood, because fusion has never been sustained for the long periods that would be required in a working reactor. We don't know and won't know about materials degradation and lifetime until we've operated a power plant. Nevertheless, important insights into these degradation problems might be gleaned from a simple experiment that generates intense neutron beams that can be used to test materials. Such facilities (particle-accelerator-based projects) have been built in Spain and in the US.

But there is still no guarantee that these material issues can be solved. If they prove insurmountable, one alternative is to make the reactor walls from liquid metal, which can't be damaged by melting and recrystallization. But that brings in a whole suite of other technical concerns, and as always, we are unlikely to relent.

Another major challenge is making the fuel for fusion. The world has abundant deuterium: this isotope constitutes 0.016 percent of natural hydrogen, so the seas are literally awash in it. But tritium forms only in small quantities naturally, and it decays radioactively with a half-life of just 12 years, so it's constantly disappearing and must be produced afresh. In principle, it can be "bred" from fusion reactions because the fusion neutrons will react with lithium to make it. Most reactor designs incorporate this breeding process by surrounding the reactor chamber with a blanket of lithium. All the same, the technology is unproven at large scales, and no one really knows whether or how well tritium production and extraction will work.

The largest fusion project in the world, ITER (International Thermonuclear Experimental Reactor) in southern France, will use a massive tokamak with a plasma radius of 6.2 meters; the entire machine will weigh 23,000 metric tons. If all goes to plan, ITER—supported by the European Union, the U.K., China, India, Japan, South Korea, Russia and the U.S.— will be the first fusion reactor to demonstrate continuous energy output at the scale of a power plant (about 500 megawatts, or MW). Construction began in 2007. The initial hope was that plasmas would be produced in the fusion chamber by about 2020, but ITER has suffered repeated delays while the estimated cost of $5.45 billion has quadrupled. In January 2023, the project's leaders announced a further setback: the intended start of operation in 2035 may be delayed to the 2040s. ITER will not produce commercial power—as its name says, it is strictly an experimental machine intended to resolve engineering problems and prepare the way for viable power plants.

There is not today a single project underway to build a fusion power plant that will produce energy. The current consensus projection (latest Venetian blind) is that fusion plants might be feeding power into the grid by around 2050 and then could become steadily more important to the energy economy in the second half of the century, especially post-2060. Several startups are also being funded now by the VCs and the billionaires. Artificial intelligence can accelerate development but we are truly playing with fire here, and there is a higher risk of disaster with entrepreneurs and uncontrollable machines.

Whether nuclear power becomes a reality or not, it is almost certain that even Africa will be armed with nuclear missiles by the end of the century. That will be a positive outcome as it will enable Africa to gradually cease resource extraction from the continent and eventually become self-sufficient and sustainable.

The Sun has been worshipped as a life-giver to our planet since ancient times. India is blessed with 250-300 sunshine days in a year, annual solar irradiance of 4-7 kWh/m2/day, to generate 5 million TWh per year of energy. Theoretically, a small fraction of the total incident solar energy (if captured effectively) can meet the entire country's power requirements. The solar energy available in a single year exceeds the possible energy output of all of the fossil fuel energy reserves in India. Several utility scale solar plants are already operational in various parts of the country confirming the techno-commercial viability of tapping India's solar potential.

As compared to other renewable sources of energy, solar potential is huge and its generation needs land, a precious and finite resource. India has estimated a potential of creating 750 GW of solar capacity on ~14,000 sq kms of wasteland, which is just 3% of the total available wasteland (467,000 sq kms). With that capacity, India will generate ~1,200 TWh of electricity, which is 6.6% of the total primary energy requirement of sustainable India. Therefore, India will definitely need to make much larger solar capacity building plans. Given that the potential of other renewable sources is much less variable, solar power generation requirements should be determined after establishing the potential generation from other renewable sources, which also have minimal land requirements.

The onshore wind potential has been estimated to contribute ~1,500 TWh of electricity in the base case. In 2019, the National Institute of Wind Energy published the wind potential atlas at 120 m height.[243] Wind is a mature sector in India and technology upgrades over a decade led to the increase in hub height from 100 m to 120 m, as well as larger turbine sizes. Out of the total estimated ~700 GW potential (base case), ~340 GW could be installed in wasteland, ~350 GW in cultivable land and ~10 GW in forest area.

The atlas base case is a little under half of the maximum potential as per the current technology outlook. In the base case, the availability of different parcels of land has been assumed to be different and the windy Himalayan region has been excluded. The base case availability assumptions are - wasteland (80%), cultivable (30%) and forest (5%).

---

[243] "India's Wind Potential Atlas at 120m agl", National Institute of Wind Energy, Chennai, Ministry of of New and Renewable Energy, Government of India, October 2019

Table 12.2 - On-shore wind power generation capacity for different capacity factors

	Unit	Base case	High case	Comments
Wind capacity at 25-28% CUF	GW	340	822	Better land availability and inclusion of Himalayan regions
Wind capacity at 28-30% CUF	GW	140	241	Better land availability
Wind capacity at 30-32% CUF	GW	82	141	Better land availability
Wind capacity at 32-35% CUF	GW	75	129	Better land availability
Wind capacity at >35% CUF	GW	57	98	
Additional generation with hub height increase	TWh	160	451	
Total onshore wind capacity	TWh	1702	3673	

30% availability of cultivable land is a very conservative assumption as wind and agriculture pair well.[244] It is possible for farmers to plant crops and graze livestock right up to the base of the turbines and therefore make use of about 95% of the land in the immediate area around the turbine. The development of wind energy has a significant positive effect on nearby crop yields. Changes to the microclimate were the primary driver for increased crop yields, with results indicating that sizable wind farms decreased the number of growing season extreme degree days (defined as days above 30°C during the growing season) by 2.2%-2.6%.

---

[244] "The Mutual Benefits of Wind Energy and Agriculture", Guidehouseinsights, MAY 11, 2021

Even the 5% availability of forest land is extremely conservative. While forests were considered absolute 'no-go' areas for wind turbines only a few years ago, forest wind farms have now become reality in many German states.[245] High hub heights and large rotor diameters enable wind farms at inland sites in southern Germany to operate profitably. At a height of 120 meters, annual mean wind speeds reach up to between 5.5 and 7 meters per second even in Bavaria and Baden-Wuerttemberg. These high-wind layers of air are also high above the tree crowns of the around 11 million hectares of German forests – mainly spruce, pine, beech and oak with average heights of between 15 and 30 meters. Given that the average height of trees in Indian forests is lower, India can more effectively realize the wind potential of forest sites.

Improving the availability assumptions to wasteland (80%), cultivable (80%) and forest (20%), leads to a 72% increase in the wind potential capacity, as outlined in the wind atlas for CUF >35%. Extrapolating the same to other capacity segments with lower CUFs, the wind power distribution potential goes up to 2,700 TWh from ~1,500 TWh.

Inclusion of the Himalayan and Northeast regions adds another ~500 TWh of potential generation capacity, taking the total wind generation potential to ~3,200 TWh in the best case. The elevated regions of Himalayan and Northeastern states have a high wind potential but due to the land suitability assumptions applied (especially with respect to elevation and slope), the technical wind potential has become negligible in those regions. But apparently there can be scattered potential pockets available for wind farm development, which can provide an additional ~237 GW to the national grid.

---

[245] "Can wind farms and forests mix?", Peter Herbert Meier, Renewable Energy Magazine, 23 February 2012

Further increases in hub height from 120 m to 160 m can also add ~400 TWh of power to the grid.[246] Wind resource quality improves significantly with height above ground. Wind speed differences translate to sizable capacity factor improvements. Although the observed variance is broad, median capacity factor gains with higher hub heights are estimated at 2 to 4 percentage points when going from 110 to 140 m. Between 140 and 160 m, median capacity factor gains are approximately 1 percentage point.

India's Exclusive Economic Zone in The Indian Ocean (within 200 kms of the shoreline) has an offshore wind potential of 140 GW in the base case, and technological potential of 195 GW (112 GW fixed and 83 GW floating).[247] The high plant load factor (40-55%) of offshore wind (relative to onshore) is ideal for large-scale renewable energy integration in the national grid and also can be well integrated with India's hydrogen mission. After removing the transmission and distribution losses (10-15%), offshore wind can contribute 500-800 TWh of electricity demand.

Hydro power generation can contribute 440 TWh to 1240 TWh of electricity for consumption. India is endowed with economically exploitable hydropower potential to the tune of 1,48,700 MW of put in capability.[248] In addition, 56 pumped storage projects have additionally been known with a most likely put in capability of 94,000 MW. Additionally, to the present, hydro-potential from small, mini & micro schemes has been calculated as 19,749MW. So, in total, India is blessed with a hydro-potential of 262 GW.[249] The existing hydro projects are operating at an average capacity factor of 38.7%,

---

[246] "Increasing Wind Turbine Tower Heights: Opportunities and Challenges", report by National Renewable Energy Laboratory US and Renewable Energy Consulting Services, Inc., May 2019

[247] "Offshore wind technical potential in India", The World Bank and Energy Sector Management Assistance Program (ESMAP); "No offshore wind project has commenced in India: Are we on track for 30 GW by 2030?", Jasleen Bhatti, DownToEarth, September 10, 2021; "High cost, challenges: Why offshore wind energy potential remains untapped", Business Standard, November 29, 2021

[248] "Hydroelectric power in India", Wikipedia

[249] "Assessment & Analysis of Hydro Power Potential in India", Bahra University Solan, International Journal of Engineering Research & Technology (IJERT), May 5, 2017

whereas the potential average capacity factor has been calculated as 60%. Therefore, in the base case (148.7 GW and 38.7% load factor), India will generate 440 TWh, but in the best case (262 GW and 60% load factor), India can generate up to 1,240 TWh of electricity with hydro. Conservation and enhancement of India's water bodies through the creation of lakes, river systems, removal of settlements from riverbanks and mountains, and development of riparian forests, can further enhance the hydro power potential.

The Indian Ocean gives India the opportunity to tap into the various forms of ocean energy. Ocean energy harvesting technologies can broadly be classified into Ocean Thermal Energy (OTE), Ocean Wave Energy (OWE) and Tidal Energy (TE).[250] According to an estimate ocean and tidal currents altogether contain about 5 TW of energy and 1-10TW of wave energy in the entire ocean. Waves provide 15-20 times more available energy per square meter than wind and solar energy. OWE is also more reliable because it is available up to 90% of the time whereas availability of solar and wind energy is limited to 20-30% of the time. In a tropical country like India, the temperature difference between the free surface of the ocean and depth of around 900 m is above 20°C. The fluctuation in this value is only 1°C round the year. Thus, OTEC can be considered as a source to depend upon for harmless energy.

The estimated OTE potential in India is around 180 GW which would contribute 1,240 TWh of electricity with a 90% load factor.

Wave energy potential for India is 40-60 GW. This energy is however less intensive than what is available in more northern and southern latitudes. The capacity utilization factor for wave energy in India is in the range of 15-20%. Therefore, wave energy can contribute 54-95 TWh.

---

[250] "An overview study of Ocean energy potential and technologies in India", Geetam Saha, Dipesh Majumdar, Virginia Polytechnic State Institute and State University, Jadavpur University, December 2020

The identified economic tidal power potential in India is of the order of 8-9 GW, with about 7 GW in the Gulf of Cambay, about 1.2 GW in the Gulf of Kachchh and less than 100 MW in the Sundarbans. With capacity factors ranging from 20-35% for typical tidal projects across the globe, India can expect 12-25 TWh of energy contribution.

The strength of India's bioenergy resources mostly lies in the agricultural sector. Crop residue and animal waste are the biggest sources of bioenergy production. The technologies for producing electrical energy from both these sources are proven and well established in the Indian environment. Consolidation of the agricultural sector will enable much higher efficiency of generation from these sources.

A large quantity of crop residue biomass is generated in India. Overall, India produces 686 MT gross crop residue biomass on an annual basis, of which 234 MT (34% of gross) are estimated as surplus for bioenergy generation. The estimated annual bioenergy potential from the surplus crop residue biomass is 4.15 EJ[251], and can contribute ~1,000 TWh of electricity after removing transmission and distribution losses.

The total moisture free form of dung (calorific value of 14 MJ/kg) has already been used for power generation across the globe. Anaerobic Digestion (AD) is the most popular and widely used energy conversion technique among all efficient energy conversion techniques. It is most suitable for converting dung-based biomass to biogas and then later to electrical energy. AD process deals with the degradation of dung or any other organic matter by microbial movement, transforming it into biogas under anaerobic conditions. The dung is collected in this system, which is already rich in microbes and mixed with required water to form a slurry, and the recovered biogas from this process and later combusted in a combustion engine to generate electricity. The

---

[251] "Bioenergy potential from crop residue biomass in India", Moonmoon Hiloidhari, Dhiman Das, D.C. Baruah, April 2014

estimation of biogas potential has been done based on the availability of dung (excluding the use for manure) from livestock species in various states of India. This underutilized net biogas potential of 212,924 million m3 per year has the capability to generate additional electrical energy of 386 TWh per year.[252] Usage of human and food waste can increase the biogas electrical energy generation potential up to 500 TWh.

The contribution of the various renewable sources (except solar) adds up to 5,100 - 9,050 TWh, with 5,400 TWh expected in the base case. Hence, solar power generation needs to fulfill the demand gap of ~16,300 TWh in the base case (total demand is ~21,700 TWh). But, in the best case (18,700 TWh of demand and 9,050 TWh from renewables), India would only need ~9,700 TWh from solar energy. Assuming 10-15% losses in transmission and distribution, India will need to generate ~10,800 TWh (best case) and ~18,700 TWh (base case) of solar energy.

Based on the capacity utilization factors of existing solar projects in India (ranging from 17.37% to 18.80%), 1 GW of solar capacity produces 1.52 - 1.65 TWh (1.60 TWh base case) of electricity.[253] Hence, for 10,800 TWh, India will need ~6,500 GW of solar capacity and for ~18,700 TWh, India will need ~11,700 GW of solar capacity. New solar projects are being developed with capacity utilization factors of above 20% reaching up to 22%.

The current target of creating 750 GW of solar capacity on 14,000 sq km of wasteland needs to be significantly ramped up, to fully meet the energy demands with renewable sources. India will need to allocate ~65,800 sq km of land in the best case, and `262,700 sq km in the base case, on the basis of

---

[252] "Prospects of biogas and evaluation of unseen livestock based resource potential as distributed generation in India", Gagandeep Kaur, Naveen Kumar Sharma, Jaspreet Kaur, Mohit Bajaj, Hossam M. Zawbaa, Rania A. Turky, Salah Kamel, 2021

[253] "Solar Capex vs Opex", Energyhive, June 9, 2020; "5 MW Solar Power Energy Plant in India: Profit, Cost & Land Requirement", Waree, July 3, 2021; "Levelized Electricity Cost of Five Solar Photovoltaic Plants of Different Capacities", Tahira Banoa, K.V.S. Rao, Department of Renewable Energy, Rajasthan Technical University, Kota, India, July 9, 2016

variation in capacity and technology assumptions. These represent 2.0% and 8.0% of India's total land area respectively. The total area of wasteland that is accessible for solar energy is 467,000 sq km. The total area of barren land in the country is 140,000 sq km.

The solar power capacity per sq m varies with technology and scale. The capacity per sq m is usually ~40 W / sq m but can reach up to ~60 W / sq m for larger installations (Neemuch, 151 MW).[254] There are two technologies that dominate the solar power industry: the Concentrated Solar Power (CSP) and Photovoltaic (PV). PV / silicon-based solar cells account for 80-90% of the world installed capacity today and market share. CSP needs almost double the area (10 acres per MW) needed in PV installations (4-6 acres per MW). CSP is suitable for direct high intensity solar radiation.[255]

The capacity factor / efficiency of solar cells seems to have plateaued, with only incremental gains expected over the next few decades. For commercially available technologies, an upper bound for the efficiency is set by the celebrated Shockley–Queisser (SQ) limit, which accounts for the balance between photogeneration and radiative recombination of thermalized carriers. Any optical, conversion, or electrical loss would result in efficiency lower than predicted by the SQ formula. Mature technologies already approach the SQ limit, but most of them show little evolution over the last five years. Photovoltaic devices have a high theoretical energy conversion limit: above 33% for single junctions, and ultimately close to 90% if suitable materials can be found. In laboratories, the 25% efficiency threshold was reached in 1999, and slight improvements have been observed since, up to more than 26.6%. Those values approach the theoretical efficiency of the silicon cells (29.4%). The silicon technology

---

[254] "Levelized Electricity Cost of Five Solar Photovoltaic Plants of Different Capacities", Tahira Banoa, K.V.S. Rao, Department of Renewable Energy, Rajasthan Technical University, Kota, India, July 9, 2016
[255] "5 MW Solar Power Energy Plant in India: Profit, Cost & Land Requirement", Waree, July 3, 2021

is therefore reaching a plateau, pointing toward the need for new conversion concepts such as multi junctions.

As of today, multijunction cells are the only concept which demonstrated performance overcoming the single-junction Shockley–Queisser limit and reaching industrial applications.[256] The idea of multijunction devices is based on the fact that a cell reaches its maximum conversion efficiency for photons at a wavelength that is equal to its bandgap, when thermalization and non-absorption are inexistent. Dividing the solar spectrum into several wavelength ranges, and covering those wavelength ranges with distinct cells of suited bandgap, allows reaching higher efficiencies. Splitting of the incident spectrum could be achieved by stacking different materials, the highest band gap material being on top of the device. III–V materials (compounds of elements of columns III and V in the periodic table) have been widely considered, since they provide a large spectrum of available band gaps covering the sun spectrum. Moreover, efficient fabrication methods are available, and many compounds provide direct band gaps (which are preferred, since their high absorption allows fabricating thinner cells, requiring less material and relaxing the constraint on transport properties). Nevertheless, one limitation is the requirement of lattice matching for keeping high material qualities. A material combination that fulfills this condition is the Germanium/GaAs/InGaP cell. Although it allows reaching high performances (41.6%), this cell is far from the condition of current matching. The bandgap of the germanium cell being rather low produces a current almost twice as large as the limiting subcell current. A device with the optimum combination of materials is therefore not readily available but can be approached thanks to various technological strategies: wafer bonding, metamorphic growth, inverted stacks, dilute nitride, and multiquantum wells. While

---

[256] "Material challenges for solar cells in the twenty-first century: directions in emerging technologies", April 10, 2018

progress has been made with the highest conversion efficiency to date, at 46%, reported using wafer bonding, the high cost of the involved devices prevents large scale application.

Table 12.3 - Energy supply: Sustainable India (FY72) base case

Source	Capacity (GW)	Primary supply (TWh)
Solar	11,700	18,700
On-shore wind	700	1,700
Off-shore wind	140	550
Hydro	150	450
Ocean Thermal	180	1,250
Ocean Wave	40	50
Tidal	10	20
Bioenergy		1,400
India - generation		**25,000**
India - distribution		**22,000**

Given that we have arrived at the base case energy balance with renewables, we should identify key sensitivities that could significantly alter the balance.

The use of air conditioners is a big demand driver. An urban household (4 people) can consume anywhere between 240 to 1500 kWh of electricity just for running their air conditioner(s). A 1.5 ton AC consumes 1.5 kWh of electricity per hour, with an average household running AC for 16-40 hours per day (hours from multiple ACs combined). While most households use AC for the four summer months, there is a growing share of the population that uses the AC for ~10 months in a year. With these assumptions, the base case electricity consumption of a household for AC comes out to be 375 kWh / month. This creates an additional national demand of over 3,000 TWh (base case), including both residential and commercial. If we use solar, we will need an additional 1.5% of India's land based on the current solar performance in India.

Industrial energy efficiency is the next most critical factor. A ~20% further gain in industrial energy efficiency, results in a ~2,750 TWh reduction of energy consumption (~16,500 TWh total in base case). In the base case, we are expecting India to reach the current energy efficiency levels of the most industrially advanced nations in the next 20-30 years. In the best case, India could be at the technology frontier along with the others. Focus on consolidation in the most energy intensive industries will deliver the maximum energy savings.

Energy transition

The transition towards sustainable energy balance would involve a gradual reduction of per capita demand requirements, rapid buildup of renewable capacity and meeting the gap (demand minus renewable distribution) with non-renewable sources.

Chart 12.4 - Energy transition (FY22 to FY72)

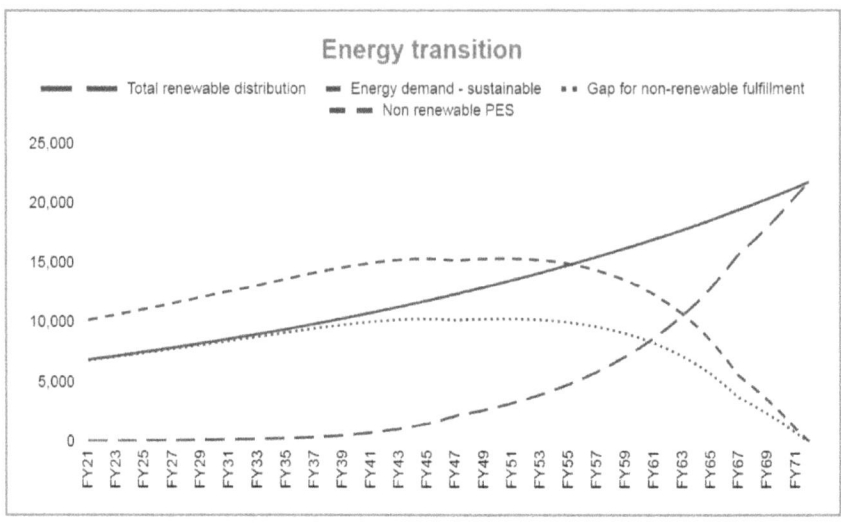

Controlling the demand assumes critical importance as in the momentum scenario, the energy demand in 50 years would be ~10x the current demand or around ~70,000 TWh, basis the expected real GDP growth. Migration to the ~130 cities, and the sustainable reorientation of industry will enable India to keep the demand under control, and only reach ~22,000 TWh by FY72.

The ramp up of renewable capacity is expected to average around ~15% over the next 25 years and continue at a steady pace to have ~25,000 TWh of generation and ~22,000 TWh of distribution by FY72. The entire demand would be fulfilled by renewables at this stage.

The gap between demand and renewable distribution increases till year 30 (to about ~10,300 TWh), and then rapidly decreases to Zero by FY72. Therefore, the non-renewable Primary Energy Supply (PES) will also be maximum in Year 30 (equivalent to around 15,300 TWh). The non-renewable PES is currently ~9,800 TWh equivalent.

Therefore, India's consumption of non-renewable resources (coal, crude oil and natural gas) will go up to 1.5x its current use during this period of transition. Even with the globally accepted value of India's coal stock (130 years basis current levels of production), India is in a strong position to keep the import prices in check throughout this period.

Energy storage - pumped hydro

In the scenario where all energy generation is done from renewables, storage becomes a critical part of the energy value chain. In energy systems utilizing high penetrations of variable renewable energy (VRE), energy storage is needed to keep the lights on and the electricity flowing when the sun isn't shining, and the wind isn't blowing — when generation from these VRE resources is low or demand is high. Energy storage can help VRE-dominated electricity systems balance electricity supply and demand while maintaining reliability in a cost-effective manner — that in turn can support the electrification of many end-use activities beyond the electricity sector[257].

Storage technologies are of four types - electrochemical, thermal, chemical, and mechanical. Some of these technologies, such as lithium-ion batteries, pumped storage hydro, and some thermal storage options, are proven and available for commercial deployment. While people commonly associate batteries with energy storage, 93% of the utility scale energy storage in the United States is done using Pumped Storage Hydropower (PSH). Pumped Hydro is a purely sustainable form of storage solution with almost negligible consumption of non-renewable resources.

Pumped storage hydropower (PSH) is a type of hydroelectric energy storage. It is a configuration of two water reservoirs at different elevations that can generate power as water moves down from one to the other (discharge), passing through a turbine. The system also requires power as it pumps water

---

[257] MIT Energy Initiative, Tom Melville, May 16, 2022

back into the upper reservoir (recharge). PSH acts similarly to a giant battery, because it can store power and then release it when needed[258].

The proposed large lakes in each of the envisaged ~130 cities, present a unique opportunity for India to leverage pumped hydro for its energy storage requirements. Given that we still have to design the lakes, we can incorporate the storage requirements into the development.

The optimal storage size would vary between 10-20% for a 100% renewable electricity storage system. With a cost optimization model, the optimal storage size has been estimated to be ~10% of the assumed annual electricity demand in Germany[259]. The requirements are larger based on a time series analysis. Occasional spillage of solar or wind electricity on sunny and windy days when storages are full is economically preferable to overbuilding storage to absorb all the generated energy. Typical spillage of solar and wind electricity in optimized hourly-resolution modeling studies is 5%–25%. The use of bioenergy as baseload or as a substitute during periods of scarcity can also increase system flexibility and reduce storage requirements.

Many existing PSH systems have been developed in conjunction with a conventional river-based hydroelectric system. Two reservoirs are created, at different altitudes, but close to each other. Often, the lower reservoir is large and located on a substantial river, while the upper reservoir is smaller, and located higher up on the same river or in a high tributary or parallel valley. Most river water passes through the system, generating electricity, and then flows down the river. Some water is cycled between the two reservoirs to create energy storage. Typically, pumping would take place by buying electricity during times when prices are low, which is when demand is low or the availability of electricity from

---

[258] Office of Energy Efficiency and Renewable Energy, The Department of Energy, United States

[259] Storage requirements in a 100% renewable electricity system: extreme events and inter-annual variability, Oliver Ruhnau, Staffan Qvist, March 2022

other sources is high (e.g., a windy and sunny day). Generation would take place during times of high demand (such as during evenings) when prices are high or during times of scarcity in the case of a renewables focused energy system. This pattern of buy-low and sell-high is called arbitrage.

Off-river PSH systems are not very common but are a highly viable and effective form of pumped hydro storage project. An off-river PSH system comprises a pair of artificial reservoirs spaced several kilometers apart, located at different altitudes, and connected with a combination of aqueducts, pipes and tunnels. The reservoirs can be specially constructed ('greenfield') or can utilize old mining sites or existing reservoirs ('brownfield'). Off-river PSH utilizes conventional hydroelectric technology for construction of reservoirs, tunnels, pipes, powerhouse, electromechanical equipment, control systems, switchyard and transmission, but in a novel configuration.

An off-river PSH system has the advantage that flood mitigation costs are minimal compared with a river-based PHES system. Heads are generally better than river-based systems because the upper reservoir can be on a high hill rather than higher in the same valley as the lower reservoir. The much greater number of off-river sites compared with on-river sites allows much wider site choice from environmental, social, geological, hydrological, logistical and other points of view.

Another advantage is that construction of off-river pumped hydro can be much faster than other storage methods. Bespoke engineering in mountainous river valleys is unnecessary. Work can proceed in parallel on the two reservoirs, the water conveyance, the powerhouse and the transmission. Construction timetables of 2–3 years are feasible for 10 GWh storages, although longer periods would be typical.[260]

The capital cost of a river-based hydroelectric system is highly dependent upon local geology, geography and hydrology. The cost of an off-river pumped hydro system is relatively predictable as compared to river based PSH. The absence of a river eliminates major flooding as a criterion, and also eliminates the environmental consequences of flooding a river. Most off-river sites are similar from key points of view, allowing a substantial element of 'copy and paste' to be employed in a large-scale storage construction program.

The cost of storage energy (\$ GWh−1) primarily relates to the cost of reservoir construction. The cost of constructing an off-river reservoir includes moving rock to form the walls, a small spillway and a water intake. Other significant costs could include road access, water access, lining the bottom of the reservoir to mitigate water leakage and placing evaporation suppressors on the water surface. Forming the walls is usually the dominant cost and can be approximated by the cost of moving rock (\$ m−3). The amount of energy stored in a hydro system is proportional to the head and to the usable water volume of the reservoirs. The important reservoir metrics are (a) the head and (b) the ratio of water impounded to the rock required to form the reservoir walls.

---

[260] A review of pumped hydro energy storage, Andrew Blakers, Matthew Stocks, Bin Lu and Cheng Cheng, Mar 2021

Figure 12.5 Indicative capital cost of 1 GW off-river pumped hydro systems with combinations of the key cost parameters: energy storage volume, head, slope and water–rock (W/R) ratio.

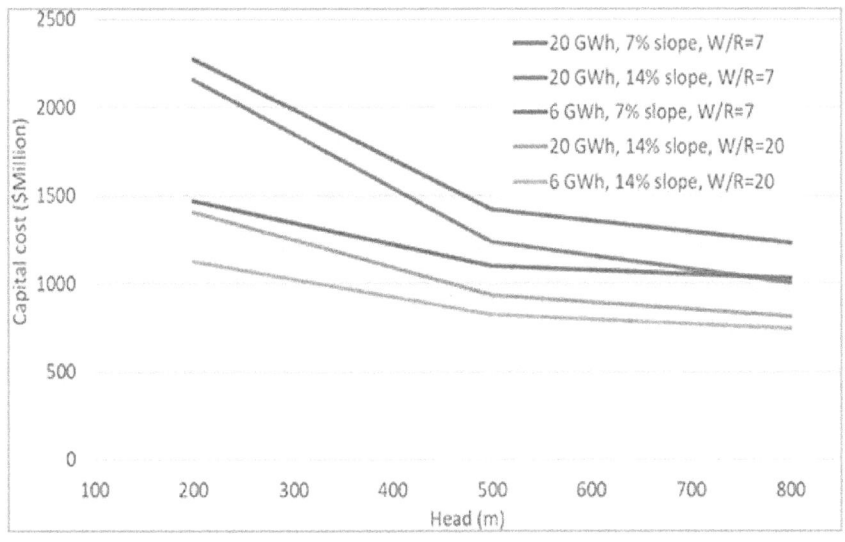

Figure 12.6 Levelized cost of storage for 1 GW off-river pumped hydro systems with combinations of the key parameters: energy storage volume, head, slope, water-rock (W/R) ratio and cycles yr−1

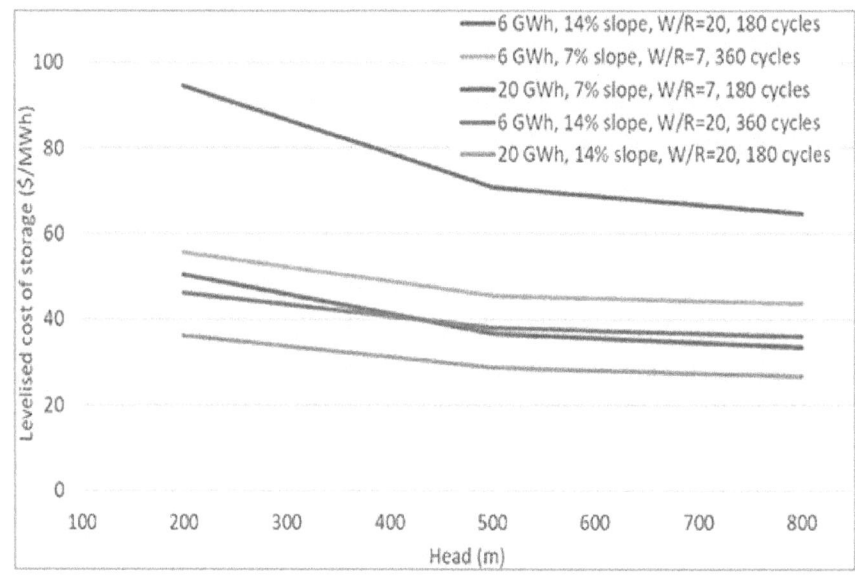

13. Indian citizen

An Indian citizen needs to be enabled and encouraged to lead a healthy and sustainable life. India must take responsibility for each of its citizens and establish a high standard of living for everyone. India should gradually move from a system of earning the daily bread, to entitlements for being a responsible healthy citizen. Instead of competing for wealth and material gains, everyone should simply be able to lead a fulfilling life.

Irresponsible procreation is one of the biggest crimes in today's resource constrained world, more so in India given that it has the highest population density amongst nations with a sizable landmass (>500,000 sq km). While it is possible to become sustainable with 150 crore people, renewable natural resources will become insufficient if we get close to the 200-crore mark. Land requirement for agriculture presents an insurmountable challenge. We estimated ~100 million hectares of arable land requirement in the natural farming scenario. Hence, there is maybe room for 10-20% increase, but that would only be at the expense of forest area and would therefore compromise the Indian climate. Irresponsible breeding also creates a huge social burden for several generations. It increases inequality, reduces system efficiency and creates unnecessary social friction. Procreation needs to be treated as sacred to the well-being of India.

Urbanization is already driving couples to make more responsible decisions as they fully bear the costs of living a high quality sustainable life. The fertility rate — average number of children born to a woman — is 1.8 in urban India and 2.4 in rural India. As India urbanizes over the next few decades, the average fertility rate will decrease from 2.2 (current) to below 2.0. Hence, urbanization would automatically solve the population problem, without the need for seemingly oppressive restrictions.

Removing key structural impediments for urbanization therefore assumes great significance. The biggest hurdle is the attachment of land and property to individuals. As we move towards greater levels of equality, ownership of land, property and other assets needs to be re-examined. Inheritance laws have also been central in making families produce more children. Succession planning is a major occupation of families even if they simply own a small shop or just a hut.

Land ownership is clearly meaningless given the finite span of human life. An individual can at most be a renter or lessee of land. Best is to keep land ownership only with government entities.

Only development companies should be allowed to lease land for a period during which it will maintain the developed structure (established practice in several developed nations). Laws should prevent land leases from being transferred to any other organization. Banks or financial institutions should also not have any recourse to land leases, in case of defaults by developers.

In case of immovable property as well, the concept of ownership needs to be discontinued. People or organizations should be allowed to lease property for an appropriate period. Individuals could lease the property for the duration of their lifetime or less. Companies and organizations should be able to lease for a fixed tenure with varying renewal clauses.

In the case of movable property, people and organizations should have ownership. These should be inherited by the legal heirs / nominees / successors.

India also needs to evolve from family owned to professionally owned companies. Non-executive shareholding should be entirely discontinued. There should also be controls to prevent unfair recruitment of family members even in private companies. Inheritance of company ownership needs to be discontinued. Only the proceeds of sale of company shares should be inherited. In the case of non-liquid shares, there should be no inheritance claim.

Urbanization and implementation of progressive asset ownership laws will likely happen over decades. During that period, India still faces the risk of reaching unsustainable population levels. Besides, even in urban settings, childbirth is treated and handled very differently by different segments. There are several localities where people are encouraged to produce more children to help maintain political control and ownership of private and public property. Even the educated and affluent urban population does not fully comprehend responsible upbringing. Flawed incentives, lack of awareness and ignorance are driving irresponsible procreation in urban environments. How can you punish someone if they don't know (or feign ignorance about) the crime they are committing? A vast majority of urban women are unable to exercise their choice in family planning. They undergo poorly supported pregnancies and are forced to bear the responsibility of child upbringing without having the necessary means and resources.

Robust family planning is therefore the need of the hour for India. India has so far adopted a very soft approach for influencing people. For the next 30-50 years at least, India should enforce strong family planning practices.

An independent Family Planning organization should be set up to ensure responsible procreation. The organization should help people effectively navigate the process and decision making related to childbirth.

The organization should make a determination of the readiness of a couple to bring a child into this world. Couples should be allowed to procreate only if they are deemed fit by the Family Planning body. The determination should be based on parent health, employment and financial status, living standards, criminal record, willingness, existing children, commitment to good upbringing, and other important considerations. Strict enforcement is the right approach here, as carrot and stick will not only leave loopholes but will also create unnecessary inequality within kids and amongst parents.

Eventually, the purpose of the Family Planning body would always be to educate people about producing healthy and responsible citizens. Parents would need to be counseled and reminded about minimum requirements and best practices around nutrition, hygiene, value system, education, physical development, grooming, parent engagement, social activities, use of gadgets etc. Couples need to understand responsibilities for nurturing children and should have a coherent plan for executing them.

Responsible family planning will reduce the variability in fertility rates across demographic segments and will become the cornerstone of an equal Indian society. The single most important factor in population growth is the total fertility rate (TFR). If, on average, women give birth to 2.1 children and these children survive to the age of 15, any given woman will have replaced herself and her partner upon death. A TFR of 2.1 is known as the replacement rate. India's TFR recently dropped to 2.0 which is below the replacement rate, suggesting that the population growth has plateaued. The urban fertility rate has dropped to around 1.7 due to resource constraints, excessive competition, high cost of living, and low wages.

By most estimates, India will reach a peak population of around 1.7 billion by 2070. In a sustainable India, the fertility rate will likely increase again as people have adequate incomes and complete social security. The fertility rate should ideally stabilize around the replacement rate in a sustainable India.

To make sure we nurture healthy and responsible citizens, India also needs to enable the entire population to meet the requirements of being a responsible parent. For that, the most important is to establish the minimum wages and benefits across all forms of employment.

By most estimates, the total size of the Indian workforce is ~500 million. The Indian labor market is characterized by high levels of segmentation and informality. Of the total employed, more than half are self-employed, and of the ~200 million wage earners, ~60% are employed as casual workers.[261]

Wages in India are abysmally low and most earn below the minimum wage. In 2018–2019, the mean monthly wage of a regular worker was Rs 16,149, and the median wage was Rs 10,000—far below Rs 18,000, the minimum pay recommendation of the Seventh Central Pay Commission. About 42% of regular workers earned below Rs 10,000 per month. The workers in the other employment categories are heavily concentrated at the lower end of the earnings distribution. 92% of casual workers and close to 60% of the self-employed earned less than Rs 10,000 per month. On the whole, 24% of Indian workers earned less than Rs 5000 per month and 63% earned less than Rs 10,000 per month in 2018–2019. In absolute numbers, of the total workforce of 480 million, 114 million workers earned less than Rs 5000 per month and 301 million workers earned less than Rs 10,000 per month.

Income inequality is high with the bottom of the pyramid earning less than 15% of the top bracket. The daily earnings across the defined occupation segments are - Legislators, senior officials and managers (INR 1052), professionals (743), technicians & associate professionals (479), clerks (446), service workers shop and market sales workers (251), skilled agricultural and fishery workers (177), craft and related trade workers (212), plant and machine operators and assemblers (254), and elementary occupations (138).

---

[261] "India wage report, wage policies for decent work and inclusive growth", International Labor Organization, 2018

The Fair Wages Committee (1948) defined three different levels of wages: living wage, fair wage and minimum wage. Among the three, the living wage constituted the highest level: covering food, clothing, shelter, education of children, health expenditure and old age insurance. Fair wage, envisaged as between the living wage and the minimum wage, includes subsistence plus standard wage. It considers national income, productivity and the capacity of the industry to pay, in the determination of its level. A minimum wage was defined as one necessary for sustenance of life and some measure of education, meeting medical requirements and for amenities for the preservation of the efficiency of the worker. It is the absolute minimum below which wages should not be set. These concepts very clearly embody the social objectives of and aspirations for a "decent standard of life".

India currently has a complex system of minimum wages, not applicable to all workers, and set up often arbitrarily, by different authorities – making it difficult to monitor and enforce the innumerable minimum wages.

In the current times, a minimum wage needs to cover food, housing, utilities (water, gas, electricity, phone and wifi), cleaning, clothing, children education, health & fitness, transportation and pension. Eventually, minimum wage should also cover maternity and childcare expenses.

For a family of four, the minimum monthly expenses for these in urban India (non-metro) would be food (INR 5,000), house rent (INR 10,000), water (INR 100), electricity (INR 750), gas (INR 500), phone (INR 500), wifi (INR 250), cleaning (INR 500), clothing (INR 500), education (INR 1,500 per student), health (INR 1,000), fitness (INR 1,000), transportation (INR 1,000 per worker) and pension (INR 1,000 per worker). These add up to ~INR 26,000 for the household.

The national minimum wage should then be INR 13,000 per month (post tax). As minimum wages would apply to all forms of employment (skilled and unskilled), both adults (in a family of four), will be able to earn. This minimum wage will also be sufficient to cover the expenses of singles. While this may seem insufficient to lead a good quality life in the current Indian metros, that is because the metros are overcrowded. In other tier 1 cities, this minimum wage will provide for a decent standard of life.

Minimum wages would need to be revised on a regular basis (ideally every two years) while taking into consideration changes in the cost of living, GDP growth and growth in labor productivity.

Mechanisms should be put in place to ensure rightful spending on urban housing, health, education and pension. HRA deduction should carry an additional incentive for renting an apartment in a high-rise. The government can provide higher deduction for living in a building with more than 15 floors. The existing system of tax benefits is well designed to ensure spending on health and education. Similarly, the government pension contribution is well structured to get people to invest in their pension.

Setting the minimum wage will automatically accelerate urbanization and consolidation. Rural and small-town enterprises will find it difficult to pay minimum wages. They will enter a cycle of manpower rationalization, migration, and local demand depletion. Small and medium sized farm owners will find it difficult to pay minimum wage to farm labor. Casual agricultural laborers are the single largest segment of the Indian workforce, and their migration to cities will trigger mass migration from rural to urban areas. Even shops and small establishments will go through the same cycle, eventually resulting in rationalization, closure or sale.

Minimum wage legislation by itself cannot ensure that minimum wages would reach low-paid workers, and efforts would need to be made to make it effective and strong enforcement mechanisms would need to be put in place. A number of strategies have been identified to improve compliance, which include conducting information and awareness raising activities, reinforcing labor inspections, strengthening the role of workers' and employers' organizations, and imposing sanctions and penalties.

Labor inspection services in developing countries are often under-resourced and under-staffed, and the challenge is even greater in the agricultural sector and the informal sector. In India, there is no effective enforcement mechanism for minimum wages, as the task falls on the inspection staff that are already entrusted with monitoring the implementation of other labor legislation. In addition, the number of staff has declined sharply over the past decade in all states. Furthermore, the inspection policy has changed since 2014, with inspections only carried out in the event of a complaint. Even in domains where inspection is a legitimate activity, lack of infrastructure constitutes a serious impediment to the effective implementation of laws. Brazil and Costa Rica have high compliance rates due to the strengthening of the labor inspection systems through considerable investment. Kerala has adopted the electronic system that logs wage payments into bank accounts, which is based on the United Arab Emirates model, and the labor department monitors it to ensure compliance. Similarly, workers engaged in MGNREGA are also paid wages directly in their bank accounts and adequate monitoring has been able to strengthen the focus on the groups that are entitled to these benefits, but also for the provision of financial services to rural areas. The strengthening of the labor inspection system along with electronic payments could help with effective enforcement of the minimum wage.

Penalties and sanctions are essential to improve compliance. However, to be effective they must be set at an appropriate level with effective institutions and procedures to administer and enforce them. If reliant primarily on criminal liability and court proceedings, they will rarely be imposed in practice because such proceedings are costly and lengthy. In China, the penalties for violations were increased from 20 to 100 percent of wages to a new range of 100 to 500 per cent to improve enforcement.

Extension of minimum wage to the informal economy, casual workers and small enterprises is critical given the heavy concentration of the Indian workforce in these segments. More than half the workforce is self-employed in informal services and one person / small family enterprises. Even medium and large enterprises have a sizable informal workforce in the form of contractors. The gig economy has taken off in the Indian cities with no social security and benefits available to the gig workers. Wages of casual workers in both the organized and unorganized sectors are much lower than regular wages. Except for agriculture, social personal services and private households, trade and hotel & restaurants, regular wages are more than double the casual wages in other industries (mining & quarrying, manufacturing, electricity, gas & water, construction, transport, storage & communication, banking & finance, real estate & business services, public administration & defense, education and health & social work).

The informal economy needs to be formalized to extend the coverage of minimum wage and other labor laws to every working citizen. The transition of workers and economic units to the formal economy needs to be done while ensuring the preservation and improvement of existing livelihoods during the transition. It calls for a combination of incentives, compliance and enforcement measures, including, for example, improving access to business services or finance as a result of transition, and reducing compliance costs for micro and small economic units through simplified tax and contribution regimes, as well as more extensive coverage of labor inspection in the informal economy. Self employed people engaged in informal services such as cleaning, cooking, security, electrician, carpenter, plumber etc. need to be brought under institutional set up (public or private) and given all the minimum benefits.

As long as the 130 cities are geared to absorb the migration, the transition is likely to be smooth. Cities will need to have organizations and transition mechanisms in place for people to get gainful employment and have a decent standard of life. Large agricultural and construction companies need to be ready to engage the workforce in large scale farming operations and in building the urban infrastructure respectively. Agriculture and food companies will need to be equipped by the government to maintain continuity of food supply and keep prices in check.

While the enforcement of minimum wages will reduce income inequality, wage dispersion across sectors and occupations also needs to be rationalized. The functioning of free markets enables accelerated development of new products and skills. The US is a free market and the center of global innovation, but also has a high Gini coefficient of 0.378 (indicator of income inequality). India has a Gini coefficient of 0.479 (10th worst globally) and South Africa has 0.577 (worst). Now while it is important to encourage skill development, education and innovation, it can be done within a narrower band of incomes.

A responsible healthy family does not need unnecessary luxuries. They don't need big bungalows, an army of servants or cars. They don't need lavish parties, wardrobes full of fancy clothing, or excessive amounts of food. Healthy people choose quality over quantity and avoid a lot of unnecessary expenses. There is basically a limit beyond which expenses become unhealthy. The aspiration of a healthy family determines the maximum income that people should aim for. They would want a high quality in everything from apartment (INR 50,000), groceries (INR 25,000), clothes (INR 5,000), phone (INR 10,000), wifi (INR 1,500), cosmetics & cleaning products (INR 20,000), children education (INR 1,00,000), health and life insurance (INR 20,000), pension (INR 50,000), transportation (INR 15,000), vacations (INR 50,000), outside eating (INR 20,000), sports & fitness (INR 50,000), entertainment (INR 10,000), household shopping (INR 20,000), and gifting (INR 10,000). They may also engage cooking and cleaning professionals (INR 30,000). Along with the other standard expenses, these add up to ~INR 6,00,000 per month (post tax including pension / savings contribution). Individual earnings beyond this upper limit should be discouraged through various means for workers as well as profit makers. India does not need the super-rich who are usually wasteful in their use of resources. India simply needs the right institutional structures and mechanisms to enable continuous progress.

To promote healthy living and high productivity, India needs to restrict working hours per day to a maximum of eight (excluding 1 hour of unpaid break), across all forms of work. The total number of working hours should not exceed 40 in a week. India should aim to bring it down to 35 hours over the next 2-3 decades. It would be best to simply not allow any overtime, except maybe in the case of national emergency projects. It is an essential change to bring Indians out of the hyper competitive and unfair work culture. People across the income spectrum are being made to toil for long hours. The youth are made to slog to earn rewards and get ahead in their careers. In doing so, people develop unhealthy lifestyles and habits. The mad race for money needs to stop with the assurance that 8 good hours of work will lead to a fulfilling life. The 8-hour restriction will also prevent companies from unfair profit making at the expense of overworked employees.

14. People love people
Formalize and institutionalize to maximize the use of human potential

The role of the services industry is to facilitate efficient and sustainable production and consumption. Services need to drive high quality, efficient and sustainable production and enable equitable, responsible and organized consumption.

The services industry (excluding technology) itself has an insignificant carbon footprint, but is responsible for building the skills, capabilities, processes and systems that govern our output and footprint.

The services industry will expand significantly along with the growth in infrastructure and manufacturing. Even with efficiency gains, the expansion will be multifold. Natural retailing and green hospitality will need greater manpower intensity.

Technology has rapidly disrupted the services industry and will continue to change the services paradigm. The developments which have taken place in information and communication technologies for the last 30-40 years have changed the traditional production processes.[262] Improvements in information technology have decreased the need for physical labor and increased the number of people who work in the service industry. Technological changes have led consumer preferences to improve and change. The extraordinary development of new technologies has played a central role in the transformation of economies and societies and affected both the structure of a great number of service activities. The combination of new information and communication with services at company level has given a

---

[262] "Service sector and technological developments", Filiz Gölpek, Hasan Kalyoncu University, Turkey, 2015

boost to the uptake of their services in the market. New technologies, at the same time, have invited many services to be more transportable and more attainable at any place in the world day and night.

Technology determines, to a great extent, the demand for raw materials and energy, the ways and efficiency of manufacturing, product performance, waste reduction and waste handling, health and safety, transportation and infrastructure, etc., thereby making significant impacts on the economic, environmental, and social dimensions of industrial development.

As long as technology innovations deliver a net improvement in resource efficiency, they are beneficial for humanity, even if that results in the substitution of manual work. Such innovations are referred to as 'creative destruction', which is defined as technological progress that improves the lives of many, but only at the expense of a smaller few. Creative destruction occurred during the industrial revolution when machinery and improvements to the manufacturing process such as the assembly line pushed out craft and artisan production.

More recently, the information revolution and technologies such as computing, the internet, mobile telephony, and information technology, are resulting in creative destruction across several service industries. Travel websites have eliminated the need for human travel agents. Tax software has eliminated numerous jobs for tax accountants. Newspapers have seen their circulation numbers decline steadily, replaced by online media and blogs. Increasingly, computer software is actually writing news stories, especially local news and sporting event results. Language translation is becoming more and more accurate, reducing the need for human translators. The same goes for dictation and proof-reading. Secretaries, phone operators, and executive assistants are being replaced by enterprise software, automated telephone systems, and mobile apps. Financial professionals such as stockbrokers and advisors have lost some of their business to online trading websites. Many banks are giving customers the ability to deposit checks via mobile apps or directly at ATMs, reducing the need for human bank tellers. Payment technologies have ushered in a new era of cashless existence, which could eventually eliminate the workforce involved in cash collection and management. Fast food companies have invested in computerized kiosks which can take orders without the need for humans. Retail cashiers have also been displaced at supermarkets and big-box stores with self-checkout lines. Toll-booth attendants have been replaced by systems like E-ZPass. Job recruiters have been affected by the growth of recruitment websites. The postal services industry is pretty much at the end of the road with the mass adoption of electronic mail for personal as well as commercial communication. The need for retailers of music and video content has been eliminated with the digitization of content.

Technological progress has mostly been incremental (especially in the 21st century) and gradual over time, involving improvements and adaptations of existing technology. However, on a few occasions in the 19th and 20th centuries, technological change has been "radical", resulting in major breakthroughs that have ultimately transformed the organizational structure of societies and economies. The first industrial revolution was characterized by the growing use of machines to replace manual labor, particularly the use of the steam engine and new industrial methods organized in factories. The second revolution was marked by the rapid adoption of electricity and other technologies in manufacturing and was enabled by growing transportation, communication, and public health infrastructure. A third revolution came from the digitalization of electronics, which enabled information to play a transformative role in the social, economic, and political spheres.

Technologies become transformative when they evolve into general purpose technologies (GPTs) that enable productivity gains across many sectors of the economy. In particular, past waves of industrialization have been associated with pervasive GPTs that resulted in growing returns-to-scale. The adoption of steam to power machines, the discovery and use of electricity, and the ease of communication permitted by information and communication technologies (ICT) are examples of applications of GPTs that were at the center of the three great disruptive periods in modern economic history. Each time, the GPTs contributed to fundamental economic transformation and helped reshape the world.

The internet will rank among the major technological movements in world history. On the scale of the discovery of fire, the wheel and cultivation of crops, the interconnection of humans is a very important step toward becoming the caretaker of the universe that we are destined to be.

Recent breakthrough developments in several clusters of technologies have led some to argue that a new technological revolution may now be taking place. A so-called Fourth Industrial Revolution (4IR) builds strongly on ICT expansion initiated during the digital revolution but is characterized by qualitatively different technologies and capabilities. Breakthroughs in many areas, including digital-tech, biotech, nano-tech, neuro-tech and green-tech, have been spurred by the growing ability of artificial intelligence (AI) systems to autonomously solve complex problems. This has been made possible by the combination of increasing computational power at decreasing costs, rapidly growing datasets, and advances in "deep learning" algorithms. The current new wave of technology innovations entails rapid transfer of new technologies (cloud computing, nanomaterials, artificial intelligence, automation, 3D printing, internet of things, blockchain) into design and manufacturing of high-performance products and services.

Although new and emerging technologies have become an engine of change and progress, the net improvement brought to the environment and society becomes questionable, if sustainability principles are not fully incorporated into the technology development and application phases.[263] For instance, although introduction of nanomaterials has created new opportunities for high performance applications and novel product introduction, there exist various concerns about long term material availability and negative impacts of their production on health and the environment.

From real scientific innovations across different fields of engineering during the 20th century, the focus of technological development during the 21st century has been in finding newer applications and improving consumer experience. While core engineering improvements continue to happen across the globe to deliver higher levels of industrial efficiency, quality and sustainability, the growth of consumer-oriented technology services and products has been exponential. Technology moved rapidly from basic digitization, large servers and computers to cloud computing, social / data platforms, predictive analytics, digitization of consumer products, mobile and mobile applications - the current frontier being machine learning, artificial intelligence, robotics, 3D printing etc. Some of these technologies are indeed making it easier for the real scientific community to advance research and product development in the areas of health, energy and manufacturing.

We are witnessing rampant development of products for everything that human imagination can fathom. Electronic products have been built to perform almost every single task - essential or not. Techies are out to accomplish everything automatically. They simply want to live in their cocoon and avoid all the agony associated with human interaction. Everything should happen as they need without any physical effort and ideally without them having to move from their

---

[263] "Technology innovation and sustainability: challenges and research needs", Yinlun Huang, July 2021

couches. Some of the latest home technology products include smart salt dispensers, Roomba for cleaning, hair coloring device, bluetooth hairbrushes, smart bathing systems, body monitors, smart baby rocker, baby poop alarms, high tech fridge, smart sleeping solutions, smart door locks, high tech washer and dryer, motion sensing faucet and other water products, bigger and brighter TVs, air purifiers, VR boxer, smart wallet, massagers, smart tracking devices, pet camera, pet feeders, smart pet door kit, special gaming monitors, video doorbell, home security lights, vacuum sealer machine, toilet lights with motion sensors, automatic sprinkler system, color changing light panels, ultrasonic eyewear cleaner, subwoofer watchers, virtual tattoos, weight loss headband, smart forks, smart condoms, ipad typewriters, smart / sleek / luxury cases for every personal device… the list is endless and mind boggling.

These smart products directly impact employment in various home-based services such as cleaning, security and childcare, increase energy and resource (water, detergent) consumption, and are detrimental to physical and mental health. Their production also consumes significant energy and precious materials. The adoption of these products by everyone is simply not sustainable. The jobs created in the production of these products are miniscule as compared to the ones lost because of them. These are innovations to protect the elite from facing the real world. By doing so, they are creating an unsustainable social divide where the rich have everything and consume excessively, and the rest, who are left with insufficient resources and amenities, are fighting to get rich. With such products, there may be improvements in some people's lives, but there are negative impacts for many, many more. A lot of these products are simply an outcome of the lack of trust between humans. Instead of working towards solving the real problems of inequality, these products are exacerbating the vicious cycle of inequality and mistrust. A healthy person will never feel the need for these things and will actually find them to be detrimental to their wellbeing.

Even commercial and industrial establishments are now flush with physical products that minimize human intervention and create a more luxurious working environment - smart postage meter, automated letter opener, coffee warmer, phone sanitizer, self-changing trash can, personal desk heater, portable air conditioner, standing desk, under desk elliptical machine, desktop vacuum cleaner, heating blanket, voice mask and so on. While the development of drones for defense made sense, we are now looking at the use of drones for home delivery, agriculture, traffic monitoring, and various other applications. We are also pretty much on the verge of having driverless cars, which may prove to replace all sorts of driving jobs, including bus and truck drivers, taxi drivers, and chauffeurs, and will involve damaging levels of resource use.

Besides these physical products, consumer technology has directly impacted various service industries. As is the case with physical products, we have a mix of technology enabled services that are good or bad. There is a set of consumer-oriented technologies that are genuinely making life more efficient and better, without creating an additional resource burden. Applications for knowledge and information gathering, content creation, communication and sharing (email, chat, video), social networking, local discovery (food, places etc.), non-delivery marketplaces (health, home services, transportation, used items, laundry, tailoring etc.), tax preparation and filing, travel bookings, weather forecasting, entertainment, and so on, have simply removed agents and made these services much more accessible, efficient and better for people, without any additional resource requirement.

But then we are also being inundated with applications that create an additional resource burden and carbon footprint, as well as result in a net reduction in employment. They also encourage unnecessary consumption and an unhealthy lifestyle. The biggest examples are home delivery applications that now span every consumer good. The delivery services add at least one additional layer of packaging (additional material and effort) for the products and are breeding a culture of instant gratification. Walking down to fetch items of regular consumption and a weekly / fortnightly family visit to the shopping center will always remain most efficient, healthy, and sustainable. It is also the best experience and keeps consumption optimal. They are also creating ad hoc employment and taking away formal employment from the physical retail sector. Unless these services operate without packaging and fuel consumption, they will be detrimental to society at large. In a dense mixed use urban environment, physical retail is most efficient and ensures planned responsible consumption.

There are also segments where we are pushing digital services without realizing the negative impact on quality and effectiveness. Education is a prime example. Online applications are attempting to replace physical teaching. While the world will benefit from the reduced use of paper and materials, there are bigger problems associated with the use of technology in education. Students are taking a shortcut in life with early exposure to technology. Learning is about change, experience, context, interlinkages and uncertainties. Physical interaction with the real world is the only way to fully comprehend the world around us and to develop deep and practical knowledge. Holistic and balanced education requires development of physical, mental and social faculties. Before students understand the working of technology systems, a technology free environment is best suited for developing healthy and vibrant personalities.

Education systems across the globe have evolved already to deliver the desired learning outcomes across all fields and subjects. Technology has only entered the education space to make it more accessible and efficient. Once we decide on urban only living, the problem of access disappears. Improving efficiency has never been an issue in learning environments, especially in primary, middle and high school. There is possibly some use case for technology when students become capable of doing simulation, design and development, but that too only once you have built the core understanding of the underlying engineering fields as well as have acquired the basics of computer technology. The use of the internet by students from an early age is well advised for the purposes of intellectual curiosity but should be limited and controlled in the school environment.

The purpose of the education system is to create responsible, capable and healthy adults who can work together to advance humanity forward. The use of technology in early years changes the social and emotional connection between students and teachers - there is difference in walking up to your buddy in the morning and in sending a 'hi' text message. The use of computers by the teaching faculty and administration to efficiently perform their jobs makes sense, and technology enablers for the same are well advised. The greatest potential for educational technology to improve education perhaps exists in support of understanding complex problems and domains. But unless it can be demonstrated or logically proven with confidence that certain kinds of improved learning outcomes are the result of specific technology, adoption should be restricted.

This unbridled technological expansion is damaging the natural environment in several ways. The current trends of digital technology development seem unsustainable and damaging for the environment. Most of the sector is based on the fundamental concept of replacement rather than repair. The fundamental business model across the sector is based on innovation to attract people to buy the latest new technology, rather than to build technology that can be reused. The hardware-software development cycle forces users to upgrade their equipment on a regular basis. Innovation in the digital technology sector means that hardware developments often make old software unusable on newer devices, and new software (particularly operating systems) requires newer hardware on which to run. This leads to massive redundancy with older equipment simply being thrown away. The net effect is that despite efforts to recycle digital technology, e-Waste remains a fundamental problem for the sector. Much e-waste contains concentrated amounts of potentially harmful products, and this shows little sign of abating. Reports in 2019 suggested that there were just 50 million tonnes of e-waste, with only 20% of it being dealt with appropriately. In recent years a substantial trade has developed whereby poorer countries of the world have become dumps for such waste, resulting in severe environmental damage. The fundamental point being that the sector as a whole is built on a model that generates very substantial waste, rather than one that is focused inherently on sustainability.

The unsustainable exploitation of many rare minerals for technology products is environmentally unsustainable. Most digital technologies rely on rare minerals that are becoming increasingly scarce. Integral to the production of information and communication technology (ICT), rare earths—magnesium, niobium, germanium, borates, and scandium—exhibit the highest supply risk of critical materials in the world's digital transformation. Minerals such as Cobalt, the 17 rare earth elements, Gallium, Indium and Tungsten are becoming more and more in demand, and as supply is limited prices have often increased significantly.

Digital technology, almost by definition, must have electricity to function, and as industry and society become increasingly dependent on electricity for production, exchange and consumption, the demand for electricity continues to rise. The overall demand for electricity from the digital technology sector is growing rapidly. ICT networks that used ~5% of the world's electricity in 2012 are predicted to use ~10% by 2020, and ~20% by 2025.[264] Most measures of electricity demand focus on the direct uses of digital technology, such as powering servers, equipment and charging mobile devices (phones, tablets, and laptops), but indirect demand must also be recognised, notably the air-conditioning required to reduce the temperature of places running digital technology. The increased emphasis on data storage, management and analysis, and the ever-growing demand for data-streaming will lead to exponential increases in energy demand of the technology sector.

Specific new technologies, notably blockchain, have been developed with little regard for their electricity demand and thus their environmental impact. Currently at the start of 2020, Bitcoin alone has a carbon footprint of 34.73 Mt CO2 (equivalent to the carbon footprint of Denmark), it consumes 73.12 TWh of electrical energy (comparable to the power consumption of Austria), and it produces 10.95 kt of e-waste (equivalent to that of Luxembourg).[265] The demand is simply driven by the design of Bitcoin technology which relies on miners frequently adding new sets of transactions to its blockchain, and then all miners confirming that transactions are indeed valid through the proof-of-work algorithm. The machines that do this require huge amounts of energy to do so.

Future projections relating to Smart Cities, 5G and the Internet of Things give rise to additional concerns over energy demand. In the case of 5G, for example, the necessary denser networks will place much heavier demands on electricity unless more energy efficient technologies are put in place. Likewise, the massive roll-out of the Internet of Things has the potential to dramatically increase energy use. Yet there are advocates who also argue that the use of these

---

[264] "Digital Technologies Are Part of the Climate Change Problem", Tim Unwin, UNESCO Chair in ICT4D at Royal Holloway, University of London, February 20, 2020

[265] "What is Web 3.0 and how it will transform the digital era", TimesofIndia, November 4, 2022; "The Environmental Impact Of Web3", Salman Zafar, EcoMENA, April 11, 2022

technologies will actually enable more efficient systems to be introduced. On balance, it is certain that most of these new technologies will themselves generate greater electricity demand, but it is only likely that systems will be introduced to mitigate such increases.

The digital sector will emit as much as 4% of total greenhouse gas emissions in 2020.[266] The impact of the large number of new cell towers and antennas that will be needed for 5G networks, as well as the buildings housing server farms and data centers also have a significant environmental impact. It is not just the electricity demands for cooling that matter, but the sheer size of data farms also has a significant physical impact on the environment. The average data center covers approximately 100,000 sq ft of ground, but the largest noted in 2018 was at Langfan in China spread over 6.3 million sq ft. Lastly, the environmental impact of the increasing proliferation of satellites also needs to be considered.

It is interesting to conjecture over the extent to which this has been a deliberate process by those involved in conceptualizing, designing and selling these technologies, or whether more generously it is an unintended consequence of actions by people who simply did not know what they were doing with respect to the environment. Digital technologies in many ways separate people from the physical environments in which they live. This reaches its most extreme form in Virtual Reality, but every aspect of digital technologies changes human experiences of the physical world. One cannot help but wonder whether digital technologies, by increasingly separating us from the "real world" physical environment, actually also serve to prevent us from really seeing the environmental damage that they are causing.[267] It is as if these technologies are themselves

---

[266] "Digital Technologies Are Part of the Climate Change Problem", Tim Unwin, UNESCO Chair in ICT4D at Royal Holloway, University of London, February 20, 2020

[267] "Leading concerns about the future of digital life", Kathleen Stansberry, Janna Anderson, Lee Rainie, Pew Research Center, October 28, 2019

preventing humans from understanding their environmental implications. Someone living in their own virtual reality in a smart home in a smart city bubble, being moved around in autonomous smart vehicles when required, and communicating at a distance with everyone, will perhaps no longer mind about the despoliation of hillsides, the flooding of valleys, the carving out of canyons to feed the machines' craving for minerals...

There are concerns over the power of large technology companies, the rise of platforms that offer services in exchange for data and marketing dollars, the potential for growing lack of human agency in the algorithm age, the potential loss of jobs as humans are replaced in workplaces, and other worries over emerging potential negatives of digital life.[268] Commercial interests propel AI, platforms and digital media. The interests of for-profit companies don't necessarily align with the best interests of earth, humanity, nations, or democracy. With significant investment in these fields, there is tremendous pressure to generate commercial products and services, and the speed required doesn't leave room to ask critical questions about a technology's impact on individuals, communities or our society. If we do not change the developmental track of AI in the present, the probability of negative scenarios will increase during the next 50 years.

Today, from the application user interface up to the economic ecosystem, platforms often exploit human foibles for profit. The first step in the journey of the next 50 years is reaching a consensus that an addictive approach to the digital world is not sustainable. And that the profit motive, like discipline, is a means to an end, and not an end to itself. Technology options can inform the journey's second step. We need to rethink the 'how' and the 'why' of digital devices for a sustainable future.

---

[268] "Leading concerns about the future of digital life", Pew Research Center, October 28, 2019

The essential component of industrial sustainability is three-pillar-based balanced development.[269] This requires that technology innovations be shaped to incorporate sustainability principles fully throughout their development and application phases. It is imperative, therefore, to conduct a fundamental study on the sustainability dimensions of technology innovation and develop systematic methodologies and effective tools for technology inventors, decision makers, and organizations to evaluate and maximize potential sustainability benefits of new and emerging technologies. In this endeavor, sustainability assessment of technology innovation, especially in its early development stage, is critical.

There is a lack of scientific framework for systematic, integrated assessment of technology innovation in different life cycle stages. More critically, there have been no systematic methods for technology assessment (TA) in the triple-bottom-line-based sustainability space. A main challenge in sustainability assessment (SA) of technology innovation is how to conduct multiple life-cycle-stage based assessment and to compare sustainability performance under different scenarios, especially when the available system information is uncertain, incomplete and imprecise.

Institutional mechanisms need to be set up and enforced to ensure a thorough assessment of new technologies before they are released to the larger public. Building a holistic perspective of the change envisaged by the new technology is essential. From understanding the status quo, necessity of the solution, techno-commercial benefits, impact on customer experience and health, resource consumption, employment, future possibilities for application and improvement, there are several aspects that need to be deliberated before a technology is cleared for roll-out.

---

[269] "Technology innovation and sustainability: challenges and research needs", Yinlun Huang, July 2021

A framework that prioritizes overall resource efficiency and impact on human health will enable the development of sustainable technologies and products. A net reduction in the consumption of resources and a net positive impact on human health should be made mandatory for any technology or product to be cleared for commercialization. Both these criteria should be met simultaneously. Only in cases where there is a positive impact on human health, technology that consumes more resources could be allowed.

For example, even though the use of Artificial Intelligence in the healthcare and life sciences industry will lead to significant energy and resource consumption, it should be encouraged as it is likely to accelerate medical advances.

The stalwarts of the Indian technology industry already have sustainability deeply rooted into their DNA and have always been the champions of equality. The industry obviously possesses the intellectual and technical capabilities to regulate itself. It simply needs clear direction from the top.

Technology will remain integral to the functioning of the services industry and will be a key driver of changes in the nature of work. But we need to avoid the possibility of technology taking control of humanity and driving it over the cliff. We need to build a harmonious interplay of industry, technology and services that is sustainable.

The services industry currently acts as a smooth facilitator of the exchange of goods, information and services, and complies with environmental regulations. We need to move to a scenario where the services industry works towards enabling sustainable, healthy and equitable consumption and production. Technology needs to support the same objective and empower the services industry to make it happen. There needs to be a fundamental shift so that those designing new digital technologies in the future do so primarily based on environmental considerations. Sustainable technology should encompass technology that has been designed specifically to remedy or prevent environmental issues, and technology that has been produced with sustainability in mind.

A move towards a low technology future will be sustainable. Resource constraints suggest a shift away from the high direction our society is taking. There is growing interest in low tech solutions that prioritize simplicity, durability, local manufacture, as well as traditional or ancient techniques.[270] Low-tech solutions often focus on conviviality. This involves encouraging social connections, for example through communal music or dance, rather than fostering the hyper-individualism encouraged by resource-hungry digital devices. Low-tech" does not mean a return to medieval ways of living. But it does demand more discernment in our choice of technologies – and consideration of their disadvantages.

Low technology refers to the need to balance a technology's performance with its environmental impact, being cautious of automation (especially where employment is replaced by increased energy use) and reducing our demands on nature. But the first principle of low-tech is its emphasis on sobriety: avoiding excessive or frivolous consumption and being satisfied by less beautiful models with lower performance. A reduction in consumption could make it quickly possible to rediscover the many simple, poetic, philosophical joys of a revitalized natural world, while the reduction in stress and working time would make it possible to develop many cultural or leisure activities such as shows, theater, music, gardening or yoga.

Recognition and formalization of all forms of work needed in the current society is critical for kickstarting the move towards a more equal Indian community. We need a systematic movement towards the planned creation of non-technological job positions as work evolves. Given that technology has the potential to replace almost all jobs, we

---

[270] Low-technology: why sustainability doesn't have to depend on high-tech solutions, Chris McMahon, translator of Philippe Bihouix's "The Age of Low Tech", Feb 2022

need to carefully deliberate on services that are essential and should be carried out by humans in a sustainable future. The essential forms of physical labor (urban gardens and forests, elder care, child care, local food production and preparation, cooking, cleaning, repairs, security) should be made a part of the emerging social structure.[271] We need to free Indians from labor that is meaningless, but have to give them work with a purpose. As long as the purpose of an organization aligns with the overall purpose of sustainability, the entity and the form of work should be retained. In the Indian context, we need to consolidate the services sector and simultaneously introduce controls that prevent individuals from exercising their free will over organizations. We need to move towards a future where the idea of huge profits and private control of massive wealth should look as grotesque as the idea of heads on pikes and guillotines do now.

The services sector is the largest sector of India. Gross Value Added (GVA) at current prices for the services sector is estimated at INR 97 lakh crore (~$1.3 trillion) in 2020-21.[272] The services sector accounts for 53.89% of India's GVA of 179.15 lakh crore Indian rupees or ~$2.4 trillion. The sector accounts for 34% of the country's employment. India's growth story has been riding on services for several decades, in contrast with the developed nations where economic growth was initially powered by manufacturing. India still does not have a national policy, department or ministry dedicated to services.

In developed countries, services contribute 60-80% of the total GDP.[273] Most advanced nations have a service contribution of 70% to 80%. In sustainable India with a manufacturing output of $4-5 trillion (2020 terms), and an agricultural output of ~$1 trillion, the eventual size of our

---

[271] "20 Industries Threatened by Tech Disruption", Adam Hayes, Doretha Clemon, Timothy Li, Jan 2022

[272] "Chapter 9 - Services Sector, India Budget 2019-20", Economic Survey, Government of India

[273] WTO Stats, World Trade Organization

services industry can be estimated to be $20-30 trillion (more than 15 times the current size).

Construction

Infrastructure development is at the core of India's sustainable transformation. Construction is therefore the foundational services sector for India. The construction industry will need to be ramped up for India to build the 130 cities (residential, commercial, industrial and public infrastructure), and the enabling infrastructure required for these cities viz. highways, intercity rail tracks, canals, riverbanks, dams, bridges, five-star destinations etc. The industry is currently worth $125-150 billion and employs around 6 crore workers. We estimated (chapter 'Live in the city') a capital outlay of ~INR 500 lac crore (2020 prices) for building the residential high-rises in the 130 cities. Given that residential real estate accounts for ~40% of the overall urban infrastructure, the total outlay for building the 130 cities would be ~INR 1,250 lac crore. Now assuming that cities would account for over 80% of the overall infrastructure development, the total capital outlay for building a sustainable India would be more than INR 1,500 lac crore. The cost of construction (excluding materials, land acquisition, clearances) varies from 25% to 50% of the total project cost.[274] Therefore the total outlay towards construction during the development phase would be ~INR 900 lac crore (~$11 trillion). If the build out is planned over the next 50 years, the construction industry should gradually ramp up to an annual industry size of around $1.5 trillion (real terms). This would also be the sustainable (post build out) size of the industry for ongoing maintenance and redevelopment. The industry will employ around 5 crore people if India steadily builds its 130 cities and achieves highest levels of productivity and scale efficiencies.

---

[274] "External, infrastructure development charges", Ashwini Kumar Sharma, Mint, October 17, 2017

Banking and Financial Services

Given the large financial requirements of the transformation, banking and financial services need to drive the transformation. By most estimates, the financial services sector is around a quarter of the world's economy. The global financial services market reached ~$22 trillion in 2021, accounting for 24% of the global GDP. With total global wealth estimated at $431 trillion, the banking and investment sector with $103 trillion AUM, accounts for just under a quarter of the world's assets.[275]

Tectonic shifts are reconfiguring the global financial system: phenomenal growth in digitization, convergence of industries, fusion of technologies, proliferation of increasingly intertwined ecosystems, and the blurring of product constructs. The new financial architecture created by digital assets will have profound consequences for banks by revolutionizing how money is created, transferred, stored, and owned.

The Indian financial sector currently comprises several segments: commercial banks, new-age fintech startups, non-banking financial companies (NBFCs), co-operatives, pension funds, mutual funds, small and medium financial entities and recently established payment banks. Financial services is much more than lending businesses, and diversified with many sub-sectors such as asset management companies, brokerages, wealth management, depositories, exchanges, insurance companies such as life and non-life insurance and other entities, including Rating agencies. Commercial banks are responsible for more than 64% of the total assets held by the Indian financial system.

We are still under-penetrated in various sub-segments of banking and financial services – be it loan products, mutual funds, demat accounts, insurance (life and non-life), pension,

---

[275] "Financial Services: Sizing the Sector in the Global Economy", Sean Ross, Investopedia, September 30, 2021

wealth management, etc. India's retail loans-to-GDP ratio stands at mere 13 per cent, whereas the same for the US stands at 76 per cent, and for the UK, at 88 per cent. The mortgage loan-to-GDP ratio of India also stands at meager 6 per cent, compared to 77 percent in the US and 59 per cent in the UK. In insurance, the sum assured as a percentage to GDP for India stands at only 19 per cent, against 251 per cent for the developed countries such as the US, while for Japan, it stood at 252 per cent. The mutual fund AUM to GDP ratio of India also stands at a meager 12 per cent, compared with 120 per cent for the US and 67 per cent for the UK.

The financial services industry needs to finance the multifold expansion of infrastructure and industry, enable industrial consolidation, create smooth mechanisms for facilitating urbanization, and maintain a sizable presence in the global financial markets.

Both infrastructure and industrial expansion will need massive capital outlays. The land buyback is expected to cost the government around $20 trillion (real 2020 prices). The high-rise urban development of the envisaged 130 cities will also need massive financing. High-rise development is expected to cost ~$8 trillion and $6 trillion (real terms) for residential and commercial respectively. Public infrastructure (transportation, utilities) will need another ~$5 trillion (real 2020 prices) for these cities. Development of urban lakes and urban green areas will also require $2-5 trillion. The total capital outlay for sustainable infrastructure development would be around $50 trillion. The tenfold industrial expansion ($400 billion to $4 trillion) will also necessitate high levels of capital expenditure (30-40% of industry revenue) throughout the build-out period.

The current quantum of gross fixed capital formation (GFCF) in India meets the year one capex requirement.[276] Gross capital formation (formerly gross domestic investment)

---

[276] "Chapter 8 - Industry and Infrastructure", India Budget 2019-20, Economic Survey, Government of India

consists of outlays on additions to the fixed assets of the economy plus net changes in the level of inventories. Fixed assets include land improvements; plant, machinery, and equipment purchases; and the construction of roads, railways, and the like, including schools, offices, hospitals, private residential dwellings, and commercial and industrial buildings. GFCF as a percentage of GDP has been steadily declining in India since FY12. The GFCF to GDP ratio has declined from 34.3% in FY12 to 28.8% in FY20. In China, it's more than 40%. But in absolute terms, GFCF was ~$583 billion in FY12 and ~$800 billion in FY20, not far off from the trillion dollars needed in year 1.

The Indian financial system simply needs to channelize the capex towards the envisaged 130 cities and large-scale industrial production. Financial institutions and the government will need to adopt several measures to move away from financing non sustainable development. A strong focus is critical not just because of the paucity of capital but also because distributed development and small-scale industrial expansion dampens the progress and returns of sustainability-oriented projects. Loans to the MSME sector and individual housing loans are also much riskier and increase the NPAs of banks. Infrastructure financing should only be made available to large developers who can build and connect the 130 cities. Households need to be provided incentives for investing in high-rises in the 130 cities instead of building individual homes across the length and breadth of the country. Bank lending for individual land purchases needs to be phased out and individual land holders should be encouraged to sell out to the government. Financial institutions will need to create attractive financial instruments to accelerate the land / property buyback and migration towards the 130 cities.

Bank credit policies should evolve to enable consolidation across various industrial sectors. Medium and small enterprises and even large ones that do not meet the scale criteria should be nudged towards selling out, with more than fair compensation. Large-scale enterprises will also need cheap capital to carry out leveraged buyouts. The Indian private equity ecosystem needs to be ramped up to facilitate the consolidation.

One of the crucial elements of the Indian capital market is the corporate bond market. Persistent effort by the government and Sebi in the last few years has enabled a nascent corporate bond market to move in the direction of maturity. The government and corporate bonds market needs to be augmented as they are ideal for raising capital for infrastructure and industrial expansion. The government is currently planning to borrow ~$155 billion in 2022-23 to meet its expenditure requirements.[277] The supply of corporate bonds in the domestic market is expected to double to ~$1 trillion by fiscal 2025 with the financial sector contributing around 50% to this growth.[278] The financial sector will contribute around 50% of the incremental supply, followed by innovation (close to 25%) and infrastructure (about 20%). The share of infrastructure bonds (private, public and PPP) needs to be significantly enhanced as infrastructure accounts for ~80% of the total capex requirement. Attracting foreign capital will also be necessary to bridge the domestic funding gap. Environmental, social and governance (ESG) profiling of Indian corporates will be important to attract much-needed foreign capital debt into the debt capital markets. Currently, retirement funds are expected to contribute ~25% of the incremental demand, followed by insurance and mutual funds contributing close to 20% each. Reforms including encouraging widespread acceptance of the INFRA EL rating scale, enhancing retail participation via tax sops to investments in debt mutual funds, fast-tracking proposed institution for secondary

---

[277] "Ministry of Finance - Government's borrowing plan", Government of India

[278] "Indian corporate bond market can double to ₹65-70 lakh cr by March 2025", Crisil, February 24, 2021; "Size of the Indian Bond Market is US$ 2 trillion!", IndiaBonds, Mar 5, 2021

market liquidity and development of corporate default swap (CDS) market, among others can help in bridging supply-demand gap in corporate bond market. Encouraging greater retail participation makes sense as the corporate bond market offers a wide variety of higher returns to individual investors. Households that transfer their huge savings to investments and in this case to a safer asset class of corporate bonds, will likely spur an exponential growth of corporate bonds and provide the funding for a sustainable India.

Real estate investment trusts (REITs) and real estate bonds have emerged as ideal financial instruments for individuals to invest in real estate. A REIT is a company that owns, operates, or finances real estate assets. They can be publicly or privately traded, and they tend to specialize in certain property types (residential, commercial, industrial, retail, hotel & resort etc.). REITs offer liquidity, diversification, and potential for capital appreciation. A bond is a debt instrument issued by real estate developers that investors can purchase. In doing so, they receive a promise from the bond issuer to receive their money back, plus interest, over a defined period of time. Investors like bonds for their relative safety and steady income.

These investment instruments can accelerate high-rise development in the envisaged cities, as well as drive people away from individual purchases of land and property. The Government and the financial services industry need to work in sync to gradually increase restrictions on individual development / purchase of real estate, and simultaneously introduce alternative options for people to invest in real estate. These instruments will also level the playing field by creating an equal opportunity for everyone to generate returns from real estate. As the rental (home / property) market takes over, the financial services industry will also need to create rental instruments (lump sum payment, escalation protection etc.).

India needs to exponentially grow the green financing market. Green financing includes green, social, and sustainability (GSS) debt and sustainability linked bonds (SLBs). SLBs are forward-looking, performance-based debt instruments that are issued with links to Sustainability Performance Targets (SPTs) and associated Key Performance Indicators (KPIs) at the entity level. SLBs can be a useful tool for issuers on a low-carbon transition trajectory as they finance whole entities in transition and help to build experience and credibility on target setting, as long as the SPTs are credible; calibrated ambitiously in line with sector-based pathways; and provide meaningful financial reward/penalty.

Indian GSS debt issuance increased more than six-fold (+585%) to reach USD7.5bn in 2021.[279] Most GSS bonds and loans currently target offshore investors, but the domestic market is also starting to have relatively large deals. Grid-connected utility-scale energy is by far the largest type of project financed but deals with a more diverse use of proceeds (UoP) are expected to increase in both number and scale. Green bonds are in the pipeline for solar rooftop assets, waste management operations, agriculture, real estate, and electric vehicle (EV) investments. Green financing is indeed the best path for India's gigantic leap on renewable energy. India needs to rapidly expand the coverage of sustainability debt / bonds to sustainable infrastructure development (green buildings, water bodies, green cover development) and sustainable transformation of all industrial sectors. India has already seen the issuance of bonds for the cement (UltraTech Cement) and steel (JSW Steel) industry. India also needs to avoid financing of non-sustainable segments such as Electric Vehicles (EVs).

The overall sustainability investing space is increasingly active and preparing to support the large issuers of the future.

---

[279] "India sustainable debt, state of the market 2021", Sandeep Bhattacharya, Neha Kumar, Prashant Lonikar, Climate Bonds Initiative, UK Government, May 2022

It is anticipated that an Indian sovereign green bond will be issued in the domestic market in 2022. This landmark transaction will draw on best practices and will significantly boost the domestic market. Policy development will create the necessary framework for the growth of the sustainable finance market in India. There is an acknowledgement of the need to align with international and domestic best practices, the need for transparency, and a greater degree of standardization. Supportive public policy has begun to emerge with the Indian Ministry of Finance (MoF) setting up a Sustainable Finance Task Force to a) develop a taxonomy of sustainable activities, b) recommend reporting and disclosure policies, c) determine appropriate financial policy and regulations, and d) devise relevant measures for market development. Enabling retail participation would be essential not just for bringing an additional source of funds but also for building broad understanding and consensus towards the sustainable transformation. India's financial industry will remain central to the growth of green financing as they will directly and indirectly structure, execute and manage the issuances of public entities, the non-financial corporate (currently account for ~75% of issuances) and financial entities.

The growth of the insurance and pension industry is critical for India. Not only are they the biggest source of funds for long term investments, they are the most important instruments for India to provide high levels of health and social security to all its citizens.

Pension

India's pension system is globally the second least sustainable, with only Greece being worse off. With pension assets exceeding $56 trillion worldwide, most prosperous nations have more than their gross domestic product (GDP), according to a recent report from the Organization for Economic Co-operation and Development (OECD). In developed countries, the average assets under management of pension funds are over 100% of GDP. In India, they stand at 14% of GDP.[280] India's poor penetration of pension funds points to a lack of interest in retirement planning. Formal retirement provisions cover less than 12% of India's active workforce (450 million). Herein lies the opportunity to provide an assured pension for all individuals planning to retire (including gig workers) and simultaneously build infrastructure in the country. When young, most of us are in a spending mode and less concerned about saving and investing. When asked about retirement, it is revealed that many in India still depend on their children. Much of India's workforce has over a couple of decades to reach retirement age. There is a pressing need, therefore, to nudge retirement planning. Only 10% of the labor force is covered currently through government sponsored or mandated schemes, highlighting the lacunae in the present system of pension. Income generated through existing programmes is inadequate for many retirees, and often does not provide for protection against the risks of longevity and inflation and the large and fast-growing informal sector is not covered under any formal pension scheme.

The presence of long-term pension funds brings stability to financial markets. While global pension funds can invest in Indian equities like any other foreign portfolio investor, they have multiple options. A local pension fund system is bound to deploy capital within India. Reforms in the pension sector

---

[280] "Why India needs a vibrant pension market", Sumit Mohindra, Mint, Jan 26, 2022

will inflate the capital markets which will require advanced techniques for managing the extra flow of funds.

The World Bank has formulated a three-pillar model, in which retirement income is from three income sources: public pensions to cover basic needs, occupational pensions for an earnings-related source and additional private savings. This model allows for risk diversification. The government needs to accordingly guide the pension funds industry towards complete financial security for all senior citizens.

To start with, India needs to introduce universal pension coverage for every citizen that provides financial security needed to cover basic expenses. In the Netherlands, with supposedly the best pension system in the world, a basic provision (instituted by the government in 1957) is paid to everyone living in the Netherlands, once they have reached the qualifying age. It is referred to as the General Old Age Pension Act (AOW). Residents of the Netherlands accrue 2% of their AOW every year for 50 years until reaching the required age. They do not have to be (or have been) in paid work to accrue AOW. The AOW should be seen as a basic minimum provision, and in most cases is supplemented with income from the other pillars. The AOW is administered by the Ministry of Social Affairs and Employment and is funded from tax revenues, and not from capital paid in by the recipient: it is a pay-as-you-go system.

For the second pillar, India needs to make it mandatory for all full-time occupations to be brought under the pension system. India can offer a flexible payment and withdrawal option to encourage more workers in the unorganized sector. This can also work for farm laborers who have no social security. The government needs to ensure strong growth of pension assets and provide incentives for private retirement savings, such as tax advantages, matching contributions, for mid and higher-income earners. Regulatory changes are needed for the industry to offer large scale products for private retirement savings on a cost-efficient and profitable basis. Employee contribution should be characterized by high default savings rates with auto-escalation. Dutch workers contribute between 21% and 25% of their pre-tax pay to their pensions. The second pillar in the Dutch pension system features collectivity, mandatory participation, efficient administration and being not-for-profit. Given the size of our population, India should introduce all three forms of occupational pension i.e., defined benefit (DB), defined contribution (DC) and collective defined contribution schemes (CDCs).

For people who are not in permanent employment or are self-employed, attractive pension products need to be introduced by banks and insurance companies. Tax exemptions are key to encourage participation in these plans. The private sector can also bundle pension products with various riders such as health, travel etc.

Reverse mortgage is a stone that will simultaneously kill two birds for India. Not only would it provide financial security to senior citizens, but it can also accelerate the shift away from individual homes in the smaller cities, towns and villages, and move towards the 130 high-rise urban centers. The Indian market for reverse mortgage is in its infancy and could be around Rs. 5,000 crores (<$1 billion) at present.[281] Reverse mortgage is a financial instrument that allows a homeowner to consume some of his housing equity by converting it into an income stream yet maintain ownership and residence in the home. Most of the retirees in India are 'home rich–cash poor', that is, they might not have enough money for covering everyday life expenses but often own and live in expensive homes. India ranks 7th in the list of countries, with a homeownership rate as high as 86.6 per cent. In India, most of the homeowner's lifetime savings are used to buy or build a house, making reverse mortgage a welcome instrument that helps them convert some or all of their rising but locked home equity into a cash stream that can comfortably sustain

---

[281] "Reverse mortgage in Indian banks - a study", Sandhya Rani Dasari, Jan 2017

them in their old age. Key to the efficacy of reverse mortgages is the development of a strong financial and regulatory infrastructure that will minimize loopholes, prevent fraud, and make this product successful in serving the needs of the senior citizens in India. Reverse Mortgage products are such products that have the potential of not only increasing the liquidity in the economy but also diversifying many risks. Besides insurance and pension products, actuaries with their long term horizon are in the position to play a leading role in designing products like reverse mortgages needing inputs both from actuarial and finance/investment domains.

Insurance

Insurance is an important part of the financial sector that contributes significantly to the economy of a country. There exists a bidirectional causal relationship in the long run between economic growth and insurance market size.[282] Insurance market contributes to economic growth as a financial intermediary and also helps in managing risk more effectively. Moreover, insurance contributes to the promotion of financial stability, facilitation of trade and commerce, management of risk in an effective manner, mobilization of savings, allocation of capital in an effective way and also it acts as a complement of Government security programs. Insurance is one of the rare mechanisms that allow for the spreading of risk over time. There are very few other industries that have such a long-time horizon as the insurance industry. In almost every developing and developed country the importance of insurance is rising due to the increasing share of the insurance sector in the entire financial sector. Insurance companies, together with mutual and pension funds, are one of the biggest institutional investors in stock, bond and real estate markets. Their impact on economic development has been growing due to aging societies, widening income disparity and globalization.

Insurance has a doubly positive impact on the savings of an economy: Firstly, it increases the general savings rate (especially through the existence of life insurance products) thus creating deeper markets and allowing for more investments. Secondly, it decreases the level of unnecessary precautionary savings (savings often not available to capital markets) and stimulates investment and consumption by reducing bound (and therefore unproductive or less productive) capital. Insurance thus helps to provide more working capital to an economy because people do not have to protect themselves against the eventuality of, for example,

---

[282] "Contribution of Insurance on economic growth in India: An Econometric approach", Dr. Sunita Mall

their home being destroyed by a fire. They just have to secure adequate cover through a fire insurance policy and be ready to pay a much lower amount of money over a longer period – a totally different mechanism. This means that the money saved in the process can be allocated to other things, more in line with the preferences of the individuals and more productively. Insurance mechanisms transform dormant capital into free capital.

Insurance plays a central part in the capitalization process of a modern economy. Insurance companies have long been a significant presence in infrastructure financing. Infrastructure investments have many qualities that are appealing to insurers, including long duration, mostly stable and secure cash flows, attractive risk adjusted returns, and low correlation to other asset classes. The stable and long-term cash flows of infrastructure assets naturally align with liabilities of insurers, particularly life insurers. Insurance companies typically invest premiums, or dollars, that are not used to pay claims and other operating expenses. Through stock, corporate and government bonds, and real estate mortgages, these investments often finance building construction and provide other crucial support to economic development projects around the nation.

Insurance, when it is provided, gives independence to people and increases their self-reliance. The ability to cope with adverse effects, which are often unexpected and might occur at the least opportune moment, is strengthened. This creates a very strong impact on future development because it enables people to become and stay active as they do not have to worry about all possible adverse effects that a certain activity might entail. While there is a direct economic effect through the financial protection of assets, there is also an additional consequence: peace of mind. People tend to behave differently – and we suppose more positively – when they know that certain risks are taken care of.

The insurance industry is, of course, a very large employer in any developed and emerging market. In addition to their own staff, insurers also generate a lot of indirect employment of numerous professionals such as agents, brokers, financial intermediaries and other services companies in areas ranging from IT to transport, from auditors to consultants, etc.

The global insurance industry collected a total premium of ~$6 trillion in 2018.[283] The industry is segmented into life (~$2.7 trillion), P&C (~$1.8 trillion) and health (~$1.4 trillion) insurance.[284] In India, life insurance premium was ~$68 billion and non-life premium was ~$23 billion in 2018-19.

India's insurance penetration (premium as % of GDP) was 3.76% in 2019, much below the global average of 7.23%.[285] The penetration in India is particularly low for the non-life (health and P&C) segment. The penetration for life insurance in India is 2.82%, and the penetration for non-life insurance is much lower at 0.94%. Globally, insurance penetration was 3.35% for the life segment and 3.88% for the non-life segment. In the developed markets, total insurance penetration is around 10%.

Taiwan has the highest coverage of life insurance (18.7%). In India, only about 3.3% of the population is covered by a life insurance policy. Health insurance has been globally recognized as the most essential form of insurance, with most developed nations having 100% of their population covered with some form (public or private) of health insurance. India has 27% of its population covered by health insurance - 21.6% covered by government plans and 5.4% covered by private plans.

India has extremely low insurance density (per capita spending on insurance) compared with global average and

---

[283] "World insurance regional review 2019 and outlook", SwissRe Institute, Nov 2020

[284] "Global Insurance Pools statistics and trends: An overview of life, P&C, and health insurance", Mckinsey, April 29, 2021

[285] Insurance Regulatory and Development Authority of India (IRDAI) Annual Report 2018-19

other comparable countries. The insurance density in India was around $78 in 2019. Density for life insurance was $58 and non-life insurance was much lower at $19 in 2019 in India. Globally, insurance density was $379 for the life segment and $439 for the non-life segment, respectively. The average insurance density of the advanced nations is >$4,000 and >$1,000 after PPP adjustment. Hence, the insurance spending per capita in India will need to increase more than 12 times to match the developed nations, which would result in a market size of at least a trillion dollars (2019 terms).

Banks and other financial institutions also have the responsibility to drive sustainable consumption through appropriate lending policies. Credit should be made more expensive and difficult for non-sustainable expenses and sustainable purchases need to be rewarded with discounts and a higher rate of returns.

Technology will play a big role in the future evolution of the financial services industry. Finance is already undergoing a profound transformation. Digital technologies are reshaping payments, lending, insurance and wealth management – a process that the COVID-19 pandemic has accelerated. Innovations in financial technology such as mobile money, peer-to-peer (P2P) or marketplace lending, robo advice, insurance technology (insuretech) and crypto-assets have emerged around the world.

Technology is making financial services more accessible, efficient, inclusive and diverse. Consumer interfaces are changing from physical branches to convenient digital access from anywhere. Technology is reducing information asymmetries and enabling progress towards greater equality. In the past decade, fintech has already driven greater access to and convenience of financial services for retail users. Meanwhile, artificial intelligence (AI), cloud services, and distributed ledger technology (DLT) are transforming wholesale markets in areas as diverse as financial market trading and regulatory and supervisory technology (regtech and suptech).[286] Big data is being used in a wide range of traditional financial services and new types of businesses to improve credit analysis, process efficiency, risk management, product design, customer service and other areas. Through mobile and smartphones, which are near-ubiquitous, technology has increased access to, and the efficiency of, direct delivery channels and promises lower-cost, tailored financial services. Advances in information and connectivity have also led to an unbundling of financial services consumption (horizontal disintegration). Customers now have more information about different providers and an increased ability to interact across providers, so they can choose different providers for the different financial products they use.

Another result of the technological advances described above has been the wide emergence of platform-based business models. Fintechs, big techs and even some incumbents have moved increasingly to a role as "matchmakers" between different users and providers on their platforms.

Leading banks are rapidly closing gaps in digitization of internal processes and customer offerings, to compete with fintechs and the large technology (big tech) firms that have also entered the fray. Innovation has introduced competition and increased inclusion, particularly in emerging markets and developing economies. Fintech seems to have thrived particularly in markets where the financial system has been less developed.

The underlying economics of intermediation combined with new technology may lead to concentration among both traditional and new financial services providers.[287] The India financial industry is well poised to benefit from digital

---

[286] "Fintech and the digital transformation of financial services: implications for market structure and public policy", Erik Feyen, Jon Frost, Leonardo Gambacorta, Harish Natarajan and Matthew Saal, July 13, 2021

[287] "Fintech and the digital transformation of financial services: implications for market structure and public policy", Erik Feyen, Jon Frost, Leonardo Gambacorta, Harish Natarajan and Matthew Saal, July 13, 2021

technologies but needs to prevent monopolistic or anti-competitive behaviors by big technology platforms and digital banks.

Technology is automating functions across the financial services value chain and will eliminate a sizable percentage of the workforce.[288] Most financial services can now be delivered directly and digitally, vastly increasing access to finance, but also eliminating a sizable chunk of the workforce. An emerging class of services and assets could in principle even be delivered without the need for an intermediary. The back and middle office are being revamped – or eliminated entirely. Technology has reduced the costs of, and need for, much of the traditional back office infrastructure, from paper processing to data centers. The back office is being revamped to lower cost and improve communication. Process automation and upgrades to software and IT systems are causing a restructuring of financial institutions and a reduction of full-time employees. Middle-office functions such as reconciliations are increasingly unnecessary. Entire processes, and many of the skills that previously had to be hired, can be replaced with automation or expert systems.

Nearly 25% of the financial services workforce requirements would be eliminated during this decade itself. The insurance industry will be the most strongly affected with 25-30% job cuts, followed by the banking industry with 22-25% of job cuts. The capital markets will be least affected, with about 15-20% of positions replaced by AI. Positions in finance trading, risk auditing, customer service and background finance are much more likely to be replaced. In banking, AI will mainly affect marketing and sales, risk control and audit, customer management and services in the front office and middle offices. In the insurance industry value chain, AI will replace positions in marketing and sales, underwriting, insurance policy management, service and claims. In the capital

---

[288] "The impact of artificial intelligence on the financial job market", David He, Michael Guo, Jerry Zhou, and Venessa Guo, March 2018, BCG

markets value chain, AI is expected to replace jobs in sales transactions, clearing and settlement. AI will have an even larger impact on supporting functions of the financial services industry such as compliance, customer service, accounting, audit, admin and logistics.

Those who solve complex problems and respond to emotional interactions or random changes in the environment will not be replaced but will be able to increase their working efficiency using AI. For example, AI and big data will improve the efficiency of banks' client managers. AI will increase efficiency in many segments of the insurance value chain such as product development, claims processing, surveying, adjustment and damage evaluation. In asset management, AI can recognize assets with the best ROI, efficiently monitor and analyze ROI and risk data, and adjust an asset portfolio in real time to maximize benefits and prevent risk to increase reaction times and efficiency in asset management operations. AI will significantly improve efficiency across the value chain of capital markets, especially smart investment decision making and asset management. In the future, AI will combine with classical economics and investment research theory to enable macroeconomic research through big data analysis to improve efficiency and accuracy.

India needs to carefully tread this journey of transformation and needs to strike the right balance between technology and human involvement. Technology should be used to increase access, efficiency, and inclusion, as well as improve customer experience. But human involvement is critical not just for providing a great customer experience but also for keeping the financial services systems in check. Client managers should be made available to everyone regardless of their current financial status. The agent model has worked wonderfully in the life insurance industry of India. Technology should simply act as an enabler for the financial workforce to efficiently serve the customer and provide a great experience. The human workforce is best equipped to formulate policies and products for a sustainable India and drive their adoption.

India will need a total manpower of ~2.5 crore (25 million) in the broad financial services industry (including insurance). The US represents the most evolved financial services industry in the world. There are around 10 million people employed in the US financial services industry. India is likely to have higher manpower intensity than the US. To provide equal services to every Indian citizen, the industry's workforce will need to be three times the US. So, in the base case, with the adoption of efficient technologies, a workforce around 2.5 times that of the US seems optimal.

Health

Global spending on health reached $8.3 trillion or 10% of global GDP in 2018.[289] The OECD countries spent 8.8% of their GDP on health, with the US spending 16.8%.[290] Given that the Indian GDP is very small for ~1.3 people, healthcare spending per capita is more relevant to estimate the potential size of the Indian industry. The Euro area spent ~$4,000 and the US spent ~$10,900 per capita on healthcare in 2019.[291] In comparison, India spent a meager ~$64 per capita on healthcare. After PPP adjustment, the per capita spending of the Euro area is more than 15 times and that of the US is more than 42 times the per capita spend in India. The current size of the healthcare industry in India is around $100 billion, suggesting a potential industry size of anywhere between $1 trillion to $4 trillion.

Healthcare is the largest employer in the US with over 20 million people employed in healthcare out of the total workforce (~130 million). While technology is continuously improving the efficiency and effectiveness of healthcare delivery, there is no real impact of technology on employment in the industry. In the developed nations, care coordination and health & wellness coaching are actually increasing the healthcare manpower requirements.

The Indian healthcare system is fragmented in many ways. The fragmentation is not just in terms of financing and provision of healthcare in the country, but also in terms of other dimensions such as alternate systems of medicine, continuum of care, quality of care standards and so forth.

India's healthcare system is currently dominated by a fragmented and highly diverse private healthcare sector ranging from large multi-specialty and corporate hospitals,

---

[289] "World Health Organization: Global spending on health: weathering the storm", December 10, 2020

[290] "Health expenditure as a percentage of gross domestic product (GDP) in selected countries in 2019", Statista

[291] "Health spending per capita - Country rankings", theGlobalEconomy.com

diagnostic centers, not-for-profit hospitals, charitable trust hospitals and nursing homes, to individual practitioner led clinics (qualified and unqualified), chemist shops and traditional healers.[292] The last decade has seen a sizable influx of capital into the private healthcare industry which has resulted in a burgeoning corporate healthcare sector pan India, displacing the earlier model of employment of healthcare professionals in small and medium-sized hospitals and individual run clinics.

Currently, the public sector in India has ~26,000 hospitals and ~700,000 beds, while the private sector has an estimated ~43,000 hospitals with 1,200,000 beds. India also has a large informal healthcare sector in rural areas, with informal providers being defined as producers of goods and services that are not authorized or registered. They are estimated to have a market share ranging from 48% to 80%.

In the Indian healthcare delivery space, public and private sectors operate mostly in isolation of each other. Public funding goes mostly for provision of care by the public sector; and the same holds true of private funding and private provision of care. The interaction between the two sectors is very limited. This is partly because of low public funding of healthcare in India and partly because the private sector, particularly the corporate hospitals, with their overriding profit orientation as well as high cost and price structures, are designed to serve the higher end of the market.[293] The low-cost public healthcare system has been developed due to the poor state of our economy. Lack of access to quality care in public health facilities forces people to turn to the private health sector and the resultant out of pocket (OOP) expenditure on health has resulted in impoverishment for vast numbers of people. India thus has one of the most highly

---

[292] "National Health Policy 2017: Addressing the "fragmentation" challenge", Rajeev Ahuja, Health Express, April 7, 2017

[293] "Analyzing Regulation of Private Healthcare in India", Dr Abhay Shukla, Dr Kanchan Pawar, Dr Abhijit More, Oxfam India, March 17, 2021

privatized and commercialized healthcare sectors in the world, along with an underfunded public health system. This combination reinforces the social and economic inequities, and often has ruinous consequences for the majority of its people, especially women, marginalized and vulnerable sections of society.

Given that healthcare is a core contributor to economic output, India needs to rapidly transform its public healthcare system and bring it at par with the private sector. Government expenditure accounts for around 80% of the total healthcare funding in most developed markets. Ramping up the public healthcare system is therefore most essential for India to improve quality of care and access, as well as to make healthcare a significant contributor to the country's economy.

Besides care provisioning and financing, health sector fragmentation exists among different systems of medicine. Allopathy, of course, is the most popular among different systems of medicine as it is able to provide cure for vast numbers of ailments/illnesses. At the same time, alternate systems of medicine such as Ayurveda, Homeopathy, Unani and so forth can also be quite effective especially in treating specific kinds of ailments/illnesses, with little or no side effects. Integration of the different forms of medicine will not only help patients get the best treatment but will also help advance medical research most effectively.

Fragmentation in the health sector also exists along the continuum of care. At present, primary care is totally disconnected from secondary and tertiary care, which is highly inefficient from a health system perspective. As a consequence, people seek primary care in a hospital setting at a later stage in the disease cycle and fail to take advantage of preventive and promotive care.

Quality of care standards is yet another dimension of fragmentation. At present there are variable standards of care being practiced by health facilities at different levels. The

Clinical Establishment Act (CEA) that prescribes basic minimum standards of facilities and services for each type of clinical establishment, has as yet not been adopted by all states. The current health policy seeks to promote early adoption of CEA by the remaining states too. Of course, there are higher standards of care too that are ensured through the process of accreditation and certification, but adoption of those standards is voluntary in nature. Strong enforcement mechanisms are essential to drive adoption and application of uniform standards across the entire spectrum of the health sector.

India's current substantial reliance on the private healthcare sector is a reason for grave concern, owing to its lack of comprehensive regulation and standardization.[294] Due to extremely weak and ineffective mechanisms for accountability and regulation, the private healthcare sector's quest for profit maximization often results in frequent unwarranted treatments, exorbitant healthcare bills and a commercialized approach towards patients. An impersonal and profit-driven corporate management style in multi-specialty hospitals, with doctors being set performance targets and incentivised for achieving numbers has had far reaching consequences on the practice of medicine – from hyperinflation in costs of healthcare, increasing instances of malpractice and corruption to a growing trust deficit between doctors and patients and incidents of violence against hospitals and healthcare workers.

A large part of health sector fragmentation has to do with the health system design issues which can potentially be fixed if sound policies and interventions are pursued. But some part of health sector fragmentation has to do with the federal structure of the country. As per the Indian Constitution, health care delivery is a state subject. Each state is free to design its own health system and is free to proceed at its own

---

[294] "Analyzing Regulation of Private Healthcare in India", Dr Abhay Shukla, Dr Kanchan Pawar, Dr Abhijit More, Oxfam India, March 17, 2021

pace in improving health outcomes. The national government can at best incentivize states to prioritize health and make technical assistance available for strengthening its health system. The different choices made by the various states results in fragmentation of the health sector at the national level.

An urban only India would be best served by a consolidated public (sizable majority) and private healthcare industry. Having a sufficient number of heavily regulated large integrated hospitals along with a dense network of pharmacies is the best model for serving all the healthcare needs of a city's population.

Education

After health, education is the most fundamental pillar of human evolution. Education is one of the vital tools that help a nation to develop. Well educated and properly trained manpower can accelerate the pace of economic development. For India to urbanize and industrialize and move towards sustainability, everyone needs to have the right perspective and manpower capabilities need to be ramped up across various sectors. The Indian education system is faced with the problem of inaccessibility and low-quality that make Indians unemployable. Due to this, India is unable to fully exploit the potential of its human capital.

Many branches of the knowledge system had their origin in India. India lost the plot on education during the subsequent invasions by the Mughals and the British. Therefore, renaissance and scientific thinking as happened in Europe didn't happen in India. Later, the British established the modern education system that is still followed in India. They replaced age-old systems of education in the country and introduced the British structure of education. Since independence, India has evolved one of the most competitive education systems in the world that enables fast, high-quality learning, capability building for effectively contributing to the modern world, preservation of cultural heritage and integration with the world.

With more than 1.5 million schools and more than 290 million enrolments, India is home to one of the largest and complex school education systems in the world along with China. There are a total of 15,07,708 schools in India, out of which 10,32,570 are run by the Union Government and state governments, 84,362 are government-aided, 3,37,499 are unaided private schools while 53,277 are run by other organizations and institutions.[295]

---

[295] "How independent education industry is a major source of employment in India", Raghav Poddar, FICCI, November 21, 2020

The literacy rate in India (~75%) still lags behind the world literacy rate of ~87%. India is home to the largest population of 287 million illiterate adults in the world. This amounts to 37% of the global total. Survival to class 5 is around ~60% as compared with the global average of ~83%.[296] There remains a considerable gap between urban and rural literacy in India – 87.7% of India's urban population is literate, while only ~70% of the rural population is literate. The Gross Enrolment Ratio (GER) in higher education in India is extremely low at 25.8% (2017-18). Lack of access is a major reason behind the low intake of higher education.

India is spending around 4% of GDP as a public expenditure and around 2.5% of GDP as private expenditure on education; together it is spending around 6.5% of GDP on education.[297] Hence, the total size of the industry is more than $150 billion currently, larger than the Indian healthcare industry. While education spending as a percentage of GDP is comparable to even the developed world, per pupil expenditure is abysmally low. Achieving spending levels similar to the developed world would result in multi-fold expansion of industry with the potential size being more than $1 trillion. The expansion would largely be in terms of quality of infrastructure and teaching capabilities.

Both access and quality of education are vastly different in urban (tier 1 and 2) and the remaining parts of India (tier 3 cities, towns and rural India).[298] Urban India has sufficient capacity to serve primary, secondary and higher education needs, and enrolment ratio is high. The remaining parts of India have insufficient capacity, poor infrastructure, lower quality of teaching staff and are influenced by various

---

[296] Annual report 2018-19, Ministry of Human Resource Development, Department of School Education and Literacy, Government of India

[297] "Private and Public Expenditure on Education in India", Venkatanarayana Motkuri and E. Revathi, Research cell on education, Center for economic and social studies, ICSSR, Ministry of Education, Sep 2020

[298] "Improving access and quality in the Indian education system", Sam Hill and Thomas Chalaux, OECD Economics Department Working Paper, July 29, 2011

economic, social and cultural factors that hamper enrolment. The scattered nature of Indian settlement results in poor efficiency of public expenditure on education. The quality of education delivered is extremely poor and students from such backgrounds remain largely unemployable in the formal sector. A move towards an urban only India will largely solve the problem of access to all forms of education.

Now even within the current Indian cities, there is significant difference between public and private education, and the difference has been increasing of late.[299] Private educational institutes have been able to charge much higher fees from the middle income and above segments of the Indian society. That has allowed these institutes to generate sizable profits, attract the best teaching staff and invest in building superior infrastructure. While private unaided schools comprise 22.38% of the total number of schools, 37.18% of the total number of teachers work in private schools.[300] India needs to gradually bring the publicly funded educational institutes at par with the best private ones. New Delhi and few other Indian cities are already leading the way in significantly improving the quality of public education. Some of the schools and higher education institutes in these cities are more prestigious and sought after than private. Even in some of the most advanced cities such as New York, the public education system adheres to the highest standards of education. Private schools largely cater to the ultra-rich in these cities. Greater allocation of public funding towards urban areas would be a good starting point for bridging the public-private gap in the cities and will also help in accelerating the process of urbanization. India should also gradually introduce regulations that facilitate a reduction in the public-private quality gap.

---

[299] "Private vs public education: Which industry is where and why?", India Today, December 7, 2020

[300] "Government Schools Have Much Lesser Teachers Compared to Private Schools", Ditsa Bhattacharya, July 11, 2021

In terms of educational content, India needs to provide greater avenues for experiential learning throughout primary, secondary and higher education. In primary and secondary years, the focus should be on conceptual understanding rather than rote learning. Universities and colleges need to build much stronger linkages with the industry to provide real world experiences. Large enterprises in both industrial and services sectors should be mandated to provide opportunities for students to experience the application of theoretical knowledge. We need to move away from a culture of competition in classes and move towards making everyone cross the threshold of learning. Instead of making students work towards maximizing their individual scores, the entire class should be incentivized to make everyone pass. As we move towards a more equitable society, it is important to discourage the ranking of professions. Everyone should be made capable and have the choice to pursue any occupation and should be equipped to swiftly move from one profession to another.

Primary and secondary curriculum needs to have a much greater emphasis on health and sustainability. Besides introducing both health and sustainability as core subjects throughout the primary and secondary years, every school should provide access to high quality sports facilities and faculty. The objective should be to make everyone participate and develop an affinity for sports, and not to create winners.

Education is one of the top employers in the country and is likely to remain so even in the wake of technological advances. The education sector currently provides direct employment to over 10 crore people (teaching, non-teaching and support staff) in India.[301] There is no technology substitute for education provided by a qualified teacher in a physical environment. Technology can possibly act as a bridge during India's urban transition and can serve to

---

[301] "How independent education industry is a major source of employment in India", Raghav Poddar, FICCI, November 21, 2020

improve the efficiency of educational delivery by the teaching professionals. The losses in non-teaching staff should be offset by the increased number of teaching staff needed for sports, extracurricular and sustainability.

Retail

Retail has emerged as the largest industry globally, generating revenue of ~$23 trillion in 2020. The industry serves as a vital link between production and consumption, and therefore assumes a central role in driving sustainability. Even though the online retail industry has made significant inroads over the last couple of decades, physical retail will remain dominant (with over 80% market share in the stable state) in mixed-use urban development. Eventually, online retail fulfillment will also be most efficient and sustainable through local retail stores. India also has the unique opportunity to completely leapfrog big box retailing and formalize natural retailing. India needs to evolve store formats, supply chain, inventory management, and customer support functions to enable purchase of packaging free products.

Retail is segmented into Food, Beverage and Grocery, Personal and Household Care, Apparel, Footwear, and Accessories, Furniture, Home Décor, Toys, Hobby and Household Appliances, Industrial and Automotive, Electronic, Consumer Durables and IT, Pharmaceuticals, Luxury Goods, and Others.

The Indian retail industry is worth around $500 billion and would expand to ~$5 trillion in a sustainable India. The current private consumption (PPP adjusted) is around one tenth of the levels in the most advanced nations.

The lack of organization in Indian retail suppresses the industry value, customer experience and worker compensation. While organized retail has over 80% share in most developed markets, it only accounts for 5% of the market in India. In 2015, there were more than 15 million mom-and-pop stores across India. The unorganized retail sector in India is largely devoid of any regulation with people simply working to earn their daily bread with oppressive working conditions and no benefits. India needs to drive organization in retail by ramping up the regulatory regime.

Scale is critical to achieve profitability in a regulated retail industry. Small independent retail operations also become unviable in an urban environment due to the high cost of real estate. Organized retail will therefore take over the retail industry as India urbanizes. Urbanization and organized retail go hand in hand and hence, a push towards organized retail will also drive migration towards the cities. In a mixed-use urban India, only the large organized retailers will have the financial and operational capabilities to get retail space at cheaper prices and stay profitable. Independent retail would largely be restricted to food or categories where the retailer is able to drive differentiation with their in-store processing capabilities.

In India, retail is the second largest employer after agriculture, providing employment to over 40 million people. However, the share of retail in total employment in India is only around 7 percent, primarily because a large part of retail is still in the traditional or unorganized sector where there is a high incidence of disguised unemployment.[302] Over 10% of the workforce works in the retail industry in most developed markets. Natural retailing will increase manpower intensiveness of retail above levels seen in the developed markets.

The Indian retail sector mainly consists of small privately-owned single stores that largely depend on family labor. These are built on the model of entrepreneurship or sole proprietorship and provide self-employment. The need for hired labor is low and, because the labor laws do not apply to the unorganized sector, workers may be paid less than the minimum wage and have long working hours. The unorganized sector is characterized by poor working conditions and lack of social security. Various Labor Acts of the central and state governments such as the Minimum

---

[302] "Employment Conditions in Organised and Unorganised Retail: Implications for FDI Policy in India", Arpita Mukherjee and Tanu. M Goyal, Indian Council for Research on International Economic Relations, April 2012

Wages Act, 1948 and the Employees State Insurance Act are applicable, but only to employees in the organized retail sector.

With liberalization, Indian corporates and foreign retailers started operating in the retail sector and modern retail evolved. Unlike the unorganized sector, modern or organized retail has a corporate management with a transparent accounting system. Modern retailers have to abide by the labor laws and employment conditions. The incidence of disguised unemployment is low. The working hours are fixed, so employees work on a rotation basis. Unless India adopts a clear stance of moving towards organized retail, India will continue to struggle in encouraging small, self-employed retailers and in increasing the living standards of the retail workforce. The government needs to create smooth mechanisms for organized retail to take over the industry.

Focus on natural retailing will also help large Indian retailers capture the multi-fold value expansion of the industry. The key capability difference between the world's leading retailers and large Indian retailers is in the areas of processing and packaging. Indian retailers have already built significant operational expertise and are adept at using technology to drive efficiencies throughout the supply chain. As long as we have a self-sufficient economy, there is no real reason to allow any form of FDI in any segment of retail.

While the urban development across the envisaged 130 cities should draw from the retail infrastructure of leading cities such as New York, retailing practices should be governed by the age-old natural retailing followed in the dense cities of India, China and some other Asian and middle eastern countries.

Logistics and warehousing

Logistics and warehousing services will remain an essential service but will be significantly optimized. India has one of the most inefficient logistics industries in the world due to the distributed nature of our settlements and small-scale production. As India moves towards urban only living and consolidates its production and processing within the cities, efficiency of logistics will dramatically increase. Localization will enable industrial production to become more flexible and responsive to market demand, thereby preventing excess production, and minimizing inventory costs and warehousing requirements. Consolidation of production (industrial and agriculture) will bring in scale efficiencies. City level production / processing will reduce long haul freight of consumer goods and durables. In India, the average distance of freight transport is around 550 km, which is higher than the EU (130 km) and the United States (~400 km). Minimization of imports and exports will also reduce logistics requirements.

That said, India has a very low density of warehousing infrastructure and will need to beef it up to minimize spillage and reduce inventory costs. Warehousing will become increasingly important, especially to manage the output of large-scale agriculture. A shift to natural supply chains and retailing will increase demand for high quality warehousing services. Retail is likely to converge with warehousing in the cities.

But overall, as the population stabilizes around 150-200 crores and Indians start becoming healthier, the quantum of consumption will remain similar to what it is today. Average freight distances will reduce, utilizations will increase, and rail will become the predominant mode for inter-city logistics. During the build stage, construction related freight will be much higher than the current levels, but local sourcing of materials (from the excavated land for lake development) would keep the average distances in check.

The Indian logistics sector is currently worth around $150-200 billion and employs 2.2 crore people. India handles 4.6 billion tonnes of goods each year that represent a variety of domestic industries and products: 22 percent are agricultural goods, 39 percent are mining products, and 39 percent are manufacturing-related commodities.

In a sustainable India, the industry could be worth around $500 billion. The increase will be driven by increased manpower costs and a ramp up in warehousing infrastructure. The industry is expected to employ ~1.0 crore people with decreases in freight manpower requirement (due to increased scale of movements) and increases in warehousing manpower.

Travel & tourism

Travel & tourism is a big adjacent industry and is increasingly converging with retail. The industry will witness significant growth as India upgrades the industry towards five-star destinations and green transportation. The size of the global travel and tourism industry is pegged at ~$8.9 trillion with the US ($2.1 trillion) and Europe ($2 trillion) having the lion's share.[303] The current size of the industry in India is ~$200 billion.

The potential size of the sustainable Indian transportation and tourism industry would be around $4.0 trillion. While on the basis of US benchmarks, the size of the industry would be around $1.5-2.0 trillion, green transportation would result in much higher manpower intensity (especially for shared car drivers). Adding up the revenue from passenger transportation (~5% of GDP), five-star destinations (~$150 billion), and city tourism ($200-500 billion) would suggest a stable industry size of ~$2.0 trillion.

In the developed world, nearly one tenth of the workforce is engaged in the travel and tourism industry. The industry has high manpower intensity in India engaging nearly 4 crore people. In the US, the industry employs around 1.7 crore people and in China, around 8 crore people. Using 10% of the workforce as a benchmark, the Indian travel and tourism industry should employ somewhere between 5 to 8 crore people in the stable state. But for green transportation, the transportation industry will need ~10 crore people. Hotels (five-star destinations and urban hospitality) will likely have a manpower of around 1.5 crore.

---

[303] "Travel & tourism, global economic impact and trends 2020", World Travel & Tourism Council, June 2020

Professional Services

A sizable chunk of the services industry in India consists of individual practitioners and small firms in a wide range of fields. Some of these require relatively high levels of knowledge and skills (consultants, doctors, lawyers, tax consultants, accountants, architects, sports / fitness trainers, art / music / dance trainers etc.), some are semi-skilled professions with short vocational training requirements (electrician, plumber, carpenter, mason, barber, beautician, tailor etc.) and some have been deemed as low skill jobs (cook, cleaner, driver, security, nanny etc.).

In the developed world, most of these services have been formalized with established institutes providing training and certification. Skilled and semi-skilled professionals earn enough to have a good standard of living and even the low skilled ones make more than the minimum wage.

In India, save for the highly skilled professionals, the rest, fall in the informal sector. The compensation is minimal in these occupations and dependent largely on the demand-supply dynamics of the local area. They pretty much work towards daily wages and have no social security or benefits. While there is a fair share of uneducated and untrained people involved in these professions, even educated youth are taking up these professions due to their inability to find employment in the formal sector.

As India urbanizes and the industry consolidates, there will be some changes in the demand for these services. We might not need architects to design individual homes, but they would always be needed by the large developers. Electricians and plumbers will always be needed, though the demand should reduce with the increasing quality of installations. We may not need as many carpenters as minimalism takes over. Individuals might no longer need tax consultants and accountants, and their role would largely be restricted to the corporate sector. The demand for trainers (sports / fitness / arts / music / dance) will increase as the average income increases and we become a more health-conscious society. Barbers and beauticians will also see higher demand as Indians start living better. The demand for domestic cleaners and drivers should increase given their critical contribution to sustainable living. The need for security personnel is likely to reduce as we move towards a more equitable society, but the reduction will not be substantial given the need for coordination in the high-rises, especially in India.

In a sustainable India, around 20-25 crore people could be employed in these professional services. We will need around 6-10 crore domestic helpers, >10 crore drivers for shared cars, trucks and other commercial vehicles, >2 crore trainers, ~1 crore handymen (electricians and electronic repair professionals, plumbers & carpenters, tailors, cobblers etc.), and over 1 crore professionals for the remaining services (legal, tax, accounting, security etc.).

For all these professionals who will form the largest segment of the country's workforce, India needs to create an institutional set up to bring them in the formal sector. Technology start-ups are attempting to organize some of these services but are unable to increase the living standard of these professionals. The gig economy is just taking advantage of their ability to control the consumer interface and the lack of formal employment opportunities, to rally the workforce in an ad hoc manner. Besides, one might be initially attracted by the proposition of a flexible working model, but in the long run, people realize the value of permanent employment and fixed working hours. India needs to have a few large companies that employ these professionals on a full-time basis and provide them with fair compensation, social security and benefits. Freelance work in these service segments should be phased out completely.

Large companies will help improve the quality of service delivery and create a formal career path for employees. These companies will be able to evolve processes and capabilities that improve quality and efficiency of service delivery. The large companies will be able to improve the working conditions in these occupations, provide a safety net and elevate the status of these professionals. These companies will also be better equipped to train the workforce and provide exposure to different areas in a field.

Technology, media and telecom (TMT)

The services components (excluding equipment) of technology, media and telecommunication industries largely round out the services industry. The combined size of these service industries globally is more than $5 trillion, with an increasing level of overlap amongst them. The industry employs over 50 million people globally, with over 10 million people working in these industries in the US itself.

Seven TMT companies are now in the ten most valuable public companies in the world.[304] A decade earlier, three energy companies, three banks, and just two TMT companies made the list, so a broad economic and social shift from physical to digital has clearly occurred. The 2010s will be known as the decade of social media, smartphones, streaming, sharing, machine intelligence, and the cloud. Many of the top TMT performers rode those trends to great heights.

Some global trends that helped propel growth in the 2010s are fading. The number of Internet users will not double in the next decade, as it did in the previous one. The rate of smartphone adoption has also begun to slow, even in emerging markets.

The TMT sector will continue to face regulatory and public scrutiny over its ability to monitor and limit unintended uses of its products and services; to control the spread of falsehoods and deep fakes; and to keep pace with unending developments on social media. At the same time, companies will be facing new scrutiny over their own carbon footprint.

The TMT sector has a dual role to play in sustainability — to transform their own organization and ecosystems, and to use their role as digital enablers to drive the sustainability journeys across sectors.[305] They are significant contributors

---

[304] "The last decade was great, but what about the next?, the 2020 value creators report", BCG, Feb 24, 2020

[305] "TMT's dual role in building a sustainable future", Praveen Shankar, EY, 2022

to global energy usage, emissions and e-waste. The information and communications technology (ICT) sector accounts for 2%–4% of global carbon emissions and up to 7% of global electricity use, with many projections signaling continued exponential increase in data traffic and potential for ICT to rise to 14% of global emissions by 2040. Meanwhile, the global volume of e-waste is rising relentlessly, with only 17% recycled. Data centers are energy-intensive, using an estimated 200 terawatt-hours (TWh) each year, more than the national energy consumption of Iran. The power requirements for emerging technologies are high and growing. 5G technology is estimated to add between 2.7 and 6.7 million tonnes of CO2 equivalents per year by 2030.

On the other hand, TMT companies have a key role in the design and execution of sustainability.[306] TMT-enabled smart technologies help quantify, monitor and predict energy usage while also driving exponentially greater efficiency. In the future, ICT solutions could reduce global emissions by up to 15%. Today's mobile technologies are enabling carbon reduction equivalent to 4% of global emissions, which is 10 times the mobile industry's own carbon footprint. TMT companies enjoy a deep and wide-ranging reach into enterprises across all industries, and they have unparalleled touchpoints with billions of consumers. These relationships put them in a unique position to deliver smart solutions for a more efficient, sustainable future. Media firms also have a role to play in pioneering sustainability and breaking many of the culture and perception barriers that exist in consumers and businesses.

The current wave of new technologies is attempting to control the operation in the physical world. Consumer tech is democratizing creation of products and services and enabling their consumption at the touch of a few buttons. But humanity needs to prevent overuse of technology and avoid its unintended consequences. The purpose of technology is to

---

[306] "Tech, media, and telecom must be a springboard for sustainability", HFS, Oct 7, 2021

make production more efficient, enable equal access, and encourage people towards responsible consumption. Consumer centricity should not lead to compromises on health and sustainability.

An urban only India presents a very different requirement from TMT. The problem of availability and access to various products and services becomes almost a non-issue in the crowded urban marketplace. There will be people all around for everything one might need and therefore technology-based services aiming to replace humans would become redundant. Discovery and technology driven transactions will remain relevant. Cities are ideal for sharing products and technology can facilitate the same and help maximize resource efficiency.

The vibrant cities will drive people away from unhealthy worthless solitary occupations such as playing video games or watching cartoons. There will be people everywhere to monitor and influence responsible behaviors thereby eliminating the need for artificial intelligence and IOT. People will be the energy, not oil, not data. Mixed use urban development powered by renewable sources of energy will eliminate the case for remote working. The forces of globalization would be neutralized by the evolution of an independent Indian economy. Healthy living will reign supreme and people across the subcontinent will work together in sync with the natural cycle.

Urban-only living also creates the opportunity to avoid the excessive use of data intensive technologies. Concentrated living in built-to-last urban high-rises will minimize the need for wireless technologies (wifi, 4G, 5G) and data intensive applications (e.g. video calling) that are creating a massive carbon footprint. High quality cable networks would not only be sufficient for connectivity (within and amongst cities), it would drastically reduce data generation, related energy use and would also be more stable and reliable.

India is pretty much at the frontier of TMT services in terms of capability and is poised for exponential growth in the next couple of decades. The size of the TMT services industry in India is around ~$150 billion, with IT services contributing ~$90 billion, telecom ~$40 billion and media & entertainment around $20 billion.

IT services is largely an export business and has a significant domestic growth potential as India industrializes and consolidates. Over a crore of the workforce is employed in these industries in India. One of the major drivers of service sector growth in the post globalization era in India has been the IT and ITES sectors. In the post-1991 period, there were several measures undertaken by the government to develop the services sector, especially through deregulation of some sub-sectors of the services sector. Foreign Direct Investment (FDI), varying from 26 per cent (in print media) to 100% in information technology (IT) sector, business process outsourcing (BPOs), e-commerce activities, infrastructure etc.), has been permitted.

Uninhibited growth on the lines of the US and Europe in the TMT sectors will possibly lead the industry to more than a trillion dollars. But if India follows the path of health and sustainability, we are likely to arrive at the optimal size of these industries much earlier. India still has a choice to shape the evolution and adoption of technology in ways that improve human lives without creating an additional resource burden. Charting a course where technology simply drives efficiency of production and consumption, and encourages healthy consumption and lifestyles, will optimize the scope of technology in our lives. Slow technological progress that is absorbed by every member of the society and allows us to move forward together will be the ideal path and lead us towards sustainable harmony.

The size of a sustainable TMT industry would still be large but built to enable superior physical experiences. Media and entertainment should take center stage with everyone having the time and opportunity to perform. Everyone should find avenues in their locality for performing arts and move away from watching television. City life should be a celebration of life with the calendar full with participation and attendance in theater, music & dance, and the creation of art.

Besides ensuring efficient and sustainable production and consumption, we also need services for building and managing our natural wealth, protecting the Indian territory and ensuring safety of every Indian citizen. Finally, we need the government to formulate and enforce policies, systems and processes to lead India towards sustainability.

Forests

In sustainable India, forests would occupy the largest percentage of land area. Ideally, India should have a very dense forest cover[307] on more than 60% of its land area. Once people evacuate the identified forest lands, significant effort will be needed to regenerate the forests and restore the natural ecosystems. While the task of nurturing 60% of the land area might seem daunting and manpower intensive, forest ecosystems thrive best with minimal human intervention. The European Union (42% forest cover out of a total 4.2 million hectares of land area) has less than 10 lac people working in forest management and exploitation.[308] While the total forest area of a sustainable India would be similar to the EU's current forest cover, the higher diversity of Indian forest ecosystems results in greater opportunities for responsible exploitation. Hence, India could have anywhere between 50 lac and 1 crore people working in various functions of forestry (responsible exploitation, research & development, restoration, monitoring and surveillance, protection against human encroachment / illegal exploitation / fire and floods, roads & pavements, human safety etc.).

Water

Management of inland water resources (rivers, canals, lakes, estuaries, ponds, streams, springs, marshes, swamps, creeks etc.) will become increasingly important as India builds a sustainable water infrastructure. While a massive effort is needed to build the ~130 city lakes and the associated river systems, maintaining the health of these water bodies will also be a significant undertaking. India needs to build robust water resource management (planning, development and management) capabilities to maintain the quantity and

---

[307] "Forest Survey of India 2022", Ministry of Environment, Forest and Climate Change, Government of India

[308] "Total employment in the forest sector: considerable socio-economic importance", Europe and the forest - Volume 3

quality of water across all water uses.[309] India will need highly advanced institutions, infrastructure, incentives, and information systems that support and guide water management. The staff ratio of various city level water organizations varies from 5 to 10 per 1000 connections.[310] Assuming a similar staff ratio for the 50 crore or so connections (including commercial) in the 130 cities, India would have around 25-50 lac people working in the core water resources industry, who would develop and manage the various water bodies. Over the longer term, the water industry could employ a much larger workforce in ancillary activities.

Waste

Waste management (including sewerage and remediation) is essential for a responsible society and critical for preventing environmental deterioration. The advanced European nations are moving towards a circular economy and have a well-established waste management industry. Germany (~8 crore population) has around 1.35 lac professionals and Netherlands (~1.7 crore population) has around 35k professionals. Even if India minimizes dry / packaging / chemical waste, there will always be a significant amount of wet waste that would need to be efficiently managed. Hence, a workforce of 30-40 lacs would be needed for waste management in sustainable India.

Fire

India also needs to be well prepared to prevent and respond to fire (building, industrial, forest). India currently has around 60k fire personnel[311] as against an estimated requirement of ~6 lac firemen (based on a 2012 fire risk report prepared for

---

[309] "Water resources management", World Bank

[310] "2007 benchmarking and data book of water utilities in India", Asian Development Bank, October 2007

[311] "India's Fire Preparedness: A FactCheck", FactChecker team, 9 Dec 2019

the Indian Government). The US has more than 10 lac firemen.

Defense

National security is likely to remain a key priority for a very long time. India currently has one of the largest armed forces in the world with over 25 lac personnel across military (>90% of the total armed forces), navy and air force. Technology development over the last few decades has dramatically changed the modus operandi of armed forces. Manpower requirement is likely to further decrease as technology continues to eliminate the need for physical deployment of troops. Armed forces should be allowed to accelerate technology development and adoption to minimize the at-risk active frontline personnel.

Police

As India becomes a more equitable and healthy society, crime rates will also gradually reduce. The role of the police will evolve from crime prevention and resolution to influencing responsible behaviors across all walks of life. India has the largest police force (>20 lac personnel) in the world but still has a relatively low police density. India is ranked 128 in police density with just ~150 personnel per 1 lac of population. Over the course of the sustainable transformation, the police will have an important role in facilitating migration to the cities and influence the development of responsible urban societies. Given that significant regulatory changes will ensue during this period, a higher police density (250-300 per 1 lac of population) would be ideal.

Government

The last but possibly the most important component of the services industry is the Government itself. Through public policy and administration, the Government is responsible for laying out the vision and driving the nation towards the same. Public administrators are employees working in government departments and agencies, at all levels of government. They are also responsible for the provision of various public services. India has somewhere between 1 to 1.5 crore people working purely in public policy and administration (excluding defense, police, railways and other PSUs) in central and state government. Given that there are several areas of public administration that need to be initiated, formalized or enhanced across various sectors, even with the anticipated productivity improvements, sustainable India will need around 2 crore public administrators.

India's Services exports recorded ~$180 billion in revenues during 2021-22. Software and IT services accounted for ~49% of the total services exports. The total value of global services trade (export) was ~$6 trillion. India is currently the 8th largest exporter of commercial services with a ~3% share of the global services trade. With a 15% share of global services, India can only reach a trillion dollars in revenues from services export. As discussed earlier, the outsourcing industry is wrought with several negative consequences for an economy and its people. Besides, expansion of the domestic services industry therefore presents a much larger potential for India.

Based on the estimated sector wise potential of the various services industries, the total size of the Indian services industry would be around $22.5 trillion. The sector wise breakup for a sustainable India would be - construction (~$1.5 trillion), banking (~$500 billion), pension (~$1 trillion), insurance (~$1 trillion), healthcare ($2-3 trillion), education (~$1.2 trillion), retail (~$5 trillion), logistics (~$500 bn), travel & tourism (~$4.0 trillion), professional services (~$3-4 trillion), TMT (~$1 trillion), forest (~$200 bn), water (~$500 bn), waste management (~$100 bn), fire (~$25 bn), armed forces (~$100 bn), police (~$100 bn), and the Government (~$300 bn).

The services industry could potentially provide employment to around 60 crore people in sustainable India, with the following breakup across the various sub-sectors - construction (5 crore), financial services (2-3 crore), healthcare (3-5 crore), education (~5 crore), retail (~10 crore), logistics (~1 crore), travel & tourism (~12 crore), professional services (~12 crore), TMT (2-3 crore), forest (50 lac to 1 crore), water (~75 lac), waste management (30-40 lac), fire (~10 lac), defense (~25 lac), police (~40 lac), and the Government (~2 crore).

Table 14.1 - Size ($ bn) and employment across various services sectors

Sector	Size of industry		Employment	
	FY 21 ($ bn)	FY72 ($ bn)	FY21 (Cr)	FY72 (Cr)
Construction	125	1,500	5.00	5.00
Demolition	1	25	-	0.05
Banking and financial services	160	2,500	0.50	2.50
Real estate - rental	160	1	-	-
Healthcare	60	1,500	1.00	4.00
Education	125	1,250	3.00	5.00
Retail	200	5,000	3.00	10.00
Logistics and warehousing	150	500	1.50	1.00
Hotels	75	500	0.25	1.50
Transport	100	3,500	1.00	10.00
Professional services	250	3,500	12.00	12.00
Technology	90	500	0.45	1.00
Media	20	250	0.60	1.00
Telecom	40	200	0.40	0.40
Energy	108	1,000	0.20	1.25
Water	5	500	0.15	0.75
Waste Mgmt	2	100	0.50	0.35
Fire	0	25	0.06	0.01
Armed forces	64	100	0.25	0.25

Sector	Size of industry		Employment	
	FY 21 ($ bn)	FY72 ($ bn)	FY21 (Cr)	FY72 (Cr)
Police	14	100	0.20	0.40
Govt and public administration	75	300	1.25	1.50
Total - Services	**1,823**	**22,851**	**31.13**	**58.05**

15. Independent economy

India is currently a dependent economy with no real muscle to control its performance. India has a sizable current account (merchandise) deficit ($102 bn in FY21) which includes an uncontrollable oil deficit of $57 billion.[312] The size of our import bill is constantly increasing (~10.5% YoY growth in the five years leading up to the pandemic). Capital inflows are continuously increasing to help maintain a surplus in the balance of payments and are resulting in a gradual loss of ownership of our enterprises and creating a massive future liability.

Post independence, India has always been dependent on the industrialized nations for engineering. In the first few decades post-independence, we exported raw materials and foodstuffs, to acquire critical engineering goods. We then followed the strategies suggested by the leading economists of the 20th century and adopted the path of import substitution industrialization (ISI) and export of manufactured goods.[313] But these strategies, instead of freeing the economy from its heavy reliance on primary exports, foreign capital and technology, has in fact aggravated the situation and nature of dependency. Increasing industrial production has created high energy dependence and lately dependence on electronics.

Economic dependence has governed India's pattern of production, resource allocation and now consumption as well. MNCs have steadily expanded and have become a key determinant of the social structure and exert strong influence on the political system as well.

---

[312] Reserve Bank of India

[313] "Economic independence: Concepts and strategies, a theoretical investigation and an empirical case study", Eqbal Al-Rahmani, University of New Hampshire, Durham, 1988

Participation as a dependent in the free play of the international market forces has largely worked to India's disadvantage. The income levels have been suppressed to maintain the competitiveness of our exports. Even the surplus that we have generated with increasing labor productivity has been transferred either to the importing nations (via a downward trend of export prices) or to the privileged class within the country. A certain fraction of the privileged class has even compromised national development and facilitated foreign expansion for their personal benefits. Foreign companies are lining up to serve the extravagant lifestyles of the rich and elite in India. These forces have resulted in the growth of unnecessary trade and hindered the development of the core industrial sector. India will find it difficult to reach the developed status if it maintains this flamboyant trade orientation.

India's economic set up and monetary policies are both outward oriented to cater to the dependent status. One of the key objectives of the RBI is therefore to manage exchange rates. To do so, it maintains significant foreign exchange reserves. Since 2001, the RBI's balance sheet has completely shifted to holding foreign securities (dollar reserves and foreign treasury securities) as the asset to back the Indian financial market. Foreign securities now account for over 96% of the asset base of the Reserve Bank of India (RBI).[314]

In contrast, Government Treasury and Agency securities account for over 98% of the assets of the Federal Reserve, the central bank of the United States.[315] That is indicative of the strength of the US Government and absence of any dependency.

But on the positive side, India has always chosen the most optimal path given the enormous constraints. Towards the overarching objective of national security, India was forced to

---

[314] Liabilities and Assets, Reserve Bank of India

[315] "Combined Financial Statements, Federal Reserve Banks", As of and for the Years Ended December 31, 2021 and 2020 and Independent Auditors' Report

make several compromises and deviate from the path of purity. But the sacrifices made so far have now brought India to a point where it can make choices to gain control of its economic destiny.

A sustainable India will obviously be self-sufficient, have complete economic freedom and will actually generate an economic surplus. But even the pursuit of sustainability as the supreme national objective is the best strategy for India to strengthen its economy in the near term. The path towards sustainability is mainly inward focused and immediately starts breaking the chains of dependency. The pursuit of sustainability simply needs an internal commitment of resources towards building the 130 cities and enabling a high-quality life for every Indian citizen. Urban-only living drastically reduces the magnitude of the problem of national security, both external and internal, and lays the foundation of creating a homogeneous Indian society. The development gives India the opportunity to build its own financial assets. Investment in its own people presents the best path for maximizing the quantity and quality of output and the size of the economy.

A Sustainable Superpower

The real GDP of the sustainable Indian economy will be ~$28 trillion in FY72 (FY21 prices and exchange rate), which translates to a 4.7% YoY growth over the course of 50 years. India is currently the seventh largest economy with a GDP of ~$2.6 trillion. In FY21, the largest economies were the United States (~$23 trillion), China (~$14 trillion), Japan (~$5 trillion), Germany (~$4 trillion), the United Kingdom (~$2.9 trillion), and France (~$2.8 trillion). The US economy is likely to reach ~$49 trillion by FY72 based on the current forecasts of its long term real GDP growth (1.5%).

Services (including construction) will be the largest component (80.7%) of the sustainable Indian economy with a real GDP contribution of ~$23 trillion, followed by manufacturing (~$3.7 trillion, 12.9%) and agriculture (~$1.8

trillion, 6.4%). The current distribution for the major developed economies is also similar - the US (80%, 19%, 1%), and the UK (79%, 20%, 1%).

Phases of transformation

The transformation journey can be sequenced into four overlapping phases - i) Concentration, consolidation, and capability building, ii) Capacity expansion, iii) Steady growth, and iv) Stabilize.

Phase I will involve concentration (realigning resource allocation towards the 130 cities), consolidation (of industrial and services enterprises) and capability building (indigenous and acquisition led enhancement of industrial efficiency and establishing sustainable methods of production).

Phase I will actually be preceded by a Phase 0 where we develop the national and city level blueprints, build consensus, enhance the public institutional set up to execute the transformation and minimize oil price risks by signing forward agreements (20-30 years).

Phase I will also involve initiation of regulatory changes for transition towards sustainable production and consumption and formal employment. Regulatory changes would need to be staggered mainly over the first two phases to keep the use of non-renewable energy and inflation within manageable limits. We assume an average YoY growth of 10% during this phase. The real GDP growth during this phase will be driven by substantial increases in government spending on infrastructure development of the 130 cities and government led investments in capability building.

After around 15 years of Phase I, we will be ready for changing gears and stepping up into the next phase of growth. While 15 years are inadequate for complete capability building across all sectors, we should be able to build threshold levels of capability that allow us to ramp up development and production without exceeding the limits of energy use.

In Phase II, we will rapidly expand capacity to reach production levels that will be close to the maximum levels required in sustainable India. We assume an average growth of 14% during this phase which should last for around 10 years in the base case. In this phase, the real GDP growth will be driven by further acceleration of government spending on infrastructure development, expansion of the large consolidated enterprises across sectors as well as by the continued investments in capability building.

In Phase III (steady growth) India will slow down the capacity expansion and continue with steadily building the cities and bringing more and more people in the sustainable living mode. We assume a 7.5% average annualized growth during these 20 or so years. Around this time, India will also be in a position to start reducing its unsustainable foreign trade. During this phase, we will see the 130 high-rise urban centers taking shape and large-scale migration to the cities. Urban blue and green will also start displaying visible growth during this phase. By the end of this phase, more than 70% of the workforce will be formally employed within these cities and would have secured a high-quality life for their families, and India would be well on its way towards sustainable production, consumption and trade.

In Phase IV, India will simply need to stabilize the economy at the growth rates of a sustainable India. Real GDP growth should stabilize around 5% and inflation should come down to below 3%. Everyone should be settled in the heavenly cities. India would be generating a surplus on all fronts and the balance sheet will be backed by its own assets.

Growth rates - overall and sector wise

The overall real GDP growth rates (base case) for the four phases are based on the target of building ~40 crore high-rise residential units in 50 years, given that we are currently clocking 300,000 units annually. The critical path activity during the complete transformation journey is the number of high-rise housing units being built in the 130 cities. All other forms of infrastructure development and industrial growth would be linked to the same. It will also determine the quantum of migration that can be smoothly facilitated. The construction workers who migrate from rural and semi-rural areas to build the cities would have an assured unit as part of their compensation.

The growth rate for individual sectors would be similar as all the sectors are interdependent, need to go through the four phases of transformation and because all of them are dependent on the rate of urbanization. But the growth rates will not be exactly the same as they are currently in different stages of maturity and have different end states. We therefore use a rationalization factor r to calculate the phase-wise growth rate for each sector. We solve for r in the following equation for each sector:

$(1+r1/r)^{15} * (1+r2/r)^{10} * (1+r3/r)^{20} * (1+r4/r)^{5} = (1+r0)^{50}$

where r1, r2, r3 and r4 are the overall real GDP growth rates for the four phases and r0 is the sector specific constant growth rate that will lead to its stable state size in 50 years.

Division of the overall growth rate for each phase by the rationalization factor will give us the sector specific growth rate for the phase.

Sector specific growth rates for the four phases are captured in the table below:

Table 15.1 - Phase wise growth rates for each sector

Sector	Capability build up (Year 1-15)	Capacity expansion (Year 16-25)	Steady growth (Year 26-45)	Stabilize (Year 46-50)
Agriculture[1]	3.11%	4.35%	2.33%	1.55%
Forestry	3.45%	4.83%	2.59%	1.73%
Fishing	2.64%	3.70%	1.98%	1.32%

Sector	Capability build up (Year 1-15)	Capacity expansion (Year 16-25)	Steady growth (Year 26-45)	Stabilize (Year 46-50)
Aggregates	7.01%	9.82%	5.26%	3.51%
Cement	4.73%	6.63%	3.55%	2.37%
Iron & steel	5.20%	7.28%	3.90%	2.60%
Aluminum	3.45%	4.83%	2.59%	1.73%
Other metals / minerals	4.97%	6.96%	3.73%	2.48%
Capital goods / heavy engg	2.43%	3.40%	1.82%	1.21%
Metal consumer products	7.01%	9.82%	5.26%	3.51%
Ceramics	2.72%	3.80%	2.04%	1.36%
Glass	5.46%	7.65%	4.10%	2.73%
Pipes	3.24%	4.54%	2.43%	1.62%
Paint	2.72%	3.80%	2.04%	1.36%
Electrical & electronics	6.10%	8.55%	4.58%	3.05%
Furniture	2.17%	3.04%	1.63%	1.09%
Textile	4.67%	6.54%	3.50%	2.34%
FMCG	4.57%	6.39%	3.42%	2.28%
Pharma	4.33%	6.07%	3.25%	2.17%
Sports goods	12.76%	17.87%	9.57%	6.38%
Toys	5.87%	8.22%	4.40%	2.93%
Automotive	4.22%	5.91%	3.17%	2.11%
Rolling stock	7.01%	9.82%	5.26%	3.51%

Sector	Capability build up (Year 1-15)	Capacity expansion (Year 16-25)	Steady growth (Year 26-45)	Stabilize (Year 46-50)
Shipbuilding	6.51%	9.12%	4.88%	3.26%
Aerospace & defense	8.08%	11.31%	6.06%	4.04%
Leather	-2.63%	-3.68%	-1.97%	-1.32%
Chemicals	-0.01%	-0.01%	-0.01%	-0.01%
Plastics	-1.92%	-2.69%	-1.44%	-0.96%
Wood panels	6.37%	8.91%	4.78%	3.18%
Paper	-0.95%	-1.33%	-0.71%	-0.48%
Construction	5.37%	7.52%	4.03%	2.69%
Demolition	7.01%	9.82%	5.26%	3.51%
Banking and financial services	5.96%	8.35%	4.47%	2.98%
Real estate rental [2]	-10.00%	-14.00%	-7.50%	-5.00%
Healthcare	7.01%	9.82%	5.26%	3.51%
Education	4.97%	6.96%	3.73%	2.48%
Retail	7.01%	9.82%	5.26%	3.51%
Logistics and warehousing	2.56%	3.59%	1.92%	1.28%
Hotels	4.08%	5.71%	3.06%	2.04%
Transport	7.77%	10.88%	5.83%	3.89%
Professional services	5.71%	8.00%	4.29%	2.86%
Technology	3.68%	5.15%	2.76%	1.84%
Media	5.46%	7.65%	4.10%	2.73%
Telecom	3.45%	4.83%	2.59%	1.72%

Sector	Capability build up (Year 1-15)	Capacity expansion (Year 16-25)	Steady growth (Year 26-45)	Stabilize (Year 46-50)
Energy	4.79%	6.71%	3.59%	2.40%
Water	10.18%	14.26%	7.64%	5.09%
Waste Mgmt	8.59%	12.02%	6.44%	4.29%
Fire	12.33%	17.26%	9.25%	6.17%
Armed forces	0.95%	1.33%	0.71%	0.48%
Police	4.20%	5.88%	3.15%	2.10%
Govt and public administration	2.96%	4.14%	2.22%	1.48%

1. Includes horticulture, animal husbandry, dairying, livestock; 2. No GDP contribution assumed from real estate rentals in stable state; Note: the actual calculations are based on a 51-year transformation period with phase I lasting for 16 years

GDP based on wage method

Now given that 80% of the eventual GDP would be from services, the transformation is essentially about people. For India to enlarge the domestic market, retain the production surplus internally and reduce inequality, it is critical for India to increase income levels and drive income redistribution. The quality of people and their productivity will be much higher in sustainable India. Every working Indian citizen should have an income that provides for a high-quality urban life.

In FY21, India had a total workforce of 56 crore (560 MM) people, out of a total population of 136 crore (1,360 MM), representing a worker to population ratio (WPR) of 41.3%.[316] The WPR is comparable to the developed world even with low women participation because of the explosive population

---

[316] "Workforce changes and employment", Niti Ayog, March 2022

growth during the second half of the 20th century. Now with the declining population growth in the 21st century, India will need an equal contribution from women in the workforce.

Sustainable India can have a WPR of 45% in the base case and 50% in the high case. Life expectancy should increase from 70 years (current) to 80 years (base case; most developed countries) and could even go up to 85 years, like in Japan. The working age would be 20-64 in the base case and 15-64 in the high case. The current working age is 21-60 in India and 15-64 in most developed countries. We can expect the employment rate to be around 80% in the base case (85% in developed countries). Hence, in the stable state when the level of fertility is likely to be at the replacement rate (equal to 2.1), the worker population ratio would simply be Average Working Years divided by Life Expectancy, and multiplied by Employment Rate, giving us a worker to population ratio of 45-50%. Equal participation from women is essential to achieve this WPR ratio in the stable state.

The income levels should be such that a couple generates more than the cost of living of a 4-member urban household, with sufficient headroom for contingencies and savings. An urban household needs around INR 14,00,000 in annual earnings to support good quality living.

Table 15.2 - Cost of living (expenses of a household with 2 adults and 2 children in a Tier 1 Indian city for good quality living; FY21 prices)

Category	Monthly cost (INR)
Rent	20,000
Utilities (water, electricity)	3,000
Groceries	10,000
Clothes	1,000

Category	Monthly cost (INR)
Phone	1,000
Wifi	500
Cosmetics & cleaning	2,000
Education	8,000
Insurance	5,000
Pension	10,000
Transportation	5,000
Hotels	2,000
Restaurants	2,000
Sports & fitness	2,000
Entertainment	1,000
Household shopping	2,000
Gifting	1,000
Professional services (incl childcare)	5,000
Saving	10000
Sum of household costs	**90,500**
Tax rate	26%
Required household monthly income	**1,22,712**
Required household annual income	**14,72,542**

The current average annual salary in India is ~INR 1,40,000, ten times lower than the annual household earning requirement for good quality urban living. In agriculture and construction, the average income is INR 1,20,000, in manufacturing between INR 1,40,000 and INR 1,60,000, more complex manufacturing (automotive, rolling stock etc.) around INR 1,80,000, in simple services (retail, logistics, transportation etc.) INR 1,20,000 to INR 1,50,000, utility services (energy, water, waste, telecom, media etc.) around INR 1,80,000, in knowledge intensive industries around INR 3,00,000, in government around ~INR 2,70,000, police ~INR 3,00,000, and armed forces around INR 8,50,000.

Table 15.3 - Sector-wise employment and average income (FY21)

Sector	Total people employed (#)	Average annual income (INR)
Agriculture[1]	15,00,00,000	1,20,000
Forestry	5,00,00,000	48,000
Fishing[317]	2,80,00,000	38,439
Aggregates	2,00,000	1,32,000
Cement	8,00,000	1,44,000
Iron & steel	8,00,000	1,56,000
Aluminum	2,00,000	1,56,000
Other metals / minerals	2,00,000	1,56,000
Capital goods / heavy engg	12,00,000	1,44,000
Metal consumer products	5,00,000	1,44,000
Ceramics	6,00,000	1,44,000
Glass	15,00,000	1,44,000
Pipes	3,00,000	1,44,000
Paint	3,00,000	1,44,000

---

[317] "Handbook on fisheries statistics 2020", Department of Fisheries, Ministry of Fisheries, Animal Husbandry and Dairying, Government of India

Sector	Total people employed (#)	Average annual income (INR)
Electrical & electronics	10,00,000	1,80,000
Furniture	5,00,000	1,44,000
Textile	30,00,000	1,44,000
FMCG	35,00,000	1,56,000
Pharma	7,00,000	1,56,000
Sports goods	5,00,000	1,44,000
Toys	5,00,000	1,44,000
Automotive	10,00,000	1,80,000
Rolling stock	1,50,000	1,80,000
Shipbuilding	1,00,000	1,80,000
Aerospace & defense	1,50,000	1,80,000
Leather	3,50,000	1,44,000
Chemicals	15,00,000	1,44,000
Plastics	5,00,000	1,44,000
Wood panels	1,00,000	1,44,000
Paper	4,00,000	1,44,000
Construction	5,00,00,000	1,20,000
Demolition	1,00,000	1,20,000
Banking and financial services	50,00,000	3,00,000
Real estate rental [2]		
Healthcare	1,00,00,000	3,00,000
Education	3,00,00,000	3,00,000

Sector	Total people employed (#)	Average annual income (INR)
Retail	3,00,00,000	1,50,000
Logistics and warehousing	1,50,00,000	1,20,000
Hotels	25,00,000	1,50,000
Transport	1,00,00,000	1,20,000
Professional services	12,00,00,000	1,20,000
Technology	45,00,000	2,00,000
Media	60,00,000	1,80,000
Telecom	40,00,000	1,80,000
Energy	20,00,000	3,60,000
Water	1,50,000	2,67,217
Waste Mgmt	50,00,000	1,80,000
Fire	60,000	2,40,000
Armed forces	25,00,000	8,73,421
Police	20,00,000	3,00,000
Govt and public administration	1,25,00,000	2,67,217
Total India	**56,00,00,000**	**1,40,000**

1. Includes horticulture, animal husbandry, dairying, livestock; 2. No GDP contribution assumed from real estate rentals in stable state

Now, given the annual household earning requirement of INR 14,00,000, average individual income should be around INR 10,00,000 in an urban only India. That translates to a real wage growth of ~3.9% YoY during the 50 years of transformation. This is simply the adjustment of wages for good quality responsible living in today's terms. The nominal wages will be higher once we factor in the inflation.

The size of the total workforce in sustainable India will be around 70 crore (700 million) resulting in a worker to population ratio of 42% (towards the lower end of the WPR range estimated earlier), which leaves sufficient headroom to engage additional workforce across sectors.

The real GDP based on the wage method [GDP = (1 / labor cost percentage) + profit] would be between $32 and $40 trillion depending on the labor percentage within the individual sectors and the level of profits assumed. Excluding profit, the real GDP based on wage method amounts to **~$29 trillion**. The following table outlines the base case assumptions and calculations for Real GDP based on wage method.

Table 15.4 - Real GDP estimate (FY72) based on wage method

Sector	People employed	Avg annual income (INR)	Real wage bill ($ bn)	Labor cost percentage	Real GDP ($ bn)
Agriculture[1]	5,00,00,000	10,02,445	675	50.0%	1,351
Forestry	75,00,000	10,56,859	107	50.0%	214
Fishing	50,00,000	9,54,115	64	50.0%	129
Aggregates	30,00,000	9,75,605	39	30.0%	131
Cement	30,00,000	9,41,360	38	25.0%	152
Iron & steel	30,00,000	10,19,807	41	17.5%	236
Aluminum	6,50,000	10,19,807	9	17.5%	51
Other metals / minerals	6,50,000	10,19,807	9	17.5%	51
Heavy engineering	15,00,000	10,64,297	22	17.5%	123
Metal consumer	10,00,000	9,41,360	13	25.0%	51

Sector	People employed	Avg annual income (INR)	Real wage bill ($ bn)	Labor cost percentage	Real GDP ($ bn)
products					
Ceramics	10,00,000	9,41,360	13	25.0%	51
Glass	25,00,000	9,41,360	32	25.0%	127
Pipes	10,00,000	9,41,360	13	25.0%	51
Paint	6,00,000	9,41,360	8	25.0%	30
Electrical & electronics	50,00,000	10,40,472	70	25.0%	280
Furniture	10,00,000	9,41,360	13	25.0%	51
Textile	25,00,000	9,41,360	32	25.0%	127
FMCG	50,00,000	10,19,807	69	25.0%	275
Pharma	15,00,000	10,19,807	21	25.0%	82
Sports goods	25,00,000	9,41,360	32	25.0%	127
Toys	20,00,000	9,41,360	25	25.0%	101
Automotive	20,00,000	10,40,472	28	25.0%	112
Rolling stock	10,00,000	10,40,472	14	25.0%	56
Shipbuilding	5,00,000	10,40,472	7	25.0%	28
Aerospace & defense	10,00,000	10,40,472	14	25.0%	56
Leather	1,00,000	9,41,360	1	25.0%	5
Chemicals	5,00,000	9,41,360	6	25.0%	25
Plastics	1,00,000	9,41,360	1	25.0%	5
Wood panels	5,00,000	9,41,360	6	25.0%	25

Sector	People employed	Avg annual income (INR)	Real wage bill ($ bn)	Labor cost percentage	Real GDP ($ bn)
Paper	2,00,000	9,41,360	3	25.0%	10
Construction	5,00,00,000	10,02,445	675	35.0%	1,501
Demolition	5,00,000	10,02,445	7	35.0%	19
Financial services	2,50,00,000	10,56,911	356	15.0%	2,373
Real estate rental [2]					
Healthcare	4,00,00,000	10,56,911	570	40.0%	1,424
Education	5,00,00,000	10,56,911	712	45.0%	1,582
Retail	10,00,00,000	9,80,584	1,321	20.0%	6,605
Logistics and warehousing	1,00,00,000	10,02,445	135	40.0%	338
Hotels	1,50,00,000	9,80,584	198	35.0%	566
Transport	10,00,00,000	10,02,445	1,351	30.0%	4,502
Professional services	12,00,00,000	10,02,445	1,621	50.0%	3,241
Technology	1,00,00,000	10,21,935	138	35.0%	393
Media	1,00,00,000	10,40,472	140	45.0%	311
Telecom	40,00,000	10,40,472	56	35.0%	160
Energy	1,25,00,000	9,88,351	166	20.0%	832
Water	75,00,000	10,65,950	108	20.0%	539
Waste Mgmt	35,00,000	10,40,472	49	60.0%	82
Fire	10,00,000	10,83,702	15	60.0%	24

Sector	People employed	Avg annual income (INR)	Real wage bill ($ bn)	Labor cost percentage	Real GDP ($ bn)
Armed forces	25,00,000	16,45,774	55	52.0%	107
Police	40,00,000	11,96,726	64	55.0%	117
Govt and administration	1,50,00,000	9,41,414	190	60.0%	317
Total India	68,63,00,000	10,11,273	9,350		29,143

Note: The average real wages for FY72 across all sectors are within the range of 9lac to 11lac, except for Armed Forces and Police. 1. Includes horticulture, animal husbandry, dairying, livestock; 2. No GDP contribution assumed from real estate rentals in stable state

Core inflation

The core inflation in the economy during the transformation will be based on the increases in factor prices or factor costs. An increase in consumption per capita does not lead to a reduction in purchasing power, if the increases in supply are gradual and similar across sectors and are met with steady and balanced increases in the income across all sectors. Therefore, it is essential for all the sectors to move forward in unison. As long as the growth in GDP, money supply and income are concentrated in the 130 cities where the cost of living would also increase simultaneously, core inflation will simply reflect the change in factor costs.

The increase in factor costs would be the sum of the increase in wages and other costs. The increase in other costs also improves the quality. We also need to factor in the efficiency gains we are likely to witness across sectors. As the efficiency gains will mainly impact other costs in a service-oriented economy, we can use the following equation to estimate factor cost increases across sectors from FY21 to FY72:

Factor cost increase multiple (sector level) = [(Wage Increase Multiple) X (Wage Cost Percentage of Total Cost)] + [(Quality Increase Multiple) X (Percentage of Other Costs) X (Efficiency Gain Reduction Factor)]

The following table summarizes the calculation of factor cost increases for each sector:

Table 15.5 - Sector-wise factor cost increase (Industrials and manufacturing)

Sector	Factor cost increase
Aggregates	3.6
Cement	2.6
Steel	2.2
Aluminum	2.2
Other metals / minerals	2.2
Metal consumer products	2.5
Heavy engineering	2.8
Ceramics	2.6
Glass	2.8
Pipes	2.6
Paint	2.5
Electrical & electronics	2.9
Furniture	3.9
Textiles	3.9
FMCG	3.1
Pharma	2.8

Sector	Factor cost increase
Sports	4.6
Toys	4.6
Automotive	2.6
Rolling stock	2.6
Shipbuilding	2.9
Aerospace & Defense	2.9
Leather	2.6
Chemical	2.6
Plastics	2.6
Wood panels	2.6
Paper	2.6

Table 15.6 - Sector-wise factor cost increase (Services)

Sector	Factor cost increase
Agriculture	6.7
Forestry	16.0
Fishing	14.9
Construction	4.9
Demolition	4.9
Banking and financial services	1.8
Real estate - rental	0.0
Healthcare	4.4

Sector	Factor cost increase
Education	4.3
Retail	5.3
Logistics and warehousing	6.3
Hotels	5.5
Transport	5.3
Professional services	5.2
Technology	3.4
Media	4.8
Telecom	4.0
Energy	4.5
Water	16.8
Waste Mgmt	5.5
Fire	4.7
Armed forces	2.4
Police	3.5
Govt and public administration	3.3

We can estimate the consumer price inflation (core) and the producer price inflation (core), by using the factor cost increases of the relevant sectors. As the inflation would be linked to the real GDP growth, we will spread the average 50-year inflation value across the four phases using the methodology outlined earlier (used for calculating sector wise GDP growth rates).

Based on factor costs, the consumer price inflation (core) can be estimated to be **3.48%** (Phase I), **4.88%** (Phase II), **2.61%** (Phase III) and **1.74%** (Phase IV).

The producer price inflation (core) would be **3.26%** (Phase I), **4.56%** (Phase II), **2.44%** (Phase III), and **1.63%** (Phase IV).

The overall core inflation in the Indian economy would be **3.38%** (Phase I), **4.73%** (Phase II), **2.53%** (Phase III), and **1.69%** (Phase IV).

Besides core inflation (linked to real GDP growth), India will experience headline inflation (linked to global commodity prices) as well as inflation due to quantitative easing (increase in money supply for land buyback and industrial consolidation). These additional inflation components will directly impact the PPP and exchange rates. Unlike core inflation, which would eventually (with minimal trade dependency) lead to currency appreciation, these additional inflation components (headline and QE) will always result in currency depreciation.

Forecasting the balance of payments is therefore essential as it will determine India's ability to control headline inflation (global commodity prices especially fuel). We will then also discuss internal measures to minimize the impact of QE related inflation.

Balance of Payments

India's balance of payments which includes merchandise, services and the capital account, is largely governed today by India's import needs. During Phase I and Phase II of the transformation, India will not be able to significantly reduce the import dependency. We are yet not at a stage to start changing our stance on foreign trade. We still need to enhance industrial capabilities for efficient production, and the ramp-up before becoming self-sufficient on energy may necessitate higher energy imports.

In the base case, we need to maintain the current trade approach for another 15 years to reach high levels of industrial efficiency and sustainability. In the three years before the pandemic, India's imports were growing at a CAGR of 10.5%.[318] So for the next 15 years, we can assume an annual growth of 7.5% on both imports and exports. Even to keep the trade growth at these levels, India will need to reduce imports of non-critical goods viz. electronics (13.5% of imports in FY21).

Post the capability building phase, India should initiate a gradual reduction in both imports and exports. India can target an annual reduction of 6% on imports and 5% on exports in Phase II and onwards. India will reach a maximum current account deficit (CAD) on merchandise of ~$380 billion in FY36 (Year 15), after which the merchandise CAD should gradually reduce to negligible levels (less than a billion dollars of deficit) by FY72.

Once the tables are turned, India will face enormous pressure to keep exporting its agricultural output. India should follow a simple principle of balancing its agri exports with agri imports.

Non-renewable energy requirements are likely to remain high till the end of Phase III (Steady Growth). We estimate new solar capacity addition by spreading the total growth across the four phases, again in the ratio of the overall growth of the phases. Growth rates (new solar capacity addition) of 13.82% in Phase I, 19.35% in Phase II, 10.37% in Phase III and 6.91% in Phase IV, will result in the required total solar capacity of ~11,000 GW by FY72. By the end of Phase III, India will have a total solar capacity of ~7,500 GW.

Therefore, to keep the oil imports within manageable levels till the end of Phase III, India will need strong regulatory interventions to control the use of non-renewable energy by industry and households, acquire and deploy efficient and

---

[318] Directorate General of Commercial Intelligence and Statistics

sustainable production technologies across all industrial sectors, and wherever possible, use coal as the preferred fuel source over oil & gas.

The current account also includes services and net transfers apart from the merchandise trade. The forecast for the services industry is based on the assumption that its stable state size will be ~$500 billion and 50% of that would be from the domestic market. For net transfers, we have assumed the same growth as witnessed over the last few years (3.2% YoY growth). With these assumptions, India should generate a current account surplus by FY43 (somewhere in Phase II). The surplus will continuously grow after that and reach levels of ~$440 billion (annual) by FY72.

The capital account rounds out the balance of payments for the Indian economy. India has sizable net inflows (~$64 billion in FY21) in its capital account.[319] The account is dominated by Foreign Direct Investment (FDI), Foreign Institutional Investment (FII) and Foreign Currency Loans. India uses the capital account to plug the current account deficit and maintain an overall surplus on the balance of payments. This provides India with some leverage to manage the exchange rate.

During the period of capability development (15 years), India should be able to maintain momentum on FDI, FII, rupee debt service and other capital. We therefore assume a 5% YoY growth for each of these components. Bank capital (foreign currency accounts in Indian banks) should be kept at the same level during the 'maintain stance' phase and should then be disallowed, like in the US.

India will need to significantly increase its foreign currency borrowing (loans) to finance the acquisition of efficient and sustainable production technologies. India needs to borrow around a trillion dollars to acquire companies that cover the entire spectrum of sustainable technologies across the

---

[319] Handbook of statistics on Indian economy, Reserve Bank of India

various sectors. Around $600 billion (real) would be needed for efficiency enhancements and nearly $300 billion (real) for green technologies, spread over ~25 years. Loan amounts starting with ~$15 billion (combined for efficiency and sustainability) in Yr1 and growing annually at the rate of 5% would meet the total M&A borrowing requirement.

With the high level of borrowing, the net inflows will peak (~$170 billion) in year 15 but will then gradually reduce as the other components of the capital account start reducing. The capital account should be insignificant by FY72, dominated largely by loan repayments. The sizable net inflows during the early phases will help maintain a surplus on the balance of payments even when the merchandise current account deficit is at its peak.

Headline inflation

Currently, inflation in India has a significant headline component besides the core inflation. The headline inflation is driven mainly by global commodity prices. India's dependency on critical imports viz. crude oil, vegetable oil, metals etc. makes it a price taker, and therefore limits its ability to control the headline inflation component. Fuel prices currently contribute nearly 40% to the overall CPI, or around 2.5% of the overall inflation (average for the last 5 years). India has therefore been forced to adopt an inflation targeting regime to keep overall inflation within safe levels. Inflation targeting has suppressed the overall inflation by an average of ~2%. The Reserve Bank of India and the Indian Government use interest rates and food prices to maintain overall inflation within the tolerance band.

India adopted a formal 'Inflation Targeting Regime' in 2016 under the new monetary policy framework which mandated keeping inflation at 4 percent (+/-2%). The reactionary operation of the dependent monetary framework results in several damaging consequences - i) the government is forced to curb the growth of food prices, suppressing the income levels of the entire agricultural, food retailing and other allied sectors, and further exacerbating the levels of inequality, ii) RBI is forced to keep high interest rates, which reduces the level of investments in the economy, and iii) the externally driven headline inflation results in depreciation against the dollar.

During Phase I (maintain the current stance on trade), India will do well to keep headline inflation within the range experienced over the last 5 years (1.5-2.5%). In Phase II and III, India will be able to gradually reduce the impact of increases in global commodity prices, as it will start ramping down import of certain commodities. By the end of Phase III, India would have built sizable solar capacity to become completely immune to movements in crude oil prices. We can assume a linear reduction (from the end of Phase I to the end of Phase III) in the translation of global commodity prices to India's headline inflation. If we assume headline inflation to be negligible by the end of Phase III, the headline inflation would need to reduce by 3.3% (100% simply divided by 30 years) every year during Phase II and Phase III.

While the headline inflation fully translates to consumer price inflation (CPI), we estimate its impact to be 80% on producer price inflation (PPI), and 90% on overall inflation.

Below is the projected headline inflation that India will likely experience during the 50 years of transformation.

Chart 15.1 - Headline inflation (FY22 to FY72)

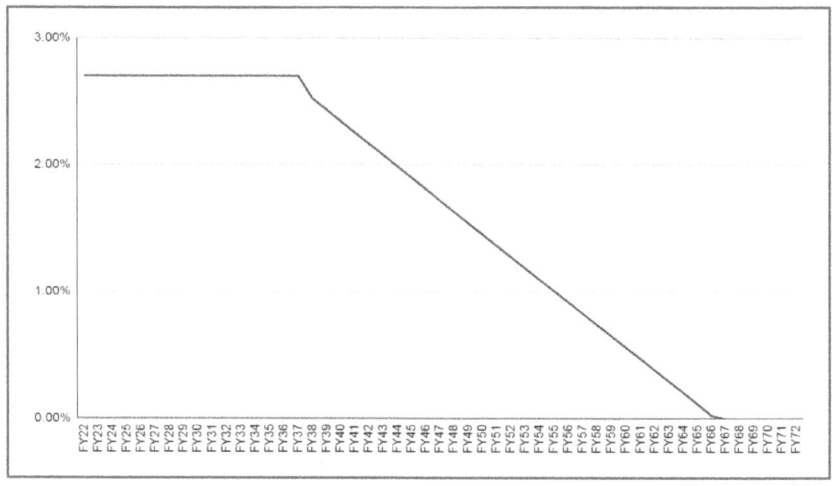

Government driven capital expenditures for facilitating the transformation

While economic expansion would necessitate significant capital expenditures by both the public and private sector, the Government needs to lead the financing of the most critical and the biggest capital expenditures. The key capital requirements are for building the infrastructure of the 130 cities, buying back agricultural land, consolidating MSMEs, and acquiring foreign companies for capability building. The Government bears the responsibility for each of these due to several reasons - i) the Government is the rightful owner of the country's land and the infrastructure created on it, ii) the Indian Government has navigated the challenges of national security and sovereignty over several centuries and has the trust of its people, iii) only the Government can muster the resources for these large scale transformations, iv) the returns from these expenditures would be generated over a very long period, v) the returns may not accrue directly to the entities that initially make these investments.

Infrastructure development of the 130 cities is the biggest capital expenditure that needs to be financed by the Government. The total infrastructure spend would include residential, commercial, public, and industrial infrastructure of each city, as well as national level infrastructure (highways, railways, rivers, canals, energy distribution etc.). The total infrastructure development expenditure will grow from ~$20 billion in Yr 1 (FY22) to a stable state expenditure of ~$10 trillion annually by FY72. The growth assumed here is the phase wise growth of the number of urban high-rise housing units we will need to reach ~40 crore units by FY72. All other forms of infrastructure are also expected to develop alongside at the same rate. The growth of all other sectors is linked to this growth rate as well.

The land buyback expenditure will grow from ~$16 billion in FY22 (Yr 1) to around ~$5 trillion annually by FY72. This is expected to achieve the buyback of 150 Mha of agricultural land and associated property. India will need to empower public entities (Ministry of Agriculture, Forest, Water (Jal Shakti), Infrastructure, Defense, Tourism and other development authorities) to acquire any land parcel or property at regulated market prices. We have assumed a 5% YoY growth in prices of land and property over the 50 year period.

India will need to regulate pricing of land and property to prevent a surge in land / property prices as well as CPI. If left unchecked, both can spiral out of control. The regulation should define a band within which the price of land and property could move. The bands should be defined for different types of land (urban, rural, agricultural, forest etc.) at the most granular level possible by the state governments. The Central Government should establish the guidelines and ranges for different parameters. The regulation could be introduced in a phased manner. The regulatory nudges will prevent price escalations, facilitate smooth buy back, discourage private ownership of land and non-urban property, maintain affordability of urban apartments and encourage equitable development.

Industrial consolidation will be a significant expense initially but will need to be largely completed in around 25 years. Consolidation is essential to bring high levels of production efficiencies, enable a shift of economic gains and opportunities from foreign to national beneficiaries, and towards a future of equal opportunities. We assume an average enterprise value to be 5 times the total sales of the entity, across the entire MSME sector. Given that typical EV / Sales is around 2.0 for buyouts across industries[320], the high multiple should be sufficient for facilitating swift and smooth consolidation. Starting with an Yr 1 expense of ~$100 billion, the expenditure will grow to ~$400 billion in Yr 25.[321] Here again, we have assumed a YoY price increase of 5% during the period of consolidation.

The loans (~trillion dollars) for acquisition of foreign companies for industrial capability building (efficiency) and sustainable production technologies will also need to be financed ideally with Government bonds.

Solar capacity building is another critical expenditure to be financed by the Government. Based on the capacity addition forecasts, solar capex will grow from $2 billion in FY22 (Yr 1) to $1.2 trillion (annually) by FY72.

The total additional capex that needs to be financed directly by the Government would be ~$160 billion in Yr1 and which will grow to around $16 trillion (annually) by FY72.

---

[320] "Industry multiples in India", Duff & Phelps, April 2018

[321] Annual report 2021-22, Ministry of Micro, Small and Medium Enterprises; "Revising the Definition of MSMEs: Who is Likely to Benefit From it?", R Nagaraj and Vikash Vaibhav, Oct 2020

Table 15.7 - Government driven capital expenditure ($ billion nominal)

	Land buy back	Consolidation	Capability	Green tech	Construction	Solar	Total
FY22	16	106	11	5	21	2	162
FY23	18	112	12	5	24	2	173
FY24	19	118	13	6	27	3	186
FY25	21	125	14	6	30	3	200
FY26	23	132	15	7	34	4	215
FY27	26	140	16	7	39	4	231
FY28	28	148	17	8	43	5	249
FY29	31	157	18	8	49	5	268
FY30	34	166	20	9	55	6	289
FY31	37	176	21	10	62	7	312
FY32	40	186	23	10	70	8	337
FY33	44	197	24	11	79	9	364
FY34	49	209	26	12	89	10	394
FY35	53	221	28	13	101	11	427
FY36	59	234	30	14	114	13	463
FY37	64	249	32	14	128	15	502
FY38	72	261	34	16	150	23	556
FY39	81	274	37	17	175	28	611
FY40	92	288	39	18	205	33	675
FY41	104	303	42	19	239	40	747
FY42	117	319	45	21	279	48	829
FY43	133	337	48	22	327	57	924
FY44	150	356	52	24	382	68	1032
FY45	171	376	56	25	446	82	1156
FY46	194	398	60	27	521	98	1298
FY47	222		64	29	608	119	1043
FY48	246				671	77	994

	Land buy back	Consolidation	Capability	Green tech	Construction	Solar	Total
FY49	273				741	87	1101
FY50	303				821	98	1222
FY51	338				910	110	1359
FY52	378				1011	125	1514
FY53	423				1126	141	1690
FY54	476				1256	160	1892
FY55	536				1403	182	2121
FY56	605				1571	208	2384
FY57	685				1762	237	2684
FY58	778				1980	271	3029
FY59	885				2229	310	3425
FY60	1011				2515	356	3882
FY61	1156				2843	409	4408
FY62	1326				3219	471	5017
FY63	1525				3653	544	5722
FY64	1759				4153	629	6541
FY65	2033				4731	729	7493
FY66	2356				5400	846	8602
FY67	2736				6175	983	9894
FY68	3091				6812	753	10656
FY69	3496				7525	839	11860
FY70	3957				8323	936	13216
FY71	4484				9218	1045	14747
FY72	5086				10222	1167	16475

Financing the transformation with Government securities

While the increased tax revenues would eventually (Phase III and Phase IV) be sufficient for financing capital expenditures, the government will need to significantly increase its borrowing in Phase I and Phase II, especially for industrial capability building, rapidly building solar capacity and for consolidating the enterprises. The expenditures on infrastructure development of the 130 cities and land buy back, would only ramp up steeply in phases III and IV.

The Government will need to increase the issuance of securities (long term maturities) to finance these large capital expenditures. The current level of Central Government expenditure on capital formation is inadequate. In FY18, the Gross Capital Formation from the Central Government budget was ~$50 billion.[322]

The Reserve Bank of India will need to lead the financing of these Government securities in the first 20-30 years of the transformation by directly purchasing a sizable percentage of the securities in the initial phases of the transformation. Currently, the Indian government borrows from the market to prevent unnecessary increases in the money supply (multiplier effect). Given that RBI assets are around 15-20% of the broad money[323], RBI can safely purchase around 20% of the Government securities without leading to spikes in the money supply.

RBI backing will provide confidence to the rest of the market. The other market participants are likely to contribute as follows - Households & private businesses (~25%), insurance companies & pension funds (~10%), banks & other financial institutions (~40%), and the rest of the world (~5%). This is based on the history of the ownership structure of the US treasury securities from 1960 onwards.[324] These treasury securities financed the development of the United States of America, and they now form the assets of their balance sheet

---

[322] An Economic and functional classification of the central Government budget, 2017-18, Ministry of Finance

[323] Handbook of statistics on Indian economy, Reserve Bank of India

[324] "Factors behind the decline in long-term government bond yields", Romain Bouis, Lukasz Rawdanowicz, Ane Katherine Christensen, OECD Economics Department, January 2014

(>98%).³²⁵ The Central Banks of Japan and Canada also have around 90% of the assets as their own Government securities.³²⁶ Even for the commercial banks in the United States, the treasury securities account for ~20% of their assets.³²⁷

India will also need to redirect the current GCF towards the envisaged 130 cities. The total Gross Capital Formation (GCF) was $866 billion in FY21, but this is distributed across the country and is creating high levels of resource inefficiency. India will need to create incentives and evolve regulations to gradually channelize the capital expenditures towards the 130 cities.

QE inflation (land buyback and industrial consolidation)

The capital expenditure on infrastructure development and industrial capability building / capacity expansion will result in real GDP growth and will not cause any additional inflation. It will result in core inflation which has been accounted for while projecting inflation related to real GDP growth.

But the expenditure on land / property buyback and industrial consolidation (buyout of MSMEs) will result in cash in the hands of families and individuals. This expenditure will lead to a significant increase in money supply, especially during the first 25 years of industrial consolidation. From ~5% in Yr1, the money supply increase would come down to around ~3.4% by Yr25 and will eventually reduce to ~2.5% in FY72.

Increases in money supply will shift the aggregate demand curve outwards and result in additional inflation (ΔP) based on the slope of the curve, if all other parameters (interest rates

---

[325] "Combined Financial Statements, Federal Reserve Banks", As of and for the Years Ended December 31, 2021 and 2020 and Independent Auditors' Report

[326] "Understanding the Central Bank Balance Sheet", Center for Central Banking Studies, Garreth Rule, 2015; "The PBOC balance sheet", Daniel H. Nielson, June 2021

[327] "Assets and Liabilities of Commercial Banks in the United States", Board of Governors of the Federal Reserve System, The Federal Reserve

and savings) remain the same. If left unchecked, this money supply increase can cause high levels of additional inflation. We can get a sense of the same by assuming a 135° slope of aggregate demand curve. The additional inflation in that case can be calculated by dividing the increase in money supply (percentage) by $\sqrt{2}$ or ~1.4.

To effectively mitigate this inflationary impact, the Government will need to introduce price controls, prevent hoarding, increase interest rates and introduce other mechanisms to incentivize saving. Price controls on food and housing would be critical to avoid any disruption in the lives of the masses and to continue the momentum towards urban living. Financial institutions (central bank, banks, mutual funds, insurance companies, pension plans etc.) along with the IRS, will need to come up with innovative financial structures to encourage people to save the sale proceeds and invest in urban housing, large companies, and in securing their health and future.

The additional inflationary impact would be significantly reduced with these measures. In the base case, we assume that 40% of the money supply increase would translate into additional inflation. Based on this assumption, the additional inflationary impact would steadily increase from ~2% in Yr1 to ~1.4% in Yr25. After the cliff in Yr25 (end of consolidation expenditure), the impact will steadily increase from ~0.5% in Yr26 to ~1.0% in Yr51 or FY72.

Increase in interest rates will be one of the primary tools for the Government to minimize the additional inflation. A key consequential challenge therefore would be to prevent the likely surge in FII inflows while maintaining healthy relations with the developed nations. This would be especially important during Phase I and Phase II when India needs to acquire capabilities. Again, as long as India is able to clearly establish the criticality of doing so for making itself sustainable, the developed nations are likely to play along.

Summary of inflation

The overall inflation in the economy will be the sum of core, headline (90% impact in base case) and money supply inflation. The overall inflation is expected to stay between 7.5-8.0% during Phase I (first 15 years), peak at the start of Phase II (~8.7% in Yr 17) and come down to around 7.7% by the end of Phase II. After the cliff in Yr26, the overall inflation will gradually decrease from ~4.5% in Yr27 to ~2.7% in FY72.

The consumer price inflation (CPI) will be the sum of core CPI, headline (100% impact) and money supply inflation. CPI closely tracks overall inflation throughout the transformation.

Producer price inflation (PPI) will be the sum of core and headline inflation. Money supply inflation is not likely to affect the producer prices.

Forecasts (50 years) for overall inflation, CPI and PPI are presented below. The first chart shows overall inflation in the economy, along with all the contributing elements i.e., core inflation, headline and money supply (land buyback and consolidation related) inflation. The second chart shows consumer price inflation (CPI) and producer price inflation (PPI).

Chart 15.2 - Overall total inflation, core inflation, headline and money supply inflation

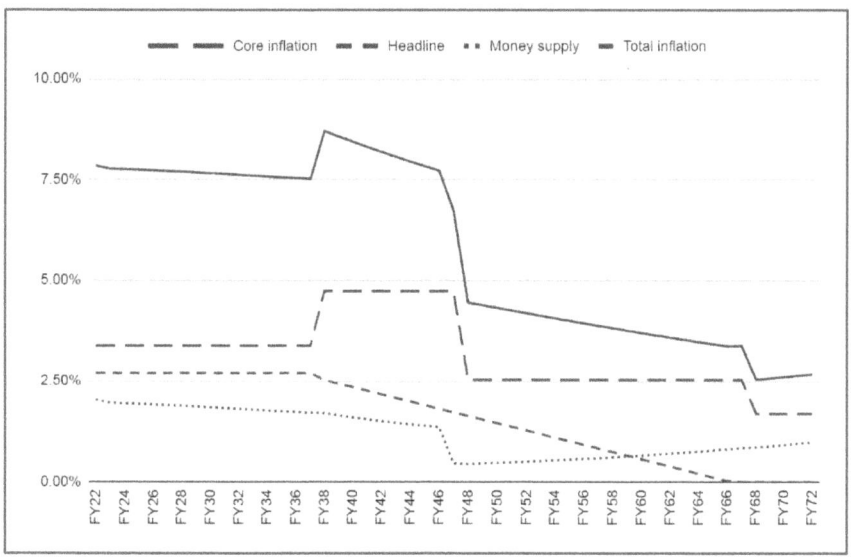

Chart 15.3 - Consumer price index (CPI) and producer price index (PPI)

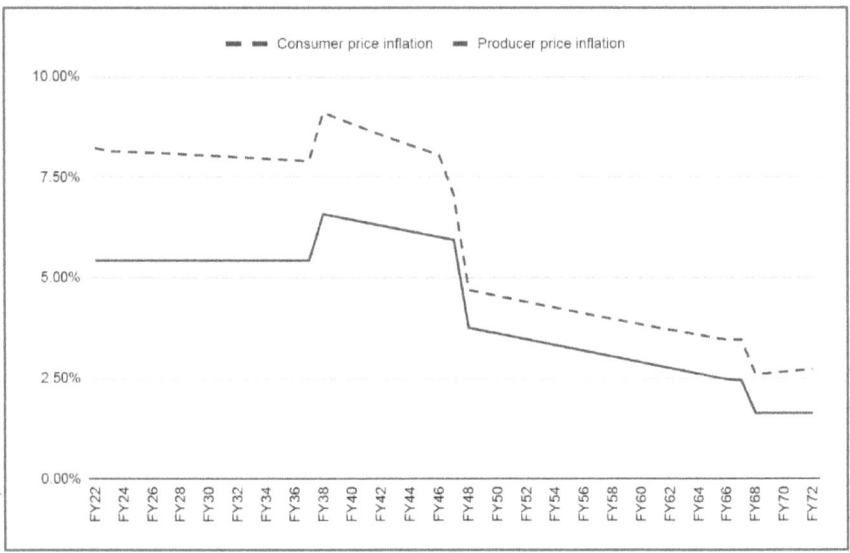

Interest rates

Interest rates tend to move in the same direction as inflation but with lags, because interest rates are the primary tool used by central banks to manage inflation.[328] The rate of inflation influences the direction of interest rates and, conversely, interest rates influence the direction of inflation.[329] If inflation is high, interest rates will typically be raised by the Central Bank to slow economic growth. If inflation is low, economic growth is generally low, and a decrease in rates is enacted in order to lower the cost of borrowing and to spur economic growth. More borrowing power can lead to spending, a stronger economy and, ultimately, inflation. The

---

[328] "Where inflation and interest rates intersect", S&P Dow Jones Indices, Heather McArdle, November 2014

[329] "Global trends in interest rates", Marco Del Negro, Domenico Giannone, Marc P.Giannoni, Andrea Tambalotti, 2018

Central Banks are tasked to optimally balance real GDP growth and inflation by changing interest rates.

Exchange rate

Higher inflation in India as compared to the US, and one that is based on real GDP growth, should lead to a real increase in the basket price, as the basket will be of a higher quality with more inputs. This in turn should increase the purchasing power of the Indian Rupee versus the Greenback (US Dollar).

LCU per international dollar (also referred to as the PPP) represents the number of local currency units (LCU) needed to buy the same basket of goods as one USD would buy.

When the quality of goods and prices are similar in two countries, the exchange rate and PPPs (measured by LCU per international dollar) converge, as seen between Germany and the US, and between the UK and the US. This relationship is further reinforced when there are no major import dependencies and there is a surplus in the capital account.

But as with inflation, the Indian exchange rate is externally driven. The law of one price holds broadly for setting exchange rates between countries with no real dependencies and where goods are broadly identical in terms of quality. In such a scenario, the exchange rates constantly adjust to maintain purchasing power parity. Such countries have the ability to walk away from trade negotiations enabling them to maintain the strength of their currency.

The exchange rate determination works very differently for a dependent country like India. India has heavy import dependency and competes with other under-developed and developing economies to export its non-differentiated goods. India is therefore a price taker on imports as well as exports, greatly reducing its ability to control its exchange rate. A relatively higher inflation in India, which is mainly headline inflation, therefore translates into a weakening of the INR.[330] Also, as most of India's foreign trade and foreign debt is dollar denominated, any strengthening of the dollar (against other currencies) gets automatically transmitted to the INR/USD exchange rate. The other key determinant for India's exchange rate is the FII. India has significant levels of FII to plug its current account deficit and maintain a surplus on its balance of payments. A reduction of import dependency and export orientation is therefore critical for India to have greater control on both inflation and exchange rate.

India will start gaining control over inflation and exchange rate after 15 years when it initiates changes in its stance on trade and capital inflows. During the first 15 years, the INR is likely to depreciate at the same rate as the rate of increase in the local prices (LCU per international dollar).

The LCU per international dollar for Indian Rupee or the PPP was INR 22.0 in FY21. We can forecast the PPP for the next 50 years by using the relationship:

PPP (n) = PPP (n-1) X (1 + Local inflation) / (1 + US Inflation), where n represents the forecast year and (n-1) represents the previous year.

Based on the overall total inflation in the Indian economy, the PPP (LCU per international dollar) increases to around INR 130 by FY72 using 2.1% as the estimated long run (50 yr) average inflation in the US. The 30-year US treasury yields have fluctuated between 2.5% and 3.0% over the last few years.

During Phase I (15 years), India will have limited control on preventing the depreciation of the Indian Rupee, as import dependency will remain high (similar to current scenario and possibly more). The exchange rate will therefore simply adjust to reflect the increase in PPP or in other words, the exchange rate will grow at the same rate as the PPP. The

---

[330] Data on exchange rates, HistoricalExchangeRates_2018-19.pdf; Data on exchange rates, Foreign Exchange Dealers Association

following formula will govern exchange rate determination during this phase:

ER(n) = ER(n-1) * (1 + domestic overall inflation) / (1 + US inflation), where:

ER = Exchange Rate

Overall inflation = Core inflation + Headline inflation + Money supply inflation (Land buyback and consolidation)

Even during Phase II, the exchange rate determination will work in a similar manner as in Phase I. The only difference being that headline inflation would have started to reduce in Phase II, as the import dependency starts reducing.

But by the end of Phase II, the current account would have turned a sizable surplus (>$90 billion), capability development would be largely complete (no need for further acquisitions in international markets), and there would be no requirement for foreign capital (FII or FDI). So in Phase III, the PPP increases driven by core inflation would gradually start translating into concomitant appreciation of the INR. We assume the leverage (ratio of core inflation translating into INR appreciation) to be zero in Yr26 and to reach 100% by FY72 with simple steady growth.

The exchange rate determination in Phase III and Phase IV would therefore be based on the below formula:

ER(n) = ER(n-1) * [1 - (Inf (Core) * Leverage] + Inf (MS) + Inf (Hl)) / (1 + US inflation), where:

Inf (Core) = Core inflation (*Please note that Core Inflation is subtracted here*)

Leverage = Percentage of core inflation translating to INR depreciation; Over the 25-year period (Phase III and IV), we have assumed that the leverage increases linearly from no leverage (-100% where core inflation translates to INR depreciation) to full leverage (+100% where core inflation translates to INR appreciation). So, starting with -100% in

Yr26, the leverage increases every year by nearly 8% to reach 100% by Yr51 or FY72.

Inf (MS) = Money supply inflation (related to land buyback and consolidation)

Inf (Hl) = Headline inflation

Based on these formulae regarding exchange rate movements during the different phases, the exchange rate will steadily increase to reach ~INR 290 by Yr26 and will continue increasing (although at continuously decreasing rate) till around Yr35, reaching a maximum of ~INR 318. From here on, it will keep decreasing and reach ~INR 235 by FY72.

The LCU per international dollar or the PPP would have reached ~INR 130. The ratio of exchange rate to LCU per international dollar would have reduced to 1.81 from 3.38 currently, with the convergence likely to continue in a sustainable India.

The year wise forecast of PPP and exchange rate is provided in the table below:

Chart 15.4 - Exchange rate and PPP (LCU per international dollar)

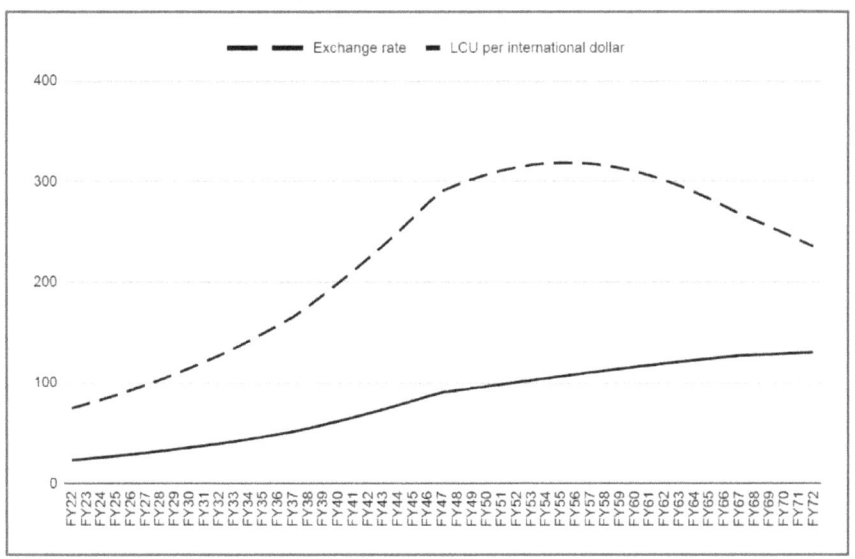

Nominal GDP (in USD terms)

Now that we have the exchange rate forecasts, we can also forecast India's nominal GDP in USD terms (provided in the graph below). The real GDP of ~$32 trillion translates to nominal GDP of **~$153 trillion in FY72**. The nominal GDP of the United States in FY72 would be ~$142 trillion. The steep rise in India's nominal GDP during Phase III and Phase IV is a result of the convergence of the exchange rate towards PPP (LCU per international dollar).

Chart 15.5 - India and US Nominal GDP ($ trillion) FY21 to FY72

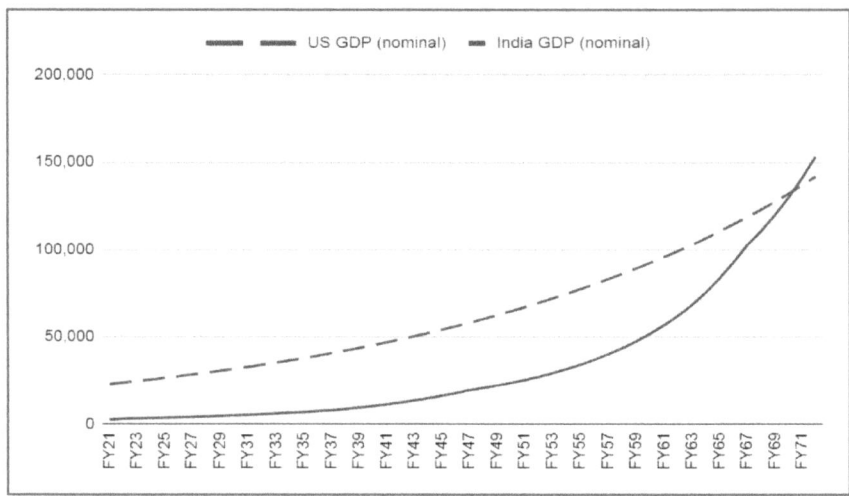

Once India becomes sustainable, it will be completely self-sufficient, and the USD would become largely irrelevant for India. There would be no trade dependency and the quality of life would be high (if not higher). The bustling Indian cities and the enhanced natural wealth would also make India an equally attractive travel destination. In any case, the USD will be much less expensive than what it is today as the exchange rate will continuously converge towards the PPP. Post FY72, the money supply related inflation would vanish, resulting in a higher rate of INR appreciation and greater convergence, assuming that the core inflation / real GDP growth would still be higher than in the US.

Nominal GDP - INR terms

After achieving sustainability, India would be an INR economy. INR will reign supreme on the subcontinent and will govern every aspect of the economy. The nominal GDP in INR terms would be ~INR 360,60,00,000 crore or ~INR 360 crore crore.

GDP per capita

The GDP per capita would increase from ~$2,000 currently to ~$92,800 in FY72. In INR terms, the GDP per capita would increase from ~INR 1,45,000 (FY21) to ~INR 2,18,00,000 in FY72. The GDP per capita would be similar to the developed world and India would achieve an equal position in its dealings with other advanced economies.

Tax revenues

The GDP expansion and formalization will also lead to an exponential increase in tax revenues of the Government. The Government's total receipts (revenue plus capital) were ~$400 billion in FY20. The Gross Tax revenue is around 11% of the GDP currently, much lower than the developed economies (~35%). The developed economies at the higher end of the tax rate also have a publicly funded healthcare system. The health spending percentage of total tax revenue is 28.8% in Canada[331], which has one of the most advanced public healthcare systems. Given that the Government will have limited ability, especially in the first two phases to fully finance high quality healthcare for everyone, there will be a mix of private and public health spending during the transition. Private health spending is likely to be significant as people get formally employed. Besides, India might also end up having a largely private healthcare system which is heavily regulated. That might be more optimal as the regulatory authorities will be able to prevent the providers from administering unnecessary care.

We can safely assume that India will reach the same levels of tax collection as the developed nations by FY72 (stable state). With health spending included the tax to GDP ratio would be around 35%, and without health spending, the ratio would be ~26%, assuming health spending to be 25% of tax revenue in the base case for India.

---

[331] "The price of public healthcare insurance, 2020, Canada", Milagros Palacios and Bacchus Barua

The Gross Tax revenue will increase from ~INR 20 lac crore (FY21) to ~INR 95,00,00,000 crore or ~INR 95 crore crore in FY72 (private health spending scenario).

Heaven on earth

Money will cease to be a concern for any Indian citizen. Everyone will have plenty of it for responsible high quality living. The avenues for irresponsible spending would have been eliminated. Life on the subcontinent will be full of entitlements with quality oozing from everything and everyone. Every Indian citizen will have high quality healthcare, education and assured pension. Work will simply be work and all forms of work will be equal. Instead of competing with each other, people would be competing with themselves. People would refocus their energies on nourishing themselves with the highest quality foods and chiseling their bodies with the abundant physical infrastructure. People in an independent Indian economy will feel more human, fulfilled and confident with greater unison between people's perspective and decisions, forces, and institutions affecting their lives. The economic barriers to human interaction would be broken. The true spirit of the subcontinent would have been liberated.

List of tables and charts

Table 7.1 - Current agricultural output and requirement for healthy diet (Metric Tonnes)

Table 7.2 - Total cropped and net sown area (Current and Sustainable India) in million hectares (Mha) and associated productivity enhancement

Table 11.1 - Size ($ bn) and employment (MM) across various manufacturing sectors - Current (FY21) and Sustainable India (FY72)

Table 12.1 - Total Final Energy Consumption - Current (FY21 / 2020) and Sustainable India (FY72)

Table 12.2 - On-shore wind power generation capacity for different capacity factors

Table 12.3 - Energy supply: Sustainable India (FY72) base case

Chart 12.4 - Energy transition (FY22 to FY72)

Figure 12.5 Indicative capital cost of 1 GW off-river pumped hydro systems with combinations of the key cost parameters: energy storage volume, head, slope and water–rock (W/R) ratio.

Figure 12.6 Levelized cost of storage for 1 GW off-river pumped hydro systems with combinations of the key parameters: energy storage volume, head, slope, water–rock (W/R) ratio and cycles yr−1

Table 14.1 - Size ($ bn) and employment across various services sectors

Table 15.1 - Phase wise growth rates for each sector

Table 15.2 - Cost of living (expenses of a household with 2 adults and 2 children in a Tier 1 Indian city for good quality living; FY21 prices)

Table 15.3 - Sector-wise employment and average income (FY21)

Table 15.4 - Real GDP estimate (FY72) based on wage method

Table 15.5 - Sector-wise factor cost increase (Industrials and manufacturing)

Table 15.6 - Sector-wise factor cost increase (Services)

Table 15.7 - Government driven capital expenditure ($ billion nominal)

Chart 15.1 - Headline inflation (FY22 to FY72)

Chart 15.2 - Overall total inflation, core inflation, headline and money supply inflation

Chart 15.3 - Consumer price index (CPI) and producer price index (PPI)

Chart 15.4 - Exchange rate and PPP (LCU per international dollar)

Chart 15.5 - India and US Nominal GDP ($ trillion) FY21 to FY72

Other sources

"Estimating energy consumption during construction of buildings: a contractor's perspective", Sandeep Shrivastava, Abdol Chini, January 2011

"Chapter 8 - Transportation sector energy consumption", International Energy Outlook 2016, US Energy Information Administration, 2016

"A wake-up call on green hydrogen: the amount of wind and solar needed is immense", Leigh Collins, Recharge, March 20, 2020

"Report on performance of power utilities 2019-20", Power Finance Corporation, August 2021

"India third largest job provider in renewable energy sector after China, Brazil", Deccan Chronicle, Oct 2020

"Factsheet Renewable Energy Employment Opportunities", Center for Science and Environment, 2019

"Future skills and job creation with renewable energy in India, Assessing the co-benefits of decarbonising the power sector", Oct 2019

"Impact of Artificial Reservoir Water Impoundment on Global Sea Level", B. F. Chao,, Y. H. Wu, and Y. S. Li, April 11, 2008

"Purchasing Power Parities and the size of Indian Economy: Results from the 2017 International Comparison Program", Ministry of Statistics and Program Implementation

"Understanding the performance on India's manufacturing sector: Evidence from firm level data", Radhicka Kapoor, Center for Sustainable Employment, Azim Premji University, March 2018

"Pocket Book of Labor Statistics 2017", Ministry of Labor and Employment, Government of India

"Combining Minimum Wage and Earned Income Tax Credit Policies to Guarantee a Decent Living Standard to All U.S. Workers", Jeannette Wicks-Lim, Jeffrey Thompson, Jan 2010

Acknowledgments

"Sustainable India" is the world's perspective on what is evidently the most pressing need of our times. The institutions and people across the globe whose publications, knowledge and data define the frontier of human understanding across the diverse range of fields covered in this manuscript, have a claim on all the acknowledgments. Here are the key segments of contributors with a few examples within each.

Google, Wikipedia, scientific research platforms (Science Direct, Springer, IOP etc.), academic publishers (Harvard, Princeton, Stanford, Cambridge etc.), industry associations, industry journals, market research agencies, consulting firms (Mckinsey, BCG, Deloitte etc.), Government institutions (Reserve Bank, all Ministries and Departments in India, government bodies of the United States and Europe), global standards, knowledge and data institutions (various UN bodies, World Bank, EEB, FSC, IFRS etc.), global and Indian sustainability organizations (IUCN, IPCC, WWF, UNEP, EPA, TERI, GWP etc.), news dailies (WSJ, The New Yorker, Times of India, Business Standard, Financial Times etc.), news agencies (BBC, Reuters etc.), business magazines (Forbes, HBR, Bloomberg, The Economist, etc.), etc.

Credit also goes to the author's teachers, managers, mentors, colleagues, seniors, classmates, friends, family and all acquaintances, for giving him the capability, perspective, opportunity, direction and the environment to undertake this responsibility with equanimity.

Author bio

Palash Tayal is a seasoned global strategy expert and an entrepreneur with a reputation of delivering value in diverse industries, functions and regions (India, United States and Europe). Palash had a fast paced and high impact consulting career with The Boston Consulting Group (Washington D.C.), Deloitte Strategy & Operations, Strategic Decisions Group and Auctus Advisors.

While working for private and public sector entities, he acquired strategic management capabilities at country, industry, and company level, spanning entry, growth, development, investment, M&A, transformation, integration, operations, supply chain, restructuring, portfolio, risk, innovation, product development, pricing, and negotiations.

His industry experience includes Technology, Infrastructure, Healthcare & Life Sciences, Consumer Goods, Retail, Manufacturing, Automotive, Energy, Transportation, Financial Services and Education.

Palash has ground level execution experience as the founder of a digital healthcare technology company. As Co-founder and CEO, he conceptualized the product, built the team (technology, healthcare and business) and commercialized the platform in India.

He graduated from IIT Bombay (B.Tech, '06) where he also led The Entrepreneurship Cell and founded E-Summit, India's largest entrepreneurship event. He earned his MBA from the University of Virginia Darden Graduate School of Business (2012-14) with courses in strategy, finance, economics, operations, real estate, policy, and water.

Palash enjoys squash, tennis, badminton, golf, running, biking, hiking, swimming, and working out. Palash lives in Vancouver with his wife (Chicago Booth MBA and IIT Bombay) and his five-year-old daughter.